NEA: The First Hundred Years

Architect's design of the NEA Center to be completed in 1958 at the corner of 16th and M Sts., N.W., Washington, D. C.

NEA: The First Hundred Years

The Building of the Teaching Profession

By EDGAR B. WESLEY

HARPER & BROTHERS   PUBLISHERS   NEW YORK

31171

CONTENTS

PREFACE

The centennial year of 1957 provides a fitting occasion for reviewing the history of the National Education Association of the United States. Its devoted founders and their worthy successors established an enduring agency for the promotion of education. As the proponent of educational ideas, as the builder of a profession, as the champion of education, and as the disseminator of educational information the National Education Association has played a major role in American life during the past hundred years.

An account of the rise and progress of the NEA in its broadest sense would be the history of American education; in its narrowest sense it would be the internal story of the growth of a great organization. Neither of these extremes did I undertake. Instead, I have reviewed the history of some aspects of American education in which the association played a prominent part. Its interests and activities therefore mark the limits of my undertaking. The account is not inclusive or exhaustive of even these selected aspects, and no claim is made or implied that the National Education Association was solely responsible for the educational progress of the last hundred years. In fact, its contributions were substantial and obvious, requiring no ingenuity of research or artistry of presentation.

The National Education Association initiated the plan of having a centennial history, selected me as the historian, and made a contribution to the expenses of writing it. The association laid down no specifications, imposed no restrictions, and exercised no censorship. The NEA offered to publish the volume, but allowed me to choose the publisher. Since the association is not publishing it and receives no part of the royalties, it has no responsibility for any statement or interpretation in the book. The only financial return that might accrue to the association is the possible profits from the sale of the NEA edition which the publishers, Harper & Brothers, have agreed to supply.

The sources for a history of the National Education Association are numerous and scattered. The *Proceedings* of the association from 1857 to 1956 are the most important single source. In fact, I deliberately chose this series as a general guide for selecting the content of the centennial history; otherwise I might have attempted a history of American education instead of a history of the NEA. The incompleteness of the *Proceedings* since 1941 forced me to a greater reliance upon other materials after that date.

Even though the *Proceedings* indicate a kind of limit, I was in no sense limited to them for facts or interpretations. Like all workers in the field of American education, I am indebted to Brubacher, Butts, Cremin, Cubberley, Curti, Duggan, Good, Kandel, Knight, Paul Monroe, Reisner, and other historians and analysts. The citations are, of course, incomplete and do not reveal the source of all the statements, ideas, and interpretations. For bibliographies of the history of American education, one must turn to the writers mentioned above.

My acknowledgments of help from organizations and persons is incomplete, but I am mentioning the principal ones. For answering inquiries, providing materials, making criticisms, or offering suggestions, I am indebted to Mrs. Doris E. Almy, Massachusetts Teachers Association; Mr. Walton B. Bliss, Ohio Education Association; Professor Lewis H. Chrisman, West Virginia Wesleyan College; Dr. Arthur F. Corey, California Teachers Association; Professor Dan T. Dawson, Stanford University; Mr. Henry Galbreth, Iowa State Education Association; Professor Clark Gill, University of Texas; Dr. Charles W. Hunt, American Association of Colleges for Teacher Education; Professor H. B. McDaniel, Stanford University; Professor Emeritus Walter S. Monroe, University of Illinois; Mr. Edward C. Pomeroy, American Association of Colleges for Teacher Education; Mr. George H. Slappey, Atlanta, Georgia; Dr. Ralph W. Tyler, Center for Advanced Study in the Behavioral Sciences; Professor Emeritus Harold Rugg, Columbia University.

For reading portions of the manuscript and making criticisms and suggestions, I am grateful to Professor Nelson L. Bossing, University of Minnesota; Professor John S. Brubacher, Yale University; Professor Michael Chiappetta, Pennsylvania State University; Professor Lawrence A. Cremin, Teachers College, Columbia University; Professor A. N. Cruikshanks, California State Polytechnic College; Professor Merle Curti, University of Wisconsin; Professor Claude Eggertsen, University of Michigan; Professor Emeritus Henry Lester Smith, Indiana University; Professor Emeritus George D. Strayer, Teachers College, Columbia University. Dr. Beulah Benton Tatum of Goucher College deserves special recognition because she read and commented helpfully on all except three chapters.

My obligation to members of the NEA staff past and present is great and I acknowledge the help that they gave with sincere appreciation: Lyle W. Ashby, William G. Carr, Miss Harriett Chase, Miss Lois M. Clark, Howard A. Dawson, Mrs. Melba Demaree, Mrs. Mildred S. Fenner, Merrill Hartshorn, Frank W. Hubbard, Norman Key, Mrs.

Martha Luck, R. B. Marston, J. L. McCaskill, Miss Hilda Maehling, T. D. Martin, Worth McClure, Miss Eva Pinkston, Glenn Snow, Miss Margaret Stevenson, T. M. Stinnett, Miss Mary Titus, Miss Elizabeth M. Thompson, Mrs. Katherine B. Watson, Howard E. Wilson, John Withall. Paul Street, director of the Centennial Commission, deserves special thanks because he bore the brunt of my many requests and either answered them or elicited the answer from his associates.

From interviews I acquired information and illumination. For counseling with me, I am grateful to Miss Cornelia Adair, president of the NEA in 1928; George Frazier, president emeritus, Colorado State College of Education; Willard E. Givens, former executive secretary of the NEA; Fred Hunter, president of the NEA in 1921; Mrs. Anna Irene Jenkins, Los Angeles; Joy Elmer Morgan, former editor of the *NEA Journal;* Professor Kenneth J. Rehage, University of Chicago; Miss Charl O. Williams, president of the NEA in 1922.

For materials and help from attendants I acknowledge my gratitude to the libraries at the University of Michigan; University of California (Berkeley); University of Texas; Library of Congress; Library of the U.S. Department of Health, Education, and Welfare; and the Library of the NEA Research Division. For the prolonged and extensive use of the Cubberley Library at Stanford University, I am deeply grateful to the librarian, Miss Emily Olson, who did more than meet routine demands. Mrs. Bess Cleaver of the same staff was also repeatedly helpful and cooperative.

Because of the kindness of the authors, I had four doctoral theses for long-continued use: (1) Albertina Adelheit Abrams, *The Policy of the National Education Association Toward Federal Aid to Education, 1857-1953,* University of Michigan, 1954; (2) Alvis Lee Sebaly, *Michigan State Normal Schools and Teachers Colleges in Transition,* University of Michigan, 1950; (3) George A. Male, *The Michigan Education Association as an Interest Group, 1852-1950,* University of Michigan, 1951; (4) Mildred Sandison Fenner, *The National Education Association, 1892-1942,* The George Washington University, 1942. All these studies were suggestive, and I made constant use of Dr. Fenner's excellent study.

For reading nearly all the chapters and giving criticisms and suggestions I am under great obligation to Mrs. Elaine Barron, Berkeley, California; and to Wilbur F. Murra, a former student of mine at Minnesota and a long-time member of the NEA staff in various capacities. Mr. Murra read, criticized, suggested, and advised. He saved me from many errors, improved many sentences, contributed many items of information, and inspired me to exertive efforts. Mr. Murra also helped prepare the final draft of the manuscript for publication and accepted responsibility for seeing the book through the press.

Last and most faithful of all my helpers is my wife, Fay Wesley. She
was the initial and final critic of every portion of the evolving manuscript.
She devised the titles of some of the chapters, did most of the research
for Chapter 10, restricted my supply of adjectives, and revised many of
my statements. She was really helpful.

EDGAR B. WESLEY
Centennial Historian
National Education Association

Los Altos, California
October 1, 1956.

PART I

Beginnings and Meetings

Milestones of NEA History

1857 National Teachers' Association organized in Philadelphia
1866 Women admitted to membership
1870 Creation of departments and change of name to National Educational
      Association
1884 Madison convention—largest and most influential of early meetings
1893 Report of Committee of Ten
      Election of Irwin Shepard as secretary—served until 1912
1895 Nicholas Murray Butler, president
1903 Charles W. Eliot, president
1906 Incorporated by act of Congress as the National Education Association
      of the United States
1910 Election of first woman president, Ella Flagg Young
1915 David Starr Jordan, president
1917 Election of James W. Crabtree as secretary and removal of headquarters
      to Washington
1918 Publication of Seven Cardinal Principles
1920 Creation of Representative Assembly
1921 First issue of NEA Journal
1922 Founding of Research Division
1923 World Federation of Education Associations founded in San Francisco
1928 Election of first classroom teacher as president, Cornelia S. Adair
1935 Willard E. Givens became executive secretary
      Establishment of Educational Policies Commission
1941 Establishment of Commission for the Defense of Democracy Through
      Education
1953 William G. Carr became executive secretary
      Construction of $5,000,000 headquarters started
1957 Centennial celebration and hundredth anniversary convention at Phil-
      adelphia

1

The American Scene of 1857

IT WAS a year of prosperity, it was a year of bankruptcy; it was an epoch of flowing oratory, it was an epoch of bitter silence; it was an era of freedom, it was an era of slavery; it was a time to settle controversies, it was a time to start new controversies; it was an age of wisdom, it was an age of foolishness; it was a period of learning, it was a period of ignorance.

In this paradoxical year of 1857 the National Education Association was born. In such a year of sweeping trends and disparate occurrences, of furious individualism and waxing controls, of expanding unity and sectional dispersion, of state rights and congressional power, of glowing patriotism and potential secession, it was inevitable that the newly formed association would reflect some of the tensions and contradictions of the age. The teachers of 1857 had grown resentful of conventional leaders and lay management; they had formed state associations of "practical teachers" who edited their own journals, held their own conventions, and nursed their own localisms. Conversely, they realized the weakness of separatism and saw the advantages of cooperation. They felt the need of a national organization that would pool knowledge, disseminate ideas, and raise standards without erasing differences or promoting uniformity. Thus the founding fathers of the NEA were unwittingly organizing against sectionalism and secession; they were unknowingly starting the work of reconstruction; they were laying the foundations of a national intelligence.

In 1857 the hourglass of events ran its destined course. James Buchanan, hesitant and irresolute, became President; the Supreme Court decided that Dred Scott was property; a pro-slavery constitution for Kansas was written at Lecompton; Douglas declared war on the southern Democrats; the Republicans were discouraged and divided; constitutional conventions met at St. Paul and at Salem, Oregon; the state capital was moved from Iowa City to Des Moines; Charles Sumner, absent for nearly a year because of wounds, temporarily resumed his seat in the Senate;

3

the legislatures of New Hampshire and New York denounced the Dred Scott decision; Robert J. Walker, territorial governor of Kansas, resigned because of Buchanan's support of the Lecompton Constitution; William Walker, filibuster in Mexico and Nicaragua, was returned by the United States Navy, in the face of indignation meetings in Mobile and New Orleans.

It was a year of expansion and prosperity, of hopefulness and enthusiasm. Cyrus W. Field started the laying of his great cable across the Atlantic. Railroads hastened to join Cincinnati and St. Louis, Memphis and Charleston. The New York *Herald* cited its increased circulation as evidence of "the dawning of exceedingly brisk and prosperous times" (February 5, 1857). Supplies were abundant; foreign trade was brisk; prices were steady. Thirty-five slaves sold for an average of $700 on the Richmond market. At Marshall, Texas, thirty slaves sold at 50 per cent above their appraised value, one prime field hand bringing $1,910; Little Allick, age 7, $810; and Flora, age 6, $695.[1] The national debt, inflated by the Mexican War, was being reduced rapidly. The tariff was bringing in so much money that every Congressman from both Massachusetts and South Carolina voted to lower its rates. Corporations were organized, banks flourished, credit was abundant, faith unlimited.

Then, almost suddenly, in midsummer it became a year of bankruptcy, unemployment, hunger, and despair.

Russian wheat, dammed up by the Crimean War, was again flowing to market, thus reducing the need for American supplies. In July the Stark Mills of Manchester, New Hampshire, suspended production because unsold bolts of cotton cloth choked their warehouses. In August the Ohio Life Insurance and Trust Company, a Gibraltar of financial strength, suspended payments. Alarmed bankers called for payments and stopped loans. Suspensions, failures, shutdowns spread, faster than fire, to Boston, Philadelphia, Chicago, Buffalo, nearly everywhere. Within the year there were 4,932 failures of banks and mercantile firms; in 1858 there were 4,225. Prosperous people lost their incomes and workers lost their jobs.

Mobs collected. They besieged mayors and boards of aldermen. They demanded jobs, money, relief. Soldiers and marines were called to protect the customhouse and subtreasury in New York. In Philadelphia and New York hunger marches and petitioning crowds were daily occurrences.

There were isolated islands of steadfastness. The banks in Louisville and New Orleans did not fail; the state bank of Indiana stood firm. And throughout the South there was relatively little suffering. In his *Commercial Review of the South* editor De Bow chuckled, "The wealth of the South is permanent and real, that of the North fugitive and ficti-

[1] Frederick Bancroft, *Slave-Trading in the Old South* (Baltimore, 1931).

tious." In the Senate, Hammond of South Carolina, exulted, "Cotton is king."

Recovery was almost as rapid as the onslaught. The nerve centers of financial life—Wall Street, the stock exchange, and the clearing houses in the large cities—were well on the road to recovery by January 1858. Only in remote places, like Minnesota and Iowa, did the depression hang on into the following years. Like all human experiences, the Panic of 1857 taught some lessons, obscured some, and left many more unilluminated.[2]

In 1857 nature was normal or abnormal, depending upon one's perspective. Violent snowstorms raged through New England, blocking roads and delaying trains. A cold wave spread from Maine to Florida, bringing temperatures to five below zero in Virginia and ten above in Florida. A violent gale swept out of the Caribbean and blew northward along the coast, overwhelming two ships and damaging others. Tornadoes, thunderstorms, and flash floods descended upon New York, Connecticut, and Massachusetts. In July hail fell upon Richmond to a depth of six inches. A damaging earthquake shook St. Louis and rumbled under Illinois and Indiana, and one tremor was felt at Buffalo.

Fires, wrecks, riots, disasters—they spread over the entire year. The state capitol at Montpelier, five hotels in Toledo, North College at Amherst, the lunatic asylum at Utica, structures in Chicago worth over half a million, twenty buildings in Brattleboro, Vermont—all burned. The fire brigade of Brattleboro was absent, attending a muster at Worcester, Massachusetts. Two killed and twenty hurt on the New York Central near Syracuse; one coach on the Cincinnati and Marietta plunged sixty feet, killing four and injuring twenty.

Laws and standards were violated. In 1857 some citizens took the law into their own hands. At Louisville a mob lynched four Negroes who had been acquitted by a jury; in Indiana a mob of four hundred tried to lynch three accused murderers but were repulsed by officials who arrested the leaders; in Iowa three men, two of them horse thieves, were lynched. The former treasurer of Ohio was found to be short in his accounts to the extent of $750,000; the Congressional Corruption Committee recommended the expulsion of three Congressmen from New York and one from Connecticut; robbers blew up the safe at the customhouse in Richmond and escaped with $20,000 in gold; rumors of slave insurrections, actual or suspected, were almost as numerous as the reports of murders, robberies, and accidents.

In New York the Five Pointers battled the Bowery Boys—eight killed, thirty wounded; the Dead Rabbits, a juvenile gang, threw stones and brickbats at the police; at Bergen Hill tunnel four hundred laborers

[2] G. W. Van Vleck, *Panic of 1857* (New York, 1943).

rioted—a feud between Munster and Connaught men; sixty convicts at Sing Sing overpowered guards and staged a riot; the Plug-Uglies from Baltimore overpowered the police and interfered with municipal elections in Washington—the Marines arrived and took over—five killed, seventeen wounded.

Tragedies on the frontier. Ink-pa-duta, Sioux chief, and his band killed thirty people in Iowa and Minnesota and carried some women into captivity. A hundred and thirty emigrants on their way from Arkansas to California were attacked by Indians and outlaws at Mountain Meadow, Utah. After a harrowing siege of four days the emigrants surrendered and gave up their guns and ammunition. When they resumed their defenseless march the attackers closed in and killed all but seventeen children.[3]

Material and cultural progress won advances and suffered reverses. The *Atlantic Monthly* and *Harper's Weekly* were started; the American Institute of Architects was organized; the United States Agricultural Society held its fifth annual meeting in Washington; the "magnificent edifice" of the Worcester County Mechanics' Association was dedicated; Edward Everett spoke at the inauguration ceremonies at Washington University in St. Louis; ex-President Tyler delivered an oration at Jamestown in celebration of its 250th anniversary; George Peabody donated $300,000 for a library, art gallery, music hall, and historical society for Baltimore; the cornerstone of a monument to Henry Clay was laid in Louisville; the Southern Commercial Convention held a four-day session in Knoxville; the first overland mail arrived in San Antonio from San Diego; a national demonstration of mowing and reaping machines was held at Syracuse; and a committee, of which Benjamin Peirce and Louis Agassiz were members, investigated the controversy between the Boston *Courier* and Dr. H. F. Gardner concerning "spiritual manifestations." The committee was quite emphatically opposed to spiritual trespasses into the material world.

In 1857 Americans took pride in their inventions and material progress and in the unbounded prospects of a vast future. The editor of the *Rhode Island Schoolmaster* was proud of the national proficiency in our language, observing that "it is undoubtedly true that the English language is more correctly spoken by the great body of the people in the United States than by those of Great Britain. . . ."[4]

In 1857 the South discussed slaves, cotton, Kansas, and secession; the North discussed business, wheat, Kansas, and secession. Everywhere they discussed politics, religion, and education. Grandiloquent pictures of human progress, particularly American, were drawn, and dire prophecies

[3] Averam B. Bender, *The March of Empire* (Lawrence, Kansas, 1952), 184-186.
[4] *Rhode Island Schoolmaster*, III, 35, April 1857.

of doom and disaster because of the decay of morality were uttered. In brief, 1857 was unique; 1857 was typical.

Such was the year in which the National Education Association was born. In its individualism, its pride of local achievements, and its fierce determination to maintain variations, the association was the child of the year. In its vision of a broader horizon, higher standards, and an informed citizenry in every state, it transcended the spirit of its birth year. Inasmuch as the NEA was the fusion of unofficial, volunteer state associations, a movement toward a degree of national unification, it was the antithesis of the idea of state rights, of the trend toward disruption. To some extent the NEA was the product of 1857; to an even larger extent it was the vanguard of a century of educational progress.

2

The Educational Scene of 1857

Sir: In accordance with the instructions of the Department, I have the honor of submitting the following Report:

The School-House. The situation of the house. is such, that with a little trouble and expense it can be made to look quite beautiful. But, as it is, there is no fence around the house; there is no playground except the highway; and a few old oak trees in the rear (in a field, where, of course, the pupils are not permitted to enter) are all that is near to remind a person of shade trees. There is no house, shed, or any thing of the kind in which to put the wood, coal, &c., used for warming the house. There is no privy, and it is deplorable that that part is nearly always neglected in building school-houses. The house is twenty-four feet long and twenty-two wide, with a ceiling eight and a half feet high. It is of brick, and was built about four years ago. There is a small wood stove in the house. In cold weather it is impossible to get the house comfortable, but with a large coal stove this might easily be done. There is no arrangement at all for ventilation, not even a trap-door in the ceiling.

School Furniture. The number of desks is sufficient to accommodate forty-eight pupils. They are of different heights; the lower are placed nearest the platform occupied by the teacher, and those that are higher, back farther. They are arranged in tiers, fronting toward the south, with an aisle between each tier. There are five tiers, and two pupils can set at each desk in three of them, but the desks in the tiers along the walls are calculated for one pupil only. The desks intended for the *smaller pupils,* are high enough for the *tallest.* They are made of white pine boards, planed smooth, but they are not painted. They have no lids, but there is a board under them where the scholar can keep his books, &c. The teacher's desk is situated at the south end of the house, on a small platform which is about eight inches high. The black-board is about ten feet in length, and three in width, and is nailed to the wall behind the teacher's desk. There is not a map, globe, chart, or anything of the kind belonging to the school furniture. At the distance of six feet from the floor there is a strip of board nailed to each wall, in which nails are driven and on these nails the hats, cloaks, shawls, &c., are hung. This is a poor arrangement, for the scholars must always get on the benches with their feet when they wish to hang up their clothes, and then do the same to get them again.

The School. This is not a graded school, but all lawful scholars are admitted. The whole number of scholars last winter was forty-five, while the average per day was only twenty-one. The scholars are well-classified. The branches taught are, Reading, Writing, Orthography, Spelling, Arithmetic written and mental, English Grammar, Geography, Music and Book-keeping. The books used, are Porter's Rhetorical Reader, Sander's Readers Nos. 1 and 2, Sander's Spelling Book: (one of the scholars had Adam's Arithmetic, and another had Greenleaf's), Davie's Arithmetic, Colburn's Mental Arithmetic, Smith's English Grammar, Morse's Geography, and Crittenden's Book-keeping. —The New Testament is also used daily, but not as a text book. The punishments are not corporal.—Government is maintained chiefly by appealing to the nobler natures of the pupils, and to their sense of duty. Three intermissions are given each day. First one commencing at 10½ o'clock A.M., and lasting 20 minutes—that is, the boys have ten minutes, and the girls ten; second, there is an intermission at noon of one hour; and third, commencing at 2½ o'clock, P.M., twenty minutes more are given. The attention paid to study by the pupils is not as great as it should be; still some of them made a good degree of advancement, but the degree of advancement of the majority of the pupils is poor, considering what it might have been, had they been more careful to improve their privileges. Their attendance is regular during the latter part of December, the month of January, and part of February, but the rest of the time, it is very irregular.

The Teacher. The teacher of this school is nineteen years of age, and was educated principally at Mifflinburg Academy. He has been teaching school three winters. He does not know yet whether he will be a permanent teacher or not. The School and Schoolmaster, Page's Theory and Practice of Teaching, the Pennsylvania School Journal, and the New York Teacher, are the principal educational books and periodicals he has read.

Miscellaneous. At the close of the term, there was an examination and exhibition, and the number of visitors on that occasion was quite large. The visits of the Directors were not very frequent. During the five months that I taught, only one Director visited the school, and he was there only twice. The President of the Board and the Secretary were on the way to visit the school at one time, but it so happened that there was no school on that day. Most of the parents visited the school once, and some of them twice, but I had to invite some of them pretty often before they did so.[1]

This unidentified teacher of Union County, Pennsylvania, belonged to that two-thirds of the teachers of his state who were under twenty-five years of age, to that 40 per cent who had taught less than three years, to that 60 per cent consisting of males, and probably to that two-thirds who were temporary teachers. His five-month term was just under the state average of five months and thirteen days. The average monthly salary for Pennsylvania teachers was $24 for men and $16.60 for women. Salaries in other states showed some variations: in Wisconsin, $24.60 for

[1] *Pennsylvania School Journal,* V, 11-12, July 1856. The report was made to D. Hekendorn, superintendent of Union County, Pennsylvania. The name of the teacher and the number of the district are not given.

men and $15.16 for women; in Indiana, $24 for men and $17 for women; in Rhode Island, $34.50 for men and $20.34 for women; in Massachusetts, $46.63 for men and $19.17 for women; in Connecticut, $29 for men and $17.25 for women; in Maine and New Hampshire, the salaries were slightly lower than those in Connecticut.

Having attended an academy, our Union County teacher had superior preparation, since more than half the teachers of Pennsylvania had attended only the elementary schools; and his reading was outstanding, for considerably fewer than half had done any professional reading whatever.[2]

Our unidentified teacher had a somewhat typical schoolhouse, possibly better than the average of his state. In 1857 there were 276 school buildings in Erie County, Pennsylvania; only thirty-two of these had privies, ten had playgrounds, three had shade trees, and only four had more than one room. According to the county superintendent, 258 were badly located and 149 were unfit for use as school buildings.[3]

Early in 1857 the editor of the *Rhode Island Schoolmaster* visited over one hundred schools in that state. He found twenty-eight "that were models of neatness and good order," but he lamented the intolerable filth, tobacco spittle, and disorder that characterized some schoolrooms. He marveled over the skill and invention that had gone into the "marks, cuts, drawings, sketches, etchings, and designs" that covered the desks. The yards were littered with pieces of wood, stones, and wind-driven sweepings. The books were torn and dog-eared; the readers were minus covers and neighboring pages, arithmetics had lost half their problems, grammars had neither beginning nor end, and other books were ghosts of their original size. Yet the observant editor commended teachers and school committeemen and noted a great improvement since his previous observations.[4]

High schools, upper schools, grammar schools, graded schools, union schools, academies, preparatory schools, preparatory departments of colleges—all these names were applied to varying forms of studies and programs beyond the eighth grade. In 1857 academies were numerous in New England, predominant in New York, and scattered all over the South. Preparatory schools in New England were attracting boys from other states, but the academies generally were losing out to the tax-supported high schools. For example, in 1857 Massachusetts had ninety tax-supported high schools and only sixty-nine incorporated academies.[5] In New Jersey and Pennsylvania academies were on the wane. West of

[2] *Pennsylvania School Journal,* V, 294-303, March 1857; VI, 271-284, March 1858; *Massachusetts Teacher,* XI, 151, 1858. The returns are for the year 1857.
[3] *Pennsylvania School Journal,* V, 225, January 1857.
[4] *Rhode Island Schoolmaster,* III, 24-25, March 1857.
[5] *Massachusetts Teacher,* XI, 71-73, February 1858; XI, 110, March 1858.

the Alleghenies high schools, popularly designated as "people's colleges," were enrolling large numbers of boys and girls, but most of those who were expecting to go to college were enrolled in the preparatory departments maintained by colleges. A small and increasing number, however, particularly in Michigan, were going from approved high schools directly into the colleges and universities. Educators were strong proponents of high schools, many of them evincing open hostility to academies—denominational, proprietary, and endowed.

By 1857 the principle of maintaining high schools at public expense had been thoroughly established in practice. Encouraged by ambitious teachers, older pupils studied subjects of a more advanced nature than these in the common-school course. Parents were delighted to have their children study these advanced subjects hitherto taught only in academies. Step by step the schools added subjects and then whole years to the program, and the high school had arrived—a growth, a process, an evolving institution—not a separate creation. The battle over high schools never involved the question of authorizing them; they already existed. The issue was over their maintenance and continuation. State after state evolved the legal theory that high schools were simply the higher subjects of the common schools, and the theory became law.

This process as it related to one state is clearly described in a resolution by the county superintendents of Pennsylvania, assembled in convention in 1857: "That the design of the School Law of Pennsylvania is to give each child in the State, so far as local circumstances will permit, a thorough education, and that there are no limits to the grade of Schools within which Directors are confined in their official capacity."[6]

The spread of advanced schools was gradual. Teachers seemed inclined to proceed rapidly to introduce algebra and Latin, and even Greek, although one county superintendent doubted that the Pennsylvania legislators ever intended that Latin and Greek be taught at public expense.[7] In Reading there was some temporary opposition to the higher branches "as a useless and unlawful expense." From Johnstown thirty or forty youths were sent away to academies at great expense, a cost that would have been saved had a higher school been established.

The attitude of the Pennsylvania teachers toward academies and high schools was expressed in a vigorous report to the state association in December 1857.[8] The report referred to academies manned by a principal and mere ordinary teachers with indifferent qualifications as "a gross cheat" upon the public and "a criminal trifling with the time and intellect

[6] *Pennsylvania School Journal*, VI, 44, August 1857. The establishment of numerous high schools in various states long before 1874 shows that the oft-cited Kalamazoo Case was neither a precedent nor an influence of any great importance.

[7] *Ibid.*, 43.

[8] *Ibid.*, 256-266, February 1858.

of the youth." Such schools "afford no advantages superior to those of our common graded schools, and their chief object is oftener tribute to the proprietor's purse than the public good." The rapid progress of the public-school system had, according to the report, "already sounded the death knell" of academies.

In Connecticut and Massachusetts echoes of this rivalry between academies and high schools were heard in 1857. Speaking at the dedication of the Norwich Free Academy, the Reverend John P. Gulliver intimated that high schools were on the wane and that their advocates were becoming apprehensive as to their ultimate success. The editor of the *Massachusetts Teacher* jumped vigorously to the defense of the public schools and reprimanded the Reverend Mr. Gulliver at length.[9] Gulliver replied and the editor rejoined. Each was polite and expressed approval of both kinds of schools, but the controversy was nevertheless an index of the strong feelings which prevailed concerning the issue. In Rhode Island the editor of the state journal remarked that he had just returned from a visit to Newark, New Jersey, and observed, "One thing which appeared eminently favorable is that the number of private schools is diminishing. . . ."[10]

Only a few months earlier, James Walker, president of Harvard University, in a speech before the American Institute of Instruction[11] rejoiced over the rise of high schools and declared that they were sending an increasing number of the "better prepared" students to college. He praised the founding of public normal schools, the rise of state universities, state scholarships, and the increasing support which the state was giving the whole system of public education.

In 1857 several new academies and high schools were started: Tuskegee High School in Alabama; Martin Academy, Jefferson, Georgia; Hicksville Academy, Hayesville, North Carolina; Hillhouse High School in New Haven; Franklin Family Institute at Topsham, Maine; Contoocook Academy in New Hampshire; Westfield Grammar School, Westfield, Vermont; Rochester Free Academy in New York; Highland Institute at Hillsborough, Ohio; Umpqua Academy at Wilbur, Oregon; and the Jesuits opened St. Aloysius Academy in Milwaukee.[12]

In the area of higher education the year 1857 was typical of its decade. Congress chartered the Columbia Institution for the Deaf and Dumb to be established in the District of Columbia; the Presbyterians secured charters for Lind University, at Lake Forest, Illinois, and Monmouth

---

[9] *Massachusetts Teacher*, X, 182-185, 321-336, April, July 1857.

[10] *Rhode Island Schoolmaster*, III, 55-56, April 1857.

[11] American Institute of Instruction, *Proceedings*, 1856, 1-18.

[12] *Report of Commissioner of Education*, 1872, II, 42nd Congress, 2nd Session, House of Representatives, Executive Document 1, Part 5, 614-635.

College at Monmouth, Illinois; Prairie College changed its name to Knox; a state-supported university was opened at Tallahassee; Central College, Fayette, Missouri, enrolled its first students; the Baptists opened a college at McMinnville, Oregon; Alfred University in New York secured its charter; Charlotte Female Institute, afterward Queens College, offered instruction; Upper Iowa University was opened at Fayette; Iowa Conference Seminary became Cornell College; St. Meinrad's College was founded in Indiana; Rock Hill College was founded at Ellicott City, Maryland; Eminence College was opened in Kentucky; Bowdon College was started at Bowdon, Georgia, and St. John's University at Collegeville, Minnesota; normal schools were started in St. Louis, San Francisco, San Jose, and Normal, Illinois.

At Harvard, in 1857, James Walker presided over a faculty whose members included Louis Agassiz (zoology and geology), Oliver Wendell Holmes (anatomy and physiology), Benjamin Peirce (astronomy and mathematics), James Russell Lowell (Spanish and French literature), Evangelinus A. Sophocles (Greek), and Charles W. Eliot (tutor in mathematics). Absence during the winter vacation could be extended to thirteen weeks for those students engaged in "keeping school." Some "pecuniary assistance to meritorious students" was extended by scholarships and a loan fund. Those who wished to enter in the fall of 1858 were asked to take the examinations in mathematics, history, geography, Latin, and Greek on July 19 and 20.[13]

In 1857 the president of the University of Michigan, Henry P. Tappan, reported that he had filled the chair of history and English literature by the appointment of Professor Andrew D. White. He explained to the regents that the falling off of students from 489 to 450 was due to the general financial conditions of the year. A committee of the faculty described the moral and religious welfare of the students as satisfactory. Daily chapel, Sunday lectures on Christian evidences, and weekly prayer meetings proved that the university was providing a religious environment. Another faculty committee implored the mayor and council at Ann Arbor to enforce the restriction against the sale of liquor to minors, observing that it would be unfortunate for the city to acquire the reputation of being an unfit place for students. The Board of Visitors declared that only Harvard and Yale were superior to Michigan and that in respect to course and design Michigan exceeded these honored seats of learning.[14]

In 1857, 447 students were enrolled in Yale University, 236 at the College of New Jersey, 274 at Indiana University, 207 at Brown Univer-

[13] *Catalogue of Harvard University, 1857-1858.*
[14] *Reports of the Superintendent of Public Instruction of the State of Michigan* for 1855, 1856, and 1857 (Lansing, 1858), 223, 224, 227, 255, 257, 263.

sity, and 160 at the University of Mississippi. Attendance at some other representative colleges in 1857 was as follows:

Amherst	221	Knox	307
Beloit	202	Mercer	c. 130
Bowdoin	199	Middlebury	82
Dartmouth	249	Rutgers	106
Emory	c. 150	Trinity	57
Franklin (Ind.)	113	Wabash	167
Georgia Female	c. 180	Waterville	69
Hanover	137	Wesleyan	149
Kalamazoo Female Seminary	210	Williams	211
Kenyon	193		

Even these apparently modest numbers must be greatly discounted, especially for the western and southern colleges. For example, the *college* enrollment at Beloit was 50, at Kenyon 102, and at Knox, 51; the others reported were in the preparatory department, the female seminary, the normal school, or the theological seminary. The *c.* in front of the southern institutions indicates that the figures are contemporary estimates.

In most of the colleges the students were closely supervised. At Kenyon College, for example, the student was admitted to a probationary period of twenty weeks, during which he was expected to establish a personal claim upon some member of the faculty, who would become his patron and adviser. A schedule of demerits for absence, tardiness, and misconduct was designed to warn the wayward. Twelve demerits evoked an admonition, twelve more a degradation, and twelve more expulsion. At Beloit, attendance at morning and evening prayers was required. In most colleges stricter rules were made for the preparatory students, a situation that provoked endless wrangles. Justifying to some extent this discrimination against the academy students was the fact that most of them, but by no means all, were younger and presumably in greater need of restrictions; another possible justification was the lower tuition of preparatory students. Tuition, board, room rent, fuel, and other expenses now appear as exceedingly low, but the annual cost of $150 to $200 was then actually prohibitive for thousands of otherwise qualified students.[15]

Miscellaneous occurrences of major or minor import for education were numerous in 1857. A. Bronson Alcott held "conversations" at Yale and inspired a troubled junior named W. T. Harris to start the study of philosophy. John Swett was the principal of a school in San Francisco; John D. Philbrick became superintendent of the Boston schools; John Eaton was superintendent of schools in Toledo. Louis Agassiz declined

[15] *The American Educational Year-Book 1858, passim; Catalogue of Kenyon College, 1856-1857; Catalogue of the Officers and Students of Beloit College, 1857-1858; Illinois Teacher, III, 392, 1857.*

the chair of paleontology at Paris, preferring to remain in America with his ovules and embryos. Thomas Hughes published his *Tom Brown's School Days*. Joseph Ray, author of arithmetic textbooks, died in Cincinnati. Henry S. Prichett and, far away in France, Alfred Binet were born. Three women were graduated from Antioch College, a bankrupt institution but a germinator of educational ideas. Instruction in scientific and practical agriculture started at Michigan Agricultural College. Also, in 1857, the legislature of Illinois created a single board of education for Chicago; the office of state superintendent of schools was established in Pennsylvania; the legislature of Massachusetts passed a law requiring the teaching of American history and another authorizing the opening of evening schools.

In 1857 William H. Johnson attended the fifth annual examination of the students of the Philadelphia Institute for Colored Youth. He was impressed by the demonstrated achievements in grammar, Latin, history, mental arithmetic, algebra, geometry, and calculus. He concluded that those who maintain the inferiority of the African race would have been troubled by the exhibition of preeminent ability in such abstruse branches.[16]

Educational publishers were numerous, active, and aggressive in 1857. Individual volumes and whole series were presented with assurance and sometimes supported by superlatives. William B. Smith and Company of Cincinnati announced "a new and greatly improved edition" of McGuffey's *New Eclectic Readers*. G. and C. Merriam brought out a new edition of Webster's *Elementary Spelling Book*, often called "the blue-back speller"; D. Appleton and Company of New York offered G. P. Quackenbos' *Illustrated School History of the United States*. The teachers' institute at Lock Haven, Pennsylvania, recommended a long list of books for adoption, including *Sander's Spellers and Definers*, Wright's *Orthography with Elocutionary Chart*, Fulton and Eastman's *Penmanship*, Pelton's *Outline Maps*, Cutter's *Physiology with Anatomical Plates*, Phelps' *Botany*, and Greenleaf's arithmetics. Again and again teachers lamented the great variety of textbooks in use and urged standardization and uniformity. They frequently recommended more maps, globes, and charts and better school furniture and equipment.

Evidence that 1857 was a typical, normal year in the history of American education is provided by contemporary appraisals of the times. T. F. Thickstun, principal of Meadville Academy and Teachers' Normal Institute, characterized his times as "a notable period . . . on account of its wonderful scientific discoveries" and "majestic schemes," deserving "the appellation of 'the fast age.' Excitement follows so quickly on the heel of excitement that a feverish restlessness has become the natural state

[16] *Pennsylvania School Journal*, V, 388, March 1857.

in which our people live. Our hot haste in the pursuit of wealth, fame, and pleasure drives us headlong from the cradle to the grave; as if our veins were coursed by the fiery fluid dreamed of in the vagaries of the ancients, and our nerves were thrilled by the subtle electric agency which dances along our telegraphic wires."[17] In less elevated style but in entire accord with orthodox tradition, a contributor to the *Pennsylvania School Journal* declared that "reading is worse taught than any other branch."[18] And he supported his contention by quoting his county superintendent as having said, "Of all the studies of our schools the teaching of reading is most lamentably deficient." In similar vein another contributor deplored the decay of handwriting: "It must be confessed that our penmanship now-a-days is very inferior in point of neatness, clearness, and legibility to what was commonly seen twenty or thirty years ago."[19]

Amid all these ideas and occurrences none has had so lasting an effect upon education as the evolving attention that was given to the preparation of teachers in normal schools and institutes and through associations and educational journals.

By 1857 normal schools had achieved a favorable status, being popularly regarded as a necessary part of the public-school system. State normal schools existed in Massachusetts, Rhode Island, Connecticut, New York, New Jersey, and Michigan; and they were on the verge of realization in Pennsylvania and Illinois. City normal schools were maintained in Boston, New York, Brooklyn, Newark, St. Louis, New Orleans, and San Francisco. Some normal schools were affiliated with high schools and academies, and some were private enterprises whose stockholders expected, and in some instances received, dividends. The private normal school at Lebanon, Ohio, under the presidency of Alfred Holbrook, was already on its way to the great prominence that it subsequently achieved. Several colleges maintained normal departments and took pride in their contribution to the supply of prepared teachers. In 1857 ninety-one students were enrolled in the normal school at Newville, Pennsylvania, and forty-five attended the one at New Castle. Through advertisements the normal school at Millersville assured prospective students that they could attend a twenty-two-week term for $36, which would take care of tuition, board, washing, light, and fuel. In May 1857, the Pennsylvania legislature provided for the eventual opening of twelve state normal schools. In Salem, Massachusetts, thirty-seven young ladies passed the examination and were admitted to the normal school for the spring term. In Rhode Island the state normal school was moved from Providence to

[17] *Pennsylvania School Journal*, V, 331, March 1857.
[18] *Ibid.*, VI, 54, August 1857.
[19] *Ibid.*, 208.

Bristol. In Ohio the teachers' association was joint owner of a normal school at Hopedale, and in Illinois great plans were making for a large and ambitious state normal school.[20]

And everywhere that there were teachers there were teachers' institutes. Institutes in nearly every county, in nearly every state. Institutes in sweltering August, and institutes in shivering January. Institutes for work and institutes for play. Institutes were normal schools on wheels, the superintendent and his high-powered itinerant lecturers serving as the faculty and the earnest, hard-working teachers as the students. And they really were students; having accepted assignments in advance, they brought their books and carried on a systematic drill.

In addition to institutes, which sometimes lasted a week or two, most teachers also attended the meetings of the local, county, or state association. Institutes tended to stress teacher participation and the discussion of concrete problems of a professional nature, whereas the association meetings usually lasted only two days and were occasions for formal speeches. Both institutes and conventions were occasions for socials, dinners, and relaxation. So prominent were the social aspects that some critics characterized institutes as frivolous and wasteful.

A tingle of excitement as teachers, speakers, leading citizens, book and supply salesmen, and crowds of women gathered around the appointed meeting place. The institute was regarded as a means of educating the public as well as the teachers. Surprisingly large numbers of lay citizens attended, in many instances outnumbering the teachers three to one. Lectures on such topics as memory, emulation, patriotism, the teacher's influence, phonetics, cube root, discipline, the use of the blackboard, and on the various subjects evoked loud praises and favorable resolutions, including the frequent recommendation that the lecture be published.

Collectively the teachers were articulate. Notwithstanding their inadequate preparation, poor pay, short tenure, and unglorious status, they were given to passing resolutions, endorsing a book or a magazine, and expressing appreciation to speakers, musicians, railroads, local committees, newspapers, and everyone who had contributed to the success of the meeting.

Some of the resolutions were by no means commendatory. On one occasion the teachers protested that a particular superintendent regarded himself as only the agent of the board rather than as also a friend and colleague of the teachers. They demanded that Saturday teaching be abolished "inasmuch as six days attendance upon school was injurious to the physical and mental faculties of both teacher and pupil" and

[20] *Pennsylvania School Journal*, VI, 5, July 1857; *Massachusetts Teacher*, X, 190, April 1857.

tended "to produce irregularity of attendance." They protested against the examining of teachers in the presence of other citizens, although one county superintendent opined that a teacher who grew nervous over a public examination would fail in a private one. They demanded an equal voice with the directors in choosing textbooks.[21] They resolved that directors fulfill the law by visiting schools, that females receive equal pay for equal work, that corporal punishment be used as a last resort, that absent teachers be admonished to attend the next institute, and that maps, charts, and dictionaries be provided every school.

In 1857 the custom of providing free lodging at institutes and conventions, especially for the women teachers, was still observed. "Notwithstanding the money pressure and stagnation of business here, the citizens of Fall River entertained the female teachers gratuitously, and in a manner that indicated that large and generous hearts are not compressed by the *pressure* of the times."[22] At Franklin, Pennsylvania, the citizens were ready to entertain three times as many teachers as came. So importunate were they that the teachers were embarrassed by being forced to choose a host. At the close of the institute at Hollidaysburg the proprietor of the American House gave a complimentary dinner to fifty teachers, who passed an enthusiastic resolution of thanks.[23]

In 1857 there were fifteen state teachers' associations. Rhode Island, New York, and Massachusetts, in the order named, organized their associations in 1845. In succession similar organizations were started in Ohio (1847), Connecticut (1848), Vermont (1850), Michigan (1852), Pennsylvania (1852), Wisconsin (1853), Illinois (1853), New Jersey (1853), Iowa (1854), New Hampshire (1854), Indiana (1854), and Missouri (1856).[24] In addition to these enduring associations scores of local and state as well as five or six organizations that were somewhat national in scope had been organized and maintained for varying periods of time.

Most of the state associations sponsored magazines, although few of them assumed direct financial and editorial responsibility. Ambitious and conscientious editors more frequently bore the burden of maintaining the journals. In a few states the superintendent of public instruction won financial support for the associations and their journals, but changes in party control often ended such arrangements. In addition to the eight or ten educational magazines already in existence in 1857, ten new ones were launched within the year. Three survived for only one issue, four

[21] *Pennsylvania School Journal*, V, 285, February or March 1857; VI, 46-47, July 1857; VI, 183-184, December 1857.

[22] *Rhode Island Schoolmaster*, III, 297, November 1857; *Pennsylvania School Journal*, VI, 60, August 1857.

[23] *Pennsylvania School Journal*, VI, 112, October 1857.

[24] NEA, *Fiftieth Anniversary Volume, 1857-1906*, 514-515.

perished within four years, and the others were sold or merged, some of them continuing under other names.[25]

Such were the educational conditions and activities of 1857. The vast majority of American teachers were working in isolated one-room schools. They taught for only a few months at starvation wages and devoted most of the year to earning a living by farming or in industry. High schools were coming into prominence; academies were declining; colleges were growing in numbers and spreading over the face of the entire nation. Publishers and suppliers were vigorously trying to meet the advancing needs of education. Normal schools were training future teachers, and institutes were providing inspiration for those in service. Teachers were organizing state associations and beginning the long, long struggle for recognition and rewards. An amazing number of educational journals were trying to provide professional guidance and encouragement. Normal schools, institutes, associations, and journals were unitedly striving to transform teaching into a profession. There could be no doubt that the American democracy had decided that education was basically important; citizens all over the country were interested in schools and schooling. But one needed element was still lacking: there was no national organization to unite these scattered and diverse efforts.

[25] Barnard, *American Journal of Education*, XV, 384; Sheldon Emmor Davis, *Educational Periodicals During the Nineteenth Century*, Bureau of Education Bulletin, 1919, No. 28, 97-98.

3

The Birth of the National Teachers' Association

FOR the summer of 1857 the editors of educational journals announced an impressive number of professional meetings. The Association for the Advancement of Education was to meet in Albany; the American Association for the Advancement of Science, in Montreal; the American Institute of Instruction, in Manchester; three state teachers' associations in August, and a dozen others in the fall.

From the vantage point of subsequent events the humble announcement that appeared in many journals, asking "practical teachers" to assemble in Philadelphia on August 26 to organize a national association, heralded the greatest educational event of 1857. After it was over, the *American Almanac and Repository of Useful Knowledge* gave the meeting a line and a half, but posterity has given it volumes and volumes—and immortality.

Four times before 1857 it seemed that a national organization of teachers was about to be realized: in 1830, when the American Institute of Instruction was formed in Boston with President Wayland of Brown University as chairman; in 1831, when the Western College of Professional Teachers was started in Cincinnati; in 1831, when the American Lyceum Association was organized in New York; and, even more assuring, in 1849, when the American Association for the Advancement of Education was formed in Philadelphia under the presidency of Horace Mann. Each of these promising organizations had a temporary success and enjoyed a degree of popularity, but for various reasons all of them failed to become the national organization of the teaching profession, the Institute because it was too sectional, the Western College because it was too remote, the Lyceum because its purposes were too diverse, and the Association for Advancement because it did not provide an active role for practicing teachers.[1]

[1] NEA, *Fiftieth Anniversary Volume, 1857-1906*, 457-474.

The "call" to hold a meeting in Philadelphia in August 1857 was issued over the signatures of the presidents of ten state teachers' associations: New York, Massachusetts, New Hampshire, Vermont, Pennsylvania, Indiana, Illinois, Wisconsin, Iowa, and Missouri.

Responsible for issuing the call were Thomas W. Valentine and Daniel B. Hagar, presidents, respectively, of the New York and Massachusetts associations.[2] Valentine, a grammar-school teacher in Brooklyn, alderman, and educational lobbyist, had twelve years earlier been one of the founders of the New York State Teachers' Association. Hagar in 1857 was principal of the Normal School at Salem, Massachusetts. The proposal to invite other state presidents to join in calling a national meeting appears to have originated in a letter from Valentine to Hagar. The call read:

To the Teachers of the United States:
The eminent success which has attended the establishment and operations of the several teachers' associations in the states of this country is the source of mutual congratulations among all friends of popular education. To the direct agency and the diffused influence of these associations, more, perhaps than to any other cause, are due the manifest improvement of schools in all their relations, the rapid intellectual and social elevation of teachers as a class, and the vast development of public interest in all that concerns the education of the young.

That the state associations have already accomplished great good, and that they are destined to exert a still broader and more beneficent influence, no wise observer will deny.

Believing that what has been accomplished for the states by state associations may be done for the whole country by a National Association, we, the undersigned, invite our fellow-teachers throughout the United States to assemble in Philadelphia on the 26th day of August next, for the purpose of organizing a National Teachers' Association.

We cordially extend this invitation to all practical teachers in the North, the South, the East, and the West, who are willing to unite in a general effort to promote the general welfare of our country by concentrating the wisdom and power of numerous minds, and distributing among all the accumulated experiences of all; who are ready to devote their energies and their means to advance the dignity, respectability, and usefulness of their calling; and who, in fine, believe that the time has come when the teachers of the nation should gather into one great educational brotherhood.

As the permanent success of any association depends very much upon the auspices attending its establishment, and the character of the organic laws it

---

[2] Although D. B. Hagar has often been regarded as author of the original call, he himself assigned the credit to T. W. Valentine. At the NEA convention in Madison in 1884, Hagar introduced Valentine as "the man who wrote the first call for the first meeting" and also as "the man who first conceived the plan for forming a national association." *Proceedings, 1884,* Part II, 26.

adopts, it is hoped that all parts of the Union will be largely represented at the inauguration of the proposed enterprise.

The call had gone out, the purpose had been declared, the teachers had assembled, the time had come. Even so, there was no haste, no overenthusiasm; instead, a solemn realization of the importance and dignity of the occasion. Those who visioned a grand comprehensive association were restrained by those who had doubts as to the success of the proposed national organization.[3]

Having issued the call, Valentine assumed the chair and called the meeting to order. He read the call and addressed the group:

Gentlemen:—We assemble here today under circumstances of more than ordinary interest. It is true that our meeting is not large in point of numbers; our coming together has not been publicly announced in flaming advertisements; nor is it at all probable that the quiet gathering of a body of teachers in this great city will create such a sensation as a political or a commercial convention, representing merely material interests, might do; and yet, in its results upon the great cause of education directly, and upon the well-being of our country ultimately, this meeting may prove as important as many of those of a more pretentious character.

. . . What we want is an association that shall embrace all the teachers of our whole country, which shall hold its meetings at such central points as shall accommodate all sections and combine all interests.

Following Valentine's remarks the meeting elected James L. Enos of Iowa as chairman and William E. Sheldon of Massachusetts as secretary. The Reverend Dr. Chalen of Philadelphia read from the scriptures and offered a prayer. After a seemly pause, D. B. Hagar offered the following resolution:

Resolved, That in the opinion of teachers now present, as representatives of various parts of the United States, it is expedient to organize a NATIONAL TEACHERS' ASSOCIATION.

Freely and openly these representative teachers discussed the resolution. Eleven persons spoke, and the tenor of all remarks was favorable toward the resolution, which was then unanimously adopted. A committee was appointed to prepare a constitution for consideration at the afternoon session. The committee to write the constitution had probably given the matter prior consideration, for the document was not only ready; it was clear, concise, brief, and logical. After minor changes it was adopted at the afternoon session and forty-three educators signed it.

The constitution contained a preamble which has survived all changes and stands today as the felicitious expression of a noble purpose: "To

[3] NTA, *Proceedings, 1857* (Bardeen ed.), 11-12; *ibid.*, 1870, 733-734.

elevate the character and advance the interests of the profession of teaching, and to promote the cause of popular education in the United States, we, whose names are subjoined, agree to adopt the following constitution."

Membership was limited to "gentlemen," although with chivalrous inconsistency they allowed Mrs. H. D. Conrad and Miss A. W. Beecher of Dayton, Ohio, to sign the constitution. And as a revelation of the spirit of the times, women could be elected honorary members and could present "in the form of written essays (to be read by the secretary, or any member whom they may select) their views upon the subject assigned for discussion." These restrictions caused reverberations at Indianapolis in 1866, at Trenton in 1869, and, far away in time, at Boston in 1910.

The officers were a president, twelve vice-presidents, a secretary, a treasurer, and one counselor from each state or representative district. Dues were fixed at $1 annually and life membership at $10. Meetings were to be held biennially at places selected by the board.

At the evening session T. W. Valentine read an address, "The Professional Organization of the Teachers of the United States," by William Russell, who was prevented by illness from attending the meeting.

William Russell, although born in Scotland in 1798, was characteristically American. Tutor, teacher, lecturer, writer, editor—distinguished and respected. Although he was at his home in Massachusetts, his words and thoughts were present in Philadelphia. His ideas were specific, his proposals challenging.

Russell wanted teachers to make their work a profession—not just an ordinary vocation. The teachers themselves should pass upon the qualifications of applicants for admission to the profession. Let a teachers' association receive a charter from the state and proceed, without further authorization, to examine and pass upon applicants for membership. It is up to the association itself to issue certificates of membership, which will also serve as legal evidence of competency to teach. That is all there is to it. Let teachers claim the right, set up proper standards, and assume the responsibility of admitting and rejecting candidates; the state and public will quickly, gladly, and appreciatively accept such an assumption of responsibility by the teaching profession.[4]

Russell's paper closed the session and ended the convention, all the sessions having been held in one day. The editor of the *Pennsylvania School Journal* scolded: "We had hoped and intended to be present and were about starting to attend the second afternoon session, when accidentally informed that the meeting adjourned at the close of the *first* day;

[4] NTA, *Proceedings, 1857* (Bardeen ed.), 15-24. This address is also reported in the NEA, *Proceedings, 1952*, 435-443.

only a few persons having attended. Where were the many hundreds of the teachers of Philadelphia?"[5]

The editor of the *Rhode Island Schoolmaster* probably expressed the restrained but earnest feelings of educators in general.

We regard the formation of this association as highly important to the teachers of our country. Those who have been accustomed for years past to attend the American Institute of Instruction can readily appreciate the advantage to be derived from an association of this kind, which shall be truly national in character and influence.

We hope the next meeting will be bourne in mind, and fully attended by teachers from all parts of our country, but especially from New England.[6]

Thus a great national organization of the teaching profession was sponsored and inaugurated by the humble state associations rather than by the semiclassical American Institute of Instruction, the eminently sponsored American Association for the Advancement of Education, or the lofty Western Literary Institute and College of Teachers. It was not Horace Mann, nor Henry Barnard, nor Francis Wayland, nor any other preeminent educator who sounded the call and effected a permanent national organization, but D. B. Hagar, Zalmon Richards, T. W. Valentine, and other practical teachers. Not that there was any hostility or resentment against great leaders, for the men who assembled at Philadelphia in 1857 recognized with gratitude their obligations to such educators and their dependence upon the germinal thinkers and eloquent advocates of the cause of education. With magnanimous impersonality Horace Mann, Henry Barnard, and other prominent educators joined the new, grass-roots National Teachers' Association and gave it unswerving support.

In another sense the National Teachers' Association itself became a lofty organization, a kind of super-holding company that coordinated the state associations by providing an annual convention where ideas, theories, and principles were discussed, leaving the practical application to the local organizations. The annual conventions became marts for the interchange of educational ideas; the annual volume of *Proceedings* recorded and disseminated the best that was thought and said in American education; common standards emerged from diversity, and in this national forum state leaders became national leaders. State systems continued, but henceforth they inevitably became to a considerable degree manifestations of a slowly evolving national policy. The teaching profession had begun the long, slow, and sometimes discouraging process of educating itself and elevating a nation.

[5] *Pennsylvania School Journal,* VI, 97, October 1857.
[6] *Rhode Island Schoolmaster,* III, 219, September 1857.

4

From Infancy to Parenthood

CINCINNATI, AUGUST 11, 12, 13, 1858

ZALMON RICHARDS, president of the National Teachers' Association, was worried. He hoped that the local committee had secured a good meeting place, that the speakers would appear, that great numbers of teachers would come, that the weather would not be too hot, that the hotels would be pleasant, that the railroads would grant free return tickets, that everything would be right for a successful meeting.

Forty-six-year-old Richards had had an active and varied career. Trained by Mark Hopkins at Williams College, he had taught in country schools and village academies. He had conducted teachers' institutes, had been principal of two academies, and in 1851 had opened his own school, Union Academy, in Washington. Restless, ambitious, forthright, and aggressive, he was interested in a simplified alphabet, phonetics, methods, teacher training, in every aspect of his profession. He was destined for even more varied and colorful experiences, but through them all he maintained his active interest and participation in the annual meetings of his association.

Much was at stake. The first anniversary meeting of the National Teachers' Association had to be a success. With a gesture of confidence the founders had chosen Cincinnati, a city distant from the birthplace of the organization. Wide swings in the meeting place were necessary to demonstrate the national scope of the association as well as to convenience the members of the successive areas. Now that the appointed time was approaching, the chairman of local arrangements and the president were eager for the meeting to begin and anxious about its success.

On the morning of August 11, 1858, President Richards had no vision of a glorious century of progress for the National Teachers' Association; in fact, he was not even sure that it could survive its first anniversary meeting. He glanced over the crowd of teachers who were assembling in Smith and Nixon's Hall. He was seeking reassurance in familiar faces,

25

but he recognized almost no one. Would the hopes of the forty-three founders who had organized the association in Philadelphia the year before be realized? Could "practical teachers," as differentiated from college presidents, state officials, and supporters in general, found and manage a great national educational organization? He hoped so, he thought so, but he was nervous as he conferred with the few leaders whom he did recognize.

President Richards need not have been anxious regarding the arrangements for the meeting. Superintendent A. J. Rickoff of Cincinnati had advertised the meetings, he had local dignitaries on hand, he had notified the newspapers; in brief, he had prepared the setting. There was a gratifying attendance of more than two hundred.

Cincinnati was glad to see the teachers. After a prayer by the Reverend Dr. Clarke, the superintendent of the city schools welcomed the delegates to the Queen City of the West; the state commissioner of schools welcomed them to the Buckeye State. Other evidences of good will and hospitality were manifested as the convention progressed. The school libraries and the Young Men's Library Association invited the delegates to visit their collections; the chairman of the local committee read off a list of hospitable invitations from various organizations and persons; Mr. Longworth sent an invitation for the association to visit his house, his gardens, and his wine cellars.

President Richards had another and understandable reason for nervousness on the morning of the first anniversary meeting. Among the large number of teachers present only five were actually members of the association. By keeping the secretary on the platform by his side and by scattering the other three members throughout the hall, he was able to keep the audience totally unaware of the actual status of member attendance. Upon the motion of one of these strategically located coadjutors, the secretary read the constitution and the president made a few explanatory remarks. The second member from another part of the audience moved that an opportunity be given forthwith for those who might not be members to join and pay their dues. The third member served as treasurer, and he and the secretary soon enrolled about seventy-five of those present. Thus relieved from the apprehended embarrassment which might have resulted from the disclosure of the actual number of members, President Richards boldly launched into his inaugural address, "The Work of the Teacher and the Agency of the National Teachers' Association in Elevating the Character and Advancing the Interests of the Profession of Teaching."

In the light of his recent anxieties and his newly acquired assurance, it is not surprising that he was somewhat challenging and aggressive. The National Teachers' Association was an accomplished fact; it would soon become *national* in reality as well as in name. Some other organizations that purported to be national were in reality local and sectional. Teaching must become a profession, one in which its own members set the standards and passed upon the applications of candidates for admission. We must have faith in the dignity and importance of our "high calling." Men are generally respected in about the same proportion as they respect themselves. Temporary and incompetent teachers must be weeded out by raising the standards of the profession, thus revealing the great gap between unqualified incumbents and successful teachers. To be successful as individuals and as an association we must win the respect and confidence of the public. In order to win its sympathy and support we must establish harmony *within* the profession. Let there be no aristocracy of rank but a spirit of equality and cooperation.

He spoke scornfully of the great number of private schools that were founded upon nothing but "flaming circulars and pretentious advertisements" and housed in any kind of room or building that would keep the children *in* and the world *out*. The profession is degraded by the existence of such so-called schools. He lamented the small number of normal schools and was dubious of the value of teacher-training departments attached to existing schools. He ridiculed the notion that teachers are born and not made; teaching ability is an attainment and not a gift. The association must take the lead in solving the problem of securing an adequate number of good teachers. He closed with an appeal for energetic and diligent service. "Our cause is good, and it requires wisdom, zeal, high purpose, forgetfulness of self, unanimity and a true devotion to our high calling."[1]

At the afternoon session Daniel Read, professor of mental philosophy, University of Wisconsin, gave an address on the educational progress of the past thirty years. He tended to ramble and reminisce over his more than thirty years of teaching. He called the roll of his colleagues and enumerated their achievements. He complimented Cincinnati upon its generous support of education and recalled how the city had built a Lancasterian school on Walnut Street in 1814. He gave a clear and emphatic statement of the place of the educator. As the watchman who guards a caravan calls out the approach of light, so must the teacher, "the appointed watchman of human progress," call out the advent of the light of increasing knowledge. Teachers must "comprehend the spirit of the times in which they live."

Professor Read enumerated and described twelve developments that had marked educational progress during the past generation:

1. The organization of state departments of education
2. The founding and spread of normal schools

[1] NTA, *Proceedings, 1858,* 35-45; *1870,* 92-93; *1891,* 118-133.

3. The rise of teachers' institutes—"purely American in origin"
4. The work of teachers' associations
5. The multiplication of books on education
6. The development of educational journals (referred to Barnard's *Journal* as being the foremost in the world)
7. The improvement of textbooks
8. The erection of better school buildings
9. The growth of libraries
10. The grading of schools
11. The development of women's education
12. The training of the deaf, blind, and feeble-minded.

While the speaker rejoiced in these developments, he was emphatic that progress consisted in the diffusion of knowledge rather than the elevation of standards. It is the function of the teacher to transform motives into action; "he has a power next to that of creation itself."

Twice during the afternoon Professor Paige sang to the delegates, one selection being "Speak Gently," which was rendered with "fine effect." Several men were elected to membership, and a few women were elected honorary members. At the evening session Professor John Young of Northwestern Christian University read a long paper on "The Laws of Nature." He described the operation of laws upon animate and inanimate nature and marveled over the wonderful instincts in insects, plants, and man. The teachers listened with respect, but their failure to discuss the paper probably indicates that they saw no definite connection between these lofty and involved ideas and their work in the classroom.

On the second day of the convention, August 12, the delegates discussed parochial schools. Cyrus Knowlton of Cincinnati saw no connection between theological dogmas and scientific and literary truths; he opposed parochial schools and denounced them as "narrow, expensive, biased." H. Tuckerman of College Hill thought that parochial schools prevented the absorption of foreigners; he feared such schools generated caste and "induced progress in circles." Horace Mann of Antioch College opposed any institution that stifled discussion and relied upon authority; an institution which forbids all inquiries into its soundness is hurtful; sectarianism is pernicious.

Some speakers were favorably disposed toward parochial schools. They had existed for years and had produced many educated persons. They arose because the public schools neglected moral instruction. This was a free country and a parent had a right to send his child to a school of his own choosing.

Although spirited, the debate was impersonal, and at its close the delegates unanimously agreed to a resolution which declared that private schools were a "most valuable and indispensable aid" and "that all teachers whether in colleges, academies, public, private or parochial schools, in every part of our land be regarded by us as brethren and fellow laborers in a common cause."

Horace Mann was on the evening program. Horace Mann, an epitome of the profession, an institution, already a tradition. With his genial austerity he rose, self-conscious in his dignity, mindful of his finely shaped head—for to the last he indulged in a dimmed but lingering faith in phrenology.

He was about to pronounce, for at least the thirtieth time, his famous lecture on "The Teacher's Motives," first given before the American Institute of Instruction in 1847. Gone were the glorious days of his educational evangelism in Massachusetts, past were his battles with the schoolmen of Boston, closed were the doors which once swung wide to a political career, remaining for the few short months of his life was the unrelieved burden of a struggling college, tangled in the snares of sectarianism. But to the end there was a resounding declaration of faith in education, a solemn charge to his colleagues. Mann told his audience that the teacher's motives start in practicality. Secure as large a salary as possible. Having made an agreement, forget the money and concentrate on becoming a master teacher. Don't disparage your students, for the teacher determines the number of dunces as well as the number of scholars. Avoid the fidgets—"twirling a pencil-case or a watch-key; stroking down a watch-guard; fumbling with a button; making the fingers ride pick-a-back; rocking the foot. . . ." Just as burnishers of steel become tubercular, tailors round-shouldered, watchmakers squint-eyed, and lawyers squint-minded, so do teachers become dogmatic and opinionated. In spite of compelling circumstances in this direction, avoid these odious defects.

Mann continued by saying that the teacher is responsible for his pupils. He presides, not over the ephemeral or temporal, but the eternal and immortal. "Not long since, I visited a prison . . . two new convicts arrived. . . . There was the Prison-book . . . a great folio of . . . five thousand pages . . . recently procured . . . only a small part of it filled." With "mournful interest . . . I looked" at its sententious columns—"two years, five years, ten years, life," and "theft, burglary, robbery. I have said that I looked with an inexpressibly mournful interest upon the sad pages of that book which had been already filled. But with a sadness more profound and solemn, did I look upon the pages which had not been filled, whose clear white sheets had not yet been blackened by the records of guilt and condemnation . . . and who are they whose names are to be written therein? . . . Teacher, you can forfend the awful handwriting, in books like these, by a sacred hand-writing upon the soul."

Teaching does not consist wholly of "doleful shadows." The picture

includes "celestial lights . . . hope . . . talents . . . benevolence . . .
fidelity . . . glorious results. 'Every man,' says Lord Bacon, 'is a debtor to
his profession.' " The good teacher dignifies his calling; he improves old
methods and devises new ones, and yet he does not mistake "his nutshell"
for "the outside of the universe." "A brighter day is dawning, and education is its day-star. The honor of ushering in this day is reserved for those
who train up children in the way they should go."

The convention wound up its session. Several letters from absent members were read. The president appointed committees to report on various
topics at the next annual meeting. The association passed resolutions of
thanks to the Cincinnati newspapers for reporting the proceedings, to
the railroad for providing free return tickets, and to the various officers
and committees for the faithful performance of their duties. The association endorsed Barnard's *American Journal of Education* and adopted a
resolution praising women and blessing women teachers. President Richards reviewed the proceedings of the convention "and declared his strong
confidence and cheering hopes of a glorious future for the Association."
He then introduced the president-elect, Andrew J. Rickoff, superintendent of Cincinnati schools, who thanked the association for the honor and
pledged "his whole heart to the promotion of the interests and objects
of the Association."[2]

WASHINGTON, AUGUST 10, 11, 12, 1859

The second meeting of the National Teachers' Association convened
in the Smithsonian Institution building. President Andrew Rickoff commented upon the unbusinesslike procedure of the business meeting and
scolded the committees for neglecting their assignments. All were in good
humor, however, when they attended President Buchanan's reception.
Rickoff introduced the members in a few words, and the President replied with the dignity and courtesy that characterized his social behavior.
On the following day he sat for an hour listening to the association's
proceedings without participating in any way.

The association debated but tabled a resolution approving the right of
a nonprofessing Christian to teach in the schools. A member announced
the death of Horace Mann, who had spoken at the Cincinnati meeting
the year before. The association passed a resolution of appreciation of
his great services to education and sent a copy to Mrs. Mann.

On the last day of the convention the members boarded the *Thomas
Collyer* to sail down the Potomac to Mount Vernon. Since proper accommodations were lacking on board, the directors postponed their business
meeting until their return to the Willard Hotel in the evening.

[2] NTA, *Proceedings, 1858* (Bardeen ed.), 107-134.

Perhaps the failure of the association to establish a magazine was the most important result of the convention. A committee had proposed the immediate establishment of an official magazine, *The National Teacher,* and made recommendations as to its policy, size, frequency, and cost. After careful debate, however, the board of directors laid the proposal on the table—and there it lay until 1920. One can only speculate how the history of the National Education Association would have been changed had the board of directors of 1859 decided to establish at once a magazine that would bridge the gap between the national organization and the individual member.[3]

BUFFALO, AUGUST 8, 9, 10, 1860

Only to a limited extent did the Buffalo meeting reflect the tensions and excitement of 1860. President John W. Bulkley of Brooklyn addressed the members, who had come from twenty states. He praised the activity of state teachers' associations and called upon Congress to establish a department of education. The association passed a resolution endorsing evening classes for adults. For diversion the members went on an excursion to Niagara Falls.

The outstanding speech at the Buffalo meeting was made by the Reverend J. N. McJilton, superintendent of Baltimore Schools. Perhaps his residence in a border state had alerted him to the trend of the times, for he was vehemently nationalistic and bitterly antisectional. He referred to the five sets of candidates in the presidential race and demonstrated emphatically that he sensed, and to an extent reflected, the rising spirit of violence. He remarked that the nation had been remiss in giving no encouragement to education; it should long ago have established a national system of public instruction or a great national school. Citizens do not inherit a knowledge of government; it must be taught. Had editors and teachers done their duty, there would now be no sectional crisis.

McJilton's strongest language was directed against potential disrupters of the Union. Federalism was of divine origin, "The most beautiful structure of government ever conceived by the human intellect, or modelled by human hands," and any attack upon such a compact is not only treason but also an offense against God and humanity, an infamy of the vilest character. He called for the halter for the neck of the impious sectionalist who would utter the word dissolution or the "demoniac term disunion."

The ambitious nature of the new organization was shown by the list of topics which were recommended for the next meeting, including free schools in all states, a professor of education in colleges and universities,

[3] NTA, *Proceedings, 1859* (Bardeen ed.), 136-178.

the necessity of professional reading, educational men for educational positions, improvement of military education, and a national bureau of education.[4]

But the next meeting was postponed. The year 1861 passed and so did 1862 without a meeting of the National Teachers' Association. For several years the spirit and attendance of the meetings were to vary in unpredictable ways.

CHICAGO, AUGUST 5, 6, 7, 1863

"Never before in all the history of this Association was there such a gathering as that at Chicago in 1863. Sixteen hundred to two thousand teachers assembled in one city to take counsel of each other. . . ."[5] Five hundred came from New England. Superintendent W. H. Wells welcomed the teachers by sections or states and called the roll of the great educators in each. He then introduced John D. Philbrick, president of the National Teachers' Association.

Philbrick had achieved a wide reputation and was destined to become known in Europe as well as America. After graduating from Dartmouth in 1842, he taught in Massachusetts in Danvers, Roxbury, and Quincy. In 1852 he was called to Connecticut, where he subsequently became principal of the normal school at New Britain and state superintendent of schools, succeeding Henry Barnard. In 1856 he was chosen superintendent of Boston schools, a position which he held for more than twenty years. His textbooks, surveys, and annual reports and his subsequent service as director at the international exhibits at Vienna in 1873 and Paris in 1878 led to honorary degrees and foreign honors.[6]

Philbrick began his presidential address by declaring that the position he held was "unsought, undesired, and undeserved." He emphasized the "strictly professional" nature of the association and urged its members to make it nonlocal, nonsectional, nonpartisan, and nonsectarian. He denounced the idea of learning by experience and endorsed as superior the method of learning from the experience of others. He recommended adequate pay, suitable accommodations, and considerate treatment for teachers. He enumerated thirteen issues or problems about which educators should concern themselves, including moral and religious instruction, local teachers' associations, a national bureau of education, a legally

---

[4] NTA, *Proceedings, 1860* (Bardeen ed.), 180-293.

[5] The quoted assertion was made in 1865 by J. P. Wickersham. See NTA, *Proceedings, 1865*, 231. The estimates vary enormously. Philbrick afterward said about 1,100 enrolled, but all agree that many came who did not register. One estimate said the men numbered 1,000 and the women 500. Another said that from the East the women outnumbered the men two to one, and from the West the men outnumbered the women two to one.

[6] For unusually full accounts of Philbrick, see NEA, *Proceedings, 1886*, 246-250, 318-331.

recognized profession of teaching, and the teaching of civics.

In accordance with President Lincoln's proclamation the association held thanksgiving exercises on August 6. McJilton of Baltimore read the scriptures, President Thomas Hill of Harvard offered the prayer, and J. M. Gregory of Michigan and two preachers spoke.

There were more than fifteen major speeches, including one by Henry Barnard, and a few informal programs, one of which was devoted to five-minute reports on the status of education in the states and sections. The business meetings interested few, and most of the resolutions were routine or axiomatic, dealing with such matters as approving the teaching of music, approving E. A. Sheldon's ideas on object teaching, electing all lady teachers present as honorary members since they were debarred from regular membership, providing for the appointment of committees, approving the teaching of history and civics, and proclaiming loyalty and condemning disloyalty to the government. One educator observed that all the "speeches teemed with loyalty," and there was not a single Copperhead in the whole convention. An innocuous resolution was passed approving better pay and more congenial surroundings for teachers. Taking its cue from a part of President Philbrick's address, the committee proposed "That the situation of the teacher must be made desirable by adequate compensation, by good treatment, by suitable accommodations, and by uniting his labors to the requirements of health and self-improvement." No one opposed such a mild restrained proposal, so it was adopted unanimously.[7]

In spite of the time and place, the great reputation of some of the speakers, and the thrilling nature of recent national events, the convention seemed to lack animation and appeal. The weather was hot, Bryan Hall was poorly ventilated, and the speeches were long. The predominant mood of the teachers ranged from patient endurance to articulate dissatisfaction. Many heard only half a program and then gathered in the foyers and wandered over the city. One editor opined that "Few persons love to sit and be talked *at* three days in succession."[8] Another complained that hundreds of teachers who came to talk had no opportunity to do so. He urged future speakers to be brief.[9]

One of the most interesting episodes in connection with the meeting occurred on Manitou Island, in Lake Michigan, far north of Chicago. The railroads and steamship lines had offered an attractive inducement to New England teachers to attend the Chicago convention. The fare from Boston by way of the Vermont Central and Grand Trunk to Sarnia, thence by steamer through the Strait of Mackinac to Chicago and return,

[7] NTA, *Proceedings, 1863* (Bardeen ed.), 297-322.
[8] *Indiana School Journal*, quoted in *California Teacher*, I, 114.
[9] *Illinois Teacher*, X, 130, March 1864.

including berth and meals on the steamer, was $20. In addition the Chicago teachers offered free entertainment for the lady visitors; so it was not surprising that several hundred teachers, preponderantly women, took advantage of the bargains, and some of the teachers made side trips from Toronto to Niagara Falls and from Chicago to Dubuque and Cedar Falls.

One steamer on which about two hundred teachers were voyaging stopped at Manitou Island to take on wood, the cutting of which was the sole occupation of the three hundred inhabitants of the island. To pass the time a group of the excursionists wandered into the woods looking for berries. They came upon a crude little structure which they assumed was a pen for calves, but, seeing some flaxen-haired children staring out of the openings, they realized that they had come upon a school. The sides and roof were covered with unplaned boards with large cracks between; there was a door and two openings for windows. One teacher estimated the cost of the building at $20.

In small groups, the teachers entered the school and were greeted by "an interesting and sprightly-appearing young lady," who had charge of the fifteen children. "The only piece of apparatus in the room was a blackboard, about two feet *short* by eighteen inches *narrow*," on which was written:

> How charming and lovely the sight
> When children their teachers obey.
> The angels look down with delight
> The beautiful scene to survey.

Impressed by the contrast between the teacher and the rude surroundings, the convention-bound delegates learned something of her story. At the age of sixteen Miss Angelica M. Buss left Lockport, New York, and went to North Manitou to live with her uncle, a man of authority and influence on the island. She was soon impressed by the fact that the children who lived on the island had no chance to learn even to read, and so she opened a school in the only available structure. For two years she received no remuneration except the satisfaction of helping forlorn children; then some of the patrons arranged for a slight compensation through subscriptions.

After leaving the island the educators discussed the situation and decided to present the teacher with some evidence of their admiration for her work, not only for her kindness in receiving them, but for the generous service she was rendering. It was agreed that a handsome gold watch would be a fitting gift. Money to the amount of $66, including a contribution from the captain of the ship, was soon raised, and a committee was appointed to buy the watch. After arriving in Chicago the committee was able to secure a hunting-case Waltham watch, which cost considerably more than the sum which had been raised, because of the liberality of the dealer, who, in view of the circumstances, allowed the committee a wholesale price and threw in a gold key as his contribution.

Upon the return voyage after the close of the convention the teachers persuaded the captain to make an unscheduled stop at Manitou Island in order that they might present the watch to Miss Buss. The surprised teacher listened to the letter of presentation and received the gift with appreciation. "The whole scene was instructive and affecting, and not a few dropped the tender tear."[10]

OGDENSBURG, NEW YORK, AUGUST 10, 11, 12, 1864

"The meeting this year seems likely to go by default, no one in the East, where it must be held, being interested enough in its success to look up a place of meeting"; so complained the *Illinois Teacher*.[11] And the president, W. H. Wells, who had recently resigned as superintendent of Chicago schools to become the western representative of an insurance company, scolded everyone in general and Detroit in particular because it did not issue an invitation for the convention. The disruption of transportation because of the war also added to the difficulties of finding a suitable meeting place. So it is not surprising that the Ogdensburg sessions were not well attended. President Thomas Hill of Harvard made a speech, and Henry Barnard made a critical report on the academy at West Point, emphasizing the high mortality rate of failure because of the poor quality of students who were appointed by congressmen. Dr. H. B. Wilbur of Syracuse read a critical, almost hostile, paper on object teaching as it was carried on at Oswego, the center of the progressive ideas of the time.[12]

HARRISBURG, AUGUST 16, 17, 18, 1865

Shadows of the Civil War lingered over Harrisburg and the meeting of the National Teachers' Association as some five hundred delegates assembled in the Dauphin County Courthouse. Joy over the end of the war had been quickly transformed into anger and grief over the murder of Lincoln. Satisfaction over the outcome of the struggle had been replaced by anxieties over the problems of reconstruction. In trying to draw comfort from the abolition of slavery, Northerners were mindful of

[10] *Massachusetts Teacher*, XVI, 285, 297-304, 341, 370-371, September 1863. Minor inconsistencies appear in the varying accounts. One commentator flippantly observed that the "party got quite enchanted with a young lady who kept school in a log cabin. . . ."

[11] *Illinois Teacher*, X, 277, July 1864.

[12] NTA, *Proceedings, 1864* (Bardeen ed.), 394-464.

their long acquiescence in its continuance. They had restricted their speech, curbed their natural feelings of sympathy, and consented to compromises which had troubled their consciences. Now that the cause of this cowardice and guilt had been removed, they felt little sense of merit or release. Whenever they tried to rejoice over a great moral victory, they were overwhelmed by the thought of four million wards living in poverty and ignorance. The challenge of the future left no time for satisfaction in contemplating the past. The feeling of guilt was soon replaced by a heavy burden of responsibility. The nation had freed the slaves; the nation must now see that they became not merely freedmen but free men. Could the National Teachers' Association help to solve the problems of a troubled nation?

Whether or not the association could help the nation, the members were keenly sensitive to its problems and bold in recommending policies. Three major addresses dealth with pressing issues—the function of education in reconstruction, the effects of the war on education, and the establishment of a Federal department of education. The association indicated its vigor and wide interest in public affairs by proposing a World Educational Convention to be held in New York in 1867, and by calling for free competitive examinations for entrance to the military and naval academies.

The first session began at 9:30 A.M. on Wednesday, August 16, 1865. After prayers, songs, welcoming addresses, invitations, and announcements, Samuel S. Greene of Providence arose to deliver the presidential address. As a citizen and patriot he was an epitome of the state of mind of the North—with a little touch of self-righteousness, a degree of bitterness toward the South, a little sectional smugness, some boasting of patriotic duties well performed, and a troubled uncertainty as to future policies of the nation. Just as a person's sense of injury is sometimes deepened and his anger renewed by receiving an apology, so victory over the South seemed to renew the realization of its original offenses and the magnitude of its rebellion in the heart of President Greene as he began the annual address.

The speaker thought that God in his providence had overridden the evil men who had attempted to contravene the eternal laws of justice. By eliminating slavery, the war had restored freedom of speech. "Can we not as educators, go boldly into the Southern States, and teach the truth and the whole truth? If not, I pray God that martial law may prevail in every Southern State, till Northern men, or any other men, may discuss educational, political, social, moral and religious topics in any part of the South as freely as in Faneuil Hall." Further evidence of the speaker's feeling is provided by his use of such words and phrases as "unprovoked," "instigators," "accursed," "cupidity," "fetters of ignorance," and "nefarious rebellion."

As an educator the speaker drew some definite lessons from the war. It had demonstrated that theory must precede practice. In spite of exceptions, the trained men of West Point had become the best generals. Fortunately teachers, in order to secure experience, do not require a battlefield; they have their fields of practice in the classrooms.

At the afternoon session letters from Presidents Francis Wayland of Brown University and Thomas Hill of Harvard University were read to the association. Wayland denounced the idea of giving education away, observing that "what men want they are willing to pay for." He characterized the late struggle as "a war of education and patriotism against ignorance and barbarism." Hill declared that the time was inviting for teachers and observed that "Pennsylvania was never more emphatically than now the Keystone State; her Governor Curtin was a wall of defense, not a veil of concealment. . . ."

Also at the afternoon session Richard Edwards, president of Illinois Normal University, said that the devastation of "the region lately blasted by slavery" called for the widespread establishment of normal schools. "The schoolmaster must finish what the soldier has so well begun. Free schools must be planted wherever the flag of the republic floats."

No speeches, resolutions, or reports on the second day of the convention. Instead, the delegates, more than four hundred of them, entrained for Gettysburg to visit the two-year-old battlefield. The reduced railroad fare, the free dinner given by the citizens of Gettysburg, and the services of informed guides tended to temper the solemnity natural to such a visit. Late in the afternoon the delegates assembled on Cemetery Ridge for a prayer, greetings, and brief speeches by five or six educators. To one Illinois teacher "The occasion was one of thrilling interest. Surrounded by beautiful, even sublime scenery, assembled on one of the greatest battlefields of modern times, educators of the nation, pledging themselves anew to more earnest efforts for the good of their country, hallowing the spot where the nation was born anew, invoking the God of Heaven to bless our coming and inspire us with holy zeal from above, were thoughts that filled the lover of his country with new life and great resolves, and made all feel that it was good to be there and drink in the glorious inspiration. It is fit that this place be made the Mecca of America."[13]

At the close of the meeting on the battlefield the delegates resolved a vote of thanks to the railroad for reduced fares and to the citizens of Gettysburg for the free dinner. After singing "America," the excursionists

[13] *Illinois Teacher*, XI, 272, September 1865.

returned to Harrisburg, where they arrived at 10:30 P.M.[14]

On the following day, however, the association resolved that excursions and visits, even though pleasant and beneficial, should henceforth be postponed until after the final adjournment of the convention.

On Friday the program proceeded. The clergy of Harrisburg were invited to sit with the association, and several women were elected honorary members. Invitations to visit the state lunatic asylum and the state capitol and grounds were received. A resolution of sympathy was passed and sent to the relatives of the late Bishop Alonzo Potter, who had been a distinguished teacher as well as theologian. A teacher from the Oswego Normal and Training School gave a demonstration object lesson with children brought in from the city. Lowell Mason, famous in the field of public-school music, demonstrated the object method in music. The association elected him an honorary member and ordered his report on object teaching to be printed as a separate pamphlet. The most important resolutions passed by the association were those urging the establishment of public-school systems in those states where they did not exist and insisting upon the organization of a Bureau of Education to gather educational statistics and advance popular education in the states.

A further instance of the activity of the association was the report of a committee on object teaching, which had been appointed at Ogdensburg in 1864. The committee of seven, including Dr. Barnas Sears, subsequently agent of the Peabody Fund, carried on correspondence and prepared an extensive report. Samuel S. Greene spent a week at Oswego drafting the report, which was analytical and impersonal. In fact, it was so largely concerned with the psychology of the learning process, the place of innate and acquired ideas, and attempts to describe objectively the process at Oswego that the hearers were probably in doubt as to the conclusions which the writer had reached.

Two major addresses—those by Andrew J. Rickoff of Ohio on the Bureau of Education and J. P. Wickersham of Pennsylvania on education in reconstruction—again emphasized the social as well as the educational functions of the association. Rickoff characterized the South as deeply hostile to the education of the Negro and warned his hearers that teachers would meet with serious resistance as soon as army bayonets were withdrawn. He cited the closing of the Negro schools by the mayor of Columbia, Tennessee, and the infliction of twenty-five lashes on an old gray-haired preacher who was teaching former slaves to read.

Wickersham, principal of the Normal School at Millersville, Pennsylvania, and president-elect of the association for the ensuing year, spoke on education as an element in reconstruction. The refrain, which ran

[14] NTA, *Proceedings, 1865* (Bardeen ed.), 221.

through considerable bitterness and recrimination, was to the effect that teachers should train the Negroes and poor whites, dispel ignorance, and thus prevent the reestablishment of slavery. He reviewed the possible causes of the Civil War and rejected such explanations as differences in rank and character among original settlers, the clash of economic interests, the problem of federalism and state rights. Instead he accepted "the antagonism between free and slave labor" as the true explanation of the cause of the struggle. "Slavery was the upas tree that bore upon its poisoning branches State Rights, Nullification, Secession, Rebellion and Assassination." It accounts for the "domineering, tyrannical aristocracy" and "a class of vassal whites, ignorant, uncouth, superstitious, and sycophantic." As for the late slaveholders, the speaker hoped that many would leave the country; "they would scornfully reject education at our hands. We must treat them as Western farmers do the stumps . . . work around them, and let them rot out." He hoped that a few would "atone for their crimes on the scaffold." He proposed that no seceded state be readmitted until its constitution provided for the establishment of a free school system. He looked forward to the time when teachers would have prepared the Negroes for all rights as citizens. He put great emphasis upon the idea that Negroes themselves should become the principal teachers of their race. He commended the Freedmen's Bureau under General O. O. Howard, but a permanent head of a national system of education was needed, for the war had demonstrated that the United States "is a nation and not a co-partnership of states."[15]

These vehement sentiments concerning the South expressed by President Greene, President-elect Wickersham, and past-President Rickoff were not calculated to soothe the Southerners. The Texas teachers, assembled in Houston on July 4, 1866, condemned the utterances of the speakers at Harrisburg and all attempts by the North to "interfere with the Negro."[16]

Following Wickersham's address, the editor of the *Illinois Teacher* relates, "it was announced that Professor Crummell, a distinguished graduate of Cambridge University, England, was present. Professor Crummell was brought forward and introduced, and to my astonishment he was as black as the ten of spades. As he moved toward the stand there were evident signs of excitement in the large audience. There was the *nigger* in our midst! What shall we do? Shy around him because he is black? Refuse him a hearing because he is a *lower order* of being? Humanity and justice triumphed!"[17]

[15] NTA, *Proceedings, 1865* (Bardeen ed.), 297.
[16] *Illinois Teacher*, XII, 393-394, October 1866. The Illinois editor thought that the Texas teachers should, in view of the day on which they met, have expressed some patriotic sentiment.
[17] *Illinois Teacher*, XI, 272-274, September 1865.

Professor Crummell, an American Negro who had been in Liberia for thirteen years, spoke briefly and fittingly of the need for education in the South and commented upon the growth of his adopted country of Liberia. "At the close of the remarks there was loud, long and enthusiastic applause."

Following the afternoon session the delegates enjoyed a free dinner at the State Capitol Hotel. The Illinois editor was overcome by such hospitality. "When the meeting occurs again at Harrisburg we desire to be counted in. Perhaps there may be more luscious peaches, sweeter cream, and more agreeable maids and matrons elsewhere; but we confess that those of Harrisburg were fully up to our standard. . . ."[18]

After passing resolutions of thanks and appreciation to the railroads, hotels, newspapers, officers, citizens, and organizations the chairman introduced the new president, J. P. Wickersham. Late in the evening the association adjourned to meet at Indianapolis in the following year.

INDIANAPOLIS, AUGUST 15, 16, 17, 1866

Oliver P. Morton, the aggressive and litigious governor of Indiana, welcomed the teachers, praised the public schools, and urged the teaching of government and patriotism. Major speeches were made by James P. Wickersham, the president of the association; Mrs. Mary Howe Smith of Oswego; Professor W. P. Atkinson of Cambridge, Massachusetts; and D. J. Sarmiento, Argentine minister to the United States, friend and disciple of Horace Mann, and subsequently the founder of the school system in his native land. One evening session was devoted to a lecture by the Reverend Jesse H. Jones on "The Psychology of St. Paul, being a new interpretation of the Flesh and the Spirit."

Resolutions were numerous: lamenting the death of Francis Wayland of Brown University and Eliphalet Nott, who had been president of Union College for sixty-two years; offering help to southern education "to establish systems of free public schools"; sending thanks to Congressman James A. Garfield for his bill to establish a department of education at Washington; and proposing a world convention for promoting the cause of education.

From the standpoint of subsequent developments the most significant achievement of the Indianapolis meeting was the change of one word in the constitution of the association, namely, the substitution of "person" for "gentleman" in defining qualifications for membership, thus clearing the way for women to enjoy the advantages of full membership. This early victory for women's rights unquestionably had a great effect upon

[18] *Ibid.*, 270.

the future of the NEA. In fact, it paved the way for another kind of victory in the far-off year of 1910.[19]

At this 1866 meeting some of the papers had been on important topics and provoked spirited discussions. There was no implication of the fact that the association would fail to meet in the following year.

NASHVILLE, AUGUST 19, 20, 21, 1868

John Eaton, chairman of local arrangements, was disappointed. He had sent out a special circular announcing the combined meetings of the Tennessee State Teachers' Association, the American Normal School Association, and the National Teachers' Association. Reflecting his position as superintendent of public instruction in Tennessee, he had urged county superintendents to come to Nashville and discuss their problems and settle their accounts. At his request the legislature passed a joint resolution, tendering the use of the capitol hall and senate chamber to the associations. He had secured free entertainment for the ladies in private homes and induced the mayor and council to pay the hotel bill for the gentlemen. He had secured free return tickets from some of the railroads. He had arranged a grand excursion and tour to Mammoth Cave on the day after the closing of the convention.

The week of the convention arrived, but many of the delegates did not come. Even some of the speakers did not show up. Few teachers came from the western and northern states. Some sent letters of explanation and regret; others did not trouble to explain their absence.

Why the small attendance? Doubtless some loss of continuity and momentum because of the failure of the association to meet during the preceding year. It is true that Nashville was far from the center of membership and that the heat was extreme. Could it be that some members regarded Tennessee as alien territory, that unrecognized resentment still smoldered in the deep recesses of their feelings? Highly improbable. Was not John Eaton, chairman of arrangements and state superintendent of schools, a northern man, a friend of the Negro, an educator, and a gentleman? And the President of the United States, whose national sentiments had been tested and tempered in the fires of local contempt and animosity, was a Tennessee man. Whatever may have been the reasons, the attendance was disappointing. All the more reason for the host to exert himself and turn disappointment into success, and that is what General John Eaton did.

In fact, it was a colorful and enjoyable meeting, memorable because of the hospitality of the people and the presence of distinguished vistors. Governor William G. Brownlow, the "Fighting Parson," famous as a bitter opponent of secession, was elected an honorary member. Ex-

[19] NTA, *Proceedings, 1866* (Bardeen ed.), 566-638.

Governor Neil Brown welcomed the teachers, and Henry Stuart Foote, ex-governor, ex-senator, ex-congressman, opponent of Jefferson Davis, historian, and educator, welcomed the teachers and urged them to strengthen the two pillars of our nation—intelligence and virtue.

Of leading educators there was no dearth. W. H. McGuffey was there, declaring, "It requires more skill to teach an infant school than to occupy a chair of moral philosophy in a great college."[20] General O. O. Howard gave a review of his work with the Freedmen's Bureau, reporting that since leaving Washington he had visited some Negro schools that were the equal of any that he had seen. The South needed help in its efforts to educate both black and white children; it needed normal schools and courageous teachers who would stand up in the face of "ostracism, pistols, threats and outrages." Paul A. Chadbourne, president of the University of Wisconsin, formerly and subsequently of Williams College, declared that the American college was "the highest institution for pure intellectual culture," and that "in its highest form" it was for "the few."

Late in the afternoon, under the guidance of ex-Senator Foote, the delegates called upon Mrs. James K. Polk and paid their respects to that gracious lady, a former mistress of the White House. They remained in the elegant parlors and on the grounds for an hour. Because of the pressure of official business and the inconvenience of the location, the association declined an invitation to visit the state lunatic asylum.

Because of the smaller attendance, or the weather, or the hospitality, the delegates discussed issues with more than usual fervor. The function of normal schools, the nature of colleges, the importance of the classics, and coeducation evoked spirited and prolonged discussions. The proposal to establish normal departments in colleges led to frank words and strong feelings. A motion to drop the discussion was vigorously rejected; in fact they voted to extend it indefinitely. Harmony finally prevailed and by a unanimous resolution the association endorsed normal schools, normal departments, normal institutes, teachers' institutes, teachers' conventions, and educational periodicals. The association heard reports, appointed committees, and passed resolutions of thanks to General Eaton, the Tennessee legislature, the citizens, the mayor, the aldermen, the musicians, and the railroads. President John M. Gregory presented his successor, L. Van Bokkelen of Maryland, and the sessions ended in a glow of good will.

Possibly the prospect of visiting Mammoth Cave the next day promoted generous feelings. Early on Friday morning some fifty members entrained for Cave City, Kentucky. Stage coaches conveyed the visitors to Cave Hotel, where they had dinner and donned suitable clothes for their visit to the cave. In the "Gothic Chapel" the delegates burst into song and

[20] NTA, *Proceedings, 1868* (Bardeen ed.), 658.

oratory, but the board of councilors that was supposed to make plans for the publication of the annual volume did not meet. The despairing secretary opined that the "Dead Sea," the "River Styx," and "Lake Lethe" made them oblivious to the past, for no sound returned, even from "Echo River," down which "the happy company of teachers glided amid strains of sweetest music and moving constellations of lanterns."[21]

TRENTON, AUGUST 18, 19, 20, 1869

Some of the members, in fact, most of them, were shocked by what Judge Richard S. Field said about religion in the schools. "You cannot give religious instruction . . . in the public schools, and this might as well be acknowledged today as ever." The schools are secular; teachers are not prepared to teach religion and should not do so, but should leave such teaching to the home and church.

The session proceeded to discuss the teaching of religion in the schools. E. E. White of Ohio proposed a "common Christianity," a consensus of the beliefs of the various denominations. Another speaker demanded that teachers be deeply religious, and a third stressed the teaching of morality. By a unanimous vote the session endorsed the reading and teaching of the Bible in the schools.

John Wesley Hoyt of Wisconsin appeared before the association and made a fervent plea for the establishment of a national university at Washington. By a unanimous vote the association endorsed his proposal and appointed him chairman of a committee to work for the establishment of such an institution.

In contrast with the Nashville meeting the sessions at Trenton were well attended. Teachers from twenty-eight states, the territory of Colorado, the District of Columbia, and Canada were present. One resolution provided for the appointment of a committee to study and report on the feasibility of establishing the decimal system of weights and measures. Another directed the board neither to ask for nor receive money from schoolbook publishers to pay for the publication of the annual *Proceedings*. So the association had to continue to take up a collection from the members when the incoming dues were insufficient to pay the printing costs.[22]

CLEVELAND, AUGUST 15, 16, 17, 1870

"I think we can hardly, at this moment, appreciate the magnitude of the work we have accomplished." So declared D. B. Hagar, president of the association, in the closing moments of the convention.[23] What had

[21] *Ibid.*, 640-690.
[22] NTA, *Proceedings, 1869* (Bardeen ed.), 692-727.
[23] NEA, *Proceedings, 1870*, 214.

been done? The small, limited, and relatively unknown National Teachers' Association had been transformed into the inclusive and potentially influential National Educational Association.

The origin of the NEA is clear. Ten state teachers' associations met in Philadelphia in 1857 and created a parent for themselves. Slowly, one by one, the other state associations and those which were organized subsequently acknowledged the parental nature of the national association. Having been created as a parent, the National Teachers' Association proceeded to increase its offspring by the simple process of adoption. The American Normal School Association, organized at Norwich, Connecticut, in 1858, became a department of the NEA at the Cleveland meeting. The National Association of School Superintendents, organized in Harrisburg in 1865 and launched in Washington in the following winter, also became a department at Cleveland. The Central College Association, organized in Illinois in 1869 as a sort of federation of state and regional associations of college men, became the Department of Higher Education of the NEA. In addition to absorbing or adopting these three organizations, the NEA created a fourth department, that of elementary education. Thus the National Teachers' Association emerged from the Cleveland meeting with a new name, the National Educational Association, and an additional function—that of coordinating the associated departments. The departments were not to be separated but joined, as President Eli T. Tappan of Kenyon College expressed it, "by a conjunction and never by a disjunctive conjunction."[24] By blending the three adopted organizations and the newly created department of elementary education into one great unit, President Hagar said, "we can preserve the advantages of each, and at the same time establish on a broad foundation an organization grand in its proportions, comprehensive in its objects, and powerful in its operations."[25]

"But it seems to me this division into sections will prove to be an elephant on our hands . . . certain sections will draw most of those in attendance and as a matter of course other sections will be very slimly attended. . . . I would much prefer that we have all our exercises in one general meeting." Such was the opinion of Zalmon Richards, who had been president of the National Teachers' Association in 1858.

But E. E. White of Ohio was sensitive and weary. He hoped there would be no "tedious discussion" nor delaying amendments. The new constitution did not require simultaneous sessions and the departments could meet on different days. He did not share the anxiety of "my friend from Washington."[26]

[24] NEA, *Proceedings, 1871*, 12.
[25] NEA, *Proceedings, 1870*, 95.
[26] *Ibid.*, 101-102.

The association agreed with White and the committee, and the new name and the new structure became an official achievement.

At the Cleveland meeting John W. Hoyt made a report for the committee on the national university; John Eaton, the recently appointed United States commissioner of education, narrated the history of the federal government's role in education; W. T. Harris, superintendent of the St. Louis schools, gave the first of 145 speeches which he was destined to deliver to the NEA before his death in 1909; and Senator Frederick A. Sawyer of South Carolina showed how a public-school system had ennobled Massachusetts and how the lack of it had degraded Texas.

Hearing that Thomas Hughes, author of *Tom Brown's School Days*, had landed in New York, President Hagar sent him a telegram inviting him to attend the remaining sessions. Alert, vigorous William H. McGuffey was there, declaring that "the teacher who can't teach his subject without a textbook can't teach it with the textbook." He lamented the transformation of textbooks into treatises which he pronounced as "etymologically preposterous." He denounced the memorizing of definitions and concluded that "committing the dictionary is the most savage kind of employment ever imposed upon children in a school." On August 6 President Grant, at that time in Cleveland, was invited to the Central High School building where the normal department sessions were being held. Upon his arrival, the members descended to the lower floor and were introduced, one by one, to the President by Commissioner Eaton. After Grant's withdrawal, the session on object teaching was resumed. One member referred to the object lesson they had just had. "If you want to know how the hand of the President of the United States feels, the only way is to feel it (Laughter)."[27]

The Cleveland meeting of 1870 had been a success. The National Teachers' Association had come through thirteen years of uncertainty and now it was certain that the joint efforts of the state teachers' associations had achieved a success denied to organizations with eminent sponsors, impressive scholarship, and multiple supporters. The teachers had done for themselves what friends, sponsors, and supporters could not do for them.

[27] *Ibid.*, 193, 173, 59.

5

Who Talked About What

As CIVILIZATION advances, ideas take precedence over deeds, theory over practice, and philosophy over practicality; the ivory tower is esteemed over the merchandise mart, the study over the office, and the library over the factory. While no sharp line is drawn between words and actions, words are recognized as the pooled wisdom of society and as guides to action.

Philosophy, theory, and method must be conceived and matured before they find application in the schoolroom. Thus the words of educators promote and reflect educational progress. Who talked, what they talked about, and what they said are significant strands in the history of American culture. The speakers at one hundred years of NEA conventions therefore reflect an important segment of intellectual history.

During the century from 1857 through 1956, the National Education Association held ninety-four conventions. No sessions were held in 1861, 1862, and 1945 because of wars; the meetings of 1867 and 1878 went by default; and the 1906 meeting, scheduled for San Francisco, had to be canceled because of the earthquake. (Instead of the 1906 meeting, the association issued a large volume commemorating its fiftieth anniversary.) The six meetings held during 1943 through 1949 were officially designated as sessions of the representative assembly only and not as conventions, but some of these—the later ones particularly—included several activities other than business sessions.

At the typical convention about 200 papers were read, making a total for the 94 conventions of about 19,000 speeches for the first century.[1] This calculation includes only those speeches that were printed, summarized,

[1] At early conventions the number of speeches was often as few as forty or fifty, but at many of the later ones the number exceeded 300. The average of 200 was reached by three different ways of calculating the number. While 200 is an approximation, it is exact enough for the purposes of comparison. Allowance must also be made for the fact that the *Proceedings* since 1941 do not list the speakers and the topics of the departmental meetings.

or indicated in the volumes of the *Proceedings*. If all the speeches given in all the separate conventions of all the departments and allied associations were included, the total number would be more than 100,000.

Who delivered these 19,000 speeches, what were the speakers talking about, and what came of it all?

The speakers can be classified and identified. They were superintendents of city and state school systems; presidents of normal schools, teachers' colleges, colleges, universities, and various other kinds of educational institutions; professors, research scholars, and specialists of divers kinds; principals and teachers from schools of every grade level; public officials, from the President of the United States to the local mayor or alderman; and invited guests of varying degrees of prominence.

Overlapping these categories, one can classify many of the speakers as officers of the NEA, United States commissioners of education, and distinguished visitors, such as diplomats, explorers, travelers, reporters, authors, scientists, inventors, business leaders, preachers, and advocates of various causes.

Another category of speakers is composed of those who made addresses of welcome, and such speeches were sometimes numerous and sometimes humorous. Governors, mayors, superintendents, school-board members, other dignitaries, and local-arrangement committees assured the visiting delegates that they were welcome to the region, state, city, and convention hall. While the responses by NEA officials were usually brief, they too were sometimes multiple. For example, when the association met at Toronto in 1891, six speakers delivered welcoming addresses, not all of them brief, and twelve NEA officers and representatives from various parts of the United States made replies—eighteen speeches, a prayer, the national hymns, and a solo as the opening program on a July afternoon. At San Francisco in 1911 Governor Hiram Johnson, Mayor P. H. McCarthy, and President Benjamin I. Wheeler of the state university welcomed the teachers, and three NEA officers replied.[2] In 1940 the governor of Wisconsin, the mayor of Milwaukee, the state superintendent of public instruction, the president of the Wisconsin Education Association, and the president of the board of education of Milwaukee greeted the association, and the secretary of the board of normal school regents expanded at some length upon the history, scenery, industries, and culture of Wisconsin.

Another group of NEA speakers may be designated as important persons. Nearly every President of the United States, from Buchanan to F. D. Roosevelt, spoke to one or more of the conventions. Buchanan invited the teachers to a reception at the White House, Grant went to

[2] One of the respondents was Josiah L. Pickard, who had been president of the NEA in 1871 and who had attended the first annual meeting in Cincinnati in 1858. In a touching manner he referred to that far-off occasion. NEA, *Proceedings, 1911,* 74-75.

the assembly hall in Cleveland in 1870 and shook hands with all those in attendance, and Garfield demonstrated his great interest in the profession by securing the enactment of the bill to establish the Department of Education in 1867 and in subsequent messages to the association. Senators, cabinet members, diplomats, judges, and others of prominence spoke to NEA conventions.

As the audiences grew larger and larger, the programs included more speakers who could discuss broad topics of general interest in a colorful and energetic manner. Thus the assembly meetings took on something of the flavor of a public forum in which competing ideas were presented. At the convention of 1940 a Democratic candidate for the United States Senate from Utah and a Republican congressman from South Dakota addressed the teachers on political issues, and H. V. Kaltenborn, a prominent radio commentator, discussed world affairs.

Not all the speakers from outside the profession dealth with such serious subjects. Poets, travelers, broadcasters, and greeters provided both entertainment and information. Among the many prominent persons who addressed the NEA conventions were Jane Addams, Booker T. Washington, Alexander Graham Bell, Samuel Gompers, Charles Lindbergh, and Earl Warren.

A number of speakers appeared on the program again and again. While frequency of speaking is not necessarily an index of ability and effectiveness, it is an indication of prominence and status. William T. Harris, St. Louis superintendent and later United States commissioner of education, spoke 145 times; Emerson E. White, superintendent and editor from Ohio, spoke 92 times; James M. Greenwood, superintendent of Kansas City, 67 times; Albert E. Winship, editor and lecturer of Boston, 61 times; F. Louis Soldan, superintendent of St. Louis, 55 times. About thirty other speakers appeared twenty-five or more times on the program. Among these were G. Stanley Hall, researcher, author, and college administrator; Charles H. Judd, researcher, professor, and college administrator; Zalmon Richards, principal and first president of the National Teachers' Association; J. W. Crabtree, president of a normal school and later executive secretary of the NEA.

What did the 19,000 speeches delivered during the first century deal with? Inclusive and specific answers to this question cannot be given, but approximations can be provided. In 1891 W. T. Harris classified the papers given at NEA conventions from 1858 to 1890 into twenty-two categories. His categories and numbers, rearranged in the order of greatest frequency, are listed at the top of page 49.

Harris's analysis gives rise to some significant interpretations. The classification of high schools with colleges was in accord with the current practice, for the few high-school teachers who attended NEA con-

SPEECHES AT NEA MEETINGS, 1858-1890

No. of Papers	Topics Treated in Papers
81	Theory and psychology
75	High schools and colleges
56	Normal schools
45	Manual training and technical schools
29	Courses of study
28	Kindergartens
27	Primary grades
25	Music education
24	Moral and religious instruction
21	Philosophy of methods
14	Federal aid to education
10	Graded and ungraded schools
10	Supervision
10	Foreign educational systems
9	Textbooks
8	Education for Indians, Chinese, Negroes
8	Examinations for teachers and pupils
8	Criticisms of schools
4	Statistical records
3	Buildings, heating, etc.
3	Compulsory attendance
2	Crime and education[3]

ventions became members of the Department of Higher Education. The popularity of normal schools is understandable, for they were growing at a rapid rate and there was a vigorous controversy as to whether they should be primarily academic or professional institutions. The great frequency of manual training as a topic is explained by its appeal to those who advocated a practical education and the subject enlisted some ardent proponents, even though Harris, Marble, and other critics denied its disciplinary value. The stress upon moral and religious issues was in accord with long-standing beliefs and did not arise from Herbart's teachings, which became influential subsequently. The ten papers on foreign school systems show that the great wave of foreign influence of the first half of the nineteenth century had subsided, and all Barnard's efforts through his *American Journal of Education* could not sustain any great interest in European education. The small attention to examinations is quite as one would expect, but the even smaller attention to textbooks is somewhat surprising, since it was a period of great dependence upon and respect for the formalized content of books. The low frequency of discussions on buildings, supervision, statistical records,

[3] NEA, *Proceedings, 1891,* 446-447.

and compulsory attendance shows that school organization and administration, in spite of marked advances, had not yet became a major interest in American education.

Without an enumeration of the topics discussed during the entire century, one can nevertheless perceive some general trends in the discussions. Some topics (1) waned in frequency of treatment, (2) some increased in frequency, and (3) some remained fairly constant.

1. The most noticeable group of topics that waned, almost to the point of disappearance by 1907, were the school subjects of Latin, Greek, grammar, algebra, history, and physics. This does not mean that the contents and methods of teaching these subjects were neglected; they were henceforth treated under such topics as curriculum, supervision, projects, and problems. Civics, citizenship, or government is a notable exception to this general tendency; it became merged with loyalty, patriotism, Americanization, and nationalism and so continued to receive repeated attention.

Another topic that lost its appeal for speakers was that of education as a profession. The almost pathological interest in proving that teaching was a profession received continuous attention during the first decades of the association. Then for many years the agitation was dropped. Within the last few years it has been revived and intensified. The recent movement is not, however, merely a wrangling over definitions but a systematic and determined effort by the educators to set the standards and requirements of their profession.

For more than fifty years educational exhibits at regional and world expositions created great interest. They were counted as among the most effective means of informing the public and inspiring the teachers. European expositions at London, Paris, and Vienna and American exhibits at New Orleans, Atlanta, Philadelphia, Boston, Louisville, Chicago, and St. Louis received great attention and were often subjects for formal reports by committees. While educational exhibits are still regarded as necessary and desirable, they no longer receive places on the programs.

Fervent and vehement speeches on the use of the Bible in schools were frequent during the first half-century (1857-1906). Its use was regarded as indispensable for the development of character, morals, citizenship, and patriotism. The Bible was also urged as a necessary preparation for the understanding and appreciation of literature, and its decline in popularity was bitterly bewailed by Nicholas Murray Butler[4] and other speakers. The same lament was embodied in a resolution of the NEA in 1908.[5] Court decisions and state laws slowly forced a diminution in the use of the Bible in schools, and consequently,

[4] NEA, *Proceedings, 1902,* 72-75.
[5] NEA, *Proceedings, 1908,* 38.

as time passed, the problem evoked fewer speeches at educational meetings.

The problem of illiteracy among the freedmen and the whites of the South provoked an almost evangelical fervor for two decades after the Civil War. The topic then declined in popularity as a subject for discussion, although it was restored for a short time after the First World War when Cora Wilson Stewart popularized the cause through the Moonlight Schools.

A few topics, somewhat restricted in duration, pertinence, and appeal, may be mentioned. For the first fifty years (1857-1906) the programs included speeches on education among the Indians and in the territories, especially Alaska. Federal responsibility was the key idea in such discussions. The crusade for phonetic spelling, which involved many speeches and great activity, waned and disappeared by about 1910. Campaigns for thrift and temperance were brief, though spirited. Coeducation had only a temporary popularity on convention programs and disappeared before the end of the first half-century. Biographical and analytical speeches about particular educators and their messages have practically disappeared from programs, although anniversaries of the birth of noted educators are still given at least formal attention.

2. Among the topics which rose markedly in frequency of discussion at conventions during the last fifty years were business education, physical education, democracy and citizenship, administration and supervision, school surveys, tests and measurements, visual and auditory aids (motion pictures, radio, television, recordings), and adult education. General curriculum problems—selecting the contents, grading the materials, and organizing the presentation—have received intense attention since the period of Herbartianism around 1890. Curriculum-making was intensified in the 1920's and shows no sign of losing its appeal to speakers. New types of school organization since about 1910—the junior high school, the junior college, nursery schools, and many specialized schools—were described and advocated by a large number of speakers. Provision for the individual pupil, although involved in Froebel's doctrine and given lip attention by early speakers, received major and rather scientific study only since about 1915. Contrary to widespread opinion, both within and outside the profession, the topic of methods received relatively little attention during the first half-century. Herbart's five steps of teaching, promulgated in the 1890's, is the outstanding exception to this generalization. The intensive study of method started with the work of Dewey, Kilpatrick, and Rugg, and, even more specifically, with the publication of H. C. Morrison's *Practice of Teaching in Secondary Schools* in 1926. These and other men promoted the development of such methods as the socialized recitation, problem, project, and unit. Within the last

decade the great growth and development of group dynamics has also enriched methods and procedures as well as techniques of human relationships. Closely related to methods are the topics of field trips and the utilization of community resources, practices that received spirited treatment in the 1930's and subsequently. Perhaps no topic is more outstandingly the possession of the last forty years than that of pupil welfare—health services, intelligence testing, personal appraisals, and guidance and counseling.

3. Many topics have maintained a high level of frequency during the whole history of the NEA. Art, music, school libraries, manual training and industrial education, character education, child study after its beginnings around 1890, and Federal aid to education in the form of land grants, special aids, and support for specific fields are among those with a steady degree of popularity. Teacher education, at first in normal schools and then in teachers' colleges and universities, has naturally been a consistently appealing topic of discussion. Juvenile delinquency has elicited an almost constant outpouring of discussion, with two high intensities following the world wars. The nature of public education and its relation to government, democracy, and civilization in general have elicited almost constant attention throughout the hundred years. Handicapped pupils—the deaf, blind, crippled, defective, and mentally retarded—were dealt with in many papers since around 1870. The Department, Bureau, and then the Office of Education was regarded as the virtual creation of the NEA; its support and functions were treated in a succession of speeches, resolutions, and campaigns. The certification, preparation, and requirements of teachers received early and constant attention; but specific aspects, such as tenure, salary, status, and conditions, came to the fore only since about 1920. The topic of college-entrance requirements received early discussion and continued until well into the present century, although the acceptance of patterns of high-school preparation rather than specific subject units has lessened the frequency of the discussion of this topic.

One additional view of the topics discussed at NEA conventions is provided by citing the numbers of papers read before selected departments during the decade 1930-1939. See tabulation on page 53.

The large number of discussions of rural education has several explanations. It was a period of school consolidation, of a migration back to the country, and of expanding services, such as libraries, health provisions, improved equipment, and a more fitting program of studies. During the depression decade many educators hoped to be able to raise standards for teachers and so discussions of teacher training were especially pertinent. The other topics, with the exception of science, were on the increase in popularity, although, as one would expect, the kinder-

SPEECHES AT NEA DEPARTMENT MEETINGS, 1930-1939

Rank order	No. of Papers	Topics
1	188	Rural education
2	91	Teachers' colleges
3	86	Supervision
4	85	Business education
5	79	Health and physical education
6	76	Adult education
7	72	Home economics
8	71	Vocational education
9	56	Science teaching
10	55	Social studies (history, geography, etc.)
11	39	Kindergarten and primary grades

garten received less attention after the merger of the two departments, kindergarten and primary, in 1927. The number of speeches on the social studies is inadequately reflected since only those of the summer meetings are counted. During this decade the Department of Social Studies met with historical associations, and in 1935 started its own conventions at which hundreds of papers were read. The same consideration applies in the cases of other departments that held separate meetings in the 1930's.

Even after reviewing all these lists and trends, one must recognize that all efforts at enumerating 19,000 speeches are bound to be unsuccessful. How, for example, can one put a speech called "The Gospel of Beauty" into a category? What is one to expect from a speaker who announces his subject as "Full-Orbed Education"? President Noah Porter of Yale provided a paper on "The Class System," which was intelligible in 1877 but now has no relevance. One speaker announced his subject as "What's It All About?" and another entitled "What, How, and How Better" evoked spirited comments. President Lotus D. Coffman of the University of Minnesota selected the neither revealing nor complimentary title "A Plea for Sanity."[6] Such titles as "Education Moves Forward," "The Great Adventure," and "Silent Forces in Education" are beyond categories.

While the speeches varied extensively in quality and style, many of them sparkled with wit and vibrated with humor. Frankness and sharp clashes of opinion were frequent, and visiting speakers were impressed with the high degree of personal objectivity in the presence of very real differences in professional opinions. In 1908 Robert A. Milliken remarked that the meeting reminded him of the fact that "the especial function of gatherings of this sort is to bring out violent differences of opinions, and

[6] NEA, *Proceedings, 1935,* 359.

under no circumstances to foster an insipid and effeminating spirit of harmony."[7] Thomas W. Bicknell made a similar observation, although he feared that the speakers were often too partisan and strident.[8]

What can be said concerning the intentions, motives, and purposes of NEA speakers? After making allowances for greeters, entertainers, repeaters, self-seekers, and those who had only good will, the vast majority dealt in sober fashion with the problems and issues of education. While many of the speeches lacked objectivity, specificity, and unity, they were permeated with noble purposes and high endeavor. The serious reader is impressed, even today, with the conscientious and earnest efforts of the early speakers to elevate the quality of the work of their "high calling." Speakers throughout the hundred years were keenly conscious of the direct connection between education and society, of the dependence of popular government upon an informed citizenry, and of the necessity of selecting pertinent studies and presenting them in an appealing manner. One may criticize the degree of objectivity, the lack of scientific methods, and the undue faith in discussion, but he cannot justly question the serious professional spirit of the vast majority of the NEA speakers.

The speeches did not escape criticism, however. Editors of state teachers' journals called repeatedly for fewer and shorter speeches and more opportunity for discussion in which the teachers could participate. And there were critics within the NEA. At the Toronto meeting of 1891 G. Stanley Hall and W. T. Harris were outspoken in their criticisms. Harris cast aspersions upon the simplicity of early speeches dealing with such topics as "The Causes of Success and Failure in the Work of the Teacher," "The Teacher and His Work," "The Teacher's Ideal," and "The Teacher's Motives," and referred contemptuously to "the old-fashioned essays read at teachers' gatherings." It is probable that Harris knew that the last title mentioned was used repeatedly by Horace Mann (see Chapter 4).[9]

Hall conceded that the general mass meetings had to deal with popular subjects in an appealing manner, but the section meetings, he felt, should "be organized for more effective work. Very much of the energy of this Association is wasted by threshing old straw, by random work, by people who have no conception of the best that has been said and done in their own subject. Nothing is more demoralizing and wasteful than to hear a half-hour paper of this sort."[10]

Recent NEA conventions have been marked by a great increase in the number of small-group sessions, meeting simultaneously. Sometimes such

[7] NEA, *Proceedings, 1908*, 986.
[8] NEA, *Proceedings, 1882*, 77.
[9] NEA, *Proceedings, 1891*, 447.
[10] *Ibid.*, 452.

sessions are planned to deal with identical subjects or different aspects of the same subject; more often they deal with a wide variety of different topics. In many cases such sessions have no formal speeches; they are panel discussions, round-table discussions, or workshops. This change in meeting pattern reflects both the vast increase in attendance at annual conventions and the desire to provide wider opportunity for individual participation.

What did the 19,000 speeches accomplish? This question inevitably merges into the larger question of the effectiveness of the whole association. To this question more extensive answers are given in various chapters of this volume. Here, however, it may be said that the speeches contributed powerfully to establishing the public schools as the agency of the state to train its future citizens; they helped to build up popular support for extending education upward to include the high school and downward to incorporate the kindergarten; they promoted the rapid growth of administration and supervision; they facilitated an adjustment between the high schools and the colleges; they disseminated a more humane attitude toward children and a better understanding of their growth and nature; they contributed effectively toward the transformation of scattered groups of poorly trained teachers into an integrated profession; they promoted the establishment of the Bureau of Education and repeatedly saved it from financial starvation; they helped to establish schools as a great moral and ethical force, divested of sectarianism; they provided for cross-fertilization of educational growth, accelerating the spread of information and exchange of experience about new developments in education such as tests, guidance, scientific curriculum-making, and the use of visual and auditory aids; they promoted the growth of *state* systems and a *national policy*. Had this last been their only achievement, it would stand as one of the greatest contributions to the growth of American nationality; and yet it is important to note that it was done by a voluntary national organization and *not* by the national government.

In the published proceedings of the NEA's annual meetings from 1857 through 1956 one can trace with considerable clarity and fullness a century of the historical development of American education. Selected aspects of this story are related in the following sixteen chapters.

PART II

Development of American Education

6

Rise of High Schools

THE dramatic success story of American education is the rise of the high school. This story is largely contained within the span of years covered by the NEA's first century. The story was, indeed, written in considerable measure by the discussions and actions of the association, its departments and committees, and its National Council of Education. It is, of course, also true that the establishment and expansion of high schools and the eventual acceptance by the American people of the ideal of secondary education for *all* youth were the result of numerous indigenous local efforts. But these efforts were stimulated and guided, and their attainment of success was hastened, by a notable series of NEA actions. No such national forum or guiding influence had had a part in the earlier story of the building of state systems of universal free public elementary schools. The key chapters in this earlier story had been largely written before 1857.

From lowly origins in the 1820's, the American high school rose in a few decades to become education's darling and problem child. Was it for the select few or was it the people's college? Was it an imitation of the academy or was it a new creation? Was it an arm of the state, a supplement to the home, an ally of the church, a prelude to vocations, an agent of culture, or a servant of the colleges? Was it dedicated to citizenship, vocational utility, ethical standards, social efficiency, mental discipline, college preparation, or general culture, or was it primarily a waiting room for maturity?

These questions plagued the founders and promoters and continued to harass those who watched the unplanned infant grow into a towering, somewhat undisciplined youth. Then, as the educators tried to answer these questions, they saw the great unmanageable institution split into junior high schools and senior high schools. While this metamorphosis solved some issues, it created others. Worries attend us still. In the meantime the high school did grow.

There were about sixty high schools in the United States in 1850, 325 in 1860, 800 in 1870, 1,200 in 1880, and 2,526 in 1890. After 1890 it is more revealing to state the growth in total enrollment.

High-School Enrollment, 1890-1955[1]
(Public and Private)

1890	359,949
1900	699,403
1910	1,115,398
1920	2,500,176
1930	4,804,255
1940	7,123,009
1950	6,427,042
1955	8,472,478

This astounding growth calls for an explanation. The institution itself, with its multiple purposes, changing curriculum, and unestablished status, provides only uncertain and inadequate explanations. The total of internal answers seems to add up to the unenlightening fact that it was for various groups whatever they wanted it to be. For the colleges it was a preparatory school; for the state it was a training ground for democracy and citizenship; for parents it was a prolongation of education within reach of the parental roof; and for the proclaimers of equality it was the people's college. Since the high school emerged from no well-integrated educational theory and served no unified social purpose, some explanation for its origin and growth must be found outside itself.

As culture rises so must the educational standard. The period following the Civil War was characterized by changes in industry, commerce, agriculture, politics, theology, and science. Darwinism forced theologians, scientists, and educators to reexamine their assumptions and reevaluate their institutions. The building of transcontinental railroads, packing plants, oil refineries, and department stores called for new techniques and skills. The dawn of scientific agriculture, the development of geology and biology, and the beginnings of corporations called for more knowledge and a higher level of popular understanding. Even the defects of American life—city bosses, the Whisky Ring scandal, the Crédit Mobilier, and strikes—showed the necessity for more education. While the high school was not a specific remedy for any particular evil, its establishment was a manifestation of the need for a higher level of general education.

To the cultural, economic, and civic reasons for high schools should be added the influence of the frontier and newer West. At Topeka in 1886 W. E. Sheldon, secretary of the NEA, announced, four years ahead of the superintendent of the census of 1890, that "there is no such thing

[1] United States Office of Education, *Statistical Summary of Education, 1949-50* (Washington, 1953), 19.

as frontier lines in this country."[2] Before these dates, however, and long afterward the influence of the frontier upon the Westerner was varied and pronounced. For one thing he had no fear of government nor any aversion to its services. In speeches of 1873 President Eliot of Harvard expressed a fear and a distrust of government aid, but President Read of the University of Missouri said that the people and the government were one. The frontiersmen was accustomed to look to government for cheap and, after 1862, free land, for the rapid extension of mail service, for help in securing railroads and roads, and for convenient courts and recording offices; he was little concerned as to whether it was the national, state, county, or local unit that provided the needed service. When he asked for schools, both common and high, he had no idea but what they too would be provided at public expense. Looking to government as the source of benefactions was a habit as well as a principle with him. It was no accident that the first fully developed state system of high schools should have appeared in Michigan, a western state, and that the high schools of the West achieved a higher status sooner than did those of the older states.

In addition to these cultural, economic, moral, and geographic explanations for the rise of high schools, one powerful factor within the educational system remains to be described. The presence of an ever-enlarging number of colleges, founded by energetic and ambitious denominations, made the distance between them and the elementary schools appear to be a gap that required immediate filling. While the colleges would have preferred traditional academies to untried high schools, they saw no chance of securing them in the West and so exerted some help in the establishment of high schools, relinquishing their preparatory departments as high schools rose to fill the gap.

The struggle to establish high schools was won, to a considerable extent, by the argument of *fait accompli*. Before taxpayers quite realized it, advanced studies were being taught by eager teachers in the upper room of the local school in response to the demands of ambitious parents and students. These scattered courses gradually coalesced into a program and an unplanned high school emerged. When alerted taxpayers finally asked questions, they were told that all the battles had been fought and all the issues settled in the campaign to establish the common elementary schools. "Any reasoning that justifies common schools justifies high schools" was the declaration of James P. Wickersham of Pennsylvania at the NEA convention of 1873.[3] Common schools increase wealth and make good citizens; so do high schools. At the same convention Richard Edwards of Illinois enumerated the arguments for high schools

---

[2] NEA, *Proceedings, 1886*, 65.
[3] NEA, *Proceedings, 1873*, 59.

and only a few of them differed from those used in the earlier campaign for common schools. High schools, said Edwards, lessen illiteracy, promote diligence and industry, provide intellectual culture, equalize opportunity, and inspire and elevate the elementary grades.[4]

In general, the high school was accepted as an extension of the elementary grades and was inaugurated in some states without additional legislation. According to a speaker at the NEA convention of 1872, the vast majority of people understood the term common schools to include the high school as well as the elementary grades.[5] In several states—for examples, Iowa and Pennsylvania—high schools were *authorized* at a particular time but not *required* until some years later. While numerous variations in programs, purposes, and support prevailed for several years, the success of the high school was never in doubt after the Civil War, and its ascendancy over all other institutions for secondary education was conceded by 1880.

The additional years above the elementary grades were designated by a variety of names—union, select, graded, upper, grammar, secondary, fitting, preparatory, and high. They were variously called institutes, seminaries, and academies. The purpose, organization, program, and support were matters of debate. Were these additional years beyond the grades a part of the common schools or were they a new creation involving a new crusade for popular support? Varying answers were given to these questions in different areas and decades.

From one standpoint high schools were the successors of the Latin grammar schools of colonial days. These schools were narrow in purpose, rigid in program, and exclusive as to admission. While they were public schools, authorized by the church operating through the state, they were not free or popular. The church-state accepted the responsibility for training the leaders of church and state, but not the followers. The academy, which slowly replaced the English and Latin grammar schools after the Revolution, was broader in purpose, program, and admission policies. It stressed practical studies, and became a terminal rather than a preparatory school. The academies, however, were not democratic; in spite of the fact that in some states they were supported in part by taxes, they were usually under the control of benefactors or self-perpetuating boards that were insensitive to popular wishes. The practical studies were slowly overshadowed by the narrow and restrictive requirements of college entrance. By the 1850's academies were widely denounced as exclusive, aristocratic, impractical, antidemocratic, and un-American.

The critics of the academy perceived the formula for creating an insti-

---

[4] *Ibid.*, 51-58.
[5] NEA, *Proceedings, 1872*, 150. See also *1914*, 498.

tution that would be responsive to their needs and suited to new conditions. The victorious crusade to allocate tax funds for the common schools could also be used to secure high schools. The idea was to extend the common schools upward, and that is what was done. The idea that the high school grew out of the academy is not only an error; it is a gross distortion. The high school strangled the academy and replaced it as the prevailing institution to provide advanced, practical terminal training for ambitious boys and girls. For a time, from about 1865 to 1893, the high school had the glorious prospect of becoming the poor man's college, the enricher of culture, the promoter of industry, the school for citizenship.

At the St. Louis meeting of the NEA in 1871 Newton Bateman, state superintendent of public instruction of Illinois, examined the question of the state's obligation to support high schools. He saw no limits to the right or power of the state to provide for the educational needs of the people, for in the long run such provision was merely insurance for perpetuating the state itself. His argument rested also upon the injustice of providing education for the few to the neglect of the many. Such a restricted program would fail to tap the human resources of the state.

The amount of latent and dormant power; of wealth-discovering and wealth-producing energy; of beauty-loving and beauty-inspiring taste and skill, that lie concealed and slumbering in the brains and hearts and hands of the keen, shrewd, capable, but untutored millions of our youth, is beyond computation. Now over all this unreclaimed but magnificent intellectual and moral territory, over all these minds and souls and bodies, with their untold possibilities of good, the State has, in my opinion, a sort of *right of eminent domain* and not only may, but should exercise it in the interest of her own prosperity and dignity.[6]

The state, according to Bateman, should provide common schools for all and high schools and universities for those who wanted them. The university lifts up and challenges the high school, and the high school provides perpetual incentive toward high standards in elementary schools. To deny a high-school and college education to the poor would perpetuate the barriers between the indigent and the affluent; it would create an aristocracy of learning to aggravate that of wealth, which was already the opprobrium of the nation. Such a restriction seems to say to the children of the poor: "Thus far, but no farther. Your utter mental nakedness shall be decently covered with homespun, but the purple and fine linen of culture are not for you." Such a policy would fail to utilize the natural abilities or capitalize the intense longings of the most promising intellects.

Even though the evolving high school grew rapidly in enrollment,

[6] NEA, *Proceedings, 1871,* 26.

broadened its program, adjusted itself to community conditions, and gave less attention to college requirements, the theory of its function did not develop correspondingly. The same perplexities that vexed the original promoters also troubled later high-school principals. In 1878 a committee of the Board of Education of Indianapolis reported in favor of continuing the high school because (1) it was the poor man's college, enabling him to fit himself for a greater variety of employment; (2) it was a powerful incentive to elementary pupils to study and continue in school; (3) it "takes even from the wealthy an excuse for patronizing private schools and prevents an indulgence of the anti-republican idea that the better class of schools should belong only to the rich."[7]

In 1896 Superintendent F. Louis Soldan of St. Louis was trying to decide upon the proper function of the high school. There were, he said, three principles or viewpoints which might guide the program maker: (1) the practical demands of life, (2) the demands of scholarly standards, and (3) the growth and development of the student. He assumed that existing programs reflected a degree of respect for each of these three viewpoints, and that the third, though probably best and most desirable, could not be adopted because of the demands of the other viewpoints.[8] In 1908 the NEA tried to solve the question of the function of the high school by passing a resolution:

Resolved that the public high schools should not be chiefly fitting schools for higher institutions, but should be adapted to the general needs, both intellectual and industrial of their students and communities, and we suggest that higher institutions may wisely adapt their courses to this condition.[9]

By 1920 the conception of what high schools should accomplish had been enlarged and matured. Reflecting the influence of the 1918 report of the NEA Commission on the Reorganization of Secondary Education (the report that set forth the "Seven Cardinal Principles"), Superintendent J. O. Engleman of Decatur, Illinois, outlined the functions of the high school: to promote health, rationalize leisure, discipline the mind, explore occupational abilities, democratize society, sensitize the civic sense, and promote living together.[10]

In contrast with Engleman's optimistic analysis, Assistant Superintendent John N. Greer of Minneapolis, speaking also in 1920, was convinced that the high schools were "saturated with college requirement rules and standards. The high school is molded and shaped in order that it might supply academic material for the academic college." He complained that college-trained teachers made the high schools mere

---

[7] *Report of Commissioner of Education, 1878,* 64.
[8] NEA, *Proceedings, 1896,* 355.
[9] NEA, *Proceedings, 1908,* 39.
[10] NEA, *Proceedings, 1920,* 209-212.

echoes of colleges in subjects and in methods. College domination caused the high rate of dropouts. The old-style manual-training schools made a temporary break in the academic domination, but they were soon reduced to preparatory schools for colleges of engineering. A similar fate overtook the work in home economics and agriculture. The academic ideal was intellectual discipline, whereas industrial education made education a social process. Greer thought that high schools should have broad enriched programs that would emphasize homemaking, business, industry, and agriculture as well as college preparation. Music, gymnasiums, athletics, and social activities should be so employed as to make the whole school a part of the community; it would then be truly the people's college.[11]

In spite of the lack of consensus as to their proper functions, the high schools continued to serve various purposes. Democratic, untrammeled by tradition, rooted in local situations, sensitive to popular demands, relatively free to evolve as conditions warranted, they began their spectacular rise. While the various names, varying number of years of work offered, and unsettled purposes make identification and enumeration of the early high schools nearly impossible, it is probable that there were about 60 by 1850 and about 325 by 1860. Following the Civil War, the number increased rapidly, as has been shown above. From Maine came the report that the high schools were absorbing both faculties and students from the academies. From New Jersey came the shamed apology that Jersey City, with 100,000 people, had not one high school. In 1890 the nation had 2,526 high schools[12] and about ten times that many half a century later.

The evolving high school encountered some opposition and suffered from the inertia that naturally sustains traditional institutions and opposes change. Unstructured and untried, it seemed raw and crude in contrast with endowed academies. No traditions of glamour hung over the upper rooms of the local school building in which the advanced classes assembled. The presence of girls, no matter how just, desirable, and politic, added nothing to the dignity and enhancement of the new institution. Religiously inclined people dimly perceived that the substitution of public high schools for denominational academies marked another step in the retreat of the churches from the educational scene. Church-supported academies viewed high schools as a threat to their existence, and private schools regarded the public high school as any business regards the rise of governmental enterprise. The colleges feared that their control over courses and programs would be impaired and college

[11] *Ibid.*, 73-75.
[12] *Report of Commissioner of Education, 1871*, 137, 163, 204, 286; NEA, *Proceedings, 1873*, 30.

faculties looked upon high schools as a threat to scholastic standards. The complaints of taxpayers slowed but did not halt the establishment of high schools. The proponents moved cautiously and in most states avoided judicial contests over the legality of using taxes to support high schools. The oft-cited Kalamazoo Case, decided in 1874, settled rather than established the principle of using tax funds for high schools. The issue had already been settled in most states by permissive legislation which did not provoke judicial contests.

A period of relative freedom, during which the high schools could have developed an independent and socially responsive program, extended approximately from the end of the war in 1865 to the Report of the Committee of Ten in 1893. During this period many schools introduced business courses, science laboratories, vocal and instrumental music, art in various forms, and, most numerous of all, programs and whole schools of manual training. The high schools were becoming people's colleges to provide instruction and training in cultural, classical, literary, industrial, and artistic fields. The people, ignorant of European educational ideas, freed from the domination of the academies, from the narrow theological dogmas that had pervaded schools, and from the superstitious awe of the classics, were working out their own educational salvation. Had the movement continued, it might have provided an indigenous institution that would have faithfully reflected and aided the growth of an American culture.

Powerful forces, however, were at work to alter, restrict, direct, and control the high schools. By the middle 1890's these forces were putting an end to the era of experimentation and self-discovery and transforming the high schools into appendages of the colleges. This period of subjugation to the colleges continued for about twenty years, until about 1918, when the National Education Association, aided by other organizations and forces, restored to the high schools something of their original freedom and autonomy.

Some of the factors that changed the high schools from an evolving institution of promise into a subservient agency of the status quo are easily identified. In fact, some of the forces operated even during the period of relative freedom from 1865 to 1893 to prevent the full realization of the possibilities of high school. Foremost in this category was the long tradition that regarded any kind of pre-college institution as basically the servant of the college. The professors who were loudest in their demands for the founding of high schools were motivated largely by the needs of the colleges rather than by the educational needs of society. Manifestly, they hoped to utilize these new schools to enhance their own institutions.

Closely related to college domination, actual and potential, was the study of Latin, which was exceeded in popularity as a high-school study in 1890 and 1900 only by algebra.[13] Such popularity reflected the persistence of the classical illusion and the power of what G. Stanley Hall called the "dead hand from the tombs of culture."[14]

Their zealous advocacy of Latin and Greek led some of the classicists into a sad misinterpretation of American traditions. They declared that the country needed and was destined to have two systems of education, one for the "ordinary citizen," consisting of the common schools, the high schools, and normal-training departments, and the other for the "highly cultured few," consisting of the common schools, preparatory academies, and classical colleges. President John P. Gulliver of Knox College decried the growing notion that the state could develop common schools, high schools, colleges, and universities, and the nation a final, crowning university, which would be acceptable to "infidels, rationalists, Jews, Atheists, and if the 'Heathen Chinese' multiply in the land, to heathen also." He declared that the high schools had failed to prepare students for college and called upon the religious denominations to found academies to supplement the deficient performance of the public high schools. President David A. Wallace of Monmouth College said that the colleges, "must labor to elevate public sentiment to demand a higher style of education." He marveled "that a Christian nation should manifest such indifference to the Greek language, in which are treasured the foundations of our religion." A few spoke up in defense of the public system, and John W. Hoyt of Wisconsin pleaded against "frittering away our energies in sectarian efforts" and called for "making all grades of our schools harmonious parts of a great national system."[15]

Another obstacle to the free development of an indigenous high school was the belief in faculty psychology. Persons who believed that one study was as good as another and that mental capacities could be whetted to a fine edge on any subject difficult enough to afford some friction were scarcely open-minded or patient enough to wait for the growth of a new educational institution. Persistently and repeatedly W. T. Harris, A. P. Marble, and other speakers at NEA conventions ridiculed the educative possibilities of manual training, shopwork, and other practical studies. Such were denounced as elementary and lacking in "mind culture."

Within a few years after the Civil War one issue gained almost a monopoly of the thought and attention devoted to high schools. Problems of support, function, curriculum, and methods were pushed aside to consider and discuss the articulation of high school and college. Thus the welfare of nine-tenths of the students was ignored in order to concentrate

13 NEA, *Proceedings, 1901,* 177.
14 NEA, *Proceedings, 1902,* 261.
15 NEA, *Proceedings, 1871,* 159-168, 181-182.

upon the college prospects of the one-tenth. College men were not interested in these other issues; they were not interested in secondary education; they were interested only in college-preparatory training. In truth, many high-school teachers had the same attitudes. Thus the educators ran from the complex problems of developing a new institution and centered attention upon a relatively unimportant issue that they could understand.

In the numerous speeches made before the Department of Higher Education in the early years of the NEA, one finds scarcely any awareness or concern with any problem of secondary education except its function of preparing students for college. In 1870 John P. Gulliver, as noted above, urged the founding of more college-preparatory academies by the churches. Immediate steps were necessary, he declared, to save liberal classical education and the millions which the churches had invested in colleges. Some of Gulliver's hearers did not share his anxiety or approve of his remedy. Professor Edward Olney of the University of Michigan said that his institution had no preparatory department and that his state had no academies. "We depend solely upon the work of the high schools, which are excellent. . . ." President David A. Wallace of Monmouth College wanted one system, either high schools or academies. Another speaker asserted that the high schools taught Latin as effectively as the academies. Still another remarked that the founding of academies would do no good, because they would immediately proclaim themselves to be colleges.[16]

At the Elmira meeting of 1873 President James McCosh of Princeton discussed the problem of preparatory schools. Like most college men of that period, he viewed the high schools primarily as stairways to college and not as terminal, vocational, general, or popular institutions. "The grand educational want of America at this present time is a judiciously scattered body of secondary schools, to carry on to our brighter youths from what has been so well commenced in the primary schools, and may be so well completed in the better colleges. How are our young men to mount from the lower to the higher platform? Every one has heard of the man who built a fine house of two stories, each large and commodious, but who neglected to put a stair between."[17] McCosh declared that there were wide regions in even the most advanced states which had no secondary education. He made no clear distinction between high schools and academies and said that the quality of work in both was poor.[18]

[16] NEA, *Proceedings, 1870,* 25.
[17] NEA, *Proceedings, 1873,* 23.
[18] *Ibid.,* 31-32.

In the ensuing discussion J. P. Wickersham of Pennsylvania called for the creation of more high schools and the abolition of the old academies. He cited one graduating class of seven boys, all of whom went to college and five girls who wanted to go, but there were no colleges to receive them. From the Lancaster high-school graduating class, nine of fifteen boys went to college. He optimistically declared that the high schools could fill the colleges and rejoiced that college men were at the convention to help solve the problem of integrating the various parts of the American educational system.[19]

The subservient position of the high schools with respect to colleges made the faculties of both institutions conscious of their status. The contempt with which many college men regarded high schools aroused a feeling of resentment in the minds of public-school men. In reporting to the NEA in 1874, a committee observed that teachers rarely asked professors to their meetings and that the two groups were alienated by condescension and envy.[20] In commenting on a new journal of higher education, the editor of the *Indiana School Journal* observed that it ought to be liberally supported, but doubted that it would be, because "so many of our higher educational men already know it all and need no more light."[21] A discussant at the 1874 meeting asserted that the best college students were trained by the high schools and the worst class of boys came from the private schools. As evidence of fact this observation has little value, but as a revelation of a feeling it is quite eloquent.[22] These and many similar instances should dispel the lingering notion that there was, back in the 1870's and 1880's, a golden period in which public-school people gratefully accepted the educational leadership of college and university professors.

The need for a "stairway" from the common schools to the colleges was supplied in four ways: by private tutoring, which was seldom used; by college preparatory departments, which were the principal means in the West and which were retained by smaller denominational colleges until after 1900; by private academies, numerous in the East and few and temporary in the West; and by the high schools, which nearly everyone regarded as the eventual means. Recognition of the emerging potential of the high school was one of the reasons why the colleges and the educators contended so bitterly over its nature and functions.

Recognizing that all college men were not unfriendly to high schools and that all high-school teachers were not understanding supporters of educational freedom, one can nevertheless say that a long educational

---

[19] *Ibid.*, 37.
[20] NEA, *Proceedings, 1874*, 11.
[21] *Indiana School Journal*, XXV, 490, August 1880.
[22] NEA, *Proceedings, 1874*, 18.

war was waged by the colleges and the high schools. The alternatives for the high schools were either educational independence *or* subservience to colleges with attendant frustration of popular hopes and expectations.

High schools generally tried to avoid domination by the colleges because they felt they had a different mission. They were to educate citizens, train workers, disseminate culture; they were to serve society and not the colleges; they were the people's college and not the college's preparatory school. This basic distinction was perceived by the public, by many educators, and by some colleges. Whereas the public and the educators accepted the situation, the colleges refused to do so. They deliberately and systematically set out to bend the evolving high schools to their own purposes, to make them mere preparatory schools, not because of evil or even selfish purposes but because they sincerely believed that a high school that served a college was better than one that developed its program for other purposes. Few college men made the distinction between secondary education and preparatory training. In fact, the majority saw no distinction. From the early days of the NEA to the present this contest has been waged. The contest was made more bitter and more involved by those college men who kept proclaiming their acceptance of the high school as a social institution with a broad function, but who also advised it to teach Latin and Greek and mathematics in order to qualify the occasional student for college.

The arguments of the college men were persuasive rather than convincing. The high school gained status in the community when its graduates could enter college. The high-school teachers, being college graduates, felt a degree of loyalty to their old institutions. The high-school teacher who trained a candidate for admission was praised as a scholar; he felt the glow that comes from approbation by one's superior. More impressive and designed to close the argument was the assertion that whatever was good preparation for college was good training for life; hence all high-school students, college-bound or job-destined, should take the same studies and learn them in the same thorough manner.

Some compromise-minded educators declared that the high school was both a fitting school and a finishing school; that it could by one and the same program prepare one boy for college and his classmate for business. W. T. Harris, James M. Greenwood, and other educators argued that whatever was good college preparation was also good preparation for business, citizenship, and home life. Some educators hesitantly took hold of this idea and tried to turn it around. They speculatively said that whatever was good preparation for life ought also to be good preparation for college, but they were reproved for their dull insight and ridiculed for thinking that manual training, which was of some value to a future cabinetmaker, was worthy of being offered as a college-entrance subject; it had, so said the orthodox educators, absolutely no value as mental discipline.

The opening campaign between the high schools and colleges was won by the high schools. With an unrealistic perception of the origin, nature, and problems of the high schools, the colleges demanded that they teach Greek because it was an entrance requirement. While the high schools rather willingly taught Latin, they were outspoken in their refusal to include Greek. Aided and abetted by their sponsors, the taxpayers, the high school said no. To a considerable extent this victory was achieved by circumstances rather than valor. The lack of prepared teachers, the necessity of courting public opinion in order to sustain the high school, and the paucity of students who wanted to study Greek rather than the fact that it was unrelated to the function of the high school and to the lives of the students caused the omission of the language. Then, too, the colleges were desperately in need of students. Repeatedly they called for the establishment of preparatory schools with a program that would conform to college requirements. Perceiving the improbability of such schools being established, they tried vainly to induce the high schools to teach Greek. While they resented the refusal of the high schools to do so, they reluctantly discovered, without too much delay, that Greek was after all a college subject and made various adjustments for taking care of those students who could be induced to study it without having had any previous preparation. By 1874 the colleges in Ohio reconciled themselves to the fact that the high schools would not teach Greek.[23] By 1878 only a half-dozen high schools in Indiana would teach it, and the state university and the colleges at Bedford, Hanover, Richmond, and Ridgeville waived the subject as an entrance requirement.[24] President Noah Porter of Yale feared that the high schools would set college standards by the mere refusal to teach Greek or geometry, or some other subject.

The task forces in the war between the high schools and colleges consisted of committees. The use of committees by educators had been well established in the NEA and its departments. In fact, the most effective committees which did battle for the colleges originated in NEA circles. The Committee of Ten on Secondary School Studies (1892-1893) was only the first of several that won decided victories for the colleges. It is not generally recognized that the most effective committee which the American Historical Association ever appointed to consider the school curriculum, the Committee of Seven of 1897, was established in response

[23] *Ibid.*, 56.
[24] *Report of Commissioner of Education, 1878*, 64-65.

to a specific request by A. F. Nightingale of the Secondary Department of the NEA.[25]

Committees were effective. They were composed of articulate leaders, men who were well informed, who knew their field, understood the educational situation, and moved with a purpose. They proceeded with caution; gathered a little information; reconciled opinions; issued strong, persuasive, convincing, specific reports; and enlisted the college officials and public-school men in carrying out their recommendations.

The idea for the Committee of Ten, whose members were selected primarily by Nicholas Murray Butler, originated in the NEA-sponsored National Council of Education at the Saratoga Springs meeting of 1892.[26] In view of the committee's dependence upon opinion and discussion, with little pretense of inquiry or research, it was fitting that it be appointed by the Council, which was itself a forum for the exchange of opinion (see Chapter 23). The committee appointed nine subcommittees of ten each. Of the hundred persons who constituted the committee that was to pronounce upon the program of secondary schools, fifty-three were college presidents or professors; twenty-three were headmasters of private schools; fourteen were high-school principals; the others were superintendents, teachers in normal schools, and holders of miscellaneous positions. Thus the college men and headmasters, numbering seventy-six, constituted three-fourths of the committee. In view of the almost unanimous agreement which followed, this preponderance in favor of the colleges may not have been important, but one cannot avoid perceiving that the committee was destined to evolve a program that was college-centered.

When the Committee of Ten was appointed, there was little feeling of rivalry between public-school leaders and college men. Even had the leaders known in advance that the committee report would put the schools under college domination, they would probably have viewed the outcome approvingly. They were accustomed to thinking that educational reforms came from the top, that the colleges shed a benign and uplifting influence over the high schools, as they in turn elevated and standardized the elementary schools. In brief, the leaders in the NEA—superintendents and college men—were quite in agreement concerning the basic principles of education. Even Francis W. Parker, usually astute, alert, and suspicious saw no great issue in the report of the Committee of Ten. In fact, he made a long speech on how to promote its dissemination and study. In other words, the prevailing educational philosophy saw no dangers in college domination, no objections to forcing boys and girls to study Latin, and looked with some scorn upon practical subjects. So

[25] NEA, *Proceedings, 1899,* 638.
[26] NEA, *Proceedings, 1892,* 754.

the report of the Committee of Ten was regarded as a great document, one that promoted better teaching, a wider curriculum, and more harmonious relations between high school and colleges. And all these ends it did achieve. Its deleterious effects were not perceived; its patronizing was not so interpreted; its establishment of subject specialists as curriculum-makers was not regarded as a misfortune. Only after the lapse of time did school men perceive that they had been taken captive by their erstwhile ally.

The nine subcommittees of the Committee of Ten, appointed to consider the various subjects, met for three-day conferences and forwarded their conclusions to the main committee. For example, the conference on history, civics, and economics, consisting of such men as Charles K. Adams, Edward G. Bourne, A. B. Hart, James H. Robinson, and Woodrow Wilson, met at Madison. The main committee claimed that the subject conferences were "distinctly conservative and moderate, although many of their recommendations are of a radical nature."[27] The committee reproved some of the conferences for trying to give their subjects weight and influence equal to Latin, Greek, and mathematics. Most of the conferences wanted their subjects taught earlier in the school program and all of them called for better teachers and improved methods and demanded that their subjects be taught in the same way to all students whether they were preparing for life or for a scientific or classical college program.

The report piously observed that secondary schools did "not exist for the purpose of preparing boys and girls for colleges."[28] It then proceeded to discuss the teaching of only those subjects which colleges did recognize, omitting any consideration of art, music, manual training, commercial subjects, and other practical courses, on the theory that such subjects had no disciplinary value.[29]

The general effect of the report was to halt the experimentation in the high school and stop all attempts to create a new institution. Just as the academy had been perverted from its practical and terminal nature and made into an alleyway to college, so would the report of the Committee of Ten force the high schools into similar subserviency. From this fate they were eventually saved by the downfall of formal discipline, by subsequent reports of a more enlightened nature, by an improved understanding of child nature and mental growth, and by curricular reforms. In the meantime, however, the report of the Committee of Ten had its effects.

Another unfortunate outcome of the report was its sanction of the idea

[27] *Report of the Committee of Ten on Secondary School Studies* (New York, 1894), 13.

[28] *Ibid.*, 51.

[29] NEA, *Proceedings, 1894*, 625-637.

that whatever a pupil studied he should study thoroughly. When this principle was actually applied, it lessened, of course, the number of subjects that a pupil could take. In other words, it was a plain denial of one of the basic principles of secondary education, namely, that it involves broad surveys, wide views, brief exposures, the exploring of varied interests, the sampling of divers topics, subjects, and areas. Instead of this reaching, expanding, and exploring, the Committee of Ten would hold the child to a prolonged exposure and a thorough mastery of the few subjects that a remote college decreed that he had to study.

Opposing voices were raised. As early as 1879 J. W. Dickinson of Massachusetts, a frequent speaker at NEA conventions, contended that when pupils had learned enough facts to understand general principles and had learned the method of studying the subject, they should be allowed to drop it and study something else.[30] Colonel Parker and other students of child nature and growth also sympathized with the idea of freedom for the student to sample, explore, reject, and pass on to something else. It is clear that the practice of holding students to the thorough completion of whatever they started was a frequent cause of their dropping out of school. In view of the fact that the original choices of what to study were made for them, it is not surprising that the number who developed a distaste for assigned tasks in prescribed studies was disturbingly large.

From the standpoint of the NEA the report of the Committee of Ten was politic, strategic, and timely; its sponsorship strengthened the association in the minds of scholars and in popular opinion. From the standpoint of educational progress, however, the report was of doubtful value; it was based upon the fast-fading psychology of formal discipline; its social vision was dim; its concern for pupil growth was nonexistent. Its total influence was designed to arrest the development of the high school as a social or community influence, and its authors revealed themselves as subject-centered, task-bound, and college-minded. In brief, it had the merits and demerits of the 1890's.

Another restrictive influence on the high schools was the work of the accrediting agencies. Beginning in 1870, the University of Michigan sent out visiting committees to pass upon the quality of work and to accredit for admission the graduates of approved high schools. In Indiana schools were inspected or rated by the state department of education and graduates recommended by the staff were admitted to the university. Within a generation most universities had established similar inspections and lists of approved schools. Beginning in the 1880's regional associations, which eventually covered the entire country, assumed the responsibility of proclaiming standards for teachers, buildings, equipment, and

[30] NEA, *Proceedings, 1879,* 24.

programs. These tangible external standards were influential in bringing the high schools up to minimum levels. In the 1930's attempts were made to include qualitative as well as quantitative standards. The mere existence of accrediting agencies had some beneficial results, but they also tended to solidify programs rather than encourage experimental growth and to perpetuate traditional subjects rather than promote enriched offerings. Thus external accreditation became a kind of substitute for internal effort, and when a school was approved, it had little incentive to develop new programs or try new methods.

High-school men began to utilize committees, not only to offset college control but also to establish their own philosophy. The Committee on the Articulation of High School and College, established in 1910, with Charles D. Kingsley of the Brooklyn Manual Training High School as chairman, set out to reestablish the freedom of the high school and incidentally to persuade the colleges to accept the broadened and popularized program which it visualized. Kingsley saw the high school as a place where students could explore diverse interests, as a social institution that should help to produce intelligent, progressive citizens, as a place for specific training as well as broad culture. He regarded mechanic arts, agriculture, and household science as rational elements, and bemoaned the fact that college requirements had turned "tens of thousands of boys and girls away from the pursuits for which they were adapted. . . ." Exclusively bookish curriculums developed false ideals of culture. Preparation to manage a home was as important, in his view, as any other kind of preparation. In brief, he visualized a functioning, popular, socialized secondary school and not a college-preparatory department.[31] In all these opinions he had the vigorous support of Charles H. Judd, a member of his committee.

Signalizing the arrival of educational maturity and independence, the educators established the Commission on the Reorganization of Secondary Education of the NEA in 1913. This large commission, operating through sixteen subcommittees, utilized the services of hundreds of public-school men and a few college professors. Between 1913 and 1921 it issued thirteen reports on such topics as civics, social studies, English, music, physical education, moral values, and guidance, which had a distribution of over 200,000. In 1918 appeared its epoch-making report on *Cardinal Principles of Secondary Education*.[32] Probably no publication in the history of education ever surpassed this little five-cent, thirty-two-page booklet in importance, both because of its fundamental nature and because of its influence.

[31] NEA, *Proceedings, 1911,* 560-561.
[32] *Cardinal Principles of Secondary Education,* Bureau of Education, Bulletin No. 35, 1918; NEA, *Proceedings, 1913,* 489-491; *1921,* 163-167.

Unlike the Committee of Ten and previous committees, the Commission on Reorganization started by examining the environmental influences that called for changes in education. Reorganization was needed because society had changed; because the student body had increased enormously, thus increasing the range of needs and abilities; because educational theory had brought new knowledge and new interpretations. Conscious of the social setting, the needs of students, the nature of learning, and the fitness of curricular materials, the commission proclaimed the seven cardinal objectives or purposes: health, basic skills, home membership, vocations, citizenship, worthy use of leisure, and character. Student-oriented, life-centered, and socially directed, these purposes marked a sharp departure from the old college-preparatory studies.

The report proclaimed a new day in secondary education, and because of its fundamental nature it tended also to socialize the elementary grades and eventually the colleges.[33] In fact, committees were appointed at once to revise the elementary program and to study the whole problem of reorganization in order to include the rising junior high schools. The basic philosophy for all these changes was in accordance with the report on the cardinal principles.[34]

Enrollments in high schools continued to grow. More attractive plants, better equipment, more appealing courses, better teaching, increasing services, more activities, the rising requirements of employers, an approving public, and the founding of junior high schools were factors in this growth, which continued through booms and depressions, war and peace, in cities and rural areas. Finally the decreasing birth rate of the 1930's had its effects in reducing high-school enrollment in the 1940's.

What did this astonishing growth in the high schools signify? According to Superintendent William McAndrew of Chicago, it meant that an institution set up for the elect, the capable, and the ambitious was now overrun by the mediocre, the mental paupers, the uninterested. It was, he said, a silk mill built to weave delicate threads now supplied with "raw materials of wool and flax, sisal, hemp, and wood pulp."[35]

McAndrew voiced the prevailing notion. As high-school enrollment doubled and quadrupled, it was assumed that the quality of students deteriorated correspondingly. This assumption was invested with the certainty of a self-revealing axiom; to doubt it was educational heresy; to act on any other assumption was educational folly. Many teachers accepted the axiom and declared that the quality of students declined perceptibly year by year. Accordingly the schools had a convenient

[33] NEA, *Proceedings, 1922,* 340.
[34] NEA, *Proceedings, 1923,* 255-257, 433-444, 1015-1016.
[35] NEA, *Proceedings, 1928,* 723. In 1912 a university president asserted that a lowering in quality was occurring at the college level. NEA, *Proceedings, 1912,* 784-785.

defense for offering formal or frivolous courses, an excuse for wavering standards, an alibi for poor student performance, and a justification for lessened efforts by teachers. Colleges tried to strengthen their entrance requirements, basing their action upon the assertion that high schools had become less select and therefore poorer.

The assumption of a constant decline in student ability rests upon the prior assumption that students of the early years were a select group. Since no objective measurements were available in those years and no convincing evidence can now be adduced for this alleged selectivity, the theory is sometimes derived from another assumption, namely, that those who went to high school in the early decades belonged to the upper socioeconomic classes. Assuming that the children from such classes were above average, one has to ask the final question, whether they went to high schools. Children, especially the boys, from well-to-do homes tended to go to private schools or college-preparatory departments. This was especially true of those who planned to go to college. When this group was removed from a school it naturally reduced the average ability. After the high schools met college-entrance requirements, this select group tended to enter the local high school instead of going elsewhere for its preparation; thus the high school may actually have risen in average ability. So it is by no means certain that the high schools of 1895 were filled with students who were superior to those of 1915. By 1930, however, many of the compulsory-attendance laws had been extended upward to the age of eighteen, and it is probable that thereafter the average ability of high-school students was lowered. Whether the decline in student quality was actual or imaginary, the steadfast belief in it had considerable effect upon the curriculum and educational standards. It led to needless sacrifices in requirements and to the too ready attitude to blame students rather than the educational process. It has provided colleges with an argument for being more selective and private schools with a slogan for recruiting students. It may be that the quality of high-school students declined markedly as they increased in numbers, but history seems to afford no specific proof for the assumption.

As high schools grew in number and size their problems also became more numerous and complex. A large percentage of students dropped out at the end of each year, the individual was lost in the crowd, little allowance was made for the growth and changes of adolescence, vocational instruction was too scanty and too late, the range in subjects and pupils from grades 1 to 7 was too great to be handled expeditiously in one organization, instruction was too formal and standardized, and even at the end of grade 12 the students were self-conscious and unsocialized.

These and other problems attracted the attention of educators. Among various plans and proposed solutions the idea of a new organization that would combine the upper grades with the first year of high school into a new school unit gained widespread approval; thus the junior high school came into existence. The idea of beginning secondary studies in the upper grades was advocated by speakers as early as the 1880's, and the Committee of Ten made such a recommendation in 1893. Several leaders, such as Calvin O. Davis of Michigan, Thomas H. Briggs of Columbia, Leonard V. Koos of Minnesota, Frank F. Bunker of Berkeley, and G. Vernon Bennett of Pomona, made special studies and experiments to show how junior high schools could facilitate the solution of many of the problems of secondary education. Under their leadership the number of junior high schools grew rapidly, from eleven in 1910, to 880 in 1920, and to 3,227 by 1954.

The junior high school was organized to promote the continuity of instruction, the adjustment of studies to the needs and capacities of adolescents, and the individualization of guidance and instruction. What looked from an outside viewpoint to be fragmentation of educational organization was in reality an arrangement more suited to the boys and girls from the age of twelve to fourteen or fifteen. As the junior-high-school program was developed in the course of time, it went far toward meeting the expectations of its founders and promoters. And from the standpoint of enrollment it participated in the success of the high school. From an enrollment of 37,331 in 1920 it grew by 1952 to 1,526,996 in separate junior high schools. By 1952 the reorganized high school of two parts included three-fourths of all secondary-school students, leaving only 1,937,210 who attended the four-year high school. Thus the junior high school has won its way, and it is established beyond doubt that American secondary education now consists of the six grades, 7 to 12.[36]

[36] Office of Education, *Junior High School Facts*, Miscellaneous No. 21, 1954, *passim*.

7

Normal Schools and Teachers' Colleges

"THE great business of all education in all its varied forms is to supply the world with teachers."[1] This sweeping statement by President Merrill E. Gates of Rutgers College reveals a perception of the truth that human progress depends upon the transmission of what is achieved. Educators of all ages have perceived this truth clearly, and all society perceives it, though sometimes dimly.

I believe that Normal Schools are a new instrumentality in the advancement of the race. I believe that without them free schools themselves will be shorn of their strength and their healing power, and will at length become mere charity schools. . . . Neither the art of printing, nor the trial by jury, nor a free press, nor free suffrage can long exist . . . without schools for the training of teachers; for if the character and qualifications of teachers be allowed to degenerate, the free schools will become pauper schools, and the pauper schools will produce pauper souls; and the free press will become a false licentious press, and ignorant voters will become venal voters; and through the medium and guise of republican forms, an oligarchy of profligate and flagitious men will govern the land. . . . Coiled up in this institution as in a spring, there is a vigor whose uncoiling may wheel the spheres.[2]

If anyone was ever entitled to pronounce a benediction upon teacher-training institutions and to utter a warning about their preservation, it was the author of the foregoing paragraph, Horace Mann, founder of normal schools. By the time of his death in 1859, normal schools had been established in nine states and were destined to spread to all existing and future states and to become an integral part of the American pattern of public education.

Colleges, academies, and upper school of various kinds had existed for two centuries in America without making any noticeable contribution

[1] NEA, *Proceedings, 1890*, 471.
[2] Horace Mann, speaking at Bridgewater, August 1846. Quoted in NEA, *Proceedings, 1872*, 31.

to the training[3] of teachers. Horace Mann saw the tragedy of their failure and devoted much of his life to the task that they had shirked. It is generally assumed that Mann and his contemporaries were greatly concerned with teaching pedagogy, methods, classroom procedures. While they did not minimize these aspects, they devoted even more thought and time to teaching young men and women the elements of an academic education. Most of the enrollees in the early normal schools, particularly the young women, had had no previous opportunity to study any subject beyond the elementary grades. So the founders of normal schools realized the situation and accepted the responsibility of providing academic training for persons who were basically untrained. Gradually they tried also to teach such simple principles of instruction as an evolving profession made available. This is the simple situation out of which grew a long and acrimonious debate as to whether normal schools were or should be institutions to teach content subjects or pedagogy or both.

Three viewpoints with respect to normal-school programs emerged.

1. The majority of schools accepted what may be designated as the academic viewpoint. Most of the entering students had great need of further training in grammar, arithmetic, geography, and other studies. Being only graduates of elementary schools, they needed first of all a review and an extension of information. Even the few high-school and academy graduates who enrolled in the normal schools needed this review almost as much as those who had come directly from the elementary schools. After a thorough grounding in content, the students studied principles of education and read simple treatises, such as Page's *Theory and Practice of Teaching*, which was little more than the comments of an intelligent teacher who retailed his experiences and threw in a few suggestions. Some schools offered a course in the history of education, but it was a dreary review of European developments and had little relevance to American conditions. The crowning course in pedagogy was practice teaching, which was supposed to afford a final test of the candidate's fitness or unfitness for teaching. It served also as the outstanding feature that differentiated normal schools from academies.

The academic program of the normal schools called forth objections from citizens, criticisms from politicians, and opposition from some colleges and academies. For fifty years the program was debated, argued, reviewed, and discussed. For fifty years it was lamented, bewailed,

[3] The word "training" is used deliberately. Only the pedant thinks he has said something when he substitutes "education" for "training." It is a tricky debater who imputes narrow denotations to his opponent and reserves large and rich connotations for himself. Shibbolethic debates over "how to think" and "what to think," teaching the child and teaching the subject, and other verbalistic joustings are all too common in education. The only reasonable attitude is to render full faith and credit to the speaker or writer and not hurry to gnaw the bones of contention.

bemoaned, and denounced by a considerable group of educators. For fifty years it was also explained, defended, justified, and endorsed. And for fifty years the academic aspect of the normal school held its dominant place in the teacher-training curriculum.

2. The second viewpoint of educators with respect to the normal-school program was the professionalization of subject matter. Those who held this viewpoint denied that the program was academic; they insisted that the entire program, including the common branches, as well as methods, was professional. They taught history, to be sure, but it was history-to-be-taught and not merely history-to-be-learned. A more thorough grasp was required, deeper insights were necessary, and a profounder knowledge of history was required for the prospective teacher than for the passive student. The future teacher was thus learning history, and at the same time he was consciously selecting materials and organizing them for future classes of his own. This procedure made history into professionalized content, quite different, so argued the supporters of this view, from the inert history that the ordinary student learned. No academy, high school, or college did, could, or would so teach its subjects. Only the normal school understood the necessity for this kind of instruction. According to this viewpoint, there was a great difference between the ability to learn history and the ability to teach it. Superintendents in considerable numbers preferred normal-school graduates rather than college graduates because they showed an aptness for teaching as well as a knowledge of the content.

3. The third viewpoint concerning the normal school held that the program should be predominantly, if not wholly, professional. According to this view, only those persons who had received a thorough training in content should be admitted to normal schools and should there devote their whole time to learning how to teach. The advocates of this kind of professional program talked a great deal about the science of education and the art of teaching. The more scholarly and orthodox educators insisted upon the superiority of the science over the art. The normal school, they said, should teach the philosophy of method rather than method itself. Principles were "seed corn that would grow," but method was baked bread with no life of its own.[4] The teaching of methods tended to produce routine teachers. Any teacher in service could acquire the needed devices and procedures, but only under wise guidance and skillful instruction could one master the science of education.

However sound in theory, the idea of a normal school devoted exclusively to education courses was quite unrealistic for two reasons. In the first place, the few persons who already had considerable academic background would teach rather than enroll in a normal school. In the

[4] NEA, *Proceedings*, 1871, 152.

second place, professional knowledge was too embryonic to merit pro-longed study. Histories of education were few and dry; the principles of learning were poorly understood and poorly described; and a course in methods of teaching was little more than a collection of anecdotes. In brief, there was no science of education from which to make a profes-sional curriculum.

In spite of this situation, about 1860 Edward A. Sheldon did make his normal school at Oswego into a professional school in which no academic subjects were taught. Since the students were teachers in service, they had already acquired a grounding in content and could properly devote their whole attention to questions of method, discipline, and curriculum. City normal schools, which controlled admission and determined subse-quent placement, tended to emphasize pedagogy over academic content.

Normal schools increased rapidly after the Civil War. In 1870 there were 75, enrolling 9,728 students. In 1874 there were 134, enrolling 24,405 students; 67 were state normals, 4 county, 9 city, and 54 private.[5] The number grew steadily, being smaller in periods of industrial dis-turbance, such as 1877 and 1893.

For a brief time it was assumed that a state could feasibly establish enough normal schools to train all the teachers, and foremost in popular thinking was the need of training rural teachers. The idea that country teachers, whose professional expectancy was only three years and who received less than $50 a month for five months of the year, would seek advanced training was chimerical. Had they done so there would have been no room in the normal schools, for at no time were there enough of them to train more than a mere fraction of the teachers necessary to supply the schools. In 1871 S. H. White of the Peoria Normal School estimated that Illinois would have to have thirty-five normal schools to supply trained teachers for that state. He emphasized the local nature of normal schools, pointing out that 80 per cent of the students lived within tweny miles of the school.[6] In 1877 C. C. Rounds of the Farmington, Maine, Normal School declared that the number of normal schools in the United States would have to be multiplied by forty in order to supply trained teachers for all the schools.[7] Even the most optimistic proponents of normal schools could not visualize a situation in which they would provide teachers for the rural schools. The person who had the ability and ambition to succeed in a normal school would not be content with a poor-paying, isolated country school. The very first graduates of normal schools were eagerly employed in village and graded schools, and the

[5] NEA, *Proceedings, 1876,* 51.
[6] NEA, *Proceedings, 1871,* 121.
[7] NEA, *Proceedings, 1877,* 161.

country schools remained in the hands of teachers with no academic or professional preparation whatever. Massachusetts established five and Pennsylvania thirteen normal schools and neither state trained more than 2 or 3 per cent of the teachers. Slowly and reluctantly educators concluded that the vast majority of teachers would never be trained so long as the pay was poor and the school sessions lasted only three, five or seven months in the year.

Some educators proposed the establishment of two kinds of normal schools, one of an elementary nature for the vast number of unprofessional, temporary teachers and one of a strictly professional nature for those who expected to become permanent teachers.

A committee of the Normal Department of the NEA made a report on the status of normal schools in 1886. In that year there were 103 state normal schools, 22 city, and 2 county, and more than 100 private normal schools. The latter were usually composite schools that included departments of music, business, art, photography, theology, and various other areas. About 60 per cent of the work was academic and the rest professional, but one school would designate all its courses as professional and another, under the same board and with a similar program, as largely academic. The committee concluded that in spite of the confusion of terms the work in the first two-thirds of the courses in all the schools was largely content. Latin was taught in one-half the schools, French and German in few, and Greek rarely. The most frequent courses in education were psychology, methods, school economy, and science of education. About one-half offered the history of education. Practice teaching was required in two-thirds of the schools and model schools were maintained by one-half of them. Only six had kindergartens.[8]

The normal schools increased rapidly in the 1880's and 1890's. In 1898 there were 166 public normal schools with 44,808 students and 165 private normal schools with 23,572 students. About 25,000 potential teachers were also enrolled in universities and colleges and high schools, bringing the total of those preparing to teach to 93,687.[9]

A committee appointed to survey normal schools reported in 1897 and 1899 that it had found distressingly wide variations and the lack of any disposition to formulate standards. Instead there was "a constant disposition to show peculiarities and specialties and oppose others in their notions just as peculiar and provincial."[10] Some of the committee conclusions: New England normal schools stressed professional work; the north-central normal schools were broader in their programs and more influential; there was little agreement on what professional courses to

[8] NEA, *Proceedings, 1886*, 393-398.
[9] *Report of the Commissioner of Education, 1898-99* (Washington, 1900), II, 1789-1842.
[10] NEA, *Proceedings, 1897*, 713; *1899*, 836-903.

teach; distressingly few normal schools maintained kindergartens. The committee recommended the observance of Tappan's Law, which held that "a teacher should be trained in an institution of a higher grade than the one in which he teaches." Thus an elementary teacher was expected to be a high-school graduate and a high-school teacher a college graduate.

There were three classes of normal schools with respect to their sponsors—state, city, and private owners. First in origin, importance, and prominence were the state schools started by Massachusetts. Since the state was responsible for education, even though it delegated part of its responsibility to counties, cities, towns, or districts, it was the natural and logical sponsor of institutions for the training of teachers. The states granted small subsidies and usually allowed free tuition to enrollees who agreed to teach within the state for a specified number of years. State normal schools were managed by state boards appointed by the governor or chosen in some other way. State normal schools remained the dominant kind and eventually outdistanced the other two classes in number and prominence.

The second class of teacher-training institution was the city normal— established in St. Louis and San Francisco as early as 1857 and even earlier than that in Boston, New York, Brooklyn, Newark, New Orleans, and possibly other cities. Such locally controlled schools could set entrance standards and could assure successful graduates positions within the city. In spite of the provincialism that such practice encouraged, it continued into the present century. In the early years the classes of city normals were usually held in the late afternoon and on Saturday.

The third class of normal schools consisted of those which were founded for purely business purposes. While two or three private teacher-training institutions were opened before the establishment of the first public normal school in 1839, the advent of the latter, with the vague but alluring word "normal," provided the real impetus to the founding of private normal schools. Their number increased steadily until 1897, when they numbered 178. More were founded in the decade of the 1880's than in any other period. After 1897 the number declined rapidly; by 1910 there were only about seventy left.

Most of the private normal schools were business enterprises, offering the students training in business, education, music, and various other fields. Only about half of the students were actually preparing to teach. Several of the private normal schools were blatant and aggressive. For example, in 1866 the South-Western Normal School of Lebanon, Ohio, proclaimed its virtues in an eight-page advertisement in the *Ohio Educational Monthly*. It ridiculed colleges for their slow, time-consuming programs, their separation of the sexes, "the most mischievous vestige of the monastic system," their rules and regulations which had to be enforced by faculty monitors and student spies, and their needlessly expensive fees. In contrast, South-Western offered a better program and more skillfull instruction at less cost, achievable in one-half the customary time.[11] Such claims were scarcely abated by 1898, when one school asserted, "If you complete our course you will be well fitted for any position in life." Several claimed to have the most healthful location, the highest scholastic record, the most successful and prominent alumni, the best buildings, the most complete apparatus, the most competent faculty, and the most unblemished reputation. Students could enroll at any time in any subject and were assured "beautiful diplomas" upon the completion of any program.[12]

Normal schools were the focuses of many problems and issues. What should be the standards of admission? Those who regarded the schools as professional or pedagogical institutions declared that only graduates of high schools or academies should be admitted. This unrealistic demand was nullified by the fact that many, and until about 1890 most, of the enrollees had had only an elementary-school training. As long as a person could study and take, and in a large percentage of cases pass, an examination for a teacher's certificate, he was loath to meet higher standards to get into a normal school merely to get ready to do what he was already legally certified to do. The city normals were able to require a high-school diploma for admission, but the state normals could regulate neither the supply of students nor their placement after graduation.

The question of degrees became an issue at an early date. Should normal schools create their own professional degree or appropriate the ones that the colleges had hallowed by tradition? In 1879 J. C. Gilcrist, principal of the State Normal at Cedar Falls, argued that a professional degree was necessary in order to identify the recipient as a member of a learned class, to encourage professional preparation, to stimulate the holders to contribute to educational literature, and to dignify the teaching profession. He reported that a variety of degrees were being given: Bachelor of Didactics, Bachelor of Scientific Didactics, Principal of Pedagogics, Normal Graduate, Master of Arts and Professional Teacher, Licentiate of Instruction, and several others.[13] Not until the normal schools became teachers' colleges was the issue of degrees settled. The educators finally made a professional degree out of the B.S., making it mean the science of education.

Another issue that provoked endless discussions and numerous reports was the place of practice teaching in teacher education. In 1895 one superintendent feelingly asserted: "When you can run a medical school

[11] *Ohio Educational Monthly*, XV, 129-136, April 1866.
[12] *Report of the Commissioner of Education*, 1898-99, II, 2464-2468.
[13] NEA, *Proceedings*, 1879, 115-117.

without a hospital for observation; when you can run a law school without moot courts; when you can run a theological school without giving the young theologians opportunities to preach to sinners—then, perhaps, you can run a normal school without practice-classes."[14]

From the first it was assumed that a school, variously called model, practice, and training—and, after about 1920, laboratory, demonstration, or experimental—was an absolute necessity. These schools, established as parts of teacher-training institutions, not only afforded future teachers necessary practical experience in their field prior to graduation, but they also enabled the faculty to assess the students' qualifications for teaching. Such schools were usually organized and conducted much as the public schools, with classes from the kindergarten level on through the high school, and with, as far as possible, typical pupils in attendance. The maintenance of such schools involved many troublesome problems. In case the normal school charged tuition for the pupils, it was in danger of not having enough pupils and also of securing atypical rather than typical children, as was required by the theory of having a school which afforded practice under normal conditions. In case the normal school used a nearby public school, conflicts of jurisdiction over its control frequently arose between the board of education or superintendent and the director of the training school.

Those who minimized the training school and practice teaching, and they were numerous, stressed the value of the study of the science as differentiated from the art of education. Those who took this viewpoint nevertheless favored some practice teaching, but they believed that the student could obtain the values by teaching his classmates and having them simulate children. This was a widespread and prolonged practice in spite of the unreality of the situation. Occasional students obtained some practice by serving as substitutes for absent teachers in nearby schools. This, too, was a far from typical situation, but it provided a kind of test of professional competence.

Late in the 1890's the demand for better teachers in rural schools became insistent. The country-life movement, the conservation idea, and urban migration seemed to emphasize the danger of the disappearance of country living and the desirability of saving it from disintegration. Michigan, Wisconsin, and several other states started the system known as county normal schools for the specific purpose of training rural teachers. These county normals were located in existing high schools, in newly built structures, or in donated buildings and were supported largely by the state, although some local taxes were required in certain states. The staff in charge of these normals was small, only one person constituting the faculty in some instances. The training program was

14 NEA, *Proceedings, 1895,* 257.

solely practical, but the hearty endorsement which these county normal schools received proves that they made a real contribution to the training of rural teachers.

Normal schools could train only a fraction of the teachers; colleges, academies, and high-school training departments could, at best, reach only a few more. The only institution of a professional nature that included nearly all teachers was the institute. Beginning in the late 1840's, this method of promoting professional development grew constantly in popularity. In scope and form it was infinitely varied. Cities, counties, townships, and states sponsored institutes, lasting from two days to two months. At some, attendance was voluntary and at others it was compulsory; some school boards allowed pay for attendance and others required the teacher to make up the lost days.

The early institute programs were designed to appeal to citizens as well as teachers. Prominent officeholders, ministers, and other public figures addressed the audiences on broad cultural topics, commended the work of the public schools, and pleaded for the support of education. In some of the early institutes lay citizens outnumbered the teachers. Institutes were held at all times of the year, but tended to center in the weeks preceding the opening of school. One speaker referred to the "annual swelter of an August institute." While attendance in the early decades of the movement was usually voluntary, a surprisingly large percentage of the teachers went. Boards and trustees soon started the practice of allowing the usual pay while attending institutes. The chance to meet fellow teachers, to participate in sociables, to enjoy free entertainment (particularly true for the ladies), to hear some well-known speakers, and to receive pay for the time spent was too appealing to be resisted. The attendance approached 100 per cent. In 1897-1898 there were 2,597 institutes with an attendance of 84,760 men and 167,008 women, making a total of 251,768 teachers.

In addition to the institute, teachers received professional help and inspiration from a number of other agencies. In the 1870's some teachers participated in the popular reading and studying circles that were formed by Dr. J. H. Vincent and his associates in the Chautauqua movement. By 1890 the circles enrolled more than a hundred thousand persons.[15] The school and university extension movement of the late 1880's was primarily concerned with adult rather than teacher education. The extension plan was started by the normal schools in 1911. Within a year the normal school at Kent, Ohio, was offering courses in thirty-five centers. Normal-school extension work was particularly popular in Iowa and some other central states. Surpassing all these in importance were the summer schools, which became popular in the 1890's and show no signs

[15] NEA, *Proceedings, 1879,* 16-17; *1890,* 243.

in 1957 of losing their appeal. Of less importance and duration were the reading circles sponsored by state teachers' associations. Selected books of a professional nature were provided at reduced prices; teachers read and discussed these books at institutes and faculty meetings. Each of these means strengthened the professional consciousness of teachers and promoted the growth of education as a subject worthy of study and respect.

The normal schools demonstrated an early interest in a professional organization. The American Normal School Association was started in New York City in 1855 and met at Springfield, Massachusetts, in 1856, at Albany in 1857, and was formally organized at Norwich in 1858 with W. F. Phelps of Trenton as president.[16] From 1866 to 1870 the normal association met with the National Teachers' Association and in the latter year became the Department of Normal Schools of the NEA. Reports on curriculums, model schools, and other topics were made by committees in various years. General surveys of normal schools were reported in 1886 and 1899.[17]

The Normal School Department did not meet all the needs of the administrators engaged in teacher education, and so a small group which met at Emporia in 1902 organized the North Central Council of State Normal School Presidents, which held annual sessions until the founding of the American Association of Teachers Colleges in 1917. In 1925 this association became a department of the NEA, replacing the normal-school department. It signalized its new status by publishing in 1926 a set of standards for teachers' colleges,[18] and soon afterward set up accrediting standards for teachers colleges. By 1940, 185 institutions were members and 158 were accredited.[19] By 1956, the department counted 314 institutional members, including schools of education and colleges of education in universities. For, in 1948, the department had enlarged its scope and changed its name to the American Association of Colleges for Teacher Education.

During the first half of the twentieth century most state normal schools became state teachers' colleges. And during the second half of this century it appears that most state teachers' colleges may become state colleges—if present trends continue.

Although the transition from "normal school" to "teachers' college" was characteristic of the early decades of the present century, the movement had actually begun earlier. In 1882 the normal school at Livingston, Alabama, became a state teachers' college; and following

[16] Massachusetts Teacher, XI, 376-377, October 1858.
[17] NEA, Proceedings, 1924, 614-619.
[18] NEA, Proceedings, 1926, 841-849.
[19] NEA, Proceedings, 1940, 337.

that the movement continued spasmodically until the decade 1911-1920, when nineteen institutions converted and the pattern of change soon swept the nation. During 1921-1930 there were sixty-nine conversions of normal schools to teachers' colleges; during the next decade, 1931-1940, there were thirty-four; and in 1941-1950 there were twelve.[20] The transition meant much more than mere change in name; for most normal schools had been two- or three-year institutions devoted to training elementary teachers, whereas the adoption of the new name was usually associated with expansion to four-year degree-granting status with programs for training secondary as well as elementary teachers.

The second transitional trend has been the conversion of "state teachers' colleges" into multi-purpose institutions with names changed to "state colleges." This transition began in earnest in the 1930's, although three institutions made the change earlier—the first being Bluefield, West Virginia, State College in 1895. By 1950 a total of thirty-six state teachers' colleges had become state colleges, fourteen of these converting between 1946 and 1950.[21] This trend continued at a more rapid pace in the period between 1950 and 1956, and it may be expected to accelerate during the next decade or two under pressure of increasing college enrollments.

The transition of normal schools into teachers' colleges involved the renewing of old controversies and the rethreshing of old issues. The proponents of teachers' colleges argued that the existing system, under which elementary- and high-school teachers were trained in different kinds of institutions, destroyed the continuity of the educational program. The elementary pupil was taught by one teacher who learned to know each individual, but when he entered high school he had four or five different teachers all of whom were subject-minded rather than student-centered. The high school was an integral part of the state system of public education, and the teachers' colleges felt that they were not only legally entitled to prepare teachers for all grades but that the unity of education would be promoted when they did so.

For several years colleges and universities were strangely reluctant to accept teacher training as one of their functions. While the original significance of college degrees as certificates of competence to teach had disappeared, the conceit that teaching ability was an inextricable accompaniment of knowledge was vitally alive. Even the recognition of the need for training ministers, lawyers, doctors, and engineers had no transfer implications for education. Teaching was not yet a profession, and training teachers to teach was not deemed worthy of a college of liberal arts or a university, even though the latter aspired to include all

[20] Rees H. Hughes, "Changing Status of Teacher Education Institutions," *Journal of Teacher Education*, II, 48-52, March 1951.
[21] *Ibid.*

knowledge. Finally, however, around 1875 pressure from the public, the example of normal schools, and the rise of high schools convinced these institutions that teacher training was an opportunity for their graduates even though it might not be an institutional obligation.

Under such circumstances it was natural, in fact almost inevitable, that the colleges began their teacher training with an inferior program and an inadequate staff. In the universities the lone professor of pedagogy was isolated from the rest of the faculty and could help only the few who chanced to enroll in his courses. Slowly, however, the colleges developed departments of education and enlisted the help of other members of the faculty. Shortly after 1900 the universities began to organize schools or colleges of education, thus finally accepting the obligation for education of teachers and placing it on par with other professional schools.[22]

The entrance of teachers' colleges into the new area of training high-school teachers naturally awakened the opposition of some private colleges, but the logic of the past and the legal bases were on the side of the teachers' colleges. The fact that they do not even yet train any large percentage of high-school teachers is due, in part, to long-established practice and the presumed competence of the colleges to provide a richer background of content than the newly developed teachers' colleges.

In the struggle to keep teachers' colleges from training high-school teachers, the liberal-arts colleges, aided and abetted by the universities, used the weapons of accreditation and the power of rejecting college applicants from unaccredited high schools. Tradition and custom favored the academic setting of the colleges for training high-school teachers over the professional training afforded in teachers' colleges. Thus the burden of proof of the capacity to train secondary teachers seemed to rest upon the teachers' colleges.

The teachers' colleges had some advantages in the struggle to win the right to train teachers for secondary schools. Unaccredited high schools, and there were many in the first two decades of this century, sent graduates to unaccredited colleges and to the state universities, which were under legal obligations to accept high-school graduates within their own states. As the teachers' colleges expanded their programs to four years and secured the right to confer degrees, they also grew in political and financial acumen. Many of them could truthfully say that their libraries, laboratories, and equipment were superior to those of many liberal-arts colleges.

Whatever the merits of the situation may have been, the outcome is clear. By 1914 one-fifth of the high-school teachers in the accredited

[22] NEA, *Proceedings*, 1905, 512-515.

schools of the North Central Association of Colleges and Secondary Schools were normal-school graduates.[23] By 1930 the teachers' colleges had won the right to train high-school teachers and the proportion so trained gradually increased.

By 1925 the training of teachers was rather systematically standardized. The teachers' colleges and normal schools trained the elementary teachers, although a few colleges of education in universities were graduating a small number of teachers for the elementary grades. Teachers' colleges, colleges, and universities were training high-school teachers, although the colleges continued to train the greater number. Selected teachers' colleges trained teachers for special fields, such as art, music, home economics, agriculture, and mechanic arts. Here and there a few voices were calling for the training of college professors.

By 1950 the period when any type of institution had a monopoly on the preparation of teachers for any teaching level or field had ended. Teachers were being prepared in all types of institutions. This trend toward diffusion of the responsibilities for teacher education is reflected in a 1952 report published in the NEA's *Journal of Teacher Education*.[24] This report showed that, of all graduates completing preparation for teaching in 1949-1950, teachers' colleges prepared 33.5 per cent of the elementary-school teachers and 16.8 per cent of the high-school teachers; public colleges and universities prepared 31.1 per cent of the elementary-school teachers and 40.2 per cent of the high-school teachers; private colleges and universities prepared 28.3 per cent of the elementary teachers and 38.9 per cent of the high-school teachers; and the remainder were prepared by professional and technical schools and by junior colleges.

[23] NEA, *Proceedings, 1914*, 531-532.
[24] T. M. Stinnett, "Accreditation and the Professionalization of Teaching," *Journal of Teacher Education*, III, 30-38, March 1952.

8

The Advance of Higher Education

"Our colleges are the choicest jewels in our national diadem."[1] In this declaration of 1870, Professor Elliot Whipple of Wheaton College intended no exaggeration. In fact, it was scarcely possible to exaggerate the importance or overstate the sentiment which then encompassed institutions of higher learning.

Colleges, seminaries, institutes, universities! From colonial days almost to the present time all such institutions were invested with halos of charm and auras of mystery; they were considered as reservoirs of wisdom and laboratories of practicality; they evoked respect and inspired awe. Both the lowly and the mighty were impressed, and all classes joined in recognizing the exalted role which institutions of higher learning played in the national life.

Colleges and universities served many exalted functions and met diverse expectations. They were regarded as shrines of wisdom, centers of faith, and springs of hope, as preservers of the past and harbingers of the future, as repositories of traditions and arbiters of standards, as guardians of truth and dispensers of culture. How these institutions operated to perform these varied functions was not well understood, but that they did so was never doubted; the assumption of their beneficent value was an article of faith.

Colleges were hallowed institutions. They were entitled to their impressive vine-clad buildings, their shaded walks, their mysterious laboratories, their lore-filled libraries, and their detachment from mundane affairs. Their gowns and ceremonies and degrees were accepted as fitting paraphernalia for a select group. They were even expected to have a touch of snobbish superiority in order to provide an aristocratic environment in which to train leaders for a democracy. Leaders, even in a democracy, were entitled to some airs and idiosyncrasies. From

[1] NEA, *Proceedings, 1870,* Part II, 27.

these nodules of learning would come social and political wisdom. Such was the faith of the people.

What the colleges taught was a matter of little concern to the public. Its faith was strong enough to believe in Latin or German, science or history, philosophy or mathematics. Professors might argue over the relative value of these studies, but such internal issues were of slight consequence to those outside. To them it made little difference whether students learned ancient conjugations, prepared for vocations, or acquired culture. Even though the colleges changed their purpose from mental discipline to general culture, or shifted their emphasis from classical languages to practical sciences, they retained their hold upon the public imagination. The accumulated fund of grace was always sufficient to offset any incongruities or foibles.

The relative immunity from harsh judgments and popular opposition which the colleges enjoyed extended in part to the students. They were presumed to be select and fortunate beings, entitled to the great privileges and rare opportunities by which they were surrounded; consequently they were accorded a leeway in conduct. The frolicsome pranks of fraternities and classes and the rowdy athletic contests between competing teams were regarded as humanizing indulgences. Just how these activities enriched life and promoted culture was veiled in obscurity, but at the end of four years the college graduate was presumed to be equipped with a subtle power that enabled him to solve the problems of life.

Many factors contributed to the lofty status that higher education enjoyed. The aura of the Middle Ages, the glory of the Renaissance, the heritage from religious reformers, the dignity and mystery of the classical languages, and the piety and aloofness associated with the training of ministers provided traditions and standards. The penury and hardships which colonial settlers endured in order to found colleges, and the courageous campaigns of frontier circuit riders to found colleges to maintain the faith, called forth respect and admiration. The resulting colleges, rather than the churches which founded them, became the recipients of good will and popular sentiment. In spite of their denominational origin, the colleges soon won a kind of nonsectarian respect that lifted them above the acrimonious arguments and fierce rivalries of the founding churches. Thus the colleges emerged as islands of culture, refinement, and neutrality in the seas of politics and sectarianism.[2]

There were some exceptions to the romantic esteem which enveloped institutions of higher learning. The agricultural and mechanical colleges created by the Morrill Act of 1862 were so unblushingly utilitarian as to

[2] For a negative view of the colleges in the post-Civil War period, see Andrew D. White's critical analysis, NEA, *Proceedings, 1874,* 60.

disqualify them as sharers of the heritage of liberal education. James McCosh of Princeton and Charles W. Eliot of Harvard cast aspersions upon them and clung tenaciously to the thoroughly erroneous notion that their function was to train farmers and artisans. The phrase "cow college" was used to imply the bucolic and backward atmosphere that allegedly clung for many years to these land-grant colleges.

Normal schools and teachers' colleges were not accepted as institutions of higher education. Since they were acknowledgedly vocational schools, they forfeited the glamour of an indefinite purpose and the romance of dubious utility. While not on a level with schools of law, medicine, and theology, teachers' colleges were like them in being devoid of the allurement of an obscure and indefinite purpose. Similarly, technical schools and specialized institutes had no share in the trailing clouds of glory that hung over colleges.

The public junior colleges, which came on the scene after 1900, were popularly regarded as higher high schools. Since the students were almost entirely local residents, there were no dormitories or fraternity houses, no students from distant states. Being local, the institution could not become cosmopolitan. It was only a vocational school or a money-saving, time-saving short cut to the junior year in some college.

The stark realities concerning colleges make the growth and maintenance of popular respect all the more remarkable. On the basis of income, buildings, libraries, courses, number and quality of students, and scholarship of the faculty, only a small fraction of the colleges merited the name. Popular sentiment, however, was indulgent; it overlooked the discrepancy between pretensions and realities; it took for granted that pretensions were statements of future facts. The woman who assumed that the building was a college because it was three stories high, and the frontiersmen who said that the logs had been cut for another university,[3] were neither facetious nor cynical; they were humble, hopeful, and trustful.

The country was well supplied with colleges at the close of the Civil War. Before the war the churches had founded 180 colleges and twenty-one states had started universities.[4] These numbers were soon increased by the thirty institutions authorized by the Morrill Act and by the continued zeal of the churches in starting additional colleges. In 1883 the United States commissioner of education reported that there were 123 universities; 247 colleges; 255 normal schools; 236 schools for women, some of which were colleges; and 30 agricultural and mechanical colleges. Only 32,767 college students were enrolled in the 370 universities and

[3] NEA, *Proceedings, 1886,* 373.
[4] Donald G. Tewksbury, *The Founding of American Colleges and Universities Before the Civil War* (New York, 1932), 90.

colleges. Almost exactly the same number (32,755) were enrolled in preparatory and other departments. The colleges thus had an average enrollment of about 89 students. The commissioner of education called attention to the large number of feeble, weakling colleges and deprecated their lofty pretensions.[5] As late as 1889, 335 out of 400 colleges still maintained preparatory departments. This practice detracted from the dignity and quality of college work, but it was continued on the assumption that high schools were not at that time prepared to meet college requirements.[6]

In 1900 Andrew F. West of Princeton compiled a list of colleges in the United States with the founding dates. According to his list, 11 were founded before the end of the Revolutionary War, 12 from 1783 to 1800, 33 from 1800 to 1830, and 180 from 1830 to 1865, making a total of 236. From 1865 to 1893 another 230 were founded, giving a total of 446.[7] After 1893 the rate of growth slowed markedly. From 1894 to 1928 the average number of new colleges per year was four, and about one-third of them were junior colleges.

Recent growth in higher education is equally impressive. During the 1930's many junior colleges were founded; and after the Second World War new institutions of all kinds were started, and existing institutions were upgraded. In 1952 there were 897 accredited colleges and universities; three years later the number was 969. In 1952 there were 480 junior colleges; three years later the number was 531, an increase of 51 in three years.

College enrollments gradually increased. From the 32,767 of 1883, they grew to 329,387 by 1916, and to 695,219 by 1927. In addition there were, in 1927, 44,165 enrolled in graduate departments and 99,424 in professional schools. Of the 695,219 college students 292,977 were women. By 1955 the figures of enrollment in institutions of higher learning were

[5] NEA, *Proceedings, 1886*, 367-385.

[6] NEA, *Proceedings, 1889*, 374. Bitter criticisms of the custom are given in *Ibid., 1890*, 99, 538, 629-633.

[7] West's report was originally prepared for the Bureau of Education. It is reprinted in Nicholas Murray Butler, ed., *Education in the United States* (Albany, 1900), 209-249. From his list the following numbers of colleges founded in each of the designated years were derived.

1865	12	1875	5	1885	8
1866	11	1876	8	1886	10
1867	11	1877	4	1887	7
1868	11	1878	7	1888	7
1869	10	1879	0	1889	4
1870	11	1880	6	1890	14
1871	4	1881	5	1891	15
1872	7	1882	9	1892	12
1873	10	1883	7	1893	6
1874	4	1884	5		

phenomenal. The teachers' colleges enrolled 243,652, universities 1,241,-101, liberal-arts colleges 712,685, and junior colleges 351,720. In universities the men outnumbered the women by more than two to one (889,360 to 351,741), in junior colleges the men were nearly twice as numerous as women (233,879 to 117,841), and in other colleges also the men exceeded women (396,955 to 315,730). Only in teachers' colleges did women outnumber men and even there the difference was not very great (129,117 women to 114,535 men).[8]

Higher education had difficulty in deciding its purposes and functions. For generations the colleges had professed to offer a liberal education, which presumably produced refined and cultivated persons. The program was untainted by materialistic or vocational elements. "No college studies are practical," according to Professor Paul Shorey of the University of Chicago in 1893.[9] The answer to practical-minded men who wanted to know what a college education was for was given by President John P. Gulliver of Knox College, who said in 1871, "that it is the business of the college to educate the leaders of society and of the public schools to educate the citizens."[10] College men would add after a little reflection that in disciplining the mind, the college produced all-round citizens. After further consideration the college men realized that the training of ministers was a major function. As medicine and law raised their requirements, college men saw their program as an excellent basis for subsequent training in the professions. As high schools grew in number and employed more teachers, the colleges saw the great opportunity and eagerly proclaimed their fitness to train high-school teachers. As time passed they added departments of commerce, art, journalism, home economics, business administration, engineering, and other vocational subjects. Thus the purposes and functions of the colleges changed with social demands. Contrary to theory, tradition, and custom and in the face of opposition by the stout defenders of liberal education, the colleges became vocational schools for many of their students.

Realizing the strength of the sentimental tradition and the hold that it had upon the popular imagination, college leaders insisted that their institutions emphasized spiritual values, character, culture, manhood and womanhood, mental development, power, and other abstract qualities rather than specific vocational purposes. Thus the colleges, pressed into serving utilitarian functions, nevertheless proclaimed their adherence to traditional ideals. Theoretically they were still the upholders of the

[8] United States Office of Education, *Opening Fall Enrollment in Higher Educational Institutions*, Circular No. 460 (Washington, 1955).

[9] NEA, *Proceedings, 1893*, 139.

[10] NEA, *Proceedings, 1871*, 165. In the preceding year he said, "The work of educating the leaders of society has been placed by Providence in the Hands of the Christian churches of the land." *Ibid., 1870*, Part II, 24.

classics and the dispensers of an impractical culture.[11]

In contrast to the shifting stand of the colleges respecting the nature of their purposes and programs, the universities were outspokenly in favor of the practical and vocational as well as the theoretical and cultural. In 1868 Chancellor J. B. Lindsley of the University of Nashville declared that a university was "a place where the whole range of human knowledge is taught—where a person may learn anything in any way, wrong end foremost, upside down, or inside out."[12] A whole succession of university presidents and founders visualized institutions that embraced colleges, technical, vocational, and professional schools, and courses in any subject that any human being wanted to learn. In addition the libraries, laboratories, and experimental farms and shops were to enable the faculty to increase knowledge as well as to disseminate it.

Andrew D. White of Cornell, J. K. Patterson of the University of Kentucky,[13] and David Starr Jordan of Stanford were only three of a larger number who cast aspersions upon ecclesiastical controls and denominational limitations and called for the unfettered pursuit of knowledge. A favorite remark of such advocates was to refer ironically to Methodist physics, Baptist geology, and Presbyterian biology. Thus the universities differed rather markedly from the colleges in the freedom of instruction as well as in the nature of the curriculum. Naturally the universities were criticized as antireligious, atheistic, godless, and worldly. For several years speakers from small colleges voiced these charges at successive conventions of the NEA. In time, however, the objectivity of science was recognized, and in dozens of ways the universities demonstrated their concern for the spiritual and personal welfare of their students.

Judged by the number of speeches and the intensity of feelings revealed, the study of Latin and Greek was the most important issue in higher and secondary education during the first half-century of the NEA (1857-1907).[14] The issue of the classics was not merely a curriculum problem; it involved a philosophy of life, the maintenance of civilization, the nature of mental faculties, and the whole concept of education. The advocates of the classical languages were extravagant in their claims, truculent in their denunciations of opponents,[15] loud in their laments over the decline of their subjects, and ready in explanation of the decline.

[11] For discussions that stress the religious functions of small colleges, see NEA, *Proceedings, 1894,* 797-806.

[12] NEA, *Proceedings, 1868,* 670.

[13] NEA, *Proceedings, 1874,* 205.

[14] The problem of college-entrance requirements received almost equal attention. This problem is discussed in Chapter 6.

[15] The tone of the classicists is indicated by their appeal of 1895, which was headed "To Teachers of the Classics and to all Friends of Sound Learning in the United States." NEA, *Proceedings, 1895,* 632.

The virtues and values of Latin and Greek were iterated and reiterated. They contributed to an understanding of English, helped in the acquisition of modern languages, provided scientific nomenclature,[16] developed correct tastes, and strengthened, expanded, and refined the mind. They were educational machines that brought "every intellectual muscle into play, observation, comparison, imagination, memory, analysis, synthesis."[17] Dr. Andrew P. Peabody characterized the classical languages as "more truly living than when they were in current use . . . and offer a surer presage of immortality than any tongue now spoken on the face of the earth."[18]

The proponents of the classics advanced some strange arguments. The student who did not want to study them was the very one who most needed lessons on humility and respect; such studies would curb his willful impulses. The classics were dry, uninteresting, and unappealing; hence they were ideal for mental discipline and developing the will. The classics were exceedingly difficult and so provided the exercise necessary for mental development. The classics were low in utilitarian elements, and so, according to Andrew F. West of Princeton, they provided a "superb sieve" to identify and eliminate those practical-minded individuals who were unworthy of pursuing classical studies.[19] James D. Butler of Madison, speaking at the NEA convention of 1874, chose as his subject "How Dead Languages Make Live Men." The classics, he said, had endured for four centuries notwithstanding "the murmurs of lazy boys" and "utilitarian men." Difficulty, he continued, was one of their great virtues, for discipline could result only from exercises with hard tasks.[20] Two subsequent speakers advanced the idea "that pupils should take languages that they don't like."[21] H. K. Edson of Denmark Academy in Iowa praised the virtue of difficulty: "But golden sands do not always sparkle in classic paths, nor are rich-paying leads at once revealed to the delver for Greek roots; although at last, when the ultimate analysis of life and labor is reached . . . classic diggins pan out well."[22] Thus a defender of the classics had to resort to American vernacular to explain the linguistic superiority of the ancient languages.

Nearly all of the advocates of the classics lamented their decline and the poor achievements of their students, and freely confessed that only an occasional one could really read Latin. The confession that the professors themselves could not read Latin and Greek was made by one

[16] David Starr Jordan ridiculed this argument for studying the classics. NEA, *Proceedings, 1893,* 135-137.
[17] NEA, *Proceedings, 1886,* 189.
[18] NEA, *Proceedings, 1874,* 154.
[19] NEA, *Proceedings, 1893,* 135.
[20] NEA, *Proceedings, 1874,* 187-204.
[21] NEA, *Proceedings, 1893,* 206.
[22] NEA, *Proceedings, 1871,* 160, 161.

frank member, A. B. Stark of Logan Female College, Russellville, Kentucky. He doubtless shocked his colleagues by declaring, "I doubt if there are ten teachers of Latin and Greek in America who can *read* them." He noted that many could *translate* but that few could *think* in the language.[23] Professor H. M. Tyler of Knox College lamented: "Men, who like enthusiastic lovers have spent their lives in unwearied devotion to classical study, may be often seen looking up with grieved expression to find that a cold unappreciative age is rudely crowding them off the stage into obscure corners, that there, unrecognized save by the pity which despises, unnoticed save by a few parting sneers, they may muse over their sorrow and watch the dying form of their love."[24]

The final outcome of studying the classics as presented by their stout defenders reminds one of the result of chasing butterflies along Tully brook as pictured by A. D. Mayo. "Clutching the flitting loveliness so fiercely at the end of the chase that there was nothing left in our hot hand but a wreck of golden wings and a stain of yellow dust."[25]

Classicists were almost unanimous in attributing the decline in popularity of their subjects to poor teaching. While lazy boys, unfriendly critics, and utilitarian philosophy were recognized as obstacles to the maintenance of Latin and Greek, poorly prepared teachers and outmoded methods were regarded as the fundamental causes of the decline. One round table devoted to the improvement of the teaching of these languages recommended more translation in writing, the help of English teachers, more demonstrations of good translations by teachers, and avoidance of pet phrases. Even while they talked of improvements, the classicists exuded only a gloomy hope of success. One speaker after another referred to the decline of their subjects, either to deny, doubt, or lament it.[26]

Critics of the classical languages were outspoken and numerous at NEA meetings. Charles W. Eliot, A. D. Mayo, W. P. Atkinson, G. Stanley Hall, Charles Francis Adams, and David Starr Jordan were a few who voiced their opposition to the traditional program. Such phrases as "antiquated system," "barren gymnastic theory," "dreary drill," "gerund-grinding," "sanctified relic," "the ghost of a ghost," "scholastic pedantry," "the bigotry of their advocates," "the grindstone theory," "fetish-worship," and "the dead and buried words of dead and buried tongues, expressing dead and buried thoughts" were used to characterize the classics and the classicists.[27] In 1876 A. D. Mayo added his opinion: "The second-class

[23] NEA, *Proceedings, 1877*, 25.
[24] NEA, *Proceedings, 1871*, 201-202.
[25] NEA, *Proceedings, 1872*, 13-14.
[26] NEA, *Proceedings, 1896*, 563-574.
[27] NTA, *Proceedings, 1868*, 659-664; NEA, *Proceedings, 1871*, 207; *1902*, 260-261, 271.

American college is now the hiding-place of a pedantic and obstinate old-time pedagogy which scorns suggestions of improvement and hugs its dreary curriculum of badly-taught classic and mathematical lore like a fetish."[28]

The decline of Latin and Greek was not caused by rebellious students, for they appeared in every generation; nor by poor teaching, for that too was a constant; nor by the critics, for they merely appraised the results; nor by the elective system, for that was only the door of escape rather than the cause of flight. The rise of the sciences, the growth of industry, the increase of knowledge, a better understanding of the psychology of learning, and the practical demands of an expanding country were more effective in changing the curriculum than faculty committees. American society was too *democratic* to accept an aristocratic tradition, too *competitive* to tolerate one program however efficacious, too *practical* to be content with theoretical values, too *intense* to endure the arid drill of formal grammar, too *impatient* to wait for deferred values, too *progressive* to study outmoded languages, too *nationalistic* to acknowledge dependence upon foreign studies, too *modern* to be awed by ancient lore, too *cosmopolitan* to depend upon the contributions of such small segments of its heritage, too *future-oriented* to be encumbered with dead languages.

Every decade brought forth hopeful prophets who proclaimed a return of the popularity of the classics.[29] They cited colleges or classes in which there were increased enrollments in Latin or Greek. Disregarding the general decreases, such prophets drew encouragement from those apparent reversals of the downward trend. This faith of the classicists in the eventual return of their lost subjects resembled the belief among the Indians concerning the return of the buffalo, and one belief was about as realistic as the other.

While Latin and Greek were fighting a losing battle for places in the curriculum, the sciences were propelled into prominence. After the founding in 1818 of the *American Journal of Science and Arts* by Benjamin Silliman and his wide achievements in the natural sciences at Yale, a number of specialists emerged to enlarge, enrich, and systematize several of the subjects. As head of the Smithsonian Institution, Joseph Henry promoted physics; the roaming, romantic J. J. Audubon elevated ornithology to an art as well as a science; at Princeton Arnold H. Guyot invested geography with a hitherto unperceived importance; and at Harvard a similar service was done for botany by Asa Gray, for biology by Louis Agassiz, and for geology by Nathaniel Shaler. In fact, the most fundamental development in higher education during the nineteenth

[28] NEA, *Proceedings, 1876,* 25-26.
[29] For examples of this recurrent faith, see NEA, *Proceedings, 1871,* 160; *1896,* 572, 574; *1911,* 557.

century was the growth of the sciences. The ideas of Darwin, the interpretations of Huxley, and the pronouncements of Herbert Spencer had
great influence in America. Even more specific were the effects of the
Morrill Act of 1862. The fact that the Federal government gave its sanction to the application of scientific methods to agriculture and industry
was overwhelmingly impressive. While the tangible results were not
generally perceptible until after the founding of the agricultural experimental stations in 1887, the influence upon popular thinking and upon
other institutions was marked and immediate. In fact, the growth of
science in colleges and universities was steady from 1862 up to the construction of the latest atomic laboratory.

Other fields than science grew in favor and almost without opposition
found places in college programs. Modern languages were soon accepted
in place of the classics. English and literature grew in popularity. And
the social sciences, including history, economics, political science, and
finally sociology, gradually won a prominent, almost a predominant,
place in higher education. Proponents of these newer subjects argued
that they, too, were liberalizing and had the added advantage of being
practical.

The growth of these various subjects resulted in the rapid expansion
of college courses. This growth evoked a strange concept—that of an
overcrowded curriculum. If the curriculum was what it purported to
be—a selection from the social heritage sufficient to maintain human
progress—it could, logically speaking, never be overcrowded; it could
not possibly exceed the culture which it reflected. But troubled professors,
seeing that the program was too much for one student, postulated the
apologetic and misleading concept of an overcrowded curriculum, as
though knowledge was at fault for outgrowing the capacities of one
person during a four-year period.

Fortunately knowledge was not restricted, nor was progress stayed,
out of consideration for the limitations of youth. Fortunately also, educators saw the necessity of an expanded program. In the words of President
William L. Bryan of Indiana University, "No one student could cover
the ground, but the catalog must do so."[30] The institutions did not evade
their obligation to society because it would raise problems for students.
Faced with more courses than they could take, the obvious solution was
to choose among them. Thus the elective system was not an invention;
it was simply the inescapable road out of a perplexing situation.[31] Misunderstanding the origin of the elective system, historians and educators
have traced its development and assigned credit or blame to Thomas

[30] NEA, *Proceedings, 1905,* 482.
[31] For an expansion of this interpretation, see Dr. Andrew P. Peabody's speech at
Detroit, NEA, *Proceedings, 1874,* 152-163.

Jefferson, George Ticknor, Francis Wayland, or Charles W. Eliot for devising it, whereas neither Eliot nor anyone else could have prevented its rise. The only credit that such educators deserve is for their early recognition of the situation and their attempts to arrange the curriculum so as to facilitate wise choices by the students.

When applied, the elective system was an immediate success. Testimony to its workability, soundness, and popularity is overwhelming.[32] After a period of almost indiscriminate choice the colleges established alternate programs and appointed faculty advisers to help students plan their schedules. By 1910 some colleges were denying the virtue of election and were trying to establish the double thesis that the student did not know what was good for him but that the faculty did. Invoking the requirements of a common heritage, general education, the humanities, minimum essentials, or basic preparation instead of the old appeal to the dictates of a liberal education, some institutions reversed some of the practices that grew up under the elective system.

The elective system received unearned praise and undeserved blame and attention out of proportion to its educational importance. It was neither a solution to curriculum problems nor a primrose path around the field of labor. The enriched and functional curriculum that the colleges established demonstrated their sensitivity to social needs, but faculty advisers, faced with the problem of making schedules for students, thought that the device of election, rather than the enlarged program, was the great educational achievement of the age. The advance of knowledge and its incorporation into college curricula were the great developments of the century—not the readjustments which they entailed upon faculty and students.

Problems of controlling students were persistent throughout the entire century (1857-1957). Colleges tried to control fraternities, regulate or eliminate hazing, supervise social activities, prevent cheating in examinations, uphold honor codes in athletics, and lead the students tactfully to eschew "slovenly speech, loud neckties, and eating with the knife."[33] The responsibility of caring for the moral and religious welfare of the students rested with great weight upon the faculties of denominational colleges. The churches that founded and supported colleges expected the faculty to maintain rather lofty standards of conduct and uphold orthodox doctrines. The burden of meeting such expectations was in-

[32] For testimony concerning the success of the elective system, see NEA, *Proceedings, 1874,* 152-163; *1895,* 658-660. Professor Edward Channing of Harvard approved it both as a student and as a professor. Noah Porter of Yale opposed the elective system, NEA, *Proceedings, 1877,* 95-105; so did Andrew F. West of Princeton, *1893,* 150-154; *1903,* 54-60. For an example of the clash between the dogmatism of liberal education and the free inquiry of science, see the brief comments of West and David Starr Jordan, *1893,* 155.

[33] NEA, *Proceedings, 1905,* 487.

creased by the fact that the colleges maintained dining halls and dormitories, and thus inevitably exercised control over most aspects of student life. To meet the problems of regulating conduct some institutions proclaimed detailed rules and established discipline committees; others experimented with advisers and faculty committees, honor systems, and various degrees of student government;[34] and in crises all of them resorted to a variety of expedients to maintain order and decorum.

College professors found some compensations for low salaries and heavy class loads. They appropriated some of the institution's dignity and applied it to their own positions, and they derived satisfaction from the belief that they were the source of educational progress. "Progress in education, like the rain and the sunshine, comes from above." As an example of the process, the speaker cited the alleged improvement in secondary teaching that followed the establishment of college-entrance examinations. Such was the trickle-down theory as expressed by a speaker at the Asbury Park meeting of the NEA in 1905.[35] The theory seems to have derived from the fact that colleges were often founded in advance of high schools, and that college men were presumably better scholars than teachers in the common schools. The theory was expanded and faith in it increased by the NEA curriculum committees of the 1890's and 1900's.

The three elements in the trickle-down theory were (1) the dissemination of knowledge, (2) the making of school curriculums, and (3) advances in pedagogy, particularly methods. It is clear that the colleges did exercise leadership in acquiring and disseminating information, and that their control of the secondary program through entrance requirements was quite complete until about 1910. It is more doubtful, however, that at any time during the century they contributed materially to pedagogical progress. In fact, college professors, especially those in universities, soon came to deprecate teaching and so naturally had little concern with motivation, interest, methods, and the whole question of teaching and learning. This indifference or unawareness of pedagogy was characteristic of even well-known individuals whose reputations as teachers depended on personality rather than upon teaching skill.

The ladder theory—that educational progress comes from below—is probably more plausible than the trickle-down theory. The kindergarten, object teaching, integration of subjects, child study, and various other reforms started on the lowest grade levels and slowly effected changes in the higher grades.

[34] For a report on student government at Illinois, see NEA, *Proceedings, 1889,* 539. For a later account of student conduct, see *ibid.,* 1912, 785-789. This account emphasizes the allegedly disgraceful conduct of students in denominational colleges.
[35] NEA, *Proceedings, 1905,* 510.

For many years the Department of Higher Education of the NEA provided the forum for college men, those from the small colleges as well as from the universities. The department grew out of the Central College Association, which had been organized in 1868. At its meeting in Oberlin in 1870 it voted to become a department of the NEA. During the years of its existence from 1870 to 1924 many prominent educators served on its programs and as officers. Charles W. Eliot and James McCosh were among its first presidents. Later presidents of the department included Daniel Read of Missouri, Noah Porter of Yale, Daniel C. Gilman of Johns Hopkins, Eli T. Tappan of Kenyon College, W. W. Folwell of Minnesota, B. A. Hinsdale of Michigan, G. Stanley Hall of Clark University, James H. Baker of Colorado, Benjamin I. Wheeler of California, Elwood P. Cubberley of Stanford, and Guy S. Ford of Minnesota.

The topics discussed at the successive meetings constitute a roll call of the problems and anxieties of the department. Those most frequently discussed were Latin and Greek, modern languages, the elective system, the national university, dormitories and student life, fraternities, the functions of universities, college-entrance requirements, alumni, athletics, schools of education, junior colleges, and war and education.[36]

Attendance at department meetings declined after about 1910, and the First World War aggravated the situation. At San Francisco in 1923 David Starr Jordan, president emeritus of Stanford University, delivered the last recorded address before the department. In the following year the board of directors of the NEA abolished the department, explaining that "the field is adequately covered by other national organizations."[37] While regional accrediting associations with their annual conferences and the newly (1918) formed American Council on Education provided help in solving problems of higher education, the small attendance of the preceding years and the failure to elect officers, rather than the adequacy of other agencies, were the main reasons for disbanding the Department of Higher Education.

The disbanding of the department and the relative neglect of higher education occurred in a period when the NEA was concentrating its attention upon teacher welfare and the public schools. This withdrawal, however, was unfortunate for higher education and for the NEA. There was no unifying organization where the problems that confronted all kinds of colleges and universities could be discussed. None of the associations of colleges, of professors, or of scholars in the various subjects met the need of a national clearing house for discussion and planning. The Second World War transformed this need into a necessity, and in 1942 the NEA

[36] NEA, *Proceedings, 1906,* 595-599.
[37] NEA, *Proceedings, 1923,* 667-688; *1924,* 565.

voted to reinstate the Department of Higher Education. A reorganization was effected at St. Louis in February 1943, and Herman B Wells of Indiana University was elected president and Alonzo F. Myers of New York University, who had been active in planning the reorganization, secretary. The department entered upon an active program of publishing bulletins and holding conferences.[38]

In 1946 the department, which changed its name in 1952 to the Association for Higher Education, started the series of national conferences on higher education which meets each spring in Chicago. Attendance and interest grew rapidly. The meeting in 1956 attracted 959 representatives from 409 colleges and universities located in 47 states. The inclusive nature of this conference is indicated by the fact that 150 public and 259 private institutions, including large universities, state and private, municipal institutions, state colleges, junior colleges, and Protestant and Catholic schools were represented. Something of the status of the participants is revealed by the presence of 117 college presidents, 74 vice-presidents, 245 deans, 163 other administrative officers, and 204 professors.[39] The results of these conferences are published in a series called *Current Issues in Higher Education*. The one covering the 1956 conference is a volume of 363 pages and presents the addresses and the opinions and conclusions of thirty-six discussion groups.

The nature of the discussions at these annual conferences provides a clear view of the great changes that have come in higher education. In 1890, for example, the Department of Higher Education discussed administration, shorter courses, chairs of pedagogy, discipline, morals of students, spiritual elements, fraternities, and admission requirements.[40] The Chicago conference of 1956 discussed class size, methods of instruction, the gifted student, student characteristics, faculty salaries, group dynamics, general education, cooperative planning, scholarships, and financing higher education.

The procedure of the two meetings differed even more than the topics of discussion. In 1890 speakers presented rather extended papers and the audience discussed them briefly. In 1956 the thirty-six groups spent many hours in arriving at conclusions which were recorded and reported.[41]

After its revival in 1942, and particularly after the initiation of the annual Chicago conference in 1946, the Association for Higher Education quickly won a unique place in American education. Without dupli-

[38] NEA, *Proceedings, 1942*, 257; *1943*, 102-103.

[39] Association for Higher Education, *College and University Bulletin*, VIII, 2, April 1956.

[40] NEA, *Proceedings, 1890*, 659-713.

[41] Association for Higher Education, *Current Issues in Higher Education, 1956: Resources for Higher Education* (Washington, 1956).

cating the work of college associations, accrediting agencies, scholarly organizations, or the association of professors, the new association provided a national forum for the exchange of educational information. The AHE, unlike other influential organizations in the field of higher education, is composed of individuals rather than institutions. And it is inclusive in its membership and in the scope of its concerns. The association makes no effort to replace the specialized associations concerned with history, chemistry, and other subjects, but it does provide a convention where professors of all subjects, administrators, deans, personnel directors, business managers, and all the varied kinds of college workers can meet one another and pool their experiences and opinions.

The return of the NEA to active leadership in the field of higher education has, in a sense, restored it to a role in which it was prominent some sixty or seventy years ago but which it abdicated for several decades. Moreover, the reactivation of the NEA's department for higher education has united—as never before was the case—both school and college personnel as colleagues in the organized teaching profession of the United States.

9

The Changing Curriculum

THE child is inclined to regard the subjects that he studies in school as eternal fixtures, mysteriously derived and passed on from time immemorial. At times he thinks of them as arbitrary tasks imposed by power-wielding adults, and so he only dimly appreciates their personal value to him. The public sees the curriculum as the changing program of studies that results from social developments. As trade increased, courses in commercial arithmetic were introduced into school programs; as America became health-conscious, courses in hygiene were added; and as traffic became fearsome, courses in automobile driving became a necessity. Philosophers and statesmen take a still broader view and seek to understand the nature of society, social purposes, and how progress may be promoted. For them the curriculum consists of those worthy skills and achievements that should be transmitted and preserved. They regard the schools as trustees and custodians of culture.

The educator accepts these viewpoints and formulates plans for identifying worthy elements of the culture and organizing information about them into teachable and learnable topics. Throughout the hundred years of NEA history, its members have been seeking to understand society and formulate programs of study that would prepare boys and girls for useful lives as individuals and as members of social organizations.

The curriculum is a product of the society in which it operates; hence educators have had to analyze society and construct programs that were faithful reflections of the times and that were within the capacities of the pupils. In successive periods leading speakers at NEA conventions reviewed the aims and purposes of society, the relation of the state to education, and the varied functions that the schools could perform.

In 1881, for example, Superintendent F. Louis Soldan of St. Louis described the social function of the school. "Thus it appears that the school should be guided by the wants of society." It is the task of educa-

107

tion, he said, to "keep pace with the development of society . . . to assimilate what is new without discarding what is good in things traditional and time-honored, to appreciate new demands and new interests without injustice to what is old and tried. . . ." The school, said Soldan, is successful to the extent that "it conceives and recognizes the noblest aims and endeavors of the century and tries to teach in accordance with them."[1] The idea that the school should be merely the unquestioning transmitter of social standards was implied in the statement cited but not endorsed by Dean Lotus D. Coffman of Minnesota: "What is good for business is good for education."[2]

Throughout the century educators saw clearly that both purposes and programs must be derived from the surrounding civilization. As social ideals changed so did the aims of the schools, and as social demands changed so did subjects taught in the schools. Educational speeches and papers abound with references to concomitant ideas and developments, such as strikes, anarchists, lotteries, the concentration of wealth, corruption in government, depressions, social reforms, international tensions, and war and peace.[3]

In successive decades various problems were singled out for attention with the hope that education could make a contribution toward their solution. Crime, juvenile delinquency, eugenics, war, depressions, racial tensions, economic strife, health, morality, and popular tastes are a few of the many problems that evoked the earnest efforts of educators and led to the addition of new courses or the modification of old ones. In the 1870's, for example, NEA speakers were greatly concerned over the relation between education and crime. While they tended to think that education lessened crime, they were not sure of their assumption. W. T. Harris took great pains to gather evidence to prove that few educated persons ever landed in jails and penitentiaries. In greeting the association at St. Louis in 1871, Governor B. Gratz Brown pleasantly but pointedly ridiculed the claim that the schools lessened crime. Education, he said, merely changed the type but not the amount of crime. W. F. Phelps of Winona characterized Governor Brown's remarks as outrageous and regretted that the members had to listen to such false ideas.[4] In spite of repeated papers and reports on this subject, the issue was never resolved.

Educators were greatly interested in the nature of the state. As the agent of society the state had to reflect faithfully the wishes of its creator and at the same time it had to direct its schools in such a way as to

[1] NEA, *Proceedings, 1881,* 144-145.
[2] NEA, *Proceedings, 1919,* 468.
[3] NEA, *Proceedings, 1872,* 141; *1888,* 102; *1890,* 616; *1894,* 32, 34; *1935,* 23-28, 540. Dozens of instances of interest in current affairs could be cited.
[4] NEA, *Proceedings, 1871,* 7-11, 222.

insure individual freedom and development. Thus the schools were potentially capable of being a conservative force to uphold the status quo
and also a revolutionary force that could remake society. Throughout
the years educators have tended to emphasize the conserving function of
education.

At the St. Louis meeting in 1871, Superintendent John Hancock of
Cincinnati presented his view of the state and its obligation to education.

A state is an organization of a community of people, not only for the protection of their persons and property, but to do those things for their mutual well-
being which can not be done at all, or can not be well done, by individual
enterprise. . . . The education of the mass of the people of a state never has
been done by individual enterprise, and perhaps never can be; and so long as
this remains a fact, such education will remain one of the proper functions of
that state. As to the scope of this education, it is only to be restricted by the
resources of the state.[5]

Educators were mindful of the contribution of education to the state
and to the general welfare. For several decades they were fond of stressing the relation of education to property and prosperity. Speaking to the
NEA convention at Cleveland in 1870, Senator F. A. Sawyer of South
Carolina contrasted "the energy, vigor, thrift, morality and civilization"
of one state that had free common schools with "the weakness, sluggish-
ness, immorality and semi-barbarism" of another state that had no public
schools. He continued: "Ignorance is poverty; education is wealth. . . .
Education invents labor-saving machinery, education utilizes material
which ignorance wastes; education husbands strength which ignorance
squanders; education dignifies labor; ignorance degrades it."[6]

In similar vein W. F. Phelps of Winona, speaking at St. Louis in 1871,
said: "Wealth is the product of intelligence. Poverty is one of the fruits
of ignorance. The best, the surest, the cheapest method of increasing the
wealth of the state is to increase the sum total of its mental and moral
power . . . educated labor is far more profitable than ignorant labor." At
the same convention W. T. Harris explained that property was secure
only in a civilized state and that it could not "exist except it be taxed
for universal education."[7]

Soldan, Hancock, Sawyer, Phelps, Harris, and dozens of other political
and educational leaders regarded education as the creator and upholder
of civilization. The existence of the state, the security of property, the
cultivation of morality, the control of crime, the success of business and
industry, and the continuation of progress all depended upon the maintenance of education. While society could not thrive without an educa-

[5] *Ibid.*, 220-221.
[6] NEA, *Proceedings, 1870*, 201, 203.
[7] NEA, *Proceedings, 1871*, 144, 35.

tional system, the schools could not rise much above the level of the society that nurtured them.[8]

The idea that education could and should contribute to social progress is as old as the institution of teaching. In 1860 J. W. Bulkley, president of the National Teachers' Association, said that the young should not be educated simply in accordance with present standards but "with a view to a future and much ameliorated condition of humanity." In 1896 sociologist Albion W. Small advised that teachers "not rate themselves as leaders of children but as makers of society."[9] Progressive educators stressed this social obligation in every decade, and its implications for the curriculum were as various as their visions of the improved society.

The limitations as well as the possibilities of social reforms through education were recognized. "We can not have a corrupt legislature and a pure judiciary; we can not have piety in the pulpit and pews and speculation and fraud in politics; we can not have false ideals and vicious practices characterizing society, and pure and lofty aims with wise and efficient methods in our schools." Such was the analysis of Professor Edward Olney of Michigan in his paper before the NEA at Baltimore in 1876. He added: "It is a fallacy to suppose that radical reform can be gotten in the school and from hence revolutionize the whole. The reform sought must be developed all along the line in order that it be possible anywhere. With society superficial and false and government corrupt it is simply impossible that the school should be in wholesome condition."[10]

Curriculum-making involved an attempt to coordinate social ideals, state policies, individual freedom, and general welfare. It was not surprising therefore that changes were frequent and that no program met universal approval. Throughout the century (1857-1957) the curriculum at all school levels from the grades to the university developed toward multiplicity and difficulty.

In the common schools some new subjects were added; but even more important, the basic studies were expanded. In 1879 Superintendent A. J. Rickoff of Cleveland declared, "The programmes of our schools are overcrowded." The textbooks, he said, had quadrupled in size and complexity, and the work of pupils was five to ten times that required in 1800. He lamented that reading, about which the public critics had been lately so articulate, was too often word-calling instead of sense-getting, the rattling of shells rather than the picking of kernels. He demanded that only the content which would have utility in adult life should be taught. He commended for imitation the instance of a British dry-goods firm which ordered its agent in China to go into the streets and observe the

---

[8] NEA, *Proceedings, 1889,* 144.
[9] NEA, *Proceedings, 1860,* 212; *1896,* 184.
[10] NEA, *Proceedings, 1876,* 31.

costumes which well-dressed people of different classes were wearing, buy the clothes off their backs, and send them to London to enable the firm to produce what the Chinese would buy. Similarly teachers might observe "the mental and moral habiliments" that successful people of various vocations were wearing. From this analysis they could make a program of studies that would have social utility.[11]

An even more extensive and radical criticism of the elementary-school program was made by J. M. Gregory, a former president of the NEA. Speaking to the association at Saratoga Springs in 1882, he asserted that the seven subjects of the elementary program—spelling, reading, writing, arithmetic, geography, grammar, and American history—had won their places by chance and had been confirmed by the industry and ingenuity of authors and publishers and the inertia of educators. Subject by subject, he pronounced them all as frivolous in content, time-consuming in their requirements, and meager in results. A child was not allowed to study the human body until he first memorized the towns of Siberia and the rivers of Patagonia; to study plants until he had mastered arithmetic. Neither arithmetic nor geography threw light upon the great moral, social, and political issues of the day. Gregory proposed the introduction of physiology, botany, chemistry, zoology, physics, geometry, technology, and political and moral and social science.[12]

The number of required subjects in the elementary schools increased from decade to decade. By 1900 the seven subjects mentioned by Gregory in 1882 had grown to a dozen. By 1930 the typical school in cities offered eighteen and by 1950 the number had grown to about thirty. Some of these so-called subjects were, of course, part-time topics and group activities.

An even more rapid growth of subjects occurred in the high school. A committee report of 1891 lists about thirty subjects. Modern and American history were conspicuously absent.[13] In 1923 a superintendent reported that one large city high school listed 168 subjects. At the normal rate of progress it would, he said, take a student fourteen years to take all of them.[14] By the 1950's the offerings were about as broad as human knowledge, but by the latter date no one tried to limit offerings to the capacities of one student. Thus the concept of an overcrowded curriculum gradually disappeared, for it was recognized that the curriculum was a reflection of social progress and not the assignment for any one pupil.

Sharp differences of opinion existed over the relative merits of the various subjects. Teachers, especially men, were popularly supposed to

---

[11] NEA, *Proceedings, 1879*, 41; *1881*, 22-29.
[12] NEA, *Proceedings, 1882*, 80-96.
[13] NEA, *Proceedings, 1891*, 313.
[14] NEA, *Proceedings, 1923*, 1015.

favor arithmetic over all other subjects and to give it an inordinate amount of time. Conversely, arithmetic was the recipient of severe criticisms of its utility and of the manner in which it was taught.[15] After visiting a large number of schools, a committee of 1890 delivered its opinion: "Arithmetic has thus become a science of difficult trifles and intricate fooleries peculiar to common schools, and remarkable chiefly for sterility and ill-adaptedness to any useful purpose."[16]

Next to arithmetic educators directed their criticisms against the overemphasis upon spelling. The oral drill was largely futile because the result was not transferable to written spelling. Superintendent Henry F. Harrington's indictment of 1875 is quite timeless in its validity: "When an elementary pupil has learned to spell correctly the comparatively few words that he is likely to use in composition during his life, he has well nigh exhausted the value of the study to him. Schools without number encourage the asinine idea that it is an immense intellectual achievement to be able to spell real jawbreakers. After mastering the 3,000 words that he will use he might as well be set to learning the language of Ugigi or Borroboola or spelling backwards tomorrow the words that he learns today."[17] Harrington lamented the time wasted in trying to learn the 10,000 words in the spelling book.

Harrington's views were not unique. In fact, they were widespread among educators of the 1870's. A realization of the discrepancy between pronunciation and spelling, and the enormous amount of time required to learn the oddities of English orthography, were factors in giving some degree of popularity to the movement for simplified spelling (see Chapter 19). It is interesting to note that later research reduced the desirable minimum of words that needed to be memorized to 1,000.[18]

The debates on the values of the various subjects reflected the long-continued controversy concerning the respective merits of the cultural, mind-training studies versus those that were presumably merely practical. "The practical," said President James H. Baker of Colorado in 1888, "dwarfs the powers, limits the horizon, degrades the soul. . . ." He feared that the smoke of factories would obscure the vision of the poet.[19] Sarcastic comments on manual training, cooking classes, and all practical courses were uttered so often that they became mere shibboleths of admission to the select group of critics. While dozens of answers were given in heated debates, one of the most telling rejoinders was that by M. R.

---

[15] NEA, *Proceedings, 1880*, 114; *1881*, 85; *1886*, 163-164; *1896*, 617.
[16] Walter Scott Monroe, *Development of Arithmetic as a School Subject*, Department of Interior Bulletin, 1917, No. 10, 127.
[17] NEA, *Proceedings, 1875*, 163. Harrington's words are rearranged and condensed. See also *ibid., 1874*, 282.
[18] NEA, *Proceedings, 1940*, 312.
[19] NEA, *Proceedings, 1888*, 172.

Trabue of North Carolina. In 1929 he observed that, in accordance with the bromidic injunction that "one should learn to live rather than to make a living," the high schools of his state were "undefiled by vocational purposes." While the factories of his state employed local high-school graduates in subordinate capacities, they turned to the technical schools of New England for their foremen and experts. Then Trabue added, "Our native graduates have presumably learned to live but their bosses from outside learned to make a living."[20]

Even when ideational differences were reconciled and agreements reached on the selection of subjects whose basic content had been somewhat standardized, the making of a curriculum was still a complex process. As time passed additional facts were added to history, arithmetic books became longer and more inclusive, new content was added to physics, and every subject became more comprehensive. So even in a curriculum of subjects some readjustments were necessary. For decades the solution was simple. Worried and harassed by the increasing fund of knowledge, educators tended to require more and more of the students. In the 1870's and 1880's they became aware of the injustice of continuous additions of new subjects and the expansion of old ones. They perceived that pupils had about reached their limits in time and capacity. What could and should be done?

What should have been done gave way to what was done. The doctrinaire and pseudo-philosophical procedure of curriculum-making in 1876 is well illustrated by the work of a committee consisting of W. T. Harris, W. F. Phelps, and Eli T. Tappan.[21] In an eleven-page report they discussed and outlined a program of studies for common schools, high schools, and colleges. At each level they used the same five basic principles to guide them in selecting appropriate subjects, namely, (1) Inorganic, (2) Organic or cyclic, (3) Theoretical or Intellect, (4) Practical or Will, and (5) Aesthetical or Phantasy. It is somewhat difficult now to see how the principle "Inorganic" pointed to mathematics, "Organic" to geography, "Theoretical" to grammar and language, "Practical" to history, and "Aesthetical" to literature, but so the committee headed by W. T. Harris saw it in 1876. No scientific procedure of curriculum-making was evolved until the 1920's.

In the meantime the curriculum problem became more complicated. The temperance reformers were among the first to confuse the problem by introducing the vicious practice of having the curriculum made by state legislatures (see Chapter 20). The example of the temperance workers was soon followed by those who advocated compulsory citizenship teaching. The complication of making a curriculum was intensified

[20] NEA, *Proceedings, 1929*, 613.
[21] NEA, *Proceedings, 1876*, 58-68.

by the increasing demand for the teaching of objectives, such as character, thrift, and health, rather than the traditional demands for the teaching of content, such as arithmetic, history, or spelling. When a legislature required the teaching of thrift, when an organization asked for the teaching of kindness to animals, and when parents demanded the inculcation of industrious habits, they were all designating purposes. The curriculum problem was to find the content and activities through which to realize objectives. Content subjects, such as American history or arithmetic, may indicate their own purposes, but thrift, kindness, and industrious habits are objectives in search of content; they are destinations without well-marked approaching paths.

Educators of the 1870's understood the problem, but they did not have specific solutions. In answer to the demand for the teaching of patriotism, they turned to poetry, biography, heroic episodes, American history, and, even more important from an educative standpoint, they turned hesitantly and reluctantly to a limited number of *activities*, such as singing, reciting, dramatizing, saluting the flag, and other individual and group activities, that would give meaning to content and that would involve more than mere perception and memory.

The public was slow to appreciate the educators' difficulty. The impatient patron seemed to think that patriotism, thrift, and kindness could be implanted by the energy and will power of the teacher. In their impatience for results the public and many teachers fell into the fallacy of confusing teaching with preaching. The typographical error in the NEA *Proceedings* of 1920 which refers to "a committee on the preaching of democracy"[22] may indicate a widespread pedagogical confusion. While no parent or teacher objects to or belittles preaching, it is imperative that a teacher recognize the difference between preaching and teaching.

The greatest development in the history of curriculum-making was the application of scientific methods. The scientific movement in education had produced intelligence tests and objective measurements of pupil achievement. In the 1920's it began to bring about revolutionary changes in curriculum-making.[23] Franklin Bobbitt, W. W. Charters, Harold Rugg, Hollis Caswell, and other professors, aided by hosts of graduate students and a few school administrators, initiated the scientific movement in curriculum reform. The method involved compiling the qualities of a good citizen, collecting the opinions of selected groups, listing the daily activities of typical workers, analyzing the contents of selected books and magazines, counting the preferences and interests of selected groups of children, listing the legal difficulties of a chosen sample of the popula-

[22] P. 162.
[23] For a brief review of outstanding quality, see J. Cayce Morrison, "The Curriculum Keeps Pace with Human Needs," NEA, *Proceedings, 1940*, 308-315.

tion, and making job analyses of various occupations. These are examples of scores of procedures for finding specific quantitative data which would indicate the topics, problems, and issues that children should study in school. The resulting curriculum would, it was assumed, be realistic, functional, and socially useful.

Curriculum-making evoked a truly remarkable outpouring of surveys, objective studies, yearbooks, and articles during the 1920's and 1930's. Beginning in 1924 the Department of Superintendence issued five successive yearbooks on various aspects of the curriculum at various grade levels and devoted the issue of 1936 to one subject, namely, the social studies. The National Society for the Study of Education devoted a great deal of attention to objective procedures for making the curriculum. Their yearbooks of the late 1920's are still used to review philosophies and derive techniques. The NEA Department of Supervisors and Directors of Instruction and the independent Progressive Education Association were also influential in the curriculum movement of the 1920's and 1930's, both groups being particularly concerned with building curriculums around learning experiences that were "functional" and that appealed to the interests of children.

Curriculum-making emerged as a distinct professional specialty. This development was signalized in 1924 by the founding of the Society for Curriculum Study, which nineteen years later was merged with the NEA Department of Supervisors and Directors of Instruction. Shortly after the merger the enlarged department adopted the name Association for Supervision and Curriculum Development. For more than a decade the ASCD has been the acknowledged leader of curriculum study and curriculum reform in American schools.

Scientific curriculum principles and procedures promulgated by a host of educators enabled the program-makers to include hitherto neglected areas and topics. For example, international affairs and current developments had been slighted, and as a consequence of these objective inquiries they were given more emphasis in school programs. The scientific movement emphasized the importance of immediate rather than deferred values. For example, pupils needed and could use information about their own communities, and in mock elections and student councils they used at once what they learned about parliamentary procedures and group techniques. The movement directed greater attention to children's interests and present needs. For example, in the elementary grades the hobby clubs provided outlets for their interest in collecting items and arranging significant displays, and at the high-school level young people were able to secure guidance in social and personal affairs.

Fully as important as the use of research methods in selecting content was their use in deleting outmoded elements. At last the educators had guiding principles for identifying nonfunctioning facts, useless words in spelling lists, unnecessary dates in history, and other excessive elements that had long encumbered the curriculum. It was discovered, for example, that the "practical measurements" in arithmetic were impractical. Slowly curriculum-makers developed the courage to eliminate inert topics and items in spite of the nostalgic laments of elders and the fretful outcries of special-interest groups.

The curriculum movement of the 1920's had two significant results—the broadening of the definition of the curriculum and the assumption by teachers of a larger role in curriculum-making. Until about 1920 the curriculum and the program of studies were synonymous. The curriculum consisted of content or subject matter. As long as this conception prevailed almost any one could, and did, suggest the inclusion of an additional subject. Curriculum-making consisted of adding American history, bookkeeping, manual training, and other subjects. As the progressive movement slowly demonstrated the fact that the subject matter was only a part of what children learned, the meaning of the curriculum expanded to include school-directed activities. Thus the curriculum was redefined; it included all those studies and activities that promoted the growth and development of children.

This new and expanded conception of the curriculum naturally required more than the old-time selection of subjects and topics; it required the steady and prolonged work of teachers, for no one else could direct the pupils through the multiple activities that were required for the mastery of skills, the acquisition of information, the practice of processes, and the growth of attitudes. As curriculum-making became more complicated and child-centered, administrators and subject-matter specialists were gradually forced to recognize their incompetence to make a curriculum. Reluctantly they left the task to teachers, aided by curriculum specialists who were also teachers.

In addition to selecting the subject matter to be studied, the curriculum-maker had to organize the content into subjects, topics, units, dramatizations, problems, and other learnable forms. Various forms of organization were popular in various periods. In the 1890's the type-study, popularized by the Herbartians, involved the selection and intensive study of a country, era, government, or person as a representative or typical specimen of its group or class. In the 1920's the fusion of two subjects, such as geography and history, or literature and history, was adopted as a method of increasing both interest and understanding. The project method involved the construction of a model or specimen; the problem procedure required the gathering of materials from varied sources to answer questions; and the unit was a collection of materials focused upon some particular topic or problem. The core curriculum was an attempt to organize several subjects into a single sequence of units. The concept of "common learnings," popularized by an Educational Policies Commission report in 1944, was an arrangement by which two or more teachers cooperated to teach a double-period class the elements of several subjects. Both core and common learnings stressed the needs and interests of pupils with less attention to traditional requirements. These and other forms of organization were tried in order to increase the appeal and learnability of the curriculum.

Since the curriculum is the reflection of social realities, the public is always sensitive to the correctness and faithfulness with which it mirrors the world of outside realities. In every decade the public seemed anxious that the basic skills be taught thoroughly. Any rumored lessening of attention to the three R's evoked a host of outspoken critics and clamorous defenders. Thus from one standpoint the public was satisfied with the old-time minimum curriculum and disapprovingly labeled new topics and activities as fads and frills. Yet in another mood these same upholders of the traditional program joined various pressure groups to induce the schools to teach a variety of new topics, causes, and reforms.

A complete list of the proposed changes during the hundred years could scarcely be compiled, but the ones that received major attention during the century are easily identified. First in frequency and popularity was the demand for the teaching of *citizenship*. This word gathered a cluster of associated concepts such as *patriotism, loyalty, law observance, democracy*, the *Constitution*, and *Americanization*. Perhaps second in frequency of advocacy and persistence was *health*. This word was often used to include physical and mental *hygiene, gymnastic exercises*, and *physical education* in all its variations. Brief views of the efforts to secure places in the curriculum for these two objectives—citizenship and health —will illustrate the process that was used to introduce dozens of similar topics and activities.

"The common school-house is not a manufactory of scholars or saints, but of good American citizens." So declared the Reverend A. D. Mayo in 1872. It was not, he added, the job of the schools to train souls for eternity but to make citizens.[24] At a later convention a speaker observed that "An important work of the schools is to make homogeneous American citizens," and another that "The state creates the school for its own purposes."[25] In 1888 W. E. Sheldon, president of the NEA in the preceding year, called for schools that would prepare "intelligent voters, fair-minded jurymen, upright judges, discreet and honest legislators, and incorruptible executive officers."[26] In 1895 the NEA endorsed "the general

[24] NEA, *Proceedings, 1872*, 12.
[25] NEA, *Proceedings, 1887*, 279-280.
[26] NEA, *Proceedings, 1888*, 148-149, 180.

movement . . . of education for American citizenship," and referred approvingly to the placing of flags in schools and the observance of national holidays. It called for systematic courses in patriotism and morality and greater respect for life and property.[27]

Some of the early educators made perceptive observations concerning the limitation of the idea of citizenship. In 1875 President W. W. Folwell of the University of Minnesota rejected the plea that the state should educate its citizens for its own perpetuation. Such a policy rested, he said, upon the debatable assumption that the state deserved perpetuation. He postulated the higher ideal of education for the maintenance of culture, which is the chief business of civilized men.[28] In 1887 E. E. White observed, "To make the end of public instruction the development of manhood is a broader view than to regard it as training for citizenship. The school does not exist for the state; good citizenship is not the end; it is not the end of the school or of any other institution."[29] In 1888 President James H. Baker of the University of Colorado said, "Education has higher aims than citizenship; it makes men and reconstructs states." He held that any state which was "not in harmony with ideal manhood must yield to progress in the interest of the individual."[30] In similar vein Dean Andrew F. West of Princeton University said in 1918, "It is good to be a true American; it is greater to be a true man or woman here or anywhere."[31]

Throughout the last fifty years, the NEA appointed several committees on citizenship and cooperated with other organizations to promote the teaching and practice of civic virtues. For fifteen years, beginning in 1909, the NEA endorsed the program of the American School Citizenship League. One committee of the 1920's formulated statements of the basic principles of democracy and secured wide publicity and discussion of them. Beginning in 1939 various committees planned induction ceremonies for new voters, and in 1940 helped to induce Congress to authorize the President to proclaim the third Sunday in May (later changed to September 17) as Citizenship Day. For a decade following the Second World War the NEA Citizenship Committee sponsored an annual conference and published manuals of citizenship. At least three departments of the NEA have published yearbooks and handbooks on citizenship.

An integral part of the campaigns for citizenship were efforts to Americanize aliens who had settled in the United States. Suspicion of foreigners and impatience with their slowness to adopt our customs were characteristic attitudes of Americans from the arrival of the first con-

[27] NEA, *Proceedings, 1895,* 32.
[28] NEA, *Proceedings, 1875,* 60-61.
[29] NEA, *Proceedings, 1887,* 278-279.
[30] NEA, *Proceedings, 1888,* 166.
[31] NEA, *Proceedings, 1918,* 90.

siderable number of immigrants in the 1820's up to the present time. Each successive wave of newcomers evoked new fears and stirred new prejudices. While many random attempts to set up ideals of American citizenship had been made before the First World War, thoroughgoing and organized attempts were first tried in the early 1920's. The NEA created the Department of Immigrant Education in 1921, state departments of education issued bulletins on Americanization, and city school systems appointed directors to see that the English language was used in instruction and that the children of immigrants were assimilated and Americanized. At the NEA convention of 1920 six speeches were made upon the topic. Said one speaker, "Americanism must be to us a political religion and teachers are the preachers of this gospel." Another speaker declared that Americanization was a process of winning hearts and minds of the foreign-born to our ways and customs.[32] While the campaign for Americanization soon waned in intensity, it left a residue of quiet determination to see that native ideals and customs were absorbed by foreigners who settled among us.

Another integral part of the citizenship movement was the introduction of democratic procedures into the educational process. Democracy in education is an example of the "curriculum as action" in contrast with the "curriculum as content." Administrators were urged, in the name of democracy, to counsel with their teachers; and teachers were admonished, in the name of democracy, to enlist the help of students in choosing problems and activities. Evidence that democracy in education had not advanced very far in 1886 was provided by the educators assembled in convention at Topeka. "The school is not really a republic or a family, or a society, but an organization, of which the teacher is the ruling and directing power," said one. Three speakers referred to the teacher as an "absolute monarch." Still another could see no fundamental difference in origin or form between the schools of a monarchy and those of a democracy.[33] Several decades passed before the idea of democracy in the classroom was given a serious hearing. When finally, however, the teacher became a key figure in curriculum-making, as he did after 1930, the pupils were given a larger share in determining the curriculum.

Still another element in the citizenship-patriotism movement was the state laws requiring the teaching of American history, the Constitution, American institutions, and civics. One study, under joint sponsorship of the NEA Department of Social Studies, showed that curriculum laws follow rather than precede curriculum changes. It reported that the program of studies, holidays, patriotic exercises, and school activities was very similar in all the states, regardless of the existence or absence

[32] NEA, *Proceedings, 1920*, 49, 439.
[33] NEA, *Proceedings, 1886*, 273.

of statutory requirements.[34] In spite of the enormous importance which pressure groups attach to curriculum laws, they have little practical effect upon school programs, being largely nuisances rather than guiding principles.

Next to citizenship, the most persistent objective in search of curricular materials and a place in the school program was health. Starting with no place in the curriculum of a hundred years ago, health has won recognition as a fundamental and pervading study at all grade levels.

"As a matter of fact, pedagogy is indifferent to physical education. This is the office of the family, civil society, or the army. The school assumes a certain degree of bodily vigor. It is not its function to teach the art of health. . . . It is a matter of history that physical education does not belong to the school." So declared W. T. Harris before the National Council of Education in 1884.[35]

"The improvement of child health is the duty of everybody; of every home, of every school, of every community, of every state, of every nation." This was the opinion of Thomas D. Wood of Columbia University, speaking to the National Council of Education in 1922.[36]

The distance between these two viewpoints is a measure of the progress of health education in the schools during the intervening years. In fact, progress beyond Harris's opinion was rather prompt. In 1891 a committee on hygiene stressed the value of good food and gymnastic exercises. In discussing this report G. Stanley Hall observed that "health is the criterion of everything in education."[37]

Some idea of the progress of health education is provided by the programs in various years. The need of such education was made shudderingly realistic by a report to the child-study department of the NEA in 1895. The speaker, a doctor, reported that the death rate from consumption of woman teachers in Boston was exceeded only by that among stonecutters. He expressed the opinion that the failure to wash the floors of the Boston schools from decade to decade was one factor in the high mortality rate. The doctor reported that the death rate among school children in London and Berlin was less than in most American cities.[38]

In 1897 a district superintendent from New York City enumerated the sources of disease and danger: impure air, poor light, unsuitable furniture, unsanitary schoolhouses, filthy outhouses, ignorance, and marks and medals which incited the pupils to unhealthful efforts to win prizes. The struggle for honors had "driven many an ambitious boy and girl to an early grave at the point of a pencil." The abstruse physiology as taught had little relation to the experiences of children. "They should be

[34] Edgar B. Wesley, *American History in Schools and Colleges* (New York, 1944).
[35] NEA, *Proceedings, 1884*, 56-57.
[36] NEA, *Proceedings, 1922*, 421.
[37] NEA, *Proceedings, 1891*, 348-356.
[38] NEA, *Proceedings, 1895*, 932-933.

taught the effect of green apples upon the stomach before they are taught the effect of alcohol upon the brain." Any teacher too delicate or refined or squeamish to deal with the needed attention to the bodily functions should "be relegated to the land of spirits to teach where mortal coil has been shuffled off."[39]

At the Chicago meeting of the superintendents in February 1909, Dr. Woods Hutchinson of New York said that the emphasis upon mind training had endangered the health of pupils. He denounced the tradition which exalted the mind and debased the body. "Ignorance and prudery are the fruitful mother of both disease and indecency."[40] Another speaker emphasized the value of playgrounds, exercise, good food, and sunshine. He cited the proverb "Where the sunshine does not go the doctor does." Superintendent W. H. Maxwell of New York recommended a department of health for each school system.

Annual examinations of school children were started in Los Angeles in 1907.[41] In 1914 the NEA endorsed health examinations and the employment of nurses by school boards.[42] School health received a great impetus during the period of the First World War. Children were induced to observe health practices by being admitted to health leagues, by games, and by posters and cartoons that popularized the Health Fairy and Cho Cho the Health Clown. It was also, as one observer labeled it, the "era of spinach."[43]

The American Association for Health, Physical Education, and Recreation, a department of the NEA, publishes yearbooks and magazines, issues bulletins on health, and sponsors national conferences. With the help of the American Medical Association the NEA and its departments carried on campaigns for both physical and mental health. In 1938 the classroom teachers' department published a yearbook on teacher health, and the Council for Exceptional Children devotes attention to the health problems of exceptional children. One of the most widely distributed of all the yearbooks issued by the American Association of School Administrators was devoted to health education. In 1950 the yearbook of the Association for Supervision and Curriculum Development, an NEA department, dealt with the fostering of mental health. Thus the NEA and at least six of its departments have devoted attention to the curricular problems of teaching and promoting health.

In addition to these two objectives—citizenship and health—which received major attention, a goodly number of other causes were also admitted to the program of various schools. Among the many that might be mentioned the following are typical: character, moral and spiritual

[39] NEA, *Proceedings, 1897,* 568-569.
[40] NEA, *Proceedings, 1909,* 263-264.
[41] NEA, *Proceedings, 1907,* 922.
[42] NEA, *Bulletin,* III, 22, September 1914.
[43] NEA, *Proceedings, 1919,* 86-88; *1920,* 78-84, 184-188, 368-371.

values, civil liberties, critical thinking, intergroup relations, conservation, consumer education, thrift (see Chapter 21), temperance (see Chapter 20), and others. Each of these causes enlisted its supporters, and each was promoted by argument, persuasion, pressure, and occasionally by law. The campaigns which were carried on to effect their entrance into the curriculum were similar to those described above in connection with citizenship and health.

Important in the history of curriculum-making in all fields, subjects, and topics and at all grade levels was the work of some of the departments of the NEA. In addition to the departmental activities in specific areas mentioned above, the Elementary Department, from its founding in 1870 until its merger with the Classroom Teachers in 1924, devoted a great number of papers and discussions to all aspects of the curriculum. The Department of Rural Education, which started in 1907, emphasized the resources of the local community as a means of enriching the curriculum and building up the morale of rural students. Naturally the subject-centered departments devoted great attention to the curriculum of their respective fields. For example, the National Council of Teachers of Mathematics, since its organization in 1920, has urged continued attention to its field through committees, conferences, and publications. In addition to its influential organ, *The Mathematics Teacher*, the department in 1954 started a new magazine wholly devoted to arithmetic. The National Science Teachers Association sponsors the Future Scientists of America (for high-school students) and has recently undertaken to restore the teaching of physics and chemistry to their former levels of frequency in secondary schools. The Music Educators National Conference and the National Art Education Association, also NEA departments, have been persistently influential in securing recognition in the curriculum for their subjects.

Through the years both the curriculum and the process of making it changed fundamentally. The guidance of tradition, the influence of abstract principles, the weight of authority, and the enumeration of opinions gradually lost favor and were replaced by studies of the social setting, the principles of learning, and student capacities. Old, inert portions were discarded from all subjects, and the remaining portions were reorganized. The fixed course of study was replaced by a changing, growing body of information, enriched and expanded by a great variety of meaningful activities. While basic skills and minimum information were never slighted, they were put into more appealing contexts. Curriculum-making has become a continuing activity, involving all members of the teaching profession and guided constructively by able leadership such as that provided by the NEA—and especially by several NEA departments.

10

Commercially Speaking

"TARDINESS is the parent vice . . . he that strolls tardily along to school is liable thereby to receive and foster impressions or form habits which may result in overwhelming ruin. . . . Let the school have a bell to be rung at a precise time before the beginning of school. . . ."[1] In these vigorous words an Illinois teacher of 1857 identified a common dereliction and suggested a remedy. For several decades after its founding in 1837 the Buckeye Bell Foundry of Cincinnati announced through various educational magazines its willingness to supply "bells for schools, churches, and farms," thus meeting the educational need indicated by the Illinois teacher.

"The stentorian commands of the old-time master, emphasized by heavy thwacks of a heavy ruler—sometimes on the desks and sometimes on the sconces of the terrified pupils—have gone out of fashion, and with them the turbulence which they caused rather than cured. The Call-Bell has taken their place, and become as indispensable an article of school furniture as the strop or the ruler used to be, and much to the relief of both teachers and taught." These were the words of J. W. Schermerhorn and Company in an advertisement of 1868, announcing a new set of nine fine-toned, silver-plated call bells for the teacher's desk.[2]

These two instances of meeting educational needs with appropriate products are indicative of the never-ceasing quest for materials that facilitate teaching and learning. Authors, inventors, designers, publishers, manufacturers, and distributors were vigilant to anticipate and eager to supply the needs of teachers, pupils, and school administrators. Making no pretensions of being charitable or disinterested but frankly embracing the motivation of the capitalistic system, these commercial suppliers of the tools of education nevertheless made contributions of great value to the cause of education.

[1] *Illinois Teacher*, III, 179, April 1857.
[2] *New York Teacher*, V, 425, October 1868.

Buildings, furniture, books, and supplies have been regarded as indispensable and their educational value as unquestionable. Whoever made a better textbook, a more comfortable school desk, or a more serviceable piece of apparatus was a benefactor of education. Educational research proved that improved equipment, more ingenious articles, and a bigger library produce more and better learning. The beneficial results from better tools were particularly impressive in home economics, the laboratory sciences, art, music, and social studies.[3] Educators have thus been aided in their efforts by publishers, map makers, and seat designers. The history of the NEA provides overwhelming evidence of the value of this cooperation between commercial producers and educators.

In 1857 schools had little demand for commercial products. A building, some seats, and a few books met the requirements of the typical school. As attendance increased and withdrawals decreased, as the school terms grew to seven and nine months, and as the number of years of required schooling increased, the material needs of the schoolroom grew in number and variety. As teachers became more adept in teaching, they required more and better books, maps, and other learning aids. As the curriculum grew and added music, art, manual training, physical education, home economics, and mechanic arts, the need for equipment multiplied accordingly. School cafeterias, health programs, and student activities have broadened the material demands of the schools still further. In fact, it is now difficult to name a product which the schools do not buy or one that has no educational utility. Thus school needs and community needs have become almost identical, reflecting the increasing complexity of both society and education. In the early years of the NEA, however, the distinction between educational materials and general commercial products was easier to perceive. A review of some of these changing needs of the schools provides another view of the growth of education in America.

Most numerous and possibly most important of the materials for education were books—pedagogical treatises, textbooks, workbooks, and the varied printed materials for pupils. Accordingly, publishers were numerous and active. In relation to the need, there were probably as many schoolbook publishers in 1857 as there are in 1957, and from the earliest years they have been active, aggressive, and competitive, eager to meet the educational needs and ambitious to publish as many books as possible. As the decades passed the number of books increased and the quality improved. A mere listing of some of the authors in some of the subjects at various times indicates the ceaseless efforts to provide suitable textbooks. Histories by Goodrich, Robert, Worcester, McMaster,

[3] See article on "Equipment" in Walter S. Monroe, ed., *Encyclopedia of Educational Research* (2nd ed., New York, 1950).

Channing, Gordy, Muzzey, Robinson, Breasted; arithmetics by Colburn, Davies, Brooks, Ray, Eaton, Robinson, Walton, Felter, Hagar, Sanford, White; readers and spellers by Sander, Sargent, Tower, Hillard, Willson, McGuffey.[4]

Competition among publishers was keen, and reviews were critical, often to the point of fault-finding and occasional hostility. The aptness of selections for readers, the kind of type used, the fine points of punctuation, and prices were all seized upon and used for and against particular books. Criticisms and rumors were used to discredit a book or a publisher, and charges of the bribery of superintendents and school boards were heard from time to time in various states. One contest, that between Willson's and McGuffey's readers, reached the height of shrill vituperation and the depths of malevolence, evoking thirty-two-page replies and rejoinders in various educational magazines during 1865. There is some basis for thinking that these fierce struggles helped to produce better textbooks, because competing companies were likely to avoid the features that evoked telling criticisms, just as seat designers and furnace manufacturers were forced by criticism and competition to develop better products.

Publishers promoted supplementary books that were not directly related to school requirements. Jacob Abbott's *Rollo's Tour in Europe* and its numerous companions enjoyed a wide and steady sale. Teachers were urged to read books on psychology, elocution, methods, and child nature and not to overlook Combe's *Lectures on Phrenology*. Collections of orations, declamations, dialogues, and selections for elocution were popular. One publisher announced that his selections were printed "with marks for emphasis, tones, inflections, and gestures." The announcement by Hinds and Noble that they could supply an interlinear translation of *Caesar* brought cheer to poorly prepared and overworked Latin teachers and doubtless also to many students who posed as teachers to secure a copy of the coveted "pony." Among the books that enjoyed at least a period of temporary popularity were F. M. Cowdery's *Elementary Moral Lessons for Schools and Families,* Froebel's *Autobiography,* and *Black Beauty,* which for a time was distributed free by the American Humane Educational Society.[5] In recent years teachers have been challenged to wrestle with Toynbee's *A Study of History.*

[4] The advertisements of the early period mentioned in this chapter were seen in scattered issues of the following magazines after 1857: *American Educational Yearbook* (1858), *California Teacher, The Fountain Electric Teacher, Indiana School Journal, Maine Journal of Education, New York Teacher, Massachusetts Teacher, Ohio Educational Monthly, Rhode Island Schoolmaster, Vermont School Journal;* advertisements in this period since 1921 were found in the *NEA Journal, Social Education* after 1937, and in various state journals (e.g., *Indiana, California*) after 1947.

[5] NEA, *Proceedings, 1890,* 54.

Magazines! Magazines for teachers, children, pupils, parents. Magazines devoted to education, to stories, to sports, to public affairs, to general culture. E. L. Godkin and Company offered prizes for the best essay for *The Nation*. Henry Ward Beecher said of it, "I wish it had a million subscribers." *Littell's Living Age, Lippincott's, Public Spirit, Harper's, North American Review* and *Atlantic Monthly* were for teachers and other adults; *The Youth's Companion, Student and Schoolmate, Little Corporal*, Demorest's *Young America, Packard's Monthly, Nursery, St. Nicholas*, and *Child Life* appealed to younger readers. In recent years student magazines and papers have been puplished by the Civic Education Service, American Education Press, and Scholastic Magazines. Teachers have been urged to make classroom use of the *Reader's Digest*, the *New Republic, Newsweek, Time*, and various other magazines. In this area as well as in the whole field of commercial products the teacher's need can scarcely be distinguished from the citizen's need or educational requirements from those of society in general.

A large number of maps and globes have been available throughout the century. In the early decades Perce's Magnetic Globes were accompanied by sets of small magnetic pieces, representing races, animals, and vegetation. Their adherence to the globe was a telling way to teach gravity. Franklin's globes were declared to be the best available, "warranted against cracking." The Pendant Globe was offered by L. P. Denoyer and Company of Appleton, Wisconsin. The Goldthwaite map was printed on white satin which could be inflated into a twelve-inch globe. In recent years sets of colored and outline maps and atlases for history and geography have been for sale by Weber Costello, Rand McNally, A. J. Nystrom, Denoyer-Geppert, and other companies.

In addition to the necessaries of the school, many miscellaneous objects and aids have been offered throughout the century to teachers and pupils. One publisher advertised Calkin's word games, a set of 250 cards containing letters, figures, and punctuation marks. In arranging these cards, children would learn words, spelling, and punctuation. Another publisher explained that his set of merit cards, certificates, and awards would gain the attention of pupils and win them to good behavior and diligent efforts. Still another recommended his set of mottoes, printed on glazed cardboards of various colors. They would ornament the walls and inspire the teacher and pupils. One dealer offered sixty-two forms and solids for use in object teaching. Others announced erasable spelling tablets, noiseless slates, and erasers. In honor of the great founder and to promote kindergartens, teachers were urged to buy Froebel souvenir spoons. Perry pictures expanded the pupil's information and promoted the development of art appreciation. No one would deny the educative effect upon children's attitudes of a set of thirty-two dolls from foreign countries.

For several years penmanship, pens, and ink probably received commercial attention out of proportion to their educational importance. Several advertisers offered copybooks, systems of penmanship, and various kinds of pens, one of which was "a nearer approximation to the real swan quill than anything hitherto invented." In the 1860's and 1870's Gillott's steel pens had center and side slits and were cross-ground to assure a steady flow of ink. Platt R. Spencer of Geneva, Ohio, designed a system of penmanship, prepared copybooks, and produced a pen. Teachers were given the disquieting information that counterfeit pens were in circulation; the only guarantee against such deceptions was to ask for the genuine Spencerian steel pen. To promote high standards of handwriting L. S. Thompson of Sandusky published his monthly *Teacher of Penmanship*. In the 1880's Hawkes' improved fountain pencil, Purdy's ever-ready fountain pen, and Wirt's "reliable writing instrument" were advertised to replace old-fashioned pens and holders. In spite of these proclaimed inventions Faber's pencils and Dixon's graphite pencils were still advertised. In the 1900's the Post self-filling, self-cleaning fountain pen was on the market, and a steady stream of improved pens and pencils, including scores of ball-point pens, have been marketed in succeeding years, culminating in today's offerings by Parker, Inkograph, Sheaffer, and other producers.

Each school subject and activity had special needs and evoked the production of special apparatus and supplies. Physical education and gymnasiums called for multiple kinds of equipment. In the 1860's Dio Lewis opened a school for girls at Lexington, Massachusetts, at which physical culture received special emphasis. From his quarters in Boston he also supplied "dumb bells, rings, clubs, and wands," a bookholder to correct stooping postures, a "spirometer" to strengthen and enlarge the pulmonary organs, and Professor Schriber's pangymnasticon, which would enable the owner to perform over a hundred beautiful and profitable exercises. Apparatus grew more varied and plentiful with each decade. In the 1920's the Fun-Ful Playground Apparatus and various kinds of gymnasium equipment were available from a number of reliable companies.

From advertisements one can trace the evolution of teaching and learning aids of a particular kind. In the 1880's James W. Queen and Company offered its optical lanterns for projecting illustrations. At the Chicago Congress of Education in 1893 a speaker reported that the elementary schools in France had used magic lanterns since 1880.[6] In

[6] NEA, *Proceedings, 1893,* 314-315.

1898 a writer observed that "the practically universal applicability of the optical lantern or stereopticon as a means of instruction from the kindergarten to the university has only recently been recognized." In 1903 the McIntosh Company of Chicago was offering the Improved School Lantern. Later came a multitude of educational films and recordings and a variety of motion-picture projectors and phonographs.

No restrictive definition of educational materials could be made, and advertisers in various decades were resourceful in implying that their products had educative values. Ferry's seeds could be used in school gardens; A. B. Dick's duplicating material provided "help for hampered teachers"; the Teen Age Book Club expanded the number of young readers and the range of their reading content; the Linguaphone promoted better pronunciation; *Compton's,* the *World Book, Britannica Junior,* and the *Book of Knowledge* helped children at home and at school; class rings and pins built pride and promoted school spirit; a Waltham or Elgin watch was useful for both teachers and pupils; Monarch bicycles might promote health and prevent tardiness; Coca-Cola, Hire's root beer, Baker's chocolate, and Hershey's candy bars could renew the flagging attention of restless pupils and sustain the efforts of weary teachers; Wrigley's chewing gum provided a release for pent-up energy and "contributed to mouth health"; a trip by plane or train would increase the teacher's store of knowledge; a teacher might be an author in need of the services of a literary agent; and many teachers made use of educational materials offered by General Motors, General Electric, General Mills, Westinghouse, the Association of American Railroads, and other corporations and organizations.

Important as were textbooks, magazines, and the varied objects and devices for classroom use, they were, commercially speaking, of lesser magnitude than school furniture, apparatus, and supplies. Such products were constantly proffered to school boards and administrators through advertisements in educational magazines. Chase's Excelsior school furniture; Hixon's revolving, tilting, and swivel chairs; Hilmes's reclining chair; Barstow's steel-plate and cast-iron furnaces; the Triumph Dovetailed desk; Grossin's ventilating stove; Kohler's hot-air furnace; the Eureka liquid slating for blackboards; Swasey's blackboards; Ross's school furniture; Prang's educational materials; Hammond, Remington, Smith, Underwood, Royal, and IBM typewriters; Nelson's pressure-tank closets; Medart's steel lockers; the American Seating Company's desks; tests for every subject, grade, age, trait, and quality, and scoring machines; musical instruments, laboratory supplies, art materials, and janitor supplies—these were only a few of the myriad offerings by the commercial firms that served the schools. These products affected school procedures, and educational innovations called for new and improved products; thus commerce and education exerted a reciprocal influence upon each other.

A great variety of advertisements and exhibits were directed specifically to the teachers. Most numerous of these appeals to teachers throughout the whole century were the calls to attend summer schools. The institutions emphasized their location and the exciting journey involved in reaching the campus as well as the professional offerings, programs of social activities, and the low costs. The teachers went. Beginning in the 1880's, the number grew larger year by year and as yet shows no signs of diminishing. Thus teachers have demonstrated their own belief in education, that it is a continuous, never-ending process.

Perhaps second in frequency among the appeals to teachers were those of teachers' agencies, promising higher salaries in some distant state. The American School Institute, founded in 1855, brought teachers and schools together, advised parents concerning the education of their children, and handled the sale of school properties. This agency had offices in New York and Boston and after 1868 in San Francisco, the latter being managed by John Swett. In 1868 one could buy a boys' school in Connecticut with 26 rooms, 3 acres of land, and 100 fruit tress for $17,000 or an academy at Lebanon, Missouri, for a smaller sum. After the 1880's the agencies became more numerous. Brockway, Albert, Thurston, Fisk, McCullough, Clark-Brewer, and a number that took the name of a city, state, or region offered to find positions in greener fields.

Opportunities, varied and alluring, were constantly presented to teachers. One advertiser of the 1860's urged teachers to sell engraved portraits of General Grant, Charles Sumner, and W. C. Bryant. Another asked them to take orders for Dr. Naphey's *Prevention and Cure,* "the best family medical book ever published," and if successful the teacher could become a state manager. William W. Glazier of Albany called for agents to sell his *The Capture, the Prison Pen and the Escape,* "a thrilling and authentic" work concerning nine Civil War prisons. Ladies, teachers, and disabled soldiers could, he asserted, easily sell from ten to twenty copies a day. One broker advertised for eighty teachers to promote gold mining properties in Colorado. Some of the advertisements frankly advised teachers to transfer into more profitable lines of work. Business colleges suggested that bookkeeping, telegraphy, and commercial law offered better prospects than teaching.

Invitations to travel were frequent. "It pays teachers to travel. They can see more in a flying trip of a few weeks than they can read about in a year. . . . Either go or return by the Pan-Handle and Pennsylvania Central. The scenery on this road is simply *grand.* The Horse-Shoe Bend is a perpetual wonder." So read an advertisement of 1880 in the *Indiana School Journal.* In the same issue the Northern Transit Company urged teachers to take one of thirty-one trips from Chicago or Milwaukee and go to Cleveland, Buffalo, Montreal, and Quebec. Tourist bureaus, railroads, steamship companies, and resort hotels extolled the educative value of travel and offered, in many instances, special rates to teachers. In 1905 E. D. Brooks of Minneapolis offered teachers a choice tour of Europe with a small private party under experienced personal direction. In more recent years airplane companies and railroads arranged tours that were thrilling, educative, and professionally advantageous. The NEA itself entered the field in the 1940's with the establishment of its Division of Travel Service, which reports that it saves NEA members from $50,000 to $60,000 annually on the tours it arranges to all parts of the nation and the world.

Teachers were admonished to learn how to appraise people, cultivate smooth manners, and develop pleasing personalities. In the 1860's *Mental and Social Culture* was advertised as a book on how to study, think, and talk, and how to be cheerful, polite, and entertaining. Its author, L. C. Loomis, was president of Wheeling Female College. In 1890 Fowler and Wells announced the publication of *Heads and Faces: How to Study Them,* a new manual on character reading. In the course of years many books on personality, power, friendship, and success were addressed to teachers as well as to laymen. Unquestionably they added to the socialization of public relations and classroom procedures.

Advertisers were mindful of the teacher's health, appearance, and general welfare. Soon after the Civil War he was advised that he could secure a perfect fit with one of Ballou's patented French-yoke shirts by providing a few simple measurements. Advertisements in state educational journals, especially at the time of the annual meeting of the state association, acquainted teachers with the latest fashions in fur coats, dresses, suits, hats, shoes, and all the requirements of any well-groomed citizen. In the early decades he was admonished to use Nature's Hair Restorative, which was "free from the poisonous drugs used in other hair preparations"; Kidney Wort for urinary diseases, female weaknesses, and nervous disorders; Scott's Emulsion for chronic coughs; Horsford's Acid Phosphate for dyspepsia, headache, and the overuse of tobacco; and Kaffe Hag for classroom nerves. In the 1860's Brown's Bronchial Troches were recommended for coughs, colds, bronchitis, asthma, and catarrh. President Edward North of Hamilton College said, "The Troches are a staff of life to me." The Stone Medicine Company of Quincy, Illinois, offered Dr. Stone's Bronchial Wafers to preachers and teachers at reduced rates.

During the first fifty years (1857-1907) of the NEA, exhibits at conventions and expositions were probably more influential than advertisements in promoting the distribution of educational materials. In fact, it is now somewhat difficult to appreciate the former enthusiasm over expositions and exhibits. School exhibits, as differentiated from commercial exhibits, consisted primarily of pupil products—drawings, compositions, maps, copybooks, and, most prominent of all, objects and articles produced in manual training, domestic science, and art classes. Pictures of school buildings, specimen textbooks, and collections of laws and regulations were sometimes included. The NEA appointed committees and heard reports concerning many of the great expositions or world's fairs of the period, those at Paris in 1867, 1878, 1889, and 1900; Vienna, 1873; Philadelphia, 1876; New Orleans, 1884; Chicago, 1893; Atlanta, 1895; and St. Louis, 1904.

Under the leadership of the resourceful Thomas W. Bicknell the NEA started its own exhibits at its annual meetings, beginning in Madison in 1884. Such exhibits were designed, as one committee expressed it, to promote "the stimulation of educational thought and the improvement of educational practices."[7] As W. T. Harris said, "The great idea of an educational exhibit is to make things talk."[8] To achieve such results the NEA appointed committees to prepare, inspect, judge, and report upon the displays. Gradually commercial exhibitors were invited to offer their products for display. As the exhibits of pupil products declined in popularity, as they did rather rapidly, the commercial exhibits grew in popular favor. At San Francisco in 1888 the committee expressed its regret that more publishers and suppliers did not display their offerings.

The decline of pupil products and the rise in favor of commercial products are clearly implied in the committee report of the Nashville meeting of 1889. After dutifully listing the twelve school systems that sent exhibits, the committee called attention to the displays of Dixon pencils, Johnson maps, and the educational and school books of Silver Burdett and Company of Boston and six other publishers.[9] Concerning the exhibit at St. Paul in 1890 one of the committee observed that "the general interest in school exhibits is evidently waning." He regretted that such exhibits could include only objects and industrial products and not achievements in the common branches. The demonstration of the art of cooking drew praise and patronage, for each day of the convention a class of girls served strawberry shortcake. The displays of the publishers of books and dealers in supplies were daily surrounded by crowds of visitors, thus showing "how valuable their presence was in promoting educational intelligence."[10]

At Toronto in 1891 the committee began its report by observing, "The exhibit of pupils' work at the Toronto meeting of the National Associa-

[7] NEA, *Proceedings, 1890*, 52-55.
[8] NEA, *Proceedings, 1904*, 183.
[9] NEA, *Proceedings, 1889*, 52-54.
[10] NEA, *Proceedings, 1890*, 52-55.

tion was small and fragmentary." The commercial exhibitors, however, presented bigger, more attractive, and more useful displays than at previous conventions. Ginn and Company occupied 250 square feet, Rand McNally and Company 48, and Milton Bradley and Company 100. Thirty-one other exhibitors displayed desks, seats, "electric multi-programme clocks and bells," a "four-ball tellurian," phonetic charts, books, globes, maps, mineral specimens, and numeral frames.[11]

After 1891 the NEA no longer sponsored annual exhibits of pupil materials, but the commercial exhibits grew in size and variety. The endless possibilities of improved school furnishings, more elaborate and teachable textbooks, and the making of hundreds of articles of educative value challenged publishers and producers to keep abreast of educational ideas and demands. In fact, the typical representative of a publisher or supply company was alert to observe and report upon educational developments. The publisher who failed to illustrate his textbooks in accordance with current standards and the seat maker who failed to keep up with the latest research were in danger of losing business to more vigilant competitors.

The suppliers of educational materials were recognized, not only as contributors to the maintenance of teaching, but as promoters of educational progress. Representatives of the major textbook publishers were often former educators who carried educational ideas and information from school to school and thus won a semiprofessional status for their new field.

From the earliest years of the NEA the producers of commercial products and educators demonstrated good will toward each other. In order to finance the publication of its *Proceedings* the National Teachers' Association adopted the custom of taking up an annual collection. The varying amounts subscribed by the members were insufficient, however, and so they called upon the bookmen to help the cause. They responded, and thus the completeness of that monumental series was due in part to such donations. Some of the members became sensitive and feared that it was questionable taste to ask persons outside the profession for help in carrying on a professional undertaking. At Trenton in 1869 it was resolved that henceforth they would not solicit funds from the publishers.[12] So far as the record shows, the members conformed to the resolution, but throughout the years the bookmen and suppliers have found many ways in which to help various educational causes.

As exhibitors became more numerous in the early years of the twentieth century, they encountered difficulty in finding suitable display booths and securing drayage and packing services. Considering it a joint prob-

[11] NEA, *Proceedings, 1891,* 255-258.
[12] NTA, *Proceedings, 1869,* 16.

lem, the NEA and the exhibitors formed an organization in 1924, named Associated Exhibitors of the National Education Association. For several years the exhibitors gave an annual dinner for the school men, but owing to the increased attendance at the conventions the guest list outgrew all reasonable proportions and gave rise to dissatisfaction. Beginning in 1939, the superintendents assigned an entire evening of the general sessions to the exhibitors, who usually employed professional entertainers or a prominent artist or musicians. The Associated Exhibitors developed a code of ethics and endeavored to assure educators that all exhibitors were reliable firms with dependable products, which they designated as "tools for education."

Year after year the exhibitors have displayed more and more varied materials. At the Atlantic City meeting of the school administrators in February 1956, there were about 440 exhibitors. In addition to the primary needs, such as books, magazines, furniture, office equipment, projection machines, and laboratory and library materials, exhibitors offered art supplies, playground equipment, travel folders, cameras, gowns, hearing aids, maps and globes, pens, pencils, tests, and teacher-placement services. There were aids and materials for teaching special topics and subjects: character, citizenship, home economics, insurance, kindergarten, music, savings programs, safety, and health.

Among these exhibitors the publishers of books were naturally predominant, numbering 87; second were the furniture dealers, numbering 59; third were the magazine publishers, numbering 32. The exhibitors of building materials, desks, films, projection machines, and special teaching aids numbered about twenty for each category.

The exhibits at the February meetings of the American Association of School Administrators and cooperating organizations are usually larger than those of the summer meetings, although the latter are by no means small. At the Chicago meeting in the summer of 1955 the exhibitors numbered 151; at Portland in 1956, the number was somewhat smaller. Since the February meetings attract a large number of administrators and many school-board members, the range and variety of the exhibits naturally exceed those of the summer meetings, which are composed largely of classroom teachers.

Progress in improving the tools of education probably kept abreast of progress in the profession. In 1874, President Noah Porter of Yale thought that textbooks were more plentiful, more attractive, and more learnable than ever and that seats were more comfortable and schoolrooms more attractive.[13] Speakers who talked to student assemblies were almost compelled by tradition to congratulate their audiences upon the superior opportunities and improved equipment which they enjoyed over those

[13] NEA, *Proceedings, 1874,* 50.

available in the preceding decade or generation. Bromidic and trite as such observations became, they were literally true.

In 1937 superintendent Homer W. Anderson made a speech about the educational significance of the exhibits.[14] The textbooks, he said, were better graded to fit pupils of varying abilities; they were more numerous than ever before and better illustrated. The seat and desk makers had realized that the arrival of the socialized recitation and the work of informal groups required movable seats and had redesigned them to fit the new development. Physiological measurements had shown that the seating height of a pupil did not necessarily correspond with his standing height; consequently seat designers had made additional adjustments to meet this more accurate measurement. A science table that would serve for biology, physics, and chemistry was on exhibit. Better projectors, radios, and public-address systems had been designed. Anderson was especially impressed by the safety features of the latest school buses. Acoustical materials made rooms quieter and warmer, and heating and ventilating systems rendered buildings more pleasant and comfortable.

The producers of educational materials made a great contribution to the nationalizing of educational practices. In spite of the division of educational functions among forty-eight states, our theories and practices were remarkably alike. This situation was described by the chief of the education exhibit at the Louisiana Purchase Exposition in St. Louis in 1904. He attributed our "national system" to the work of the Bureau of Education and the National Educational Association.[15] Other factors were also influential in achieving this result—the work of teacher-training institutions with nationwide enrollments, the wide circulation of educational books and magazines, and, of course, improved transportation and communication and other unifying influences that operated upon all aspects of American life as well as upon education. Perhaps equal in importance to any one influence were the contributions of the publishers of schoolbooks and the manufacturers of school equipment and supplies. Through advertisements, exhibits, and traveling representatives they helped greatly to unify American education.

[14] NEA, *Proceedings, 1937*, 464-467.
[15] NEA, *Proceedings, 1904*, 346-347.

11

Hails and Wails

"WE FURTHER believe that schools and schoolhouses, methods of study and methods of discipline, at the present day, are far superior to those of fifty or twenty years ago."[1]

"The readers and speakers admitted into the grammar schools within the past two years, or since this reading furor has existed, are not equal to those of former years."[2]

This optimistic statement of faith was made in 1863, and the lament over the decline in the quality of students was written in the following year. These two utterances illustrate the human tendency to rejoice and to bewail. A recital of some of the commendations and criticisms of the schools and the teaching process will afford views of the two extremes— the presumed good and the alleged bad. Each view affords an element of truth. Any attempt to strike a balance between hails and wails is destined to fail, because the result would be, like the appraisals themselves, merely an impression derived from impressions. The number of law observances far outweighs the number of crimes. Law observance is so frequent and commonplace as to call for no comment. Similarly, commendation for routine performance elicits no attention, whereas criticism, like crime, is often newsworthy. Even though no balance can be achieved, the rehearsal of past opinions is valuable, for they, as much as the events themselves, are the essence of history. So contemporary appraisals, favorable and unfavorable, constitute a kind of index of popular and professional reactions toward education and the schools.

The historical value of felicitations and laments does not depend upon their reasonableness, soundness, or acceptability, or upon the status or profession of their authors. The critical report of a committee of educational specialists, the complaint of a lonely rural teacher, and the impatient outburst of an indignant parent—all have their value in recapturing the spirit and mood of the times.

[1] *Massachusetts Teacher*, XVI, 406, November 1863.
[2] *Illinois Teacher*, X, 140, May 1864.

Most, but not all, of the commendations and criticisms quoted on the following pages were uttered by speakers at conventions of the NEA. The speakers reflected popular as well as professional opinion, and many of their laudations were made to answer or offset popular criticisms. The most discriminating praise and the most vigilant and thoroughgoing criticisms of education have been made by educators. The lay critic sometimes has an advantage of greater perspective or a clearer perception of basic principles than a practicing educator, but in general the educational critics of education have the advantage of more information, deeper insights, and untrammeled motives. The tempered restraint that characterizes the criticisms of medicine by doctors and of law by lawyers is unknown in the teaching profession. Perhaps it is that educators, having been convinced of their lowly status by centuries of condescension, neglect, and contempt, are likewise unrestrained when they view their own profession.

Educational critics do not restrict their criticisms to education. They see clearly that their effectiveness as educators is conditioned by the nature of the surrounding homes, churches, business, and governments. Inevitably they become critics of the society in which they operate. Politics affects the schools; so the educators seek to influence political decisions. The citizen who admonishes the teacher to stick to his classroom and let public affairs alone is advising him to neglect a large area of his professional obligation. Public affairs are the raw materials of education, and so educators are not meddling when they participate in community matters; they are merely attending to the larger setting.

It would be easy to prove that every period is an age of criticism. Each successive generation thinks that the critics have suddenly increased in numbers and grown more devastating in their criticisms. In 1904 Nicholas Murray Butler observed that critical attacks upon public education had a cash value. In 1941, Donald DuShane in his presidential address to the NEA in Boston declared, "there is a marked increase in unjust and destructive criticism of teachers, textbooks, courses of study, and school expenditures by certain individuals and organizations. Perhaps the most destructive at this time are the attacks upon the loyalty and patriotism of the teaching profession. These attacks are being made by enemies of public education, by well-meaning minority groups or organizations that do not understand the purposes and methods of effective education, and by individuals who have been misinformed as to the soundness of American education."[3] Certainly those who have followed popular criticisms of education during the 1950's infer that no preceding period could have equaled it in virulence or surpassed it in inclusiveness. In the long view,

[3] NEA, *Proceedings, 1941*, 33.

however, it seems that criticism, like evil, is sufficient unto the period thereof.

An examination of some specimen judgments, favorable and unfavorable, will illustrate the range, quality, and persistence of this human tendency to praise and blame. Belief in progress, rapid, far-reaching, and inevitable, was sometimes voiced. "We write it down as a part of our moral, social, and political creed that the world is wiser and better than it ever was before, and that it will be wiser and better a hundred years hence than it is now." So declared a Massachusetts teacher in 1863.[4]

While progress might be universal, its manifestation took on unique features in America. According to the energetic editor, organizer, and optimist Thomas W. Bicknell, subsequently president of the NEA, "The American people surpass all others of ancient or modern times in quickness of apprehension, openness of mind, intelligence in all matters relating to the conduct of life, and the power of adaptation to circumstances."[5]

In 1901 James M. Green, long-time president of the normal school at Trenton, expressed great pride in American schools: "While we have no strictly national educational system, the education of our nation is more nearly uniform and has produced more uniformly good schools than that of any other country in the world."[6]

In greeting the NEA at Minneapolis in 1928 Governor Theodore Christianson of Minnesota pictured the teacher as the master builder of the ages. "So if you ask me where America was made, I will say that it was made where its principles were cherished, its ideals vivified and its purposes made clear. It was made where character was strengthened, loyalty deepened, intelligence expanded, and patriotism intensified . . . for America was made in the schoolroom."[7]

These articulate optimists were more than counterbalanced by a succession of bewailers who viewed education with apprehension and deplored existing conditions in general and a variety of things in particular. Lamentation on a high level that concerns itself with human nature, mankind, and all his deeds has a great tradition, untrammeled by petty worries and ordinary irritations. While the authorship of "*O tempora! O mores!*" is assigned to Cicero, his copyright soon expired and thousands of unwitting plagiarists have echoed his sentiment throughout succeeding generations. American contributions to this tradition are numerous.

In his commencement address of 1873 President James C. Welling of Columbian University, Washington, referred to the period as "a day of intellectual giddiness and revolt, when many run to and fro throughout

[4] *Massachusetts Teacher*, XVI, 406, November 1863.
[5] NEA, *Proceedings, 1882,* 83.
[6] NEA, *Proceedings, 1901,* 62.
[7] NEA, *Proceedings, 1928,* 20.

the land, crying 'Lo! here' and 'Lo! there,' as they give heed to seducing spirits."[8] Another general and somewhat vague alarm was reported by Superintendent James M. Greenwood in 1898. "Startling theories are advanced in some quarters now and boldly maintained that we are deteriorating with a rapidity never before known in the world's history. . . . it is argued that the nation is on the verge of collapse, and national death is written in large letters over the faces of the people."[9]

One type of lament was interwoven with nostalgia for past periods or conditions. In 1863 a Massachusetts teacher feelingly contrasted his own degenerate age with the sterner standards of a previous day. "If a man committed a crime, they did not explain it away upon the supposition of insanity or somnambulism. The dogma that all criminals are insane and more sinned against than sinning had not been broached in the last generation. These mawkish, sentimental notions about crime and criminals, which would shield the knave and the miscreant from the consequences of his folly or his sin, are modern inventions. . . ."[10]

Juvenile depravity and disrespect for authority evoked many and fervent outbursts in successive periods and generations. In 1865 the editor of the *Ohio Educational Monthly* bewailed "that serious defect in the character of American youth, a want of reverence." He opined that "Since the epidemic of moral suasion swept over our country some twenty years since, most children have done about as they pleased. . . . Boys twelve and thirteen years of age . . . throng our billiard and drinking saloons, ten-pin alleys, loaf about railroad depots and steamboat landings, even during school hours, often with the consent and frequently with the tacit approval of their parents."[11]

For the next forty years the character of youth continued to distress educators. The following wail of 1905 may be designated as an official lament since it was embodied in a resolution by the NEA: "There are in the minds of the children and youth of today a tendency toward disregard for constituted authority; a lack of respect for age and superior wisdom; a weak appreciation of the demands of duty; a disposition to follow pleasure and interest rather than obligation and order."[12] Evidently little improvement resulted, for a speaker at San Francisco in 1915 observed that "the majority of our youth have respect for very little in this world . . . they are an indulged, entertained, undisciplined group, sadly prepared for the art of living to some worthy purpose. . . ."[13]

[8] Bureau of Education, *Circular of Information*, No. 5, 1873, 26.
[9] NEA, *Proceedings, 1898*, 58-59.
[10] *Massachusetts Teacher*, XVI, 406, November 1863.
[11] *Ohio Educational Monthly*, XIV, 123, April 1865.
[12] NEA, *Proceedings, 1905*, 43. The same wail in almost the same words appears in a speech on p. 291 of the same volume.
[13] NEA, *Proceedings, 1915*, 658.

It must not be concluded from these quotations that all educators concentrated their criticism on the failings of pupils without reference to the failings of schools. On the contrary, short of calumny, no one can utter more reprobative judgments or scathing strictures concerning schools than those made in 1870 by W. F. Phelps, head of the teachers' college at Winona and subsequently president of the NEA.

They [the elementary schools] are mainly in the hands of ignorant, unskilled teachers. The children are fed upon the mere husks of knowledge. They leave school for the broad theater of life without discipline; without mental power or moral stamina; with minds distorted; too often with hearts corrupted, to swell the ranks of the lawless and to recruit the army of ignorant voters who are ever a menace to the peace and security of the country. . . . Poor schools and poor teachers are in a majority throughout the country. Multitudes of the schools are so poor that it would be as well for the country if they were closed. They add nothing to the intelligence or moral power of the country. They teach nothing positively good, but much that is positively bad. They are little else than instruments for the promotion of mental and moral deformity. . . . They afford the sad spectacle of ignorance engaged in the stupendous fraud of self-perpetuation at the public expense. . . . Hundreds of our American schools are little less than undisciplined juvenile mobs. . . .[14]

No wonder these outbursts provoked rebukes. B. G. Northrop, secretary of the state board of education of Connecticut and subsequently president of the NEA, pronounced them "a libel upon the schools." After denying some of Phelps's assertions, Northrop committed the fallacy of irrelevance by saying that the enemies of common schools would be delighted with Phelps's remarks.[15]

Criticisms of the curriculum and the manner in which subjects were taught were frequent and varied. Handwriting was a matter of anxiety in the early decades of the NEA. In 1857 one speaker gave utterance to widely held fears and opinions. "Writing or the art of penmanship seems to be to some extent neglected. . . . The general introduction of the metallic pen no doubt has its influence. . . . It is truly mortifying to see the declining tendency of this beautiful branch of education. Many of the teachers of our schools are absolutely not able to write a legible hand; and the fewest number any longer able to make a pen; consequently if scholars have no metallic pens, they must go uninstructed. As a general matter, the handwriting of the present age will not compare with that gone by. . . ."[16]

Another critic, in 1864, was interested in another subject. "Probably no branch of study in our common schools is so poorly taught or so indefinitely understood as Geography. Scholars often commit to memory

[14] NEA, *Proceedings*, 1870, 13, 17.
[15] *Ibid.*, 21.
[16] *Pennsylvania School Journal*, V, 225, January 1857.

many detached facts, unimportant descriptions, and long lists of names of towns, capes, gulfs, rivers, etc., but gain no conception of the principles and laws that underlie this important science."[17] History came in repeatedly for lashings and flailings. The criticisms varied from laments over the dry-as-dust catalogues of names, events, administrations, battles, and dates to scorn of teachers who did not teach and pupils who did not remember these same decried isolates.

The disdainful outcry and the smug condescension of the speaker who reported upon the ignorance of a high-school graduate of 1896 are probably typical of a whole succession of bewailing information-mongers. The speaker reported that a girl who had already been admitted to college did not know (1) how to bound Iowa, (2) the capital of Nebraska, (3) the main products of Kentucky. The next in line, a young man, did not know (1) the second President of the United States, (2) the first secretary of the treasury.[18]

In the face of attacks on the value of spelling, the traditional and orthodox view of it was loftily conceived and vigorously hailed by a Massachusetts teacher of 1863. He declared that spelling need not be a mechanical or monotonous drill, but it could become an attractive intellectual exercise "pursued not merely to learn the literal elements of words, but for the higher aim of *cultivating the eye and conceptive faculty*, acquiring the power to bring before the mind's eye *the form of a word as a unit*, as it looks on the printed page, just as one would so carefully examine a robin, a dog, a rose, or a painting, as to be able vividly to recall the image of the object."[19]

Spelling, handwriting, geography, and history pale into insignificance in contrast with the question of reading. In spite of its professional and technical nature, the method of teaching and learning to read has elicited streams of admonition and deplorations which have continued for a hundred years and show no sign of drying up. In 1857 a Pennsylvania teacher announced that words should be taught before letters; he had devised a set of flash cards and declared that he had had great success with the word method.[20]

The advocates of the letter method, the phonic method, the sentence method, and the word method carried on decades of argument. In 1871 E. E. White, Ohio editor, author, and superintendent, stressed the desirability of seeing the word as *idea*, as *sound*, and as *form*, of perceiving the elements of phonetic sounds, and eventually the letters which constituted the form.[21] About the same time Dr. Edwin Leigh advocated a reformed

[17] *Maine Teacher*, quoted in *New York Teacher*, IV, 183, February 1864.
[18] NEA, *Proceedings, 1896*, 160.
[19] *Massachusetts Teacher*, XVI, 262, June 1863.
[20] *Pennsylvania School Journal*, VI, 207, 1857.
[21] NEA, *Proceedings, 1871*, 91-93.

alphabet that would simplify spelling and pronunciation and thus facilitate the task of learning to read,[22] and Zalmon Richards, the first president of the NEA, advocated a revision of the English alphabet.[23] Thus
the teaching of reading became intermingled with the spelling-reform
movement.

The problem of learning to read was equaled in perplexity by the
question of what to read, and the latter has evoked many admonitions and
warnings. In 1865 a general lament over the reading program and its
treatment in the schools was uttered by the editor of the *Illinois Teacher*:

In recent years there has been a great change. . . . Knowledge has been so
simplified that it has been converted into something very like ignorance.
Juvenile literature has been reduced to an endless and barren jumble of baby
talk. It has imparted no nourishment; it has not thrilled the soul with new
energy. Care has been taken to introduce no word with which the child is not
already familiar. Hence, he walks an everlasting round without rising much.
His intellectual food is diluted and reduced to the merest namby-pamby. All
manliness, all sterling vigor, is washed out of it.[24]

The uplifting qualities of good literature, the character-building elements of heroic stories, and the civic values of our national history were
commended to young readers again and again.

The depravity of juvenile literature provided a wailing wall for two
sessions of educators in 1875 and 1881.[25] Such phrases as "evil books,"
"dime novels," "poisonous influences," "vicious literature," "noxious tales,"
"degrading lessons," "exploits of highwaymen, gamblers, vagabonds,
pirates, and desperadoes," "villainous pictures," "yellow covered novels,"
and "pernicious pages" were uttered with evidences of sincerity and
alarm. The questionable books in Sunday-school libraries were mentioned
by two speakers, the degrading influence of crime reports was lamented
by another, and a third speaker declared that adventure tales in a New
York paper had caused boys to run away from home, carrying cards,
revolvers, and dime novels in their pockets.

Bad literature seemed to be widespread, deplorably effective, and
practically unassailable. One worrier reported that near every large
school building some shopkeeper, in addition to pencils and schoolbooks,
carried a stock of trashy novels and sensational papers. Those with the
most lurid pictures of murders and Indian outrages were placed in the
window. The evil results of such reading showed up in slang language,
disrespect for old people and parents, low ideals, and insubordination.
One writer opined that it was easier "to rid our orchards of insect pests

[22] NEA, *Proceedings, 1873*, 207-219.
[23] NEA, *Proceedings, 1877*, 175-180.
[24] *Illinois Teacher*, XI, 341, November 1865.
[25] NEA, *Proceedings, 1875*, 186-188; *1881*, 104-117.

than to protect the minds of youth against the sting of the curculio of bad literature." The mayor of Philadelphia was quoted as having said that the destruction of bad literature would almost empty the station houses and prisons of youthful inmates.[26]

The cure for the evil of bad literature was the substitution of good literature. History, biography, stories from good magazines, and the memorizing of gems from great poems were hailed as remedies for low tastes. Authors, books, and particular passages were cited as interesting and uplifting examples of inspiring literature. The high-water mark of optimism was probably registered by a speaker who declared that "no one who has tasted the genius of Chaucer or Milton can be induced to read these nauseous tales."[27]

Laments over educational policies, public-school costs, and criticisms of criticism appeared at various times. The record of one session of the NEA in 1875 reads almost like a catalogue of discontent and defense. Superintendent A. P. Marble of Worcester recited the criticisms of schools and reviewed the reviewers. The critics characterized free tuition above the elementary level as indiscriminate charity; they complained of the great cost of school buildings; they criticized undifferentiated instruction for classes of varying abilities; they did not want dullards and geniuses averaged; they objected to the pure child being thrown into contact with the coarse and vulgar.

Speaking for the proponents of public education, Marble made vigorous rejoinders to each charge. He called for an educational ladder from the kindergarten to the graduate level, all of its steps supported by public taxation. A jail to house a hundred criminals cost three times as much as a school building for the same number of pupils. He denounced the idea of separate schools for children of different nationalities, religions, and social cliques as Brahminism. "What has any boy's inheritance or prospects got to do with his learning arithmetic or grammar?" The lapidary, he observed, polished all stones without ever trying to average them. With ironical seriousness he declared that those born to greatness would survive even public-school instruction; that it was better to establish foundling asylums for those stray children of the angels than to try to adjust instruction to the level of geniuses. To the charge that the schools merged the refined and the unrefined into one mass, Marble replied that pure children did not live on certain streets nor attend certain schools. While immorality and vulgarity had been discovered in public schools, he said that the grossest instances of such conduct had been uncovered in private schools.[28]

[26] *Indiana School Journal*, XXV, 131-135, March 1880.
[27] NEA, *Proceedings, 1875*, 188.
[28] NEA, *Proceedings, 1875*, 22-32.

Two speakers of 1879 were troubled over the great investment in education. "The conviction in many minds is becoming stronger and stronger every year that, considering the amount of time, labor, and expense bestowed upon our schools, the fruits do not correspond with the immense outlay. . . ." The other said that popular voices were saying "that these results are not commensurate with the time and money spent obtaining them." The reported results were that the average high-school graduate could not read, he had developed no taste in reading, he knew no literature, he could not write, he knew nothing thoroughly.[29]

A speaker of 1894 reported that American boys and girls of eighteen were no farther along in their training than European youth of fifteen. In 1902 Nicholas Murray Butler deplored "the neglect of the English Bible" which "incapacitates the rising generation to read and appreciate the masterpieces of English literature, from Chaucer to Browning. . . ."[30] Payson Smith's ironical summary in 1907 of pupil achievement is almost timeless in its applicability. "I take it for granted that we all know that children can't spell as well as they used to spell, that only one in a hundred can add and subtract with the facility of our fathers when they were boys, and that the schools are weakened and vitiated by all the frills, fancies, and fol-de-rols which our hard-headed ancestors would have ridden out of school on the same rail with the teacher who had dared to introduce them."[31]

Educational theories and teachers were weighed by C. C. Rounds in 1879 and found wanting. "I am tired to utter weariness of the unending iteration and reiteration of exploded theories, the presentation and representation of educational machines which will not work, but which must be tried upon successive generations of children. . . . In comparison with such slaughterers of the innocents, Herod deserves canonization."[32]

A survey in 1913 of the opinions of sixty-five superintendents concerning beginning teachers shows that the latter were most lacking in scholarship, a deficiency that weakened their organization and presentation of materials. The next weakness specified by a large number of the superintendents was the predominance of methods over content. Others observed that the young teachers could not write legibly, speak correctly, or accept new ideas. Some lacked common sense and yet a goodly number of them were so overconfident as to prevent their accepting criticism or learning by experience.[33]

The condition of higher education troubled more than one university

[29] American Institute of Instruction, *Proceedings*, 1879, 13-14.
[30] NEA, *Proceedings*, 1894, 136; 1902, 72.
[31] NEA, *Proceedings*, 1907, 173.
[32] C. C. Rounds, in American Institute of Instruction, *Proceedings*, 1879, 69-70.
[33] NEA, *Proceedings*, 1913, 524-525.

administrator. In 1883 President W. W. Folwell of the University of
Minnesota observed, "The present state of higher education in America
can be briefly comprehended in one word—chaos." He lamented the fact
that higher education was a part of the apparatus of denominational
evangelization. He referred to Americans as "the most common-schooled
and the least-cultured people in the civilized world."[34] According to Guy
Potter Benton, president of Miami University in Ohio, the situation in
higher education had not improved by 1911. "If status means standing
that is in any sense permanent, then there is no status of higher education
in the United States . . . there are no universal standards or fixed policies.
. . . The whole system of education in our country, from the kindergarten
to university, is subject to indictment for capriciousness."[35]

Part of the fault in the weakness of higher education was traceable to
poor teaching. A speaker in 1927 thought so. "I know no more illiberal
men in the teaching profession than can be found in the liberal arts colleges, no more dehumanized teaching, no more complete lack of human
interest, than is to be found in the classrooms of some of the teachers of
the humanities."[36]

The public rather than the schools was to blame for the discouraging
situation in the teaching of Americanization and citizenship, said a vehement teacher of 1922. "A wave of suspicion, prejudice, and intolerance
seems to have spread over the country—religious, racial, social. This, together with congressional stupidity, makes difficult the efforts of those
who are working to mould attitudes and ideals, to develop love for this
country and its people."[37]

The intimate and causal connection between society and education
implied in the preceding lament was more fully stated by an English
critic of 1866. In fact, his analysis and description are almost as applicable
in 1957 as they were in the year of their original utterance. The two
great principles of American life, according to the English commentator,
were "perfect social equality and absolute religious freedom." The salient
phenomena are restlessness and activity, versatility, the absorbing interest
in political affairs, ambition to rise, ceaseless flow of commerce, and the
spirit of speculation. The national temperament is intense, impatient, and
versatile. The dominant lesson which the American learns "is to be dis-
contented with his station." All these characteristics and qualities are
reflected in the schools.

The American school is a microcosm of American life. There reigns in it
the same spirit of freedom and equality, the same rapidity of movement, scarce

---

[34] NEA, *Proceedings, 1883*, 127-128.
[35] NEA, *Proceedings, 1911*, 191.
[36] NEA, *Proceedings, 1927*, 794.
[37] NEA, *Proceedings, 1922*, 944.

leaving time for work to be thoroughly well done; the same desire of progress, eagerly catching at every new idea, ever on the look out for improvements; the same appeals to ambition, the same sensitiveness to praise and blame, the subordination of the individual to the nation, the same prominence given to pursuits of a refining aim, the same excessive and exhausting strain on the mental and physical powers, the same feverishness and absence of repose; elements of strength and weakness, of success and failure, mingled together in proportions which made it almost impossible to find any one discriminating epithet by which to characterize the resultant whole.[38]

The wails of educational critics have not only been uttered, and answered, by a procession of speakers before NEA conventions from the beginning; they have also been the object of official concern and action by the association as a whole and by several NEA committees, commissions, and departments. Such concern and action have been particularly evident in recent years.

Chief spokesman for the profession in defending education against its critics has been, since 1941, the NEA's National Commission for the Defense of Democracy Through Education, which has investigated, exposed, and refuted a host of vocal critics. In so doing it has often provoked attacks on itself. Speaking as chairman of the commission, Harold Benjamin told the NEA convention of 1950 that the entire profession must be alerted and mobilized to counter the "attacks" of education's "enemies."

Preventive measures, designed to forestall public accusations and actions against schools and colleges by building understanding and good will, have been persistently pushed by many NEA bodies during the past two or three decades. The post of "assistant executive secretary for lay relations" was created (and from the first it has been filled by Glenn E. Snow, former teacher and state legislator in Utah and former president of the NEA); the Defense Commission sponsored a series of layman-educator conferences; the American Association of School Administrators and the Department of Classroom Teachers emphasized, in many meetings and publications, the role and techniques of educational public relations; and the National School Public Relations Association, which had been founded in 1935, became a department of the NEA in 1950.

The National Commission for the Public Schools, composed of eminent leaders in American life, in the 1950's led a nationwide campaign to arouse public interest and support. Although this commission was composed entirely of laymen, and operated in complete independence of educational organizations, it came into existence as a result of an idea

[38] *American Educational Monthly*, IV, 402-403, October 1867.

that originated with the Educational Policies Commission of the NEA and the AASA.

The Policies Commission took note of the then current wave of hails and wails when in 1955 it issued its statement, *Public Education and the Future of America*. Instead of bewailing the wails, the EPC said that they were a healthy symptom of public interest in education—a "reappraisal of American educational policies and practices," which it termed "a helpful and hopeful thing." The commission added: "That there are inadequacies in American education, no one doubts. Current reappraisal should identify these inadequacies and look toward their elimination; the reappraisal should also lead to reaffirmation of faith in the achievements and values of the educational system and to planning for their further development during the era now emerging."[39]

Throughout the century of educational controversy, the self-criticism of educators has repeatedly sparked improvement and reform. Within any group the will to believe is so strong that only a minority is disposed to think otherwise, and it is fortunate that this minority is vigorous and articulate and so disposed as to be willing to provide the group with what it does not naturally want—criticism. Whereas commendation tends to perpetuate existing conditions and practices, criticism promotes dissatisfaction and so tends to bring about changes. Criticism can thus be an agent of progress, while commendation is a guardian of the status quo. Wails as well as hails need to be uttered.

[39] P. 82.

PART III

Educational Reforms

12

Object Teaching

FOR more than a hundred years American education, like other segments of our national life, has undergone constant change. Unquestionably, many of these changes were synonymous with progress; others were probably cyclical changes that brought old ideas and practices into use again; and a few may have been actual regressions. To which category any particular change should be assigned is often a matter of controversy, but others can be classified with the assurance of general agreement. The series of reforms, beginning with object teaching in the decade of the 1850's when the NEA was founded and extending to the present time, can confidently be classified as educational progress. While these reforms are presented largely as they were discussed at NEA conventions, no claim is implied that they were contributions of the association. Instead, the association was the agency for disseminating information and encouraging its absorption into current practices; it was thus the synthesizer rather than the creator of educational change.

These reforms have touched many phases of education. *Object teaching* was primarily a reform in the teaching of young children, a method of developing the senses and ensuring the growth of a specific and meaningful vocabulary. The *kindergarten* was concerned with the growth of preschool children; it utilized play to develop skills and personalities. It was far more than a method; it was a revolution in adult thinking about children. In fact, its effect upon the primary grades, upon teachers of all grades, and upon educational philosophy was even greater than its effect upon pre-school children. The reform known as *learning by doing* was primarily a change in the conception of the learning process. It had far-reaching effects upon teachers and pupils, laboratories and equipment, curriculum and method. *Herbartianism* was, first of all, a reform in teaching procedure, but it also stressed the values of different subjects, thus giving the curriculum a new importance. The *child-study* movement threw light upon the learning process, assembled facts about child growth, and provided insight into what children could learn at various ages. In a broader sense it was part of the trend toward liberating children from adult domination within the school and the home. *Other reforms*—the activity movement, testing and measurement, guidance and counseling, socialization practices, curriculum improvement, and progressive doctrines—enlisted their proponents and vitalized various aspects of American education. The story of these reforms is the record of an evolving, growing profession. By providing conventions and promoting publications, the National Education Association and its departments played a large role in these improvements.

An impatient observer or a disillusioned teacher is impelled to ask why a particular reform did not accomplish its purpose permanently. Why did some of the same aspects of education need to be reformed again and again? The answer is that any particular reform dealt with only some of the elements in the educative process, and reforms themselves tended to lose their vitality and become formalized and barren. Thus in time the effects of even a desirable and successful reform were absorbed into the general stream of educational progress and were no longer identifiable as distinct changes.

Why were so many reforms necessary? What is the lowest level toward which education is constantly slipping? The condition from which the schools must be constantly rescued can be described rather than labeled. It is the condition in which information and a well-stocked memory are accepted as the desirable outcomes instead of skills, processes, understanding, character, and social competence; in which buildings, supplies, and books are inadequate; in which poorly paid, poorly trained teachers are weak in scholarship, method, the psychology of learning, and understanding of children; in which routine assignments, formal recitations, and external conformity are mistaken for educational realities; in which preparation for the next grade or school predominates over the development of personality and preparation for life; in which society imposes alien and extraneous functions upon the schools or in which the schools assume unwarranted obligations.

To save the schools from slipping into this formal and ineffectual condition, a succession of educational reformers was needed. Fortunately, each generation has produced a reasonable number of dissatisfied and resourceful educators who have advocated changes, proposed reforms, and introduced experiments. Thus educational progress is a blending of traditional practices and effected reforms.

"Conceal the object and address the children. I have something in my hand. . . . It is natural, opaque, impressible, odorous, sapid, edible, wholesome, juicy, refreshing, spherical, rough, reddish yellow." What is it? The children guess; they finally agree that the object is an *orange*.

This procedure was part of an object lesson as taught by Kate H. Davis at Oswego, New York, in 1862.[1] Object teaching required the presence of a fruit, plant, coin, tool, animal, toy, or object, or at least a model, picture, or drawing of the object. Only when the child could hear, see, touch, taste, or smell the object did it become real to him. He was then able to understand and make proper use of words describing the object and its various qualities and uses, and his perceptions could be abstracted, transferred, and applied to other objects. In this way the child acquired a rich fund of meaningful concepts and was prepared to talk with intelligent understanding and to learn from others, through talking and reading. Object teaching was a fundamental method because it substituted the direct experience of the child with the object for verbalization about it by the teacher. The child became more alert, made more numerous and more accurate observations, acquired a meaningful vocabulary, and talked more freely because he had acquired a sense of the reality of what he was talking about. Thus object teaching was designed to sharpen the senses, build vocabularies, and develop personalities.

Object teaching was the popular educational reform of the 1860's. From a visit to Toronto, Edward A. Sheldon, reformer, teacher, administrator, carried back to Oswego an idea that transformed his life and the lives of countless children. Clear-eyed, conscientious, zealous, Sheldon was trying to make schooling more meaningful in the lives of his pupils. Led by a sense of duty, he had at the age of twenty-five organized the Orphan and Free School Association. When the children responded and filled a room, Sheldon could find no teacher. He assumed the burden and opened "the ragged school" for the neglected Irish and French waifs of Oswego. Abandoning his intention of going to a theological school, he devoted himself to teaching the underprivileged of the city. Sheldon was practical as well as idealistic. His activities did not go unnoticed and prominent people came to his rescue. Within a few years he was superintendent of the schools of Oswego.

Sheldon devised uniform examinations for all of his pupils, held teachers' meetings on Saturdays, and searched for ways of improving the schools. On his visit to the National Museum in Toronto he saw a collection of pictures, charts, books, maps, and objects that seemed to provide the missing link of reality. He bought a set of such materials and returned to Oswego and inaugurated the great reform of object teaching.

Recognizing Pestalozzi as the source of inspiration, Sheldon employed teachers who had firsthand knowledge of that great educator's work. From London he brought a teacher who knew Pestalozzian principles

[1] Ned H. Dearborn, *The Oswego Movement in American Education* (New York, 1925), 157.

and methods, and shortly afterward he engaged Herman Krusi, son of one of Pestalozzi's trusted helpers at Yverdon. Within a few years the Oswego system with its inspiring normal school became the great proponent of not only object teaching but also of progressive educational practices in general.

Sheldon traveled widely, spoke frequently, and wrote extensively. In 1863 he gave a paper on object teaching before the NTA in Chicago.[2] In 1864 the NTA appointed a committee to study the Oswego system and report its findings. This report, delivered at Harrisburg in 1865, was almost wholly favorable to the practices carried on by Sheldon and his able associates.[3] As a member of the NEA, Sheldon attended many meetings and appeared on the program or participated in discussing problems of teacher training in the sessions of 1893, 1895, 1896, and 1897.[4]

In the meantime the Oswego movement broadened its purposes and extended its program. It began to stress oral instruction in language, elementary science, local geography, and industrial and manual arts. Its work in the training of kindergarten teachers was notable, and graduates of Oswego were eagerly chosen as principals, superintendents and teachers in normal schools. Students came in considerable numbers from New England, Pennsylvania, and all the western states, and graduates spread out into every state in the union. Thus, Oswego became the mecca and Sheldon the prophet of those seeking new and progressive ideas in teaching and learning. The normal school became the redistributing center of Pestalozzian ideas in America.[5]

Della A. Lathrop of Cincinnati, who read a paper on object teaching at the Cleveland meeting of 1870, defined an object lesson as one that involved the use of the senses and conversational comments by the pupils. It was designed to sharpen observation, facilitate expression, and prepare for subsequent reading. She scornfully rejected the idea that a teacher who cut an apple into pieces to teach fractions was engaged in object teaching. The use of illustrations and apparatus was not object teaching.[6]

Sheldon, who heard Miss Lathrop's paper, joined in the succeeding discussions and asserted that "the ideas of external objects can only be gained through the medium of the senses." It was, he declared, impossible to get ideas through language. From objects one gained basic ideas, learned the appropriate words, and was henceforth able to make infinite combinations and arrangements of the sense impressions. While Sheldon

[2] NTA, Proceedings, 1863, 93-102.

[3] NTA, Proceedings, 1865, 245-270.

[4] NEA, Proceedings, 1893, 387-391; 1895, 228; 1896, 226, 651-661; 1897, 63-70, 282-283.

[5] Dearborn, The Oswego Movement in American Education.

[6] NEA, Proceedings, 1870, 49-58.

believed in object teaching, he thought that "it might be more properly called subjective than objective. . . . When the boy gets a clear idea of the horse, it is not necessary to trot him in before the school that he may see him." When one has obtained a clear conception, "there is no longer any necessity for the object itself." Mental pictures are more convenient and better than the objects themselves. When the ideas are clear and distinct, "throw the objects out of the window and appeal to that which he must use all through his life, the pictures or objects as they exist in his mind."[7]

In one of the discussions at the Cleveland meeting William H. Mc-Guffey, editor of readers and university professor, said, "I am a thorough convert, sir, to object teaching, but I want to have the object very frequently one which you can't hear, nor see, nor smell."[8] The eventual superiority of mental images over sense perceptions was also expressed by a speaker at a subsequent meeting, who quoted the couplet:

> What hears is mind, what sees is mind;
> The ear and eye are deaf and blind.[9]

This concept of object teaching as a temporary, preliminary step, one which could subsequently be discarded when it had achieved its purpose, was well presented by a committee which reported in 1886. From concrete reality to learning from reading the committee listed the steps as (1) the object, (2) the model, (3) the picture, (4) the diagram, (5) the experiment, (6) language, (7) the printed or written page. In commenting upon this report, Superintendent John Hancock of Cincinnati stressed the desirability of learning from others by remarking, "First hand experience is very important, but mainly as a means of acquiring second-hand knowledge."[10]

Object teaching made a delayed and somewhat transformed reappearance in the nature-study movement of the 1890's and early 1900's. Speakers saw its applicability in the firsthand study of animals, insects, minerals, plants, and geographic features. Why study the definitions in books of islands, capes, alluvial fans, deltas, and other features which could be learned firsthand in a short field trip? Some called it nature's laboratory and expanded upon the greater sense of reality that would arise from using it in preference to reading from books. The elements of botany, the mysteries of biology, the practicability of physics and chemistry were to become clear and vivid by the direct field approach. These observable phenomena were variously labeled as objects, sources, and originals, and

[7] *Ibid.*, 61-63, 84-85, 87.
[8] *Ibid.*, 172.
[9] NEA, *Proceedings, 1890*, 560. In a discussion of manual training, the speaker stressed the value of objects and direct experience. *Ibid.*, 834-842.
[10] NEA, *Proceedings, 1886*, 271, 274.

were regarded as preferable to museums and school laboratories. "To the child the book of nature is a book of revelation." It should be studied as it unfolds and functions; structure and classification should be at the end and not the beginning of nature study. While the nature-study movement made its appeal primarily to the elementary grades, its principles were declared valid at the college and graduate levels.[11]

L. H. Bailey of Cornell University said that the nature-study movement, strangely enough, was an effort to put the child in contact with his own environment. He lamented the fact that teaching in elementary schools was academic, that the ladder of learning had been let down from the university, and observed quite simply that a ladder should rest on the ground. "Education always should begin with objects and phenomena" instead of textbooks and museums. He insisted that nature study was not another subject, not an addition to the curriculum, not more work; instead, it was an attitude, a point of view, a new method.[12]

In spite of its great appeal and widespread popularity nature study was not enduringly successful. Some regarded it as a fad; some science professors declared that nature work in the elementary schools inculcated error and sentimentality; other critics said that the study was doomed to failure because the typical teacher did not know enough to guide the pupils.[13] One weary teacher doubtless reflected her experience when she observed, "In the schools, as they exist at present, it is hard to do such work in a way which will satisfy both Mother Nature and the superintendent." She cited another difficulty by quoting the opening sentence of a chapter in a high-school biology text: "The class mammalia is definable as those which have two occipital condyles, with a well-ossified basioccipital. . . ."[14]

Object teaching had a curious and unforeseen application to advanced work in science. Whether Louis Agassiz, Nathaniel Shaler, or other American scientists knew anything of Pestalozzi and his object lessons or not, their methods were based upon the same philosophy. The well-known story of Shaler's agonizing ordeal of studying a dead fish, exuding fumes of formaldehyde, for days and days under the stern, uncommunicative eyes of Agassiz is a dramatic instance of the presumed values of prolonged and minute examination of a specific object.[15] Agassiz and Shaler denounced textbooks, belittled lectures, and ridiculed questions on assigned readings. They were ardent believers in the method of catching or finding a specimen and studying it until it yielded its secrets, or going

[11] NEA, *Proceedings, 1894*, 191-204; *1900*, 404-416, 592-608; *1904*, 889-896.

[12] NEA, *Proceedings, 1903*, 109-116.

[13] NEA, *Proceedings, 1900*, 592-608.

[14] *Ibid.*, 602. The article abounds in specific suggestions for nature study.

[15] Nathaniel Southgate Shaler, *Autobiography* (Boston, 1907). The story of the fish has been included in school readers.

into the field to observe nature. This procedure they identified as the true scientific method, but it was basically the object lesson of Pestalozzi elevated to the adult level.[16]

Like all reforms, object teaching was susceptible to abuses. Some enthusiastic proponents carried the idea to absurd extremes. With only a piece of leather for the children to examine, some teachers went far afield to discuss animals, skins, and the process of making leather. Such a procedure was a distortion of the basic principle that the children were expected to learn from the object only what it revealed. The teaching of additional information was, of course, desirable, but such extensions were not a direct part of object teaching. Such misuses led to misunderstandings and unmerited criticisms of the basic ideas of object teaching. At a meeting of Pennsylvania teachers in 1864 one speaker referred to "a teacher of object lessons" as "a cannon loaded to the muzzle with facts to shoot through the children."[17] A few years later E. E. White, practical, reasonable editor, speaker, and educator, observed that "three-fourths of the object lessons are mere cramming lessons, and become a means for giving the children facts and information about a variety of things, many of which are superficial, illogical, and heterogeneous."[18] It thus appears that a basic reform such as object teaching could be diverted from its true function and used as a pretext for returning to the artificial practice of collecting random information. Failing to understand that objects had only limited, specific values and served only temporary purposes, and mistakenly assuming that the method was useful at all grade levels, some teachers criticized it for failing to do what it was never designed to accomplish.

Object teaching achieved its greatest popularity in the 1860's. Something of its philosophy and method was appropriated by the kindergarten, which became popular in the 1870's, and by the learning-by-doing movement, which reached its zenith in the 1880's. While the necessity of object teaching now appears to be so obvious as to elicit no comment, the lesson was sadly needed in 1860. Object teaching made a permanent contribution to educational progress.

[16] NEA, *Proceedings, 1872,* 232-239; *1874,* 136-137; *1903,* 848-852.
[17] *Illinois Teacher,* X, 393, October 1864.
[18] NEA, *Proceedings, 1877,* 188.

13

The Kindergarten

Over all educational reforms of the nineteenth century—object teaching, freedom for the child, activity rather than assignment—hung the spirit of that bungling, impractical, lovable genius Johann Heinrich Pestalozzi (1746-1827). From him emanated such doctrines as the basic role of sense perception, the educative value of activity, the desirability of early training, the importance of the mother as a teacher, and the proper sequence of object and word, the known and unknown, perception and reflection. From him came not method or psychology or system, but insight, sympathy, love, and faith in the child and in teaching. Refracted through Froebel, Parker, Sheldon, Peabody, Alcott, and others, the source was nonetheless found in the humble, pathetic schoolmaster of Yverdon and Burgdorf.

While Pestalozzi was the grandfather of the kindergarten, its creation, as well as its name, was the work of his greatest student, Friedrich Froebel (1782-1852). Lonely, neglected, mistreated, the child Froebel turned to nature and to his own inner life for solace and strength. With stubborn determination and insufficient funds he secured an education and became interested in the problems and philosophy of teaching children. Like Pestalozzi, his great mentor, Froebel continued to be impractical, impolitic, visionary, and introspective, but his genius enabled him to evolve out of failure and frustration the institution which was designed to promote the happiness of countless children. At the age of fifty-five, he found the word; it was *kindergarten*.

Although German in origin, the kindergarten was instantly recognized as international in application and timeless in its mission. Kindergarteners of all lands looked to Froebel with respect and affection and sought guidance in his writings.

Eager to appropriate his teachings, Froebel's followers ran into several difficulties. In the first place, Froebel was not systematic in his plans or clear in his writings. Many of his ideas were intangible and untransferable to other cultures, and his philosophical and speculative mysticism was hard to understand even in the original language. All these difficulties were increased by the complications that arose in trying to translate these ideas into other languages. The word kindergarten itself was only the beginning of misconceptions. In German *garten* had the connotation of rest, relaxation, and recreation rather than the idea of utility that it then had in English. So it is not surprising that the effort to maintain Froebel's original ideas and practices encountered difficulties and eventually resulted in failure. In fact, his educational, social, and political ideas were inclusive as well as complex, and even his closest followers at times confessed their perplexity as to the position of their master on a particular point. Even a devoted follower referred to "the chaotic mass of ideas left by Froebel." By 1900 kindergarteners were reassuring one another that Froebel's spirit still survived even though the details of his system had been lost in obscurity.

In spite of all these facts, the basic teachings of Froebel were tangible and clear. They emphasized the place of the mother, the importance of early training, the necessity of a happy, carefree atmosphere, the need of kind, patient teachers, the place of objects which he called gifts, the development of simple skills, the growth of the child's vocabulary, freedom of individual action, the development of a socialized group feeling, the absence of constraint, and the omission of books and study.

The gifts, to which Froebel attached importance, were to be used in a specified order. The first consisted of a box of six woolen balls, each a different color. The second gift was a box containing a cube, a sphere, and a cylinder; the third gift was a boxed cube cut once in each direction, making eight small cubes to be used as building blocks. Each of the gifts, totaling twenty altogether, represented gradual advances toward complexity and involved greater skill on the part of the teacher and more understanding by the children.

All the gifts—balls, blocks, cubes, cones, tablets, corks, sticks, seeds, peas, strings, straws, paper, etc.—were invested with mystic symbolism. The ball implied unity, the oneness of humanity; the circle into which the children gathered implied equality, brotherhood, understanding, good will. Froebel's whole philosophy of education was suffused with faith and devoutness.

The first kindergarten in America, a German-speaking one, was established at Watertown, Wisconsin, in 1856 by Mrs. Carl Schurz, a former student of Froebel. Within a few years other German-speaking kindergartens were started in Columbus, Newark, Louisville, and Detroit. The first English-speaking kindergarten in this country was founded in 1860, in Boston, by Elizabeth Peabody. In 1872 Boston established a kindergarten in connection with the public school, but it was soon suspended.

To St. Louis goes the honor of instituting the first kindergartens which were integrated with the public-school system. Managed by Susan Blow and supported by the great influence of Superintendent W. T. Harris, they became a part of the city school system in the 1870's. Emma Marwedel of Hamburg, aided a little later by the writer Kate Douglas Wiggin, Colonel Francis W. Parker, and others, established kindergartens in all parts of the country from Boston to Los Angeles and San Francisco.

"Madame Kriege and Miss Alma Kriege announce the opening of a normal class for theoretical and practical instruction of kindergarten teachers on November 1, 1868, at 127 Charles Street, Boston."[1] This announcement heralded the beginning of training schools for kindergarteners in America. Maria Boelte in New York, William N. Hailmann in Milwaukee, and W. T. Harris in St. Louis opened similar schools within a few years. Thus, the movement did not suffer for the lack of trained teachers.

Shortly after the beginning of kindergartens in America, the question of their nature and function came before the NEA. At the Boston meeting of 1872 William N. Hailmann discussed Froebel's educational system and called for the appointment of a committee to report upon its adaptation to American institutions. A notable group of persons commented upon this resolution—Adolph Douai of Newark, Elizabeth Peabody, A. Bronson Alcott, B. G. Northrop, and Henry Barnard.[2] The resolution was adopted and the committee made its report at Elmira the following year. This official and semiauthoritative report was signed by John Kraus, Douai, Hailmann, Harris, and others. It made several recommendations: (1) that the purpose of the kindergarten was to make children happy through play; (2) that Froebel's gifts should be utilized; (3) that the child learns through his own activity; (4) that for social purposes a kindergarten requires a group of children; (5) that the teacher should be a young woman of even temper; (6) that a room, playground, and a garden should be available; (7) that liberty, not uniformity or constraint, should prevail; (8) that reading, writing, and ciphering be excluded; (9) that the qualities and characteristics of the gifts should be noted and designative words therefor be learned; (10) that children learn weaving, plaiting, stringing, stitching, and lacing; (11) that kindergartens and teacher-training schools, both public and private, be established; (12) that the children tend flowers and plants; (13) that teachers study Froebel's system.[3]

Because of its early appearance in the growth of kindergartens, this report, with its sketchy review of Froebel's system, had considerable

[1] *New York Teacher and American Educational Monthly*, V, 420, October 1868.
[2] NEA, *Proceedings, 1872*, 141-148.
[3] NEA, *Proceedings, 1873*, 230-237.

effect. It indicated a kind of official sanction of kindergartens by the NEA and unquestionably led to further study and discussion.

Since all kindergarteners wished to be true Froebelians and since few of them could agree as to what beliefs and practices were basic, it is not surprising that debates, recriminations, and charges of heresy were common. For fifty years loyalty to Froebel was almost an obsession of his followers and also the source of misunderstandings. Proponents of orthodox views, and most kindergarteners so regarded themselves, were quick to sense deviations and swift to denounce offenders.

John Kraus, a signer of the 1873 NEA report and one of the most vigorous proclaimers of orthodox Froebelianism, demonstrated his sincerity, courage, and orthodoxy and also his undiplomatic bluntness at the NEA meeting at Louisville in 1877. "One could just as well speak about American Christianity, American Beatitudes, American Sermon on the Mount, American Golden Rule, etc., adapted to American wants, as to speak about an American Kindergarten, adapted to American wants."

Growing weary of Froebel's plain, unadorned balls, cubes, and bricks, some American kindergarten teachers had substituted toys and dolls. These Kraus denounced with vehemence. "Ready-made playthings hinder childish activity, and train to laziness and thoughtlessness. . . . The impulse to activity turns to the destruction of the ready-made things and becomes at last a real spirit of destructiveness." He criticized Dr. E. Seguin of New York for confusing object teaching with kindergarten activities; he derided "a gentleman from Ohio" who returned from a hasty visit and a superficial inspection of German kindergartens declaring that such institutions were suited for only the poorest classes of our crowded cities; and he ridiculed a kindergartener for proclaiming that she had made improvements upon Froebel's plan. Kraus referred feelingly to dabblers, quacks, and impostors and lamented the unsympathetic attention which educators had given to the kindergarten. With scorn he observed that "the popular mind has a strange and erroneous idea that the kindergarten is a school." From reading, writing, reckoning, spelling, textbooks, and memorizing, Kraus hoped to save the children until their seventh year. "The first seven years should be the growing age, not the thinking age. . . . Play is the normal occupation of children. Play is work without a practical object. . . ." He invoked the spirit of Froebel and called upon the teachers to recognize the kindergarten as a place where happy, normal, healthy, good-natured children learned to play and grow.[4]

The contrast between Kraus's orthodox views and the philosophical

[4] NEA, *Proceedings, 1877*, 186-207. This long, vitriolic speech contains many keen observations, but it also abounds in pedantic fault-finding and censorious remarks that seem incongruous in a disciple of Froebel.

and practical interpretation of W. T. Harris is striking. Harris, sponsor, expounder, and defender of public-school kindergartens, had original views. He referred to the kindergarten as providing "sub-primary education," characterized the child's play as "caprice," referred with a lack of understanding to Froebel's "system of discipline and instruction," speculated upon how the kindergarten could promote subsequent progress in school studies, and assumed that at the age of seven the child would discard kindergarten symbolism and accept conventional school procedures involving yielding to others and learning from the printed page.[5]

The gentle, orthodox, and enthusiastic believer W. N. Hailmann was pained by Harris's views. He lamented "schoolishness" in kindergartens and observed that some of them had "degenerated into sub-primary schools in which learning and now growing is the chief concern." The "weeds of traditionalism," according to Hailmann, were thus planted in the very institution that was designed to be free of conformity and external authority.[6]

The early leaders of the kindergarten movement in America came from Germany and brought with them the ideas of Pestalozzi and Froebel. It naturally followed that the first kindergartens established in this country were German-speaking ones. John Kraus, born in Nassau, Germany, in 1815, came to America in 1851 carrying with him a testimonial of his "judicious manner" in teaching. Had the writer of the testimonial stressed the qualities of zeal and integrity, he would have been on sounder ground, for Kraus was deficient in tact and quite lacking in the "judicious manner." During the Civil War he lost his property, including his library and manuscripts, in a fire, but he saved several letters which Froebel had written to him in 1851 and 1852. In 1867 Henry Barnard, the newly appointed United States commissioner of education, invited Kraus to join his staff in Washington, where he prepared elaborate reports upon the kindergarten.

In the meantime another German kindergartener, Maria Boelte, in whose career Kraus was destined to participate, had studied in the household and seminary of Froebel's widow and had taught in various schools in Germany and England. In 1872 Miss Boelte was invited to open a kindergarten in New York. Her first assistant and apprentice, Susan Blow of St. Louis, subsequently became the founder of public-school kindergartens and their most influential advocate. Among the many who came to New York to observe Miss Boelte's work was John Kraus, who returned at the end of the year and induced her to become his wife. They opened a kindergarten and training school in New York and continued active careers of writing, speaking, and teaching. Mrs.

[5] NEA, *Proceedings, 1879,* 146, 150.
[6] NEA, *Proceedings, 1890,* 565-573.

Kraus-Boelte spoke to the NEA several times and was president of the Kindergarten Department in 1899.[7]

Kraus and his wife were not the only orthodox Froebelians in America. Even before the name of kindergarten had been created, Elizabeth Peabody of Salem had taught little children in the midst of objects and pictures and on walks about the school which was presided over by Bronson Alcott, who in his abstract and philosophical manner loved children as much as Froebel did. Years later Miss Peabody heard about kindergartens from Mrs. Carl Schurz and others. After opening her kindergarten Miss Peabody soon realized her lack of training and her dim insight into the symbolism and philosophy of Froebel. To overcome her deficiency she spent a year in Europe and returned to conduct kindergartens, edit magazines, make speeches, and instruct teachers. In fact, she devoted the remainder of her ninety years to the cause of childhood education.

In addition to the Krauses there was another couple who rendered long and distinguished service to the cause of kindergartens—William N. Hailmann and his wife Eudora L. Hailmann. Hailmann was born in Switzerland in 1836 and came to the United States in 1852. He opened an academy in Louisville and on a visit to Zurich in 1860 became interested in the kindergarten. Upon his return he and his wife added, in 1865, a kindergarten to their academy.

In the same year Hailmann represented the Kentucky Teachers' Association at the Harrisburg meeting of the National Teachers' Association.[8] In 1874 he became principal of a German-English academy in Milwaukee, where he opened another kindergarten and began in 1876 the publication of the *New Education,* a magazine devoted to childhood education. A few years later he became superintendent of schools at La Porte, Indiana, where he and his wife established a summer school for kindergarteners. In 1894 he became superintendent of Indian schools and introduced kindergartens among the tribes.

During their long and fruitful careers Hailmann and his wife edited magazines, wrote books on Froebel, trained kindergarteners, and lectured at many teachers' conventions. He was the first president of the Kindergarten Department of the NEA and presided at its 1885 meeting at Saratoga Springs. In 1898 he was president of the Elementary Department. Mrs. Hailmann was president of the Kindergarten Department in 1888.

The founders and supporters of kindergartens quickly organized local, state, regional, and national associations. Some of these organizations

---

[7] Nina C. Vandewalker, *The Kindergarten in American Education* (New York, 1908), 29; NEA, *Proceedings, 1877,* 187, 207-216; *1896,* 229-230.

[8] NEA, *Proceedings, 1865,* 220.

were designed to support kindergartens and others were designed to promote the discussion of the professional problems of kindergarteners. In 1877 Elizabeth Peabody organized the Froebel Institute of North America. Two years later the Western Kindergarten Association was started in Detroit. These and other local associations participated in the Madison meeting of the Institute in 1884. Several prominent persons were on the program—Colonel Francis W. Parker, President Irwin Shepard of the normal school at Winona, and W. N. Hailmann, president of the Institute. The NEA *Proceedings* contain this almost cryptic entry: "The Froebel Institute was authorized to organize as a Department of the Association."[9] Hailmann was elected president of the new department.

The new Department of Kindergarten Instruction was launched upon its long and active career. Year after year it enlisted the contributions of faithful supporters and leading educators. At Saratoga Springs in 1892 a group of active leaders organized the International Kindergarten Union in order to enlist the support of private kindergartens, spread information to other countries, and promote the program and exhibit for the Columbian Exposition of 1893.[10] The Union held annual meetings and by 1903, when it met in Pittsburgh, it had a membership of over 8,000 located in twenty-seven states, Canada, and South America.[11] The Union and the Kindergarten Department worked cooperatively, and both joined in the request to change the name in 1927 to the Department of Kindergarten-Primary Education.[12] After several years of relative inactivity, during which leadership in the field passed to the Association for Childhood Education International, the NEA revived the dormant department during 1955-1956.

A variety of topics and issues were discussed at the annual meetings of the Kindergarten Department. Those of greatest frequency were (1) Froebel and his teachings, (2) child study, (3) materials and equipment, (4) methods and activities, (5) relationships with the primary grades, (6) relationships with mothers and the public, (7) the training of kindergarteners, and, in the years after about 1930, (8) nursery schools. The scope of the topics was, of course, broadened after the inclusion of the primary grades in 1927.

Among the most frequent speakers at the kindergarten meetings were William N. Hailmann and Colonel Parker. Other speakers included Elizabeth Peabody, W. T. Harris, Mrs. Kraus-Boelte, Elizabeth Harrison of Chicago, Kate Douglas Wiggin, Anna E. Bryan of Chicago, Michael V. O'Shea of Wisconsin, Maria Montessori of Italy, Patty Smith Hill of

[9] NEA, *Proceedings, 1884,* Part I, 23, 74-75.
[10] NEA, *Proceedings, 1892,* 254-257.
[11] NEA, *Proceedings, 1903,* 406.
[12] NEA, *Proceedings, 1926,* 526.

Columbia University, J. L. Hughes of Toronto, and Nina C. Vandewalker of Washington.

Kindergartens increased in number and enrollment. In 1888 the enrollment was 31,227, divided almost equally between public and private schools. By 1900 the number was 225,394 with about 60 per cent enrolled in public kindergartens; in 1930 the total number was 777,899, with less than 7 per cent in private schools. Then, during the depression years, the enrollment in kindergartens declined; in 1940 it was less than in 1930. During the depression the Federal government sponsored nursery schools,[13] and during the Second World War all pre-school agencies revived. By 1944 kindergarten enrollment was 733,974, slightly more than that of 1930. By 1951 the enrollment was 1,272,000, with every indication of growing more rapidly. Notwithstanding this marked growth, kindergartens have never enrolled as much as 50 per cent of those in the eligible age group.

For decades the revolutionary nature of the kindergarten was dimly perceived. In its early years it was tolerated because it concerned itself with a period which most adults regarded as barren and troublesome. Even the early kindergarteners were strict constructionists and emphasized the separateness and difference of their institution, while primary teachers who had consecrated themselves to schedules of phonics and number combinations were frankly skeptical of the value of a year or two of play and fervently hoped that the experience would not incapacitate the child for the serious discipline of mental training that lay ahead of him. These attitudes and ideas were slowly abandoned. Child study proved that the early years were not barren but influential on subsequent development.

While educators were concerned about the nature and function of kindergartens, the public was having difficulty deciding just where the kindergarten fitted into the social scene. Some regarded it as a nursery to care for the children of working mothers, a kind of social-service institution for poor people. Others regarded it as the newest luxury to entertain the children of rich people, replacing governesses and servants. Some years passed before it was identified as a means of child growth, regardless of social status and economic condition. As soon as the kindergarten became a part of the public-school system, its identification with any particular social class disappeared.

For a full half-century or more the Froebelians waged a losing struggle to maintain the original gifts, the symbolism, and the unfoldment idea. In spite of emphatic restatements of the faith in almost every decade, the institution of the kindergarten was greatly modified. The Montessori system, which was brought to America around 1910, emphasized the

[13] Nursery schools increased from 98 in 1928 to 965 in 1942.

individual, taught the child some useful skills, and introduced reading and writing. Some kindergarten teachers who had drifted into class drills, class games, and group performances claimed that these activities allowed more freedom to the individual child. More influential in the long run in modifying the kindergarten than the Montessori system was the activity idea, which had been sponsored by Parker, promoted by the child-study groups, and systematized into philosophy by John Dewey. Eventually the idea of freely chosen activities destroyed the previously selected gifts of Froebel. In fact, the abstract ideas of shape, contour, form, lines, corners, wholes, parts, and edges had appealed to the teacher rather than to the child; and when the progressives demonstrated this fact, the whole structure of Froebelian mysticism and symbolism crumbled. Several speakers before the kindergarten section of the NEA analyzed the unreality of older practices.[14] W. H. Kilpatrick's critical examination of Froebel, published in 1916, may be viewed as the virtual end of the old orthodox ideas.[15]

It would be difficult to overstate the effect of the kindergarten upon the reconstruction of the curriculum and upon popular attitudes toward children. The name "Department of Kindergarten-Primary Education" indicates an integration that extended far beyond the primary grades. The kindergarten method of direct experience, self-activity, self-expression, and group cooperation spread at once into the primary grades and in time affected methods at all grade levels. The kindergarten was largely responsible for the child-study and nature-study movements; it hastened the decline of whipping; it demonstrated anew the great truth that learning was a concomitant of doing; it demonstrated the social as well as individual values of play; it kept alive the principles of object teaching; it showed that freedom was more effective than coercion.[16] Its emphasis upon health and growth accelerated the widespread development of child-welfare clinics whose intensive research programs promise to expand and enrich the whole program for the pre-school child.[17] In fact, the kindergarten revolutionized all pre-school education. Its success is somewhat obscured by the extent to which its philosophy has been accepted and applied. The kindergarten was the liberator of the child from adult domination. Merged and absorbed into a prolonged continuum of child culture, it stands forth as the greatest humanizing institution in the history of education.

[14] NEA, *Proceedings, 1913*, 435-445; *1914*, 406-413; *1915*, 647-653.

[15] W. H. Kilpatrick, *Froebel's Kindergarten Principles Critically Examined* (New York, 1916).

[16] NEA, *Proceedings, 1888*, 354-357; *1896*, 378-390.

[17] For an excellent appraisal of the growth and influence of kindergartens, see Patty S. Hill, "Changes in Kindergarten Education," NEA, *Proceedings, 1925*, 484-492. See also *1937*, 307-310.

14

Apostles of Childhood

In 1863 a number of Boston teachers met in the Educational Room at No. 119 Washington Street to exchange professional experiences. The abbreviated record of what was said makes clear some prevailing attitudes toward corporal punishment in the schools.

Wm. Reed of the Brimmer School opened the topic "Corporal Punishment." In theory he was opposed to whipping, but in practice he rigidly adhered to it.

Lewis B. Monroe,—I had to use the rod when I taught, and could not get along without it.

Granville B. Putnam, Quincy High School,—I *never* use the rod—I think it may be necessary in some cases.

Samuel W. Mason, Eliot School,—My *theory* and practice are to use the rod . . . if any of my teachers send a boy to me for punishment, he will surely get it without a question. . . .

D. B. Hagar, Jamaica Plain High School [one of the founders of the NEA and president in 1870],—I think I have not punished as many scholars as I have taught years.[1]

At an association meeting at Altoona in August 1864, one teacher, apparently growing weary of discussions of textbooks, object teaching, and moral culture, "sighed for the good old times, and believed the only way to bring up children is to *whip them into doing right and being good.*"[2]

Actual or potential opposition by parents to corporal punishment aroused the anger of an Illinois editor of 1865. "We have many proofs of various kinds to the effect that the race of fools has not become extinct; but of all the actual demonstrations of this fact, the course of some parents in regard to the conduct of their children in school seems to us the most unequivocal. When will parents learn that whenever they interfere with the discipline of their children at school they are sowing

[1] *Massachusetts Teacher*, XVI, 65, February 1863.
[2] *Illinois Teacher*, X, 393, October 1864. Italics in original.

the seeds of future trouble to themselves,—trouble, too, of the saddest and most heartrending character?"[3]

Prior to about 1870 the subject of corporal punishment was discussed with great frequency at institutes and conventions. While a few educators denounced corporal punishment and expressed a sympathetic attitude toward children, thus evidencing the ameliorating influence of Rousseau, Pestalozzi, and Froebel, the prevailing mood seems to have been one of rigor and harshness. The evangelical doctrine of original sin and the necessity of an abrupt conversion had its influence upon educational thought. The child was presumed to be prone to evil, inclined to oppose authority, and disposed to resist instruction. The teacher was thus faced with a collection of actual or potential rebels, and his success was determined by his firmness, his physical strength, and his will to dominate. In such a climate it is not surprising that punishment loomed large in pedagogical thinking and held a prominent place on the platforms of educational gatherings.

President Eliot said that in the Boston Latin School the principal disciplinary motive which operated upon him as a student was "fear—fear of the rough tongue of the teacher, fear of the harsh construction put on the childish motive, and the childish conduct, and fear of physical pain as an inducement to an unnatural quietness and to mental application." He attributed the advent of a milder regime to the slow emancipation "from the terrors of systematic theology."[4]

Late in the 1860's Syracuse[5] and other cities began to experiment with rules against whipping. While each such innovation provoked outbursts of criticism and laments over the decline in the behavior of young people, the general trend away from punishment was unmistakable. After 1870 there was a steady decline in whipping and in the number of discussions of corporal punishment. In 1872 W. T. Harris said that the practice was on the way out and would be gone by 1900.[6] Many factors contributed to this trend. Rousseau's gospel of the natural rights of children; the rise of the kindergarten; humanitarian reforms in the treatment of paupers, criminals, and the insane; the weakening of the influence of stern Calvinistic doctrines; the freeing of the slaves; and the agitation for women's rights had their effects upon school discipline. One teacher cited the abolition of corporal punishment in the army and navy as causing its practical elimination from schools.[7]

The decline and practical disappearance of whipping did not, however, immediately usher in a period of good will toward children or an under-

---

[3] *Illinois Teacher*, XI, 297, September 1865.
[4] NEA, *Proceedings, 1900*, 197.
[5] NEA, *Proceedings, 1870*, 150.
[6] NEA, *Proceedings, 1872*, 265.
[7] *Illinois Teacher*, XII, 313, October 1866.

standing of childhood. An occasional teacher or administrator still proclaims a lingering faith in the efficacy of corporal punishment. A delegate
to the Chicago convention of the NEA in 1955 declared his faith in "the
back end of a rubber shoe." As a last resort he regarded it as a solution
to the problem of juvenile waywardness.[8] Discarding the use of corporal
punishment did not necessarily mean discarding the assumptions behind
its use. Taking an example reported by a speaker in 1914, a teacher
betrayed an expectation of his pupils' evil tendencies by listing the
anticipated crimes along with the penalties on the blackboard on the
first day of school. For each offense the number of minutes of detention
were prescribed: dropping books, five minutes; scraping shoes on the
floor, five minutes; talking out loud, ten minutes; whispering, fifteen
minutes; kicking or cuffing, twenty minutes; marking desk, twenty
minutes.[9]

The transition from severity to kindness required not only time but
the active preachments of a host of crusaders and apostles who loved
rather than feared children and tried to understand rather than dominate
them.

"Both intellect and heart are naturally depraved." So asserted John P.
Brooks, superintendent of public instruction of Illinois in his report of
1864.[10] The idea was neither new nor original, and Brooks was neither
the first nor the last to utter it. It was stated as an axiom and provided a
basis for describing the guiding and reforming work of the teacher.

An opposing idea was also astir. "One of the most remarkable . . .
one of the most hopeful features of this progressive age is the increasing
dignity of the child." So asserted Professor Eben Tourjee of the Con-
servatory of Music in Boston in a speech before the NEA at Cleveland
in 1870.[11]

At Cleveland a group of educators discussed the nature and handling
of children. "I would like to ask the gentleman whether by the plan he
suggests, he would succeed in breaking the will of the child, or whether
it is necessary to do so in the good old orthodox way?"

"The will of the child should never be broken (Applause). The will
of the child is his mainspring in life; he needs it as long as he lives. The
idea of crushing the will of the child is barbarous." Such was the vigorous
reply of J. L. Pickard of Illinois.

But E. E. White of Ohio, next to W. T. Harris the most frequent
speaker in the history of the NEA, wanted to qualify the principle. "I am
not certain that . . . the will of the child is never to be curbed or checked.

[8] Chicago *Sun-Times*, July 7, 1955, 6.
[9] NEA, *Proceedings, 1914*, 425.
[10] *Illinois Teacher*, X, 266, July 1864.
[11] NEA, *Proceedings, 1870*, 133.

. . . In the moral training of the child, the first act sometimes is to let him know that there is a will to which his will must bend (Applause)." White thought that it was occasionally necessary to use the rod. "The truth is that before the heart-power of the teacher can enter into the heart of the child, there must be a subjection of the child unto the authority of the teacher."

Another speaker that day thought that "A school should be a place where pupils can live and live well, cheerfully, happily, and profitably; and until we make our schools such, we are not in the highest sense educators."

President E. T. Tappan of Kenyon College prefaced his remarks with an observation almost required by the conventions of the time: "This is the most important question which has been brought before this association. . . . This contest between the parent or the teacher and the child, as to which one shall give up, is frequently a mere contest of pride on the part of both, and the parent's pride and the teacher's pride is that which impels them on, and is a trait characteristic of devils, and makes devils." He then discussed the motives of fear, reward, patriotism, and love which could be used in training children.

President Henry Fairchild of Oberlin lamented the artificial incentives that prevailed in school and feared that they did not train for correct behavior in society. With respect to school discipline he advised the teacher to foresee and avoid a clash of wills. The teacher should not seek opportunities to assert his power; on the contrary he should cherish magnanimous and generous feelings toward his pupils, who will generally respond with similar sentiments.[12]

By 1870, when these men were discussing the status of children, the ideas of Rousseau, Pestalozzi, Basedow, Froebel, Robert Owen, and Herbart were operating to soften popular attitudes toward childhood. Edwin A. Sheldon of Oswego, Elizabeth Peabody of Boston, and others were trying to provide a kinder atmosphere and a more tolerant understanding of childhood.

Apostles of childhood had to oppose many prevailing beliefs, attitudes, and practices. They opposed the doctrine of innate depravity; they regarded childhood as a stage of life and not merely one of preparation for living; they resented restrictions upon freedom of movement and choice of activity; they respected the dignity and integrity of children and so opposed punishment, particularly whipping; they believed that a fixed program of studies was detrimental to personal growth. In brief, they opposed the attitude summarized by a speaker at an NEA convention:

[12] *Ibid.*, 145-149. Even in the next decade a speaker asked, "In fact, do not teacher and parent both seek, first of all, to crush the *child's will?*" NEA, *Proceedings, 1882*, 126.

"Many adults believe that they have the inalienable right or sacred duty to shape, check, repress, or coerce the emotions and thoughts of children to their own individual whims and prejudices."[13]

One of the earliest American liberators of children was Amos Bronson Alcott, philosopher, teacher, idealist, visionary. Thoroughly imbued with faith in children and convinced of the boundless possibilities of education, he pursued his impractical way, heedless of poverty and hardship which engulfed him, his wife, and four daughters. Back in the 1830's, long before the NEA was organized, he peddled goods and ideas, engaged in lofty conversations, and opened schools. His schools were charming rooms where flowers, pictures, and art objects surrounded the children. His mystical soul was entwined with noble sentiments, many of which were beyond the grasp of the children, but they never doubted his kindness and goodness. Stubborn in his gentleness, he sacrificed his schools and his living, but not his ideas. In one of his schools a Negro girl was enrolled as a pupil, and when the patrons demanded her dismissal Alcott was sorely troubled that they did not recognize that the little Negro girl was also a human being, but he never thought of yielding to their demand. His school gradually faded out of existence.

The child was the center of Alcott's thinking. There was nothing unique in this. All systems of education look to the child, but the state sees a future citizen, the church a future communicant, business a future participant, the army a future recruit. Alcott saw a free human being, worthy of help and attention for his own sake and only secondly for the sake of society.

Alcott regarded children as innately good. "I said Christianity, art, beauty, all are in the soul of the child, and the art of the teacher consists in drawing it out. . . ."[14] He abolished punishment and substituted discussion; he refused to consider spelling as worthy of separate study; he taught arithmetic with beans; and he taught English by the simple device of having children practice correct talking. He believed that happiness and learning were concurrent, and so rejected authoritarian domination, previously conceived tasks, and the bending of childhood to conform to adult preconceptions.

Alcott's program was too revolutionary for his contemporaries. He became the butt of jokes and ridicule, and was actually regarded by some as a dangerous and vicious person who was undermining the foundations of decency, religion, and morality. Despite poverty, opposition, and hostility he pursued his placid way, grieved and hurt, but unyielding in his principles.

When the NEA assembled at Boston in 1872, Alcott had outlived

[13] NEA, *Proceedings, 1928*, 429.
[14] NEA, *Proceedings, 1872*, 134.

calumny, regained status, and achieved an Indian summer of popularity. There he stood, eager and willing to participate in the discussions although he had been assigned no formal place on the program. Far in the past was the publication of his *Conversations with Children on the Gospels,* which preachers branded as heretical and editors as indecent; forgotten was his rebuff by the abolitionists, who feared to employ him as a speaker; unknown or ignored was Horace Mann's refusal to let him speak at a teachers' institute in his home town of Concord; forgiven was his aberration of the vegetarian experiment at Fruitlands. Befriended and supported by Emerson, Alcott had slowly and finally won national recognition as a traveling missionary of culture by his "conversations," and he was loved and respected as the father of Louisa, whose *Little Women* and *Little Men* had captured the hearts of the people.[15]

In fact, Alcott spoke five times in the discussion sessions of the Boston meeting. Concerning the teacher, he asserted that knowledge and books were of less significance than a magnetic temperament, one which enabled the teacher to communicate with his pupils by looks, manner, or even by silence. In discussing object teaching, Alcott referred to the pictures and pleasant surroundings of his Masonic Temple school, which he had conducted in Boston in the 1830's. He recalled with pride that the other teachers in his school were Elizabeth Peabody and Margaret Fuller. In discussing normal schools, Alcott said he would go to ancient Greece for a model rather than to Germany. He believed in idealists as well as practical men, for one must be in the clouds to see what is going on. "Common sense is valuable, but uncommon sense is more so."[16]

At the business session the NEA elected Alcott an honorary member, a recognition which he richly deserved and appreciated and an act that reflected credit upon the association. In spite of the fact that Alcott was an extremist, a visionary, a thoroughly impractical educator, the members respected his integrity, his generosity, and his tenacity, and a reasonable number of them were convinced of the truth and practicability of many of his teachings.

Next in prominence among the protagonists of childhood was Colonel Francis W. Parker—teacher, reformer, crusty debater,[17] an institution, and above all a personality. Born on a farm in New Hampshire in 1837, he became a student of his environment, studying flowers, animals, birds,

---

[15] Dorothy McCuskey, *Bronson Alcott, Teacher* (New York, 1940), 102, 138, 140.

[16] NEA, *Proceedings, 1872,* 84, 214.

[17] While Parker is usually recalled as an amiable, good-natured person, he could be vitriolic and disagreeable when aroused in defending a cause or rebuking an opponent or critic. See, for example, his castigation of John S. Clark, which ended thus: "I take no pleasure whatever in this discussion. I regret that I have said one word in criticism of the essay of this drawing-book publisher. Hereafter . . . I will only discuss questions which are fairly and honestly presented." NEA, *Proceedings, 1895,* 846-851.

rocks, and landscapes. He afterward declared that no shop or laboratory could ever equal a well-managed farm as a constructive educational environment.[18] And he later lamented with sad bitterness the harsh teacher who squelched his early attempts at drawing.[19] He taught district schools from the age of sixteen to twenty-one and in 1858 became principal of the school at Carrollton, Illinois. At the outbreak of the Civil War he enlisted and became a colonel, a title that clung to him in spite of its inappropriateness, for no person could have been less military.

Following the war he became principal at Manchester, New Hampshire, and then a teacher in a normal school at Dayton, Ohio. He spent three years in Germany, studying at the University of Berlin, and in 1875 he returned to America to become superintendent of schools at Quincy, Massachusetts. From 1883 to 1899 he was principal of the Cook County Normal School and in 1899 principal of Chicago Institute, which became the School of Education of the University of Chicago.

At the center of all of Colonel Parker's thinking and educational planning was the child. He saw the child, not as a little man, not as a carte blanche to be inscribed with adult ideas, not even as a potential learner, but always and ever as a doer, a worker, growing in skill and power because of his own activity, living now, not just preparing to live as an adult at some future date. Parker was properly hailed as "the devoted apostle of childhood."[20] Unlike the conventional teacher who endeavored to transform active, restless, individualistic children into quiet, obedient, conforming classes, Colonel Parker seemed to love children and reversed the procedure by transforming pupils back into children.

"The ideal school is an ideal community—an embryonic democracy. . . . The child is not in the school to learn, not in there for mere knowledge; but he is in there to live, to learn to live—not a preparation for life so much as real living."[21] "Eye has not seen what God has in store for those who study the child." "Anything in the way of the child's action is wrong." "Human growth comes only by human activity." "The function of education is to bring about the conditions for conscious growth."[22]

"But I say the child loves to do good at the very beginning, and it is our duty to foster that tendency." "Every child is a born worker. . . . There never was a lazy child born in God's busy world. The child is a born naturalist."[23]

[18] NEA, *Proceedings, 1897*, 535.
[19] NEA, *Proceedings, 1889*, 481.
[20] By E. E. White of Ohio. NEA, *Proceedings, 1902*, 406.
[21] NEA, *Proceedings, 1895*, 408.
[22] NEA, *Proceedings, 1887*, 381-382.
[23] NEA, *Proceedings, 1889*, 479-482.

Next to the child himself Parker stressed freedom, freedom from adult tyranny, freedom to choose activities, freedom to learn. Such freedom could not be achieved without giving prior freedom to the teacher. Parker believed in the latter so sincerely that, according to one commentator, he praised work that was "abominable and indefensible" except that it represented originality and honest effort.[24]

Colonel Parker did not expend all his energy on revising popular attitudes toward children and freedom. He devoted equal energy to enriching the curriculum and methods of teaching. He stressed objects rather than words, activities rather than textbooks, growth rather than knowledge. He installed a manual shop for elementary-school children; he taught pupils how to run a printing press and turn out simple publications; he endorsed drawing in connection with all subjects; he led children on field trips to see industries and to study local geography. He met public criticisms with courage and maintained that drawing and clay modeling, which had been branded as fads and frills, were as important in the education of the child as the three R's.

No wonder the effervescent, unpredictable, inconsistent Colonel Parker was a pain and a puzzle to conventional educators. At Chautauqua in 1880 he said that the Quincy Method had been criticized because it contained nothing new. He admitted the charge and claimed that its virtue was that it was old—the accumulated experience of a hundred years. "It is claimed that I stole all my ideas. The thing I commend in that charge is that it is solid truth. I did steal—stole it all. I stole it from Cleveland, Cincinnati, Aristotle, Pestalozzi, Spencer, and everybody else I could find in possession of anything worth stealing."

"Do nothing twice alike. Don't do things you have done before. If the child stood up before, have him sit down now. Whatever you do, do something different. Have no patterns. Uniformity is death—variety is life."[25]

The editor of the *Indiana School Journal* was present when Colonel Parker spoke at Chautauqua. His impressions were subsequently recorded in his publication:

Colonel Parker of Quincy fame, put himself forward as a champion of freedom. The Colonel who has risen to no little notoriety in educational circles within the last year or two, is a round-faced, jolly looking fellow, who always comes up smiling, and in a slashing off-hand manner generally brings down the house several times in the course of his few remarks. He is a splendid story teller, and both in manner and appearance reminds one a little of the great infidel Bob. Indeed as Col. Robert aspires to smash Moses and the prophets, even so Col. P. seems to be ambitious to lay out all the carefully

[24] NEA, *Proceedings, 1902,* 403.
[25] NEA, *Proceedings, 1880,* 49-50.

wrought educational systems and methods that have come into existence since the days of Pestalozzi.[26]

Parker declared that pronouncements, discussions, courses of study, and programs should be marked "for this day only."[27] He denounced loyalty to any educational philosophy and ridiculed discipleship as professional stultification. Although steeped in the idea of European educators, he made his own interpretations. "I am neither a Froebelian nor a Herbartian. I don't like the word 'follower.' "[28] The greatness of Pestalozzi, Rein, Ziller, and other educators was not in their theories, systems, or methods, but in the divine zeal with which they tried to understand the mind and soul of the child.

In 1902, when Colonel Parker died, his colleagues had difficulty in assessing his educational contribution. The man who delivered the memorial address saw that Parker the man was greater than Parker the educator, and remarked that his absence was a personal as well as a professional loss. "He was the arch-infidel of orthodoxy in educational creeds." "He was an uncompromising foe to all forms of conventionality." "Bound by no conventions and fettered by no traditions, creating none himself, he was ever free to take fresh points of view and to inaugurate new lines of action . . . absurdly inconsistent, his were the inconsistencies of growth."[29]

Colonel Parker's influence was profound, especially in the West, where he spent the greater portion of his professional life. He influenced John Dewey and in turn was markedly influenced by that great philosopher, whose contributions were just coming into prominence when Parker died. Parker accelerated the child-study movement, helped to banish whipping from the schools, challenged educators to keep the schools abreast of society, and promoted the concept of a growing, changing, functional curriculum.

Sheldon, Alcott, Elizabeth Peabody, and Parker were by no means the only adults who looked upon childhood with kindly eyes. In fact, the latter years of the nineteenth century became in theory at least the age of the child. Many persons gave evidence of the changing viewpoint. At the Chicago meeting of 1887 a speaker declared "that the *whole* child is worth educating. . . . The principle that a child's most complete development is through his activities is everywhere accepted."[30]

At San Francisco in the following year C. H. McGrew of San Jose said: "The child should be the center of all educational work. The child's

[26] *Indiana School Journal,* XXV, 432, August 1880.
[27] NEA, *Proceedings, 1895,* 419.
[28] *Ibid.,* 549.
[29] NEA, *Proceedings, 1902,* 399-408.
[30] NEA, *Proceedings, 1887,* 206.

nature is sacred, and its harmonious culture . . . should be our highest aim."[31] In 1890 Henry Sabin, state superintendent of Iowa schools, expressed similar sentiments. "I desire to enter a plea for the child; to recall the almost forgotten fact that the supreme object of the child's education is the child himself. . . . We sometimes speak of teaching the child to think. It is as natural for the child to think as it is for a tree to grow. It is not the part of the teacher to wake up the mind, but to avoid putting it to sleep; it is not to administer stimulants, but to avoid administering narcotics."[32] In 1891 a speaker said: "Nature made the child a questioner, a seeker after truth; the school makes him an answerer. . . . In the school of the future the pupil will originate most of the problems."[33]

In 1895 the editor of *Primary Education,* speaking at the Denver meeting, observed. "Half a century ago the children in our primary rooms were only so many little people on their unattended way from childhood to manhood. . . . The man or woman who does not talk the child today is a fossil."[34] Even more emphatic were the observations of Professor Martin G. Brumbaugh of the University of Pennsylvania, speaking in 1898. "A child can think. A child does think. He needs no more exhortation to think than he does to eat. He enjoys the prolonged exercise of both processes. . . . The best school is the one that sends the child into life eager to know and equipped to learn."[35]

Many other individuals made their contributions to the growing recognition of children. In fact, nearly all who studied kindergartens, practiced object teaching, promoted child study, believed in learning by doing, and tried to make an interesting, practical curriculum were also liberators of children. By 1902, the year in which Colonel Parker died, the various doctrines that tended toward the liberation of children were widely, though by no means universally, accepted. The educational scene was ready for the embodiment of these doctrines in the philosophical system of John Dewey. Lofty, apparently impractical, often circumlocutionary, his writings nevertheless integrated the diverse and apparently unrelated teachings of earlier reformers into an integrated system—one in which the child was the center of solicitude and attention.

In the following decades, various aspects of childhood, freedom, interest, and functional studies were restated and reemphasized by new apostles—Maria Montessori (1870-1952), with her educational apparatus and didactic equipment, renewed popular interest in play and work,

[31] NEA, *Proceedings, 1888,* 339.
[32] NEA, *Proceedings, 1890,* 228, 232.
[33] NEA, *Proceedings, 1891,* 96, 97.
[34] NEA, *Proceedings, 1895,* 1004.
[35] NEA, *Proceedings, 1898,* 344, 347.

learning, and doing;[36] William H. Kilpatrick (1871————), interpreter of
Froebel, Montessori, and Dewey, and in his own right a teacher of
democracy and democratic living, promoted a more tolerant and understanding attitude toward children;[37] Superintendent Carlton W. Wash-
burne (1889————) of Winnetka demonstrated that a curriculum could
be both fundamental and interestingly appealing to children without following conventional procedures.[38] Harold Rugg of Teachers College,
Columbia University, built a fused program which respected children's
interest more than it did the predilections of scholars, and yet reflected
social realities better than conventional programs. His rediscovery of
the child and the refocusing of attention upon children's interests, needs,
and capacities was reminiscent of the earlier apostles of childhood.[39]
Apostles all, and their messages are still available for those who would
love, understand, and teach children.

[36] NEA, *Proceedings, 1912,* 609-621; *1915,* 661-667; 717-722, 1121-1130.
[37] NEA, *Proceedings, 1922,* 683-685.
[38] NEA, *Proceedings, 1932,* 370-371; *1934,* 713-717.
[39] NEA, *Proceedings, 1927,* 771-776.

15

Coeducation

In 1890 a committee of the NEA observed that "the question of coeducation in every grade of schools in this country, in its practical aspects, is settled. Individuals may deny the soundness of the theory, but the public mind is made up, and is not likely to be shaken in its convictions."[1]

"Some things are so axiomatic in their very nature that they require neither proof nor defense. Such a one is coeducation in the high school, which has so commended itself to the people of our country that 98 per cent of the public high schools" were coeducational by 1903.[2] In fact, as early as 1891 only fifteen cities out of 628 reported separate schools for boys and girls.

Coeducation was never a problem of practical import for American public schools. As the common schools added advanced subjects and then additional years and straggled into the evolved, rather than contrived, institution of the high school, the idea of excluding girls, or having separate schools for girls, was rarely advocated. The very idea of establishing separate schools for girls and boys was educational fantasy and fiscal folly. Only a few cities ever adopted the non-American practice of separating the sexes. Nevertheless, many speakers before NEA meetings during the association's first half-century argued the question of coeducation with the ardor of dedicated "reformers."

Why was coeducation such a live issue for over fifty years? The explanation of the popularity of the question of coeducation is involved and complex. In the first place, the most important factor was its attraction as a problem in theory. The typical American of 1857 or 1875 had had no experience with separate schools for the sexes. When he heard of the idea, he was intrigued rather than impressed or troubled. He began to speculate, to opine, to imagine, and to conjure up all sorts of notions

[1] NEA, *Proceedings, 1890,* 339.
[2] NEA, *Proceedings, 1903,* 451, 456.

about the nature of boys and girls and their effects upon each other. He may even have tried to imagine what the separation of the sexes, which he had never seen in practice, might accomplish. Educators were not immune to such ruminations. They too began to talk and some of them to debate, for they knew something of the second factor in the popularity of the question of coeducation, namely, the separation of the sexes in eastern academies and colleges.

While some of the early academies in New England had admitted both boys and girls, the practice of maintaining schools for boys only became popular, and by 1850 such schools were numerous enough to be typical. The colleges, which had been founded in periods when advanced education was for men only, naturally did not subsequently open their doors to women. Having the start in time and the prestige of location, the colleges inspired the unperceiving with the notion that their exclusion of girls was in some mysterious manner the explanation for their prominence and success. So the examples of academies and colleges for men only were regarded as impressive demonstrations of the advantages of sexual segregation.

The third factor in the appeal of the coeducation question was the rise of state universities and coeducational colleges. This development provided the only touch of practicality which the issue has ever had in America. With a keen insight into the popular ideas on this subject Anna C. Brockett declared in 1874, "For the masses, coeducation and the higher education for women are one and the same thing."[3] Thus it is that discussions of mixed education as carried on at Oberlin, Antioch, Alfred, Cornell, and Michigan and separate instruction given at Vassar, Smith, and Mt. Holyoke are all parts of the subject of coeducation, and were so regarded by the public.

It is a curious fact that interest in coeducation was greatest in the areas most remote from its practice. In the East, where considerable segregation prevailed, educators were critical, suspicious, and even hostile toward the widespread practice of coeducation west of the Alleghenies; they marveled over the unconcerned naturalness with which it was regarded in the West, and felt that such a venturesome practice merited excited and prolonged comment. On the other hand, educators in the West were equally curious as to the practice of segregation in the East and seemed to feel that life at Dartmouth or Vassar could provide interesting and revealing materials for a fresh examination of the whole subject of the education of the sexes.

Coeducation around 1870 was, as indicated above, somewhat regional in character. In the West it was general although not universal; in the South it was prevalent, but there were many exceptions, especially in

[3] NEA, *Proceedings, 1874,* 128.

schools of secondary rank; in the East separate schools were the dominant practice, although there were numerous exceptions. Coeducation was proclaimed at the University of Vermont in 1865, although the records of 1871 show no females enrolled. Bates College made a vigorous statement of its status as a coeducational institution when it was founded in 1865. Coeducation also prevailed at Cornell University from its beginning in 1868, at Boston University and Swarthmore College at their openings in 1869, at Syracuse University in 1871, and at Muhlenberg College in 1873. Alfred College, Lebanon Valley College, Palatinate College, and Westminster College were also coeducational. At least a few girls were admitted to Allegheny College, Mercersburg College, and Franklin and Marshall College. Western Maryland College, founded in 1867, was coeducational to the extent of having the same instructors, but the sexes "do not recite together, meeting only in chapel services and at meals in the dining hall, where the professors are also present. The ladies' course is also shorter by a year than that arranged for gentlemen."[4] In 1872 and 1873 four female students were enrolled at Wesleyan University. In an entirely different kind of school, that of Agassiz' summer session on Penikese Island, girls were admitted.

In 1871 there were 504 so-called colleges, although it is more than probable that many of them were in reality secondary schools. They were classified as follows, although the commissioner of education had considerable doubts about the accuracy of the classification: 136 exclusively for women, 99 coeducational, and 269 for men only.[5]

Practically all discussions of coeducation, including the separate education of the sexes, began with a review of the accumulated stock of generalizations about women, their differences from men, their meritorious qualities, and particularly their frailties. The following collection of aphorisms about the sexes had the charm of eternal freshness, the virtue of half-truths, and the vitality of error.

Boys are given to skepticism, girls to belief; girls are fond of details but have only a dim grasp of matters of large import. Girls are docile, respectful, earnest, enthusiastic, diligent, accurate, and conscientious. Woman is more observing but less reflective than man; she has more taste, feeling, fancy, and imagination but less understanding, judgment, and reason; she is imitative rather than inventive; in fact, her creative power is feeble. While women may appreciate literature and art, they are forever debarred from any deep insight into logic and philosophy. Man wants an education but woman is satisfied with information. A

[4] Bureau of Education, *Circular of Information*, No. 5, 1873, 23-24.
[5] *Ibid.*, No. 3, 1873, 17, 26, 44, 90, 110; *Report of the Commissioner of Education, 1871*, 638-649, 55.

woman's intuition enables her to solve problems that defy man's reason.[6]

From these basic assumptions and assertions speakers were inclined to move on to an enumeration of the advantages and disadvantages of coeducation. Some of the asserted advantages were as follows: joint education is the way of the family and of nature; the presence of either sex restrains and softens the behavior of the other; boys are stimulated to better scholarship by the presence of girls; coeducation promotes an understanding and practice of the social amenities; it promotes a healthy emulation; it raises the moral tone of the school; without coeducation the girls would have fewer educational opportunities; coeducation does not compel identical education; elective studies provide for sex differences of taste; coeducation facilitates the use of teachers of both sexes; separate schools promote morbid ideas and eventual immorality; the self-will, violence, and rudeness of boys are restrained by the presence of girls; the different tastes of the sexes promote a balanced program of studies; much stricter surveillance is required in separate schools.

Judging by the frequency with which it was cited and quoted, the pronouncement on coeducation by Jean Paul Richter was a convincing argument in its favor. "To insure modesty I would advise the education of the sexes together; for two boys will preserve twelve girls, or two girls twelve boys, innocent, amidst winks, jokes, and improprieties, merely by that instinctive sense which is the forerunner of natural modesty. But I will guarantee nothing in a school where girls are alone together, and still less where boys are."[7]

Arguments for coeducation sometimes assumed fanciful forms. Mental dissimilarities did not imply a need for diversity in food and air, and female bread, female salad, and female pickles would be no more absurd than female algebra, female botany, or female history. Subjects have no sex and ideas are neither male nor female.

One illuminating comment about the value of educating girls was made by a Choctaw chief about 1857.

When I lived among the Choctaw Indians, I held a consultation with one of their principal chiefs respecting the successive stages of their progress in the arts and virtues of civilized life, and, among other things, he informed me at their first start they fell into a sad mistake—they only sent their boys to school. They became intelligent men, but they married uneducated and uncivilized wives; and the result was that the children were all like the mother, and soon the father lost his interest in both wife and children. And now, if we could

[6] NEA, *Proceedings, 1874,* 115; *1886,* 302-304.
[7] This quotation appears twice in the NEA, *Proceedings, 1874,* 129, and *1903,* 458; it also appeared in Kiddle and Shem's *Cyclopedia of Education* and in several state teachers' journals.

educate only one class of our children, we would choose girls; for when they become mothers, they would educate their sons.[8]

The chief's opinion was echoed by a speaker at the NEA meeting of 1868 who argued that women should be given higher training because they were shut up in the house and had little opportunity to increase their stock of knowledge. Furthermore, mothers diffuse their learning, whereas men do not pass it on freely to others, not even to their own children.[9]

The arguments against coeducation were also numerous and varied: instruction can be better adapted to classes of one sex; girls are tarnished by the rude manners of the boys; coeducation promotes sexual precocity; familiar daily association brings disenchantment; it brings the sexes together when they should be separated to allow for normal physical and psychological growth; it makes boys effeminate and girls masculine; the girl especially needs protection during her formative years against the confusion of ideals; the awkward, semiarticulate boy deserves protection against the girl of nimble intellect and glib tongue; the strain upon girls to keep up in their studies is a serious detriment to their health;[10] girls do not have the physical and mental strength to keep up with the boys; sex differences are ineradicably stamped upon the brain, thus calling for differentiated treatment; in view of the differences between men and women, coeducation is an injustice to both.

The opponents of coeducation drew many of their arguments from Dr. Edward H. Clarke's *Sex in Education,* which stressed physiological differences and warned educators about the danger to women's health in case they were forced into competition with men. More lasting arguments against coeducation were made at a much later date by G. Stanley Hall.[11]

Sessions for the discussion of coeducation took on something of the flavor of revelations, confessions, or exposés, and the speeches were sure to provoke vigorous approvals and dissents. One of the longest papers on the topic was given by Professor J. K. Hosmer of the University of Missouri at the Detroit meeting in 1874. He reported some of the results of an informal inquiry which he had made among his associates as to the success or failure of coeducation at various institutions. At Institution Z the young ladies were given to inattention, whispering, and playing.

---

[8] *Rhode Island Schoolmaster,* III, 176, August 1857.

[9] NEA, *Proceedings, 1868,* 686.

[10] NEA, *Proceedings, 1903,* 457. One speaker commented sarcastically upon a series of letters which had appeared in the *Ladies' Home Journal* about girls losing their health by overstudying. He opined that all these protesting letters had been written by the same mother and summarized their tenor as follows: "Mary, just budding into sweet womanhood, entered the high school. She became ambitious in her studies, and now she is an angel in heaven."

[11] NEA, *Proceedings, 1903,* 446-451; *1904,* 538-542.

At Institution X they cheated in examinations, and at Y an honor student was detected prompting a less capable classmate. Also at Y on April 1 some young ladies tied the doors to classrooms, imprisoning instructors and students. Following a snowstorm, some young men invaded a building and pelted the girls on the upper landing with snowballs. The girls threw chips and boards in return. Windows were broken and classes disrupted. Also at Y a party of young ladies was found playing cards in the library during study hours, and at X a young lady and a gentleman were discovered playing a solitary game in the laboratory. At these same institutions young ladies encouraged young men in such pranks as hanging a skeleton from the ceiling of the chapel, tolling the college bell at midnight, placing an alarm clock in the pulpit to ring during the chaplain's prayers, and releasing a bekettled dog in the girls' dormitory.

The danger of improprieties and scandals loomed large in the thinking of college administrators of coeducational institutions. At Z the young men flavored their allusions to their lady fellow students with a taint of vulgarity just short of indecency. At X a headstrong young lady chose to room with a family of the village rather than live in the college buildings. She was attractive and indiscreet, receiving young men in her room and attracting an undue amount of attention on the streets. At K the faculty had few troubles in the early part of the year, but as the winter waned the young men and ladies grew weary of studying and became interested in each other, making the spring term a period of watchfulness and anxiety for matrons and chaperons. On Saturdays and holidays young men and women formed a band for a long walk under the charge of a matron or teacher. In the woods couples invariably ignored their chaperon and wandered off to themselves and eventually came home by twos and twos.

In spite of these conditions, however, the presidents of Iowa, Michigan, Oberlin, and Fredonia Normal School denied any difficulties at their institutions and made light of the problem of regulating a student body because it was composed of both men and women. At an afternoon session, following the delivery of Hosmer's speech in the morning, President Daniel Read vigorously asserted that Hosmer's observations were not derived from the University of Missouri, over which he presided.[12]

At the same convention at which Hosmer disclosed the delicate situations which existed in coeducational institutions, Professor James Orton read a paper entitled "Four Years in Vassar College," thus presenting a view of segregated education, the other aspect of the broad concept of coeducation.

Objective, factual, and enumerative, Orton's speech was nevertheless a vigorous argument for the segregated education of girls. Four-fifths

[12] NEA, *Proceedings, 1874,* 118-135.

of the applicants for Vassar were destined for at least a term in its two-year preparatory program. The major purpose was education for mental power and so the program stressed languages and sciences.

Information about the students was specific. The average age of the graduating class was twenty-two, about the same as for Amherst, Yale, and Cornell. The average weight was 121 pounds and the height 5 feet, 4 inches. The graduates numbered 42 out of a starting class of 84, while at Amherst 62 out of 95 and at Cornell only 65 out of 261 survived. Orton observed that "no girl coming to Vassar need sacrifice the roses on her cheeks." In fact, he declared that the girls were better off than at home, since they got regular exercise and sleep and an abundance of plain food and pure water. The average cost of the senior year was $600, about the same as Amherst's $617, but much below Yale's $1,133.[13]

As may be inferred from some of the earlier discussions, the lack of practical import did not diminish the zeal of the speakers on coeducation, pro and con, and hyperbole and dogmatism flourished along with pronouncements of faith. President Paul A. Chadbourne of the University of Wisconsin declared that he would not, under any considerations, preside over an institution where man and women were given common training together.[14] S. Prettyman asserted that, having been head of a ladies' seminary for thirty years, he understood the matter and "knew" that young ladies should be educated separately.[15] President W. W. Folwell of Minnesota, of opposing viewpoint, said, "When asked, as I sometimes am, 'When were women first admitted to your university?' my reply is 'Never. They were never excluded.' They came at the beginning and took their place as a matter of course."[16] R. H. Jesse, president of the University of Missouri, was a true believer in coeducation. "Quickly converted to coeducation, I have stood firm in the faith for thirteen years. Nothing that wise men of the East may say would shake that faith. . . ."[17]

Worried and harassed by the discussion over coeducation, one alarmed speaker declared in favor of education for boys. "It is too late a day to discuss the question of coeducation. There are a few fossil institutions that do not admit women, but they do not represent the spirit of the times. I am fearful lest the boys will not obtain coeducation with the girls . . . girls are to become the educated sex. . . . Educate the men as well as the women."[18]

Among the more sober remarks in the discussions of the half-century

---

[13] *Ibid.,* 109-117.
[14] NEA, *Proceedings, 1868,* 685.
[15] *Ibid.,* (Bardeen ed.), 686.
[16] NEA, *Proceedings, 1875,* 72.
[17] NEA, *Proceedings, 1904,* 544.
[18] NEA, *Proceedings, 1890,* 344.

of debate over coeducation was that made by F. Louis Soldan of St. Louis, who said in 1890 that he favored coeducation for great social purposes rather than for mere educational reasons. He therefore thought that the sexes should have equivalent but not necessarily identical education.[19]

A fairly inclusive review of sex differences and their alleged significance for education was given by three speakers at the meeting of the Child-Study Department of the NEA in Boston in 1903. One speaker asserted that such differences as existed between boys and girls were derived from social custom and training, from differences in assigned tasks, from traditional practices in clothes, toys, and behavior as well as from genuine sex differences. He thought that no distinctions were necessary until the students reached the secondary level, and then the differentiation should be no more marked that those observed in the home and church. A second speaker also minimized the biological and physiological basis of sex differences and reported a series of studies that had convinced him that the differences between the sexes, while real, were slight, much less than the variation within each sex. The third speaker feared that coeducation stimulated the premature development of social life; he believed that girls should be given more time to complete a given course, and hence separate schools were desirable.[20]

Quite unexpectedly, the most able and sweeping condemnation of coeducation came near the close of the period of debate, in 1904. G. Stanley Hall argued that the training of women interferes with physical development, postpones and prevents marriage, and throws boys and girls of the same age unequally together. The girls, being more mature and insightful, develop a disdain for boys. Girls are more intuitive, less discursive, and have richer emotional lives. Sex differentiation should be accented instead of minimized.[21]

Among the last, if not the last, of the discussions that dealt with coeducation were the papers by the principals of the boys' high school and the girls' high school of Louisville, given before the superintendents in 1906. Reuben Post Halleck of the boys' high school retrod the old grooves, reechoed the old clichés, and reaffirmed the old faith that boys are, or should be, manly, brave, and aggressive, although he was haunted by the fear that American men were becoming effeminate. On this point he quoted the Mosley Educational Commission of England, which visited the United States in 1903, "that the boy in America is not brought up to punch another boy's head, or to stand having his own punched, in a

[19] Ibid., 344-345, 346.
[20] NEA, Proceedings, 1890, 344.
[21] NEA, Proceedings, 1904, 538-542; also 1903, 446-460.

healthy and proper manner; that there is a strange and indefinable feminine air coming over the men; a tendency toward a common . . . a sexless . . . mode of thought."

Halleck lamented the preponderance of women teachers and protested against the decline of rivalry among boys, although he doubted that it was necessary for girls. Boys prefer a bullfight to a love story, a Kipling poem of blood to a Tennysonian idyll, a wild tale of war to one of sentiment. In these preferences Halleck rejoiced and climaxed the argument by telling how enthralled they were by the story of a dogfight.

Miss Anna J. Hamilton of the girls' high school in Louisville saw that the times called for an education that would fit girls for earning a living as well as being wives, mothers, and housekeepers. She endorsed intellectual training but thought that character-building was even more important. She lamented the dearth of women heroines and blamed historians for the shortage. She thought that women lived most fully on the emotional, personal, and social level and that modern girls are as competent as those of former generations, and are, in addition, equipped for a larger service to humanity.

The unconvincing nature of these two papers is well reflected in the comment of Superintendent F. Louis Soldan of St. Louis, who dismissed all the implied advantages of training boys and girls in separate schools and asserted that such ideas were "discarded long ago."[22]

The great interest in coeducation gradually subsided. The feeling evidenced by Superintendent John Hancock in 1890 now seems quite outdated. "Vassar, Smith, and Wellesley will yet admit young men. I predict that in less than fifty years young men will be knocking at their doors for admission. It was a mistake to establish separate colleges."[23] Interest had already waned by 1891, when the National Council of Education transferred its standing committee on coeducation into one on moral education. Everyone began to realize that the country did not have to become either all coeducation or all separate instruction. The matter was settled by allowing all kinds of variations. Within a decade after 1900 the educator who wanted an argument had to choose some other topic. Instead of rousing a quickened pulse and an argumentative mood, the word "coeducation" was more likely to evoke a bored stare or a yawn of indifference.

[22] NEA, *Proceedings, 1906*, 58-72.
[23] NEA, *Proceedings, 1890*, 347.

16

The Herbartian Movement

"METHOD determines the quality of instruction and discipline—the success of the teacher; without method or with bad method no one should presume to impart instruction." So said United States Commissioner of Education John Eaton in 1871.[1]

While every educator admitted the truth of Eaton's observation concerning the importance of method, few gave it specific attention. Discussions concerning philosophies and theories of education overshadowed the problems of classroom instruction. In fact, classroom procedure was regarded as a kind of mechanical or personal matter, quite beneath the dignity of major attention from leading educators. The teacher was thus left to work out the application of theories and philosophies, and when he failed to understand philosophic principles and resorted to devices and mnemonics, he was scolded and ridiculed for being superficial and unperceiving. In spite of the supposed emphasis which normal schools placed upon methods, the fact was that specific procedures for use in the classroom were neglected. This neglect of methods helps to explain the great popularity of Herbart in America, for he had a formula, a procedure, a set sequence of steps that promised tangible outcomes and provided guidance and assurance for the teacher.

The teacher's problems of classroom method was made difficult by generations of pronouncements and years of accumulated prejudices. The scholar tended to say that "He who knows the subjects can teach"; the educator tended to say, "He who knows how can teach"; the protagonist of children tended to say, "He who knows children can teach"; and the psychologist who studied the learning process began to say, "He who knows how pupils learn can teach." The teacher who believed one of these pronouncements was sure of a degree of success, but the one who believed all four of them and found a way to harmonize and blend them was sure of a greater success. Hence the teacher was always in search of

[1] NEA, *Proceedings, 1871,* 179.

a pattern, a formula, a procedure, a method that would help him to solve the perplexities of a complex situation, that would reveal the degree of truth in each of these pronouncements.

With the growth of normal schools and the passing of laws requiring professional preparation for certification, methods of teaching became more important at all grade levels. Books on classroom procedures, the ones that told "how to do it," were sure of a popular reception. So it was natural and logical that Pestalozzi, Froebel, and Herbart were successively hailed as the prophets of a new day in teaching. When the Herbartians proclaimed their answers to the problems of purpose, child nature, the psychology of learning, and the true function of subjects, and at the same time offered a new dignity for the teacher, they enlisted an enthusiastic following and initiated the era of Herbartianism in America. Educators eagerly listened to their own leaders, such as Horace Mann, W. T. Harris, E. E. White, Francis W. Parker, and John Dewey; they were also willing to receive help from abroad and looked particularly to Germany.

After about 1820 American education was greatly influenced by the three German-speaking educators—Pestalozzi (1746-1827), whose influence was felt most in the primary grades; Froebel (1782-1852), whose influence was greatest upon children of the pre-school age; and Herbart (1776-1841), whose authority was greatest at the secondary level. From Pestalozzi came a new concept of the child, his worth, dignity, and individuality, a new emphasis upon the role of the senses in learning, and the basic reform known as object teaching. His influence on American education began with John Griscom's visit to Switzerland in 1819 and continued with varying degrees of intensity until about 1870, although it has never vanished altogether. From Froebel came a still more sympathetic understanding of the child and an even greater respect for his personality, and emphasis upon the importance of the mother as an educator, and the epoch-making influences of the kindergarten. The period of Froebel's greatest influence on America was from about 1855 to 1890, although he was to a considerable extent responsible for the enormous child-study movement that began about 1890. From Herbart came the unifying influence of a single dominating purpose, namely, the formation of character. From Herbart also came a new conception of the importance of the teacher, greater emphasis upon the role of the content of the program of studies, and, most influential of all, a formalized method of teaching. The Herbartian period lasted from about 1890 to 1910, although large segments of his doctrines became permanent possessions of all subsequent educators.

Through visitors and disciples Pestalozzi and Froebel directly promoted their doctrines in America, but Herbart, who died in 1841, had at the time of his death almost no following here. His influence in this country came many years after his death. The Herbartian movement was the work of a zealous band who had studied in Germany and returned to America to spread the doctrines with an almost evangelical fervor.

The Herbartians organized a club at the Saratoga Springs meeting of the NEA in 1892, and reorganized it in 1895 under the name of the National Herbart Society for the Scientific Study of Education. For the next twenty years the Herbartians wrote most of the educational books, took complete possession of several educational journals, proclaimed the issues for debate, and dominated professional discussions. Almost every prominent educator of the period endorsed all or some of the Herbartian doctrines, but the most active disciples were those who had been students of Dr. Wilhelm Rein at Jena and who were located at one time or another at Illinois Normal University—the brothers Charles A. McMurry and Frank M. McMurry, Charles DeGarmo, and C. C. Van Liew. Others who supported the movement, but with some reservations, were Nicholas Murray Butler, John Dewey, and the editors of two school journals, George P. Brown and A. E. Winship. While many educators criticized one or more aspects of Herbartianism, the only outright critic of most of its principles was W. T. Harris, United States commissioner of education.

Although Herbart's doctrines and their modifications in America were numerous and complex, his basic teachings were clear and tangible. Foremost in importance was his insistence upon the development of character as the major purpose of education. This emphasis upon individual character was expanded to include social behavior.

The development of character depends upon the presence of good ideas or interesting thoughts, which are derived from the program of studies. Those ideas that nourish character must have an enlivening, quickening effect; hence the subjects that are interesting and appealing are the ones that mold character. Routine studies, such as writing, spelling, figuring, and the mechanics of reading, can never inspire interest; therefore literature, history, and science must find a place in every grade. Fairy tales, legends, myths, songs, and such narratives as *Robinson Crusoe*[2] and *Hiawatha* were regarded as suitable for building permanent interests. And since the teacher determines what ideas and thoughts are derived from the content, he too becomes a builder of character, almost equal in importance to the content of the subjects.

Herbart stressed the necessity of *concentration,* that is, the selecting of one subject, such as history or geography, as the core of the curriculum, and the *correlation* of all subjects. Thus the arithmetic lesson could

[2] For the educational values of Robinson Crusoe, see DeGarmo's panegyric, NEA, *Proceedings, 1891,* 177-179.

utilize the facts given in geography, and the reading lesson, the spelling lesson, and the writing exercise could be derived from a passage in the history textbook.

Herbart solved the problem of the grading of materials, i.e., their arrangement in a desirable sequence of learning, by assuming that each child's progress paralleled the growth of the human race from savagery to civilization. G. Stanley Hall, who was no Herbartian, accepted the doctrine and did much to popularize it. This principle, known as recapitulation or the culture-epoch theory, seemed to throw light upon the question of the proper order for studying the various subjects. In order to know what subject or content would appeal to a given pupil, it was necessary merely to estimate his location on the scale of ascent from savagery to a complex culture.

Finally, the crowning contribution of the Herbartians was the formalizing of a classroom method of teaching. This rested upon Herbart's psychology of apperception—the process of acquiring basic experiences through the senses and relating all subsequent experiences and lessons to the already acquired apperceptive mass. It was an obligation of the teacher to promote the absorption of new materials by showing how they fitted onto what had already been learned. With this basic psychology in mind, the teacher was ready to teach, and in order to teach effectively he needed only to follow the five prescribed steps:

1. Preparation—the teacher recalls the appropriate experiences of the pupils.
2. Presentation—the new materials are outlined, indicated, or summarized.
3. Association—connections, comparisons, and contrasts between the old and new ideas are emphasized.
4. Generalization—general rules, laws, and principles are derived from the new materials.
5. Application—the new generalizations are tested by applying them to specific instances.

These formal steps, in spite of their apparently arbitrary and mechanical nature, provided not only a systematic but an inspiring procedure for those who had faith in it. Even when they were used with incomplete understanding, they were probably an improvement upon the random and structureless procedures of many teachers. While few teachers followed them faithfully or for long periods, they did provide a sound pattern of the necessary elements in teaching and learning.

By way of summary, the principal ideas of the Herbartians were (1) character as the aim of education, (2) content as the means through which character was achieved, (3) the necessity of interest, (4) the importance of the teacher in creating interest and molding character, (5) the desirability of correlating all studies into one big unity, (6) the

usefulness of the culture-epoch theory, (7) the psychology of apperception, and (8) the guidance of the five formal steps in classroom teaching.[3]

Such were the principal ideas of Herbart and the Herbartians. Fundamental, inclusive, controversial, they provided bones of contention and
points of divergence for twenty years. Such a thoroughgoing revision
of educational thinking had not been proposed since the days of Rousseau.
The Herbartians, eager, enthusiastic, hopeful, and possibly a bit con-
tentious, were willing to argue.

Perhaps the outstanding defender of the status quo and so a potential
opponent of Herbartianism was William T. Harris. With his Hegelian
philosophy of analysis and synthesis, his insistence upon subjects, textbooks, and recitations, his scant respect for the originality and capacity of
children, and his laudatory commendation of vicarious experience, he
towered over the educational scene for many years, first as the resourceful
and successful superintendent of the St. Louis schools (1867-1880), as
editor of the *Journal of Speculative Philosophy* and lecturer at Alcott's
Concord School of Philosophy, and then as United States commissioner
of education from 1889 to 1906. He sponsored kindergartens; promoted
teacher training; wrote vigorous and influential reports; served on numerous committees; was president of the NEA in 1875 and spoke on
nearly every topic, problem, and issue in the field of education. When he
declared that Herbart was useless as a philosopher and refused to accept
the new terminology, the Herbartians had to contend with the great
William Torrey Harris.

At the Boston meeting of the superintendents in February 1893, a
subcommittee on "the co-ordination of studies in primary and grammar
schools" was appointed with Harris as chairman.[4] It made its report to
the superintendents at Cleveland in February 1895. There was a chorus
of dissent and criticism. Frank M. McMurry of Buffalo said that the
report ignored the child, rejected the type of studies recommended by
the Herbartians, and reemphasized reading, writing, and arithmetic.
Colonel Parker said that the committee had ignored its assignment of
dealing with the correlation of studies. "The report is a grand statement
of facts long known to all of us." He objected to the dogmatic assertion
that there should be two reading lessons a day for six years. He moved
that a committee of fifteen be appointed to revise Harris's report.[5]

President Charles DeGarmo of Swarthmore College, a leading Herbartian, asserted that the report on correlation rejected correlation. It
"should be called a discourse on 'Educational values.'" It treated educa-

[3] NEA, *Proceedings, 1892*, 421-433; Dorothy McMurry, *Herbartian Contributions to History Instruction in American Elementary Schools* (New York, 1946).
[4] NEA, *Proceedings, 1894*, 254.
[5] NEA, *Proceedings, 1895*, 344.

tion as a series of parallel tunnels, crossed at regular distances by other tunnels. The natural interrelation among studies was ignored or denied.[6]

Charles A. McMurry remarked that the report was "essentially an analysis and isolation of the branches of study." Could Dr. Harris find any dictionary that would sanction the use of the word correlation to mean the isolation of the different studies? "I feared that Dr. Harris would take refuge in meta-physical distinctions." The speaker then flatly accused Harris of misrepresenting Herbart's whole position.[7]

Professor B. A. Hinsdale of Michigan entered the discussion and tried to effect a reconciliation of the different viewpoints. He believed in isolation and analysis, along with Harris, and also in grouping and co-ordination, along with the Herbartians.[8]

Tall, austere, and courteous E. E. White of Ohio professed a degree of ignorance of Herbartianism and then pronounced in favor of a blending and unification of the school subjects at the elementary level, but in favor of an increasing differentiation among subjects as one ascends the scale of the grades. He feared that Herbartianism meant a return to individual instruction and an abandonment of schools and classes.[9]

Nicholas Murray Butler of Columbia University, favorably disposed toward Herbartianism and almost worshipful in his respect for Harris, hesitated to criticize the report, but was compelled to say that he was "greatly disappointed" with it. He characterized it as "extremely unfortunate" and lamented Harris's refusal to accept the prevailing definition of correlation as indicating the interrelationship among the studies rather than the relationship between the school and the social environment. He said that in the effort to construct the curriculum by philosophical discussion Dr. Harris had done more than "any other single person, living or dead," but that he had failed to explain how it should be "correlated or coordinated or concentrated." He decried the attempt to derive a curriculum solely by analysis and favored the most careful inquiry into the nature and needs of children as another procedure for finding the proper studies. The child sees the world "as a correlated and concentrated whole"; it is the adult philosopher who has analyzed and separated the elements that the Herbartians are now trying to put back together.[10]

Another speaker declared that if correlation had made the kindergarten what it was, he wanted the principle carried up the scale to include all the grades.

Dr. Harris closed the discussion by restating his definition of correlation as the relating of the pupil with the world. He blessed child study

[6] *Ibid.*, 344-345.
[7] *Ibid.*, 345.
[8] *Ibid.*, 346.
[9] *Ibid.*, 346-347.
[10] *Ibid.*, 347-349.

but denied that it alone would answer the problem of deciding what to teach.[11]

Critics of Herbart and at least potential opponents of Herbartianism were found in great numbers among the followers of Froebel. At the Denver meeting of the NEA in 1895 Inspector James L. Hughes of Toronto gave a paper on the contributions of Froebel and Herbart. A few excerpts will show his preference for the former. "Herbart studied the child to mold it; Froebel studied it to guide it in its growth. Herbert studied the child as a philosopher; Froebel studied it as a sympathetic friend. Herbart saw the need of control much more clearly than the need of freedom; Froebel saw the harmony between freedom and control. Herbart made instruction the basis of virtue; Froebel made morality depend upon true living in the home and in the school. . . . Herbart made will result from action; Froebel made action result from will."[12]

In the discussion which followed Hughes' paper, Mrs. Eudora Hailmann, a leader in the kindergarten movement, marveled that Herbart made no mention of Froebel and speculated that it was because of Herbart's failure to recognize the educational value of the early years of childhood and his blindness to woman's share in education. Herbert stressed the school life of the child and did not emphasize the training of the senses. W. N. Hailmann seconded some of the criticisms made by his wife and remarked, "I think one of the chief hindrances to the development of Herbartism is its name. We have in the kindergarten gotten entirely rid of Froebel." He said that Herbartism deals with a course of study, mere instruction, whereas Froebel dealt with education.[13] Colonel Parker expressed his appreciation of both Herbart and Froebel but preferred the democratic freedom of the latter to the class education of the former.[14]

In a paper read before the National Council of Education at the Chicago meeting of 1895, Charles A. McMurry summarized the influence of Herbart upon the course of study in the common schools. The program of studies emphasized literature and history "because they contain in potent educative solution the rich culture influences" which best promote moral and ethical development. While the program stresses American geography, history, and literature and is therefore national and patriotic, it also utilizes large portions of European culture. Herbartian padagogy stresses the use of science lessons in every grade and so is quite abreast of modern developments. While it proposes no special changes in the teaching of language and arithmetic, it insists upon combining all subjects into an integrated whole. Thus the Herbartians opposed in theory and practice the old idea of formal discipline; they did not accept the

[11] *Ibid.*, 349-350.
[12] *Ibid.*, 544.
[13] *Ibid.*, 545-546.
[14] *Ibid.*, 549.

theory that one subject was as good as another. And lastly, McMurry praised the systematic method of teaching advocated by the Herbartians.

In answer to questions which followed the presentation of his paper, McMurry emphasized the desirability of using the full text of the *Sketch Book* or *Hiawatha* or *Evangeline* in class, thus providing the pupils with stronger, fuller impressions than could be derived from the sketchy excerpts given in school readers. He saw the teacher's task as the assembling from the cultural heritage of those elements that would prepare the child for the social order in which he was to live. He saw no conflict between child study and Herbartian doctrines. While he thought the culture-epoch theory was helpful in placing materials in a proper sequence, he attached no great importance to the theory.[15]

As the foregoing account has shown, the Herbartians had a profound effect upon American education. The course of study gained a new dignity and importance; character development received increased attention; training for social adjustment became a more clearly recognized function of the schools; and, most tangible if not most enduring or important, a new method was popularized. In time the culture-epoch theory was discarded as a quaint illusion, charming and colorful but basically untrue, and inapplicable if true. The doctrine of apperception was accepted and absorbed into subsequent theories of learning.

With the widespread acceptance of most of the Herbartian doctrines, there was a natural decline in the vigor and activity of the movement. Debates and discussions henceforth involved modification and utilization rather than the validity of the basic doctrines.

The National Herbart Society changed its name to the National Society for the Study of Education, under which name it has continued to the present time. For many years it has been best known for its series of yearbooks of wide range and high quality. Although never structurally linked to the NEA, the society has always been closely identified with the association through overlapping of membership and concurrence of meetings. The society's meetings have usually been held in connection with the school superintendents' department of the NEA. Aaron Gove, one-time president of the NEA, referred to the society as "an affiliated department" of the NEA "without official connection with the association."[16]

Today it can be observed that many of the contributions of the Herbartians have become permanent possessions of the whole teaching profession. For Herbartian reforms, like the movement designed to effect their realization, have been slowly assimilated into the general stream of educational progress.

[15] *Ibid.*, 475-481.
[16] NEA, *Proceedings, 1899*, 36.

17

The Progressive Movement

PROGRESSIVE ideas in education were uttered in every decade of the history of the NEA. In 1866 W. P. Atkinson wrote that "education properly considered is the development of the whole man and the whole woman." He vehemently denounced the classics as mere mental discipline and characterized the teaching of words to boys who were interested in objects and nature as "useless and perverse." He regarded the claim that the classics provided a liberal education as a fraud and an impediment to acquiring a really liberal education through science, literature, and modern languages.[1]

In 1872 E. E. White of Ohio lamented the widespread notion that education was primarily the cultivation of the intellect and added, "It is impossible to send the intellect of a child to school and leave the heart at home." W. F. Phelps of Minnesota remarked upon the inadequacy of relying wholly upon intellectual training and explained that education was "a vital, organic process, laying hold of body, mind, and soul. . . ."[2] At Topeka in 1886 Superintendent L. R. Klemm of Hamilton, Ohio, enjoined the teachers to "individualize" their teaching. "Competition is a curse, because it treats children as if they were all endowed with the same aptitude . . . competition is immoral, because it is based upon the law of the survival of the fittest, which, however natural it may be, is not a moral law." After denouncing "soulless memorizing of the printed page," he concluded by marveling over "the incongruities which exist between the requirements of life and those of the schoolmaster."[3]

In addition to circulating progressive ideas, there were a few educators who put them into practice. William B. Powell (1836-1904), brother of the well-known Major John Wesley Powell of Grand Canyon fame, was superintendent at Peru and Aurora, Illinois, and Washington, D. C.,

[1] *Massachusetts Teacher*, XIX, 365-374, November 1866.
[2] NEA, *Proceedings*, 1872, 25, 35.
[3] NEA, *Proceedings*, 1886, 153, 155, 159.

from 1862 to 1900. He introduced drawing, art, science, nature study, health, and other subjects that had not been popularly accepted. In Washington he established a business high school, probably the first in the country. "Any school is not what it ought to be where children do not attend as willingly as they will hunt squirrels or go fishing or play tennis."[4] In the manner of later progressives, he denounced imposed tasks, condemned parsing, and emphasized doing. Colonel Parker at Quincy, Massachusetts, John Dewey at the experimental school at Chicago, and occasional superintendents put some progressive ideas into practice before 1900.

Next to object teaching and the kindergarten, the most important principle in the evolution of the progressive movement was the idea of learning by doing. "If I were to reduce to a single maxim the concentrated wisdom of the world on the subject of education, I should enunciate . . . the principle that in educating the young, you serve them most effectually, not by what you do for them, but by *what you teach them to do for themselves.*" Such was the admonition of Bishop Alonzo Potter, churchman and educator, speaking to teachers in 1857.[5]

Bishop Potter did not originate the idea of learning by doing, but his statement of it shows that the principle was current in the very year in which the NEA was founded. The situation that gave rise to the principle of learning by doing was well understood. In 1877, a speaker at the NEA convention described it: "The book is taught instead of the subject; words are taught instead of the relations of thoughts or of things." He listed other difficulties which hampered the pupil's progress: too many subjects; studying the abstract, such as algebra, instead of practicing skills; stressing logical subtleties instead of practical operations. The basic cure recommended for all these defects was the practice of doing instead of pursuing the intangible values of mental discipline.[6]

In 1894 Charles B. Scott gave expression to the learning-by-doing principle in a manner worthy of Colonel Parker himself. "As we watch the kicking, creeping, toddling little child and note from day to day his life and actions, his growth and development, two characteristics which impress us above all others are his almost incessant activity . . . and his marvelously rapid development. From morning till night, during every waking moment, he is *doing, doing, doing* and *learning, learning, learning.*" Like many other educators, Scott lamented that nature's method of freedom and activity was replaced by the confinement and restraint of the schoolroom. He called for self-development rather than

[4] NEA, *Proceedings, 1897,* 154-157; *1898,* 454-462; *1904,* 361-365.
[5] *Rhode Island Schoolmaster,* III, 176, August 1857. Italics in the original.
[6] NEA, *Proceedings, 1877,* 219-220.

the acquisition of facts and emphasized nature study, the use of plants, rocks, soil, animals, and insects.[7]

In 1898 C. C. Thach of Auburn Polytechnic Institute reported that students who entered college were illiterate. "Ungrammatical expressions, faulty spelling, defective or vicious taste that characterize the pupil at this age will generally stick, like the shirt of Nessus, thru life." They could not translate Latin because they knew too little English. Their translation English was a language that never was on land or sea. The only hope which the professor saw was to use "more of the method of the gymnasium, of the studio, and of the laboratory; i.e., the method of learning to do a thing by doing it."[8]

Some educators believed in the principle of learning by doing, but feared that, if carried to its logical extreme, the doctrine would leave no place for teaching and guidance, for vicarious experience which is the short cut to learning. Superintendent John Hancock of Ohio, speaking at Topeka in 1886, endorsed the principle of learning by doing, but he regarded the method as subsidiary to vicarious learning. "First hand knowledge is very important, but mainly as a means of acquiring second hand knowledge."[9]

In 1885 the Reverend A. D. Mayo, orator, educator, traveling missioner, and preacher, delivered a long, critical speech at Saratoga Springs on the subject of learning by doing. He cited the self-made man who achieved a commendable success in the pine woods of Florida by practicing the precept of learning by doing, but had he known what other people had done, had he appropriated their achievements, he would have saved time and made greater progress. The adage of wise old Comenius, "We learn to do by doing," did not mean, Mayo said, that we learn only or even chiefly by doing, but that doing is the completion of learning, the evidence that it is a success.[10]

At the convention of 1887 Nathan C. Schaeffer of Pennsylvania gave an extensive paper on the maxim "We Learn To Do by Doing." He insisted that one does not learn to do by every kind of doing; neither does one learn one thing by doing another. He insisted that the doing must be guided by an intelligent will. There is a distinction between a science which must be learned in advance and an art which is acquired only by practice. The doing is necessary, but it must be enriched and guided by knowledge, or else man is no better off than creatures that are guided wholly by instinct.[11]

[7] NEA, *Proceedings, 1894*, 191-195.
[8] NEA, *Proceedings*, 1898, 94-97.
[9] NEA, *Proceedings, 1886*, 274.
[10] NEA, *Proceedings, 1885*, 102-108.
[11] NEA, *Proceedings, 1887*, 374-380; *1888*, 195.

Those who believed in learning by doing applied the principle to the learning of words. Experience, they said, should precede or accompany the acquistion of a vocabulary. Pupils should learn words as they need them to designate objects, actions, and qualities. When words are used in advance of experience, they often become mere verbalisms. Teachers of every generation have noted instances of this gap between verbal learning and understood experiences. Torn between amusement and desperation, teachers have cited numerous examples of the bewildered pupil, lost in everglades of words. To such pupils words obscure rather than reveal realities; they are decoys to confusion rather than guideposts to understanding. One speaker cited the instance of a high-school girl who assumed that "a forced march" was a maneuver by which a general pushed his troops right through the enemy's army. A boy thought that the soldiers who "slept on their arms" leaned against their muskets as they snatched a nap.[12] The phrase "possession of the heights commanding Washington" was interpreted to mean "General Washington was in command." Another speaker provided other examples of verbalisms. "The class was reading the 'Old Oaken Bucket.' The lesson was completed in good order. Pronunciation, enunciation, position, modulation, quality of tone, all near standard. After the exercise was finished, the teacher with a gratified look requested me to ask the class some questions. I asked how many buckets were in the well. The reply came quickly from several that there were three—the old oaken bucket, the iron-bound bucket, and the moss-covered bucket."[13]

Perhaps the current status of the idea of learning by doing was foreshadowed by Dewey. His definition of learning as the reconstruction of experience involved the utilization of all past doing in learning any new fact, skill, pattern, or idea. Thus all experience becomes a treasury from which the learner draws words, ideas, and elements and reconstructs them according to the new pattern which a book or a speaker is presenting. Experience is the raw material which can be used for further and more complicated learning. The doing experience is indispensable, but in and by itself it is incomplete and uncompleted. Subsequent introspection, reconstruction, and modification of behavior are necessary in order to complete the learning process.

Learning by doing is another form of the old emphasis upon the necessity of sense experiences. One learns what he sees, hears, says, writes, reads, feels, imagines, draws, acts, plays, tastes, touches. In this sense *learns* really means the accumulation of experience. From this collection of accumulated experiences one can draw elements and recombine them into new patterns. Directly, one cannot learn a principle, a general-

[12] NEA, *Proceedings, 1880*, 206.
[13] NEA, *Proceedings, 1879*, 141.

ization, or an interpretation by doing, but without the accumulated elements of sense experiences one cannot understand or learn such abstractions.

Learning by doing was basically a reform in methods of teaching; it emphasized the learner—his needs, interests, abilities, and limitations—rather than the lesson, task, assignment, or subject. It helped to effect a reconciliation between the age-old dichotomy of the individual and society, between what one wants to do and what others say one must do. Learning by doing did not sacrifice the ultimate goal of social adaptability and social usefulness; it simply interposed a more successful and appealing method of leading the pupil, through his inclinations rather than by forced requirements, to a satisfactory adjustment. Thus under the new banner of learning by doing the old doctrine of the basic necessity of starting with sense experiences, as proclaimed by Comenius, Locke, Rousseau, Pestalozzi, E. A. Sheldon, Colonel Parker, and John Dewey, received renewed emphasis and widespread acceptance.

Object teaching, the kindergarten, and learning by doing were important elements in the slowly evolving progressive movement in education. Even more important in this movement, however, was the highly promoted child-study development of the 1890's. In 1885 G. Stanley Hall reviewed the studies of "the systematic observation of infants" and found a reasonable number of creditable efforts in Germany and America.[14] Organized societies, institutional sponsorship, and the involvement of teachers, however, began in the 1890's.

According to G. Stanley Hall the child-study movement in the United States started in the kindergartens of Boston in 1879.[15] In the early 1890's child-study societies were organized in a number of states. These were sponsored and promoted by parents as well as educators. Universities, colleges, normal schools, state departments of education, and a few school systems joined in the movement. The objective, scientific, disinterested observation of the child became popular and widespread. While specialists, such as G. Stanley Hall, Earl Barnes of Stanford, and Colonel Parker, provided the patterns and plans, studied the data, and wrote conclusions, many classroom teachers made the observations and supplied the detailed information. They compiled biographies of children; recorded thousands of miscellaneous facts; made measures of height, weight, and growth; collected drawings and compositions; and supplied other data.

A view of some of the details of child study is provided by the record of the Denver meeting of the NEA in 1895. From Iowa came the report that the society for child study was promoting investigations into ear-

[14] NEA, *Proceedings, 1885,* 506-511.
[15] NEA, *Proceedings, 1893,* 717.

and eye-mindedness to find which sense provided the better basis for learning to spell. Another study involved the testing of eyes and ears to ascertain the percentage of defective pupils. A third undertaking was to discover the relationship between height and weight and success in school studies. Tentative results indicated that good spellers were eye-minded, that defective vision increased alarmingly as pupils ascended the grades, and that a large physique was no indication of precocity. Child study had aroused the teachers to a greater interest in their pupils and to a closer observation of their individual characteristics. The discovery of deficiencies led teachers to reseat the pupils with reference to their sight and hearing. Above all, child study had made the teachers more sympathetic and enabled them to deal more successfully with "bad boys and girls."[16]

From New York, Indiana, Minnesota, and California came reports of a great variety of investigations and studies. Many were concerned with physical measurements, with testing the alertness of the senses and motor skills, and with pupil characteristics, attitudes, and ideas. One couple kept "a psychological diary" of their two-year-old child; a professor studied children's ideas of punishments, of heaven and hell, of property, and of fear; many normal-school students observed pupils to ascertain "their power and habit of attention, perception, apperception, imagination, memory, conception, reasoning, and volition." The curve of fatigue, the retention of foreign words, the effect of parents' occupations, and the manifestation of self-control and determination were studied by various professors. Children's sense of time, of money, of right and wrong, of justice, and of fair play; their interest in nature study, machinery, places, and persons; their tendency to imitate, to concentrate, to become angry, to persist, to construct; their attitudes toward music, poetry, stories, and animals; their preferences in play, toys, and studies—these and other topics and problems were studied by eager, enthusiastic advocates of the educative values of child study.

Conclusions of varying degrees of importance and certitude were reported. A class of country children showed marked preference for learning by ear and lost interest in a topic when asked to read about it. Other studies showed that eye-mindedness increased as children ascended the grades; girls were fatigued in handwriting sooner than boys; some practice in writing with the left hand speeded improvement with the right hand; movements of young children should be large and free because exercises requiring delicate coordination and close attention were injurious to young children; play is one of the greatest educative forces; bookish eye-minded education dulls the senses and produced premature

[16] NEA, *Proceedings*, 1895, 893-895.

fatigue; it is unnatural and injurious for children to remain inactive and quiet.[17]

Earlier reforms in education had lessened harshness and punishment; schools were becoming more pleasant and attractive. The child-study movement raised the child to a new dignity and importance; he had become a live specimen for scientific study. As a specimen, he was accorded the freedom of naturalness, for the observer did not want to pervert his findings. This objectivity and detachment were often transformed into personal interest and resulted in greater attention to individual instruction. The child, the individual child, became the center of the educational system.

The child-study movement was naturally enveloped in sentiment, and its early proponents made exaggerated claims of its values for teachers. In 1903 Superintendent F. E. Spaulding of Passaic presented an ironical summary of the progress of the movement. "A few years ago, when the child-study epidemic was at its height, the most noisy and enthusiastic heralds of this movement" ridiculed the whole teaching procedure as "based on habit, tradition, accident, and guesswork." According to Superintendent Spaulding the child-study experts provided directions for observing, measuring, and tabulating, while other authorities assured teachers that there was nothing in the child-study movement for them, even going so far as to declare that "psychology was not for teachers. . . . today the very name child study has become almost a reproach. But in reality, only the bubbling foam has burst and subsided; the underlying currents of the movement are stronger now than ever."[18]

Another speaker at the convention said that the child-study movement had shown teachers that their task was "to teach children—not studies, nor classes, nor averages, but individuals."[19]

Child study evoked a spate of books, articles, study guides, and reports. To provide a clearinghouse for developments in the field, some of the leaders organized the Department of Child Study of the NEA in 1894.[20] By 1906 a total of 135 speeches, papers, and reports had been presented at its sessions. In the following year a speaker summarized the major results of child study. While some of the findings have since been discarded, the spirit of the report is revealed by the speaker's key words and phrases—"importance of the larger muscles," "detection of physical defects," "health," "games," "play," "interest," "boys' societies," "emotional nature," and "social relations." The speaker concluded: "The old theo-

---

[17] *Ibid.*, 895-914.
[18] NEA, *Proceedings, 1903,* 762-763.
[19] *Ibid.*, 765-769.
[20] NEA, *Proceedings, 1894,* 995.

logical notion that children are conceived and born in sin is dying out and child study has hastened its coming extinction."[21]

The department enlisted the cooperation of a number of prominent persons, such as Leonard P. Ayres, Lewis M. Terman, Judge Ben B. Lindsey, and Henry H. Goddard. Interest shifted from general studies to those concerning health and mental welfare, and in 1911 the department changed its name to the Department of Mental Hygiene.[22] It is interesting to note that at the twenty-fifth anniversary meeting of the department in 1918, three of the original members were present and participated on the program—G. Stanley Hall, Earl Barnes, and William H. Burnham of Clark University.[23] In 1924 the department was merged with the Department of Physical and Health Education. The child-study movement was no longer identifiable as a general educational development. Its aims and purposes were taken over by clinics and institutes of child welfare, whose findings continued to influence educational practice.

By 1900 the necessary elements for a progressive movement seemed to be present. Educational knowledge was sufficient, the leaders were available, and the public seemed to be tolerant. The fact that the emergence of object teaching in the 1860's, the spread of the kindergarten in the 1870's, the acceptance of learning by doing in the 1880's, and the formal development of child study in the 1890's did not produce a general progressive movement until after the First World War is evidence of an educational lag. The delay was caused in part by the Herbartian movement, the beginnings of the scientific study of education, and the unpreparedness of teachers. In the meantime the NEA sponsored committees on curriculum revision, teachers' status, and the democratization of the association. Such progressive ideas as community study, group cooperation, and an integrated curriculum were widely proclaimed and accepted. While the organization of the Progressive Education Association in 1918 is sometimes regarded as the formal beginning of the progressive movement, its origins are found, as recounted above, in previous decades.

By its ingenious convention programs that involved a large percentage of the audience, by enlisting the cooperation of a great many laymen and parents, and by an energetic program of publication, the Progressive Education Association asserted and assumed leadership of the progressive movement. The association rediscovered the child and elevated him to a unique place, assigning him hitherto unrecognized qualities of independence, leadership, resourcefulness, energy, imagination, and ethical insight. This emphasis upon the child was the predominant theme of the first

[21] NEA, *Proceedings, 1907,* 910-914.
[22] NEA, *Proceedings, 1911,* 870.
[23] NEA, *Proceedings, 1918,* 323.

decade of the association.[24] The upsetting experiences of the depression years soon crowded the child into the background; the association was forced to recognize that the human environment was not then adjusted to nurture or sustain the progressively trained child. The implication was that society needed reformation; hence social reconstruction, planning, rebuilding, became the dominant theme of the progressives of the 1930's.

Educational progress owes a great debt to the numerous attempts to teach atypical children. Seguin's school for idiots, Binet's work with the insane, Alexander Graham Bell's concern for the deaf, and Braille's alphabet for the blind made their contributions to the instruction of normal children. Truants, delinquents, slow learners, gifted children—all kinds and classes have received the attention of educators. Binet, Montessori, and other experimenters tried to transfer the methods that were successful with deviates to the teaching of normal pupils. While the transfer was incomplete, some remarkable advances in teaching techniques have resulted from such attempts. By an open-minded consideration of children, all kinds of children, educators gained new insights and discovered new methods. The progressives were especially alert to the possible transfer values from experiments with atypical children.

Educational progress, particularly progressive education, owed an even greater debt to Charles W. Eliot, Colonel Francis W. Parker, John Dewey, William H. Kilpatrick, Harold Rugg, and numerous other leaders in the NEA. Educational reforms of two generations were blended by these leaders into the progressive movement. The movement expressed itself in meetings and publications of the NEA and NEA departments as well as in the organization specifically devoted to its promotion: the Progressive Education Association. Parents and teachers, philosophers and administrators, united to reconstruct the school and change the attitude of the community toward both the children and the school.

Progressive educators were defenders of children. They were tolerant and sympathetic. No child was a failure, even though a school or a teacher might so label him. Children were regarded as busy and tireless beings, seeking outlets for their energy through play and finding self-development through activities. They merited respect regardless of their talents and abilities. Progressives talked repeatedly and extensively about freedom, opportunity, initiative, creativeness, health, and growth. They stressed activities and the need for shops, kitchens, gardens, studios, gymnasiums, laboratories, and libraries. They wanted the teacher to be a guide rather than a taskmaster, an arbiter rather than a judge. They had scant respect for binding traditions, resented arbitrary standards, and

[24] Angelo Patri summarized progressive principles at Cleveland in 1920. NEA, *Proceedings, 1920,* 428-431. See also H. G. Good, *A History of American Education* (New York, 1956), 391-396.

believed that the pupil, under proper conditions, would develop good habits of study and sound codes of conduct.

Some progressive educators objected to a predetermined curriculum, but all of them were committed to selecting those topics and problems that had present rather than future utility. The word *functional* became a touchstone for testing the acceptability of curriculum content. Criticisms of outmoded topics, inert facts, and static lists were frequent. Harold Benjamin's *Saber-Tooth Curriculum*,[25] which appeared in 1939, was a hilarious account of teaching tiger-scaring long after the tigers had all disappeared. It was a devastating analysis of teaching materials that no longer functioned. In fact, the concept "functional" was immensely popular in various aspects of American life, being applied to art, architecture, house furnishings, and other areas.

Assuming the utility of a topic and the pupil's need and interest, the progressive teacher tried to reorganize it in such a way as to facilitate learning. Therefore problems, projects, units, field trips, committee reports, and a geat variety of activities were utilized. The curriculum and methods were reorganized and revised. The whole institution became a child-centered school.[26]

This curriculum formula was closely related to the social setting. The progressive teacher regarded curriculum-making as a threefold process, involving (1) the transmission of large portions of the social heritage, (2) the discarding of outmoded and harmful aspects of our heritage, and (3) the promotion of changes and improvements. The second step inevitably made social appraisers out of teachers, and the third implied planning, rebuilding, social reconstruction. This aspect of progressive education excited comment and provoked opposition. Many critics did not want any planning or reconstruction by any one or any class. For teachers, who were presumed to be the willing transmitters of existing culture, to participate in making significant changes was a radical departure from tradition that naturally stirred opposition.

During the 1930's the progressive movement, aided greatly by the Progressive Education Association, made some advances. A number of administrators and teachers accepted and put into practice many of its principles. A shocking reversal, however, was just ahead. Criticisms, ignorant and extreme, well-intended and malicious, local and national, inside and outside the profession, began to appear. Absurd and preposterous caricatures of progressive education became almost daily fare for readers of newspapers and magazines. Jokes and episodes, presumed to illustrate the extremes of progressive practices, were told and retold.

[25] Harold Benjamin, *Saber-Tooth Curriculum* (New York, 1939).
[26] Harold Rugg and Ann Schumaker, *The Child-Centered School* (New York, 1922).

The public soon acquired the picture of gangs of noisy, spoiled children, dawdling away school hours in frivolous activities, while an approving teacher acquiesed in the slightest whims of his willful wards. The critics industriously circulated the notion that the basic skills were neglected, that progressive practices caused juvenile delinquency, and prophesied that national illiteracy would overwhelm the nation in the next generation. They changed the schools from child-centered to critic-centered and created the assumption that whatever is, is wrong. To make these strictures sound plausible they asserted that progressive practices were widespread, rampant, and unrestrained. While pupils, teachers, and patrons of any particular school were keenly aware of the persistence of traditional practices and the slight extent of progressive reforms, they uncritically assumed that other schools had actually adopted the practices that had been so persistently ridiculed. Thus the nation was alerted to oppose and destroy what scarcely existed.

In the heated controversy over the value of progressive principles it was difficult to distinguish the thoughtful critic from the hostile opponent. Understanding the nature and intensity of the criticisms, many educators mistakenly assumed that they were directed solely against the progressive movement and added their professional criticisms to the popular outcries. The progressive-education movement suffered a crushing defeat and all educational innovations became suspect. In the face of what appeared to be popular demands, some teachers disclaimed progressive ideas and abandoned some of the newer practices. Yielding to the wave of hostility, the Progressive Education Association changed its name to the American Education Fellowship in 1944 and later, after resuming the name Progressive Education Association for a brief period, it disbanded.

In the meantime the attacks upon education continued, reaching a crest of violence during the wave of McCarthyism about 1953. Educators began to realize that the surrender of the outer ramparts of progressiveness had not satisfied the hostiles nor stilled querulous, faultfinding voices. They realized that they had to defend freedom for progressive education whether they approved or opposed it professionally. Just as freedom of speech enables the foolish to say foolish things, so educational freedom enables a teacher to run ahead or lag behind modal practices. Professional freedom for teachers, with whatever risks are involved, is the price of educational progress.

Educators were ready to defend educational progress; many were ready to defend progressive practices. The NEA through its various agencies, especially its Commission on the Defense of Democracy Through Education, provided the facts, answered criticisms, and exposed some self-seeking individuals and tax-conscious organizations. Educators united in defending school boards, administrators, and teachers and called vigorously for a spirit of good will and for a better understanding of education.

The critics won a kind of victory. A few conscientious professional educators, publicity-seeking writers, academics who had strayed beyond their competence, enemies of public education, and organizations nourished by discontent achieved the downfall of progressive education as an organized movement. With all their animus and influence, however, they could not resubjugate children, repeal the laws of learning, destroy projects, problems, and units, reinstate arid drills, reimpose fruitless tasks, push teachers back into subserviency, restore the so-called liberal education, or convince any one, child or adult, of the all-sufficiency of the three R's; they could not reverse time or restore the past. The progressive gains of a century could not be destroyed. Pestalozzi, Sheldon, Froebel, Parker, Dewey, and a host of educational reformers still live.

PART IV

Lost Causes

18

The National-University Movement

Presiдent Charles W. Eliot of Harvard University was quite aroused; he accused, insinuated, criticized, and ridiculed. The members of the National Educational Association, assembled in the Elmira City Hall on the afternoon of August 5, 1873, had no difficulty in following his arguments. He lambasted the NEA Committee on the National University, shredded the bills to establish a national university which were then before Congress, and proclaimed the evils of government support of higher education.[1]

In criticizing the committee on the national university, which had been appointed at Trenton in 1869, Eliot was particularly severe upon its chairman, John W. Hoyt. In spite of the fact that the committee had, according to Eliot, done "nothing whatsoever during the year," its chairman, presuming to speak for the committee, had made a glowing and colorful report about a nebulous university to the association at Cleveland. And in 1871 Hoyt had made another report at St. Louis and had secured the appointment of a permanent committee of fifteen. Eliot charged that only nine of the members had assembled for a hasty meeting at St. Louis, that others had been appointed without their knowledge or consent, and that since this permanent committee had never been organized, it had no authority to speak in the name of the association. "I congratulate the association that it is thus far free from all responsibility for whatever may have been done since August, 1871, about a national university."[2]

Turning to the bills before Congress, Eliot found fault with many of their provisions. The Howe Bill failed to guard against political appointments and opened the door to a national-university ring to match the agricultural-college ring and other pressure groups. The provisions for admission to the proposed university were absurdly vague; the system of student fees was quite un-American; and the proposed model farm in the

[1] NEA, *Proceedings, 1873,* 107-131.
[2] *Ibid.,* 109.

agricultural school would be a sheer waste of funds. The Sawyer Bill proposed that the university be governed by a board of fifty-five regents, a council of seventeen educators, and an assembly of faculties. Such an arrangement was expensive and cumbersome. Eliot surmised that neither senator had introduced his bill with the faintest expectation that it would ever become law. In fact, the whole procedure, according to him, was "comical," "loose, crude, hasty, undignified and unworthy of the subject."[3]

Turning to the principle of government support of higher education, Eliot found no more justification for establishing a national university than for establishing a national church. The notion that a beneficent government should provide such an institution rests upon the theory of divine right. The habit of relying upon the government to provide even good products, such as churches, universities, and railroads, is a most insidious evil. The "essence of republicanism is self-reliance."[4] Education, whether primary or university, cannot guarantee the continuance of republican institutions. The only security is the development of traditions and habits through the practice of self-control.

The speaker saw no reason why a university, supported by the Federal government and located at the capital, would be any more national than any other American university. He characterized the hankering for a big national university as "childish." "There is an attractive comprehensiveness and a suggestion of public spirit and love of country in the term 'national,'" but the adjective actually narrows and belittles the noble conception associated with the word "university." "Letters, science, art, philosophy, medicine, law and theology are larger and more enduring than nations."[5] Just for good measure Eliot threw in the assertion that the climate of Washington was not healthy, and that Congress and its hangers-on did not make the city a better place for young men in the formative stage of life.

The Department of Higher Education of the NEA, to which Eliot addressed his remarks, was teeming with men who could and who did answer his arguments, point by point. In fact, the debate continued for years. The proposal which the delegates at Elmira debated with such fervor had had a long history.[6] In January 1787, preceding the meeting of the Constitutional Convention, Dr. Benjamin Rush published his "Address to the People of the United States," in which he proposed a Federal university that would accept only college graduates. He thus

[3] *Ibid.*, 117.
[4] *Ibid.*, 118.
[5] *Ibid.*, 119.
[6] The following summary of the early evolution of the national-university idea is drawn in part from Edgar B. Wesley, *Proposed: The University of the United States* (Minneapolis, 1936).

visualized an institution of a high level, and most subsequent advocates of the idea took an equally elevated view of its nature. In the Constitutional Convention, Charles Pinckney and James Madison asked that the establishment of a national university be listed among the powers delegated to Congress. Gouverneur Morris argued that such a provision was unnecessary in view of the exclusive jurisdiction which Congress would have over the Federal district. Morris' explanation prevailed and the power to establish a university was not stated in the Constitution, but no one is on record as opposing the university or as questioning the power of Congress to establish it.

George Washington was an ardent advocate of the national university, mentioning it in several letters, recommending its establishment in his first address to Congress in 1790 and in his last in 1796. The crowning proof of Washington's interest in the national university was his bequest in his last will and testament of July 9, 1799, of fifty shares of the Potomac River Company for the purpose of helping to establish such a university. What became of these shares is an unsolved mystery, but the fact is definitely established that the treasury never received either the shares or any money arising therefrom. The failure of the bequest to eventuate in money, however, in no wise changes the fact of Washington's sincere interest in the university, nor does it lessen the nobility of his generosity.

President Jefferson twice recommended the university to Congress, and Madison made three such requests. Monroe seems to have had doubts about the power of Congress to establish a university, but John Quincy Adams had no such doubts and recommended its establishment to Congress in 1825. In addition to these presidential efforts there were numerous bills, committee reports, hearings, memorials, petitions, proposed amendments, and speeches. While the cause was never even in sight of fulfillment, it at least manifested the vitality of survival.

After the Civil War the national-university movement was ready for a hero, one who could clarify its purpose, broaden its appeal, and enlist popular support. The man who most nearly fulfilled these conditions was John Wesley Hoyt, lawyer, doctor, professor, editor, agriculturist, territorial governor, university president, and commissioner of educational exhibits at Paris and Vienna.[7]

As United States commissioner to the Paris Exposition of 1867, Hoyt visited the major universities of Europe. From these experiences he developed the idea of a national university that would operate on a high plane of research, instruction, and public service. This idea he elaborated into a specific proposal which he presented to the National

---

[7] "John Wesley Hoyt," *Dictionary of American Biography;* scattered items from Hoyt's *Memorial,* and from his speeches in NTA and NEA, *Proceedings, passim.*

Teachers' Association at Trenton in 1869. The association endorsed his proposal and appointed him chairman of successive committees. It was this series of resolutions and reports that President Eliot criticized so severely at Elmira in 1873.

The immediate replies to Eliot were the beginning of a debate which was removed at Detroit in the following year. In fact, the 1874 meeting was dominated by this debate. Three major addresses and several impromptu speeches were devoted to the national university and the related issue of governmental aid to education. So spirited and forthright were the utterances that they subsequently led Governor Cushman K. Davis of Minnesota to observe that a reading of the proceedings at Detroit had convinced him that the National Educational Association was not "a mutual admiration society."[8]

Hoyt was entitled to make a major reply, because he had been singled out for severe, almost slanderous, criticism and because he was not present when the indictment against him was delivered at Elmira. In the interval he had prepared a detailed refutation, and it appears that the passing of months had not lessened his resentment.

In his reply Hoyt patiently reviewed the actions of the association and of the committees on the national university declaring that the report of his committee reflected the combined judgment of a number of persons. Eliot was, according to Hoyt, guilty of "gross injustice" in his criticisms of the association, the committee, and the chairman. His charge of haste in presenting the bill to Congress was "so absurd as to seem like irony." Hoyt's use of such words and phrases as "unfairness," "legedemain," "unqualified misstatements," "garbled extract," "quirk of logic," "semblance of an argument," "misrepresentations," and "sophistry" indicate both the fullness and spirit with which he answered Eliot's report.

In addition to defending the association and the committee against Eliot's criticisms, Hoyt advanced many explanations and arguments. Perhaps the most significant point was his proposal that the national university become a kind of accrediting and standardizing agency. According to his plan the university would admit only those who had already obtained a college degree from a "recognized" college. In determining the quality of the college from which an applicant had graduated, the university would necessarily make inquiries concerning programs and standards, thus becoming "a potent means for the elevation and coordination of all our schools and colleges."[9] This proposal for an accrediting agency is significant, partly because it antedates by more than a quarter of a century the actual beginnings of this important function.

At the same 1874 meeting, Andrew D. White, president of Cornell

---

[8] NEA, *Proceedings, 1875,* 2.
[9] NEA, *Proceedings, 1874,* 178.

University, with no personal dispute to settle, dealt vigorously and clearly with the basic issues of higher education.[10] White said that we have drawn an utterly illogical line between secondary and higher education. Below this line both the state and the nation have shown a deep concern, and our schools have flourished in the deep, rich soil of popular needs and feelings. Above this line we have turned education over to scattered sects; nourished in the wretchedly thin soil of sectarianism, our higher education has attained a miserably scanty growth. While primary education requires the diffusion of resources, advanced education requires the concentration of resources. This principle America has violated. Whereas England has four universities and Prussia eight, we have 360 so-called colleges and universities, which with few exceptions have inadequate faculties, impoverished equipment, and paralyzing sectarian control. The idea is sect growth and not indiivdual growth. Dull, unsuccessful preachers find asylums in the professorships of such colleges and go about the country denouncing science and taking up collections to perpetuate this mortifying system.

White declared that we have had sufficient experience. The present system has been tried for 250 years and has produced no laboratories, museums, art collections, or programs of advanced study such as abound in Germany. Private efforts under sectarian control have failed; only public civil action is equal to the occasion. The Morrill Act of 1862 was the first comprehensive effort, and the only school of natural science in America of first rank is the one at Cambridge, fostered by the state of Massachusetts. While supplementary gifts are commendable, the great danger is that education will be fettered by the dogmas and whimsies of living donors or dead testators.

White regarded the arguments against governmental aid to education as absurd. If private giving is so uplifting, why not let the state call on its citizens for donations with which to build the state capitol? If any building at all eventuated under such plan, it would resemble our educational system—a Roman tower here, a Gothic spire there; a Greek pediment here, a Renaissance cupola there; a Doric column here, a Corinthian column there. In accordance with the philosophy of private control, the donors might designate the occupancy and use of the building forever. Public support and sponsorship do not forestall private contributions; on the contrary, they encourage and guide such bequests. The concentration of the land-grant money upon Cornell University evoked gifts several times greater than the original sum. Look at the situation: a telescope in one place, an observatory at another; a geological collection in one college, a professor of geology in another; a herbarium in one institution, a professor of botany in another.

[10] *Ibid.*, 58-76.

White thought that our existing public-school system leads logically to an advanced institution. The system must be complete. We sponsor military training to preserve our national existence; with equal logic we should sponsor a national university. We are now engaged in industrial warfare with other nations; to win we must have technical education. To leave education for this warfare to the driblets which can be wheedled out of sectarian donors is to lose the race to more foresighted competitors. Our political interests as well as material welfare depend upon education. In general the men who have received advanced education have not yielded to corruption. The preliminary training which many have received has merely sharpened their claws and tusks; they have not reached the higher levels that provide ideals and standards from which they can regard corruption with the scorn that it deserves. President Barnard has shown the declining number of men of advanced education in public life. As this number has declined, corruption has increased. The relation is not mere concomitancy but cause and effect.

White concluded by pleading for the completion of the sound policy which had been started. Congress has granted land for primary and secondary schools, for state universities, and, in 1862, for colleges of science. Every state should strengthen these public institutions, for not one sectarian institution has been established beyond the original thirteen states that has even a third-rate library, laboratory, or observatory. Sectarianism has prevailed. It has driven a president from Harvard and a large number of professors from various colleges, and prevented many other competent men from securing positions.

White was interested primarily in establishing the principle that higher as well as lower education was the responsibility of government, both national and state. He was in favor of one or several national universities, whatever would most effectively provide a high quality of instruction that would meet the needs of a growing and expanding society.

The discussion of White's paper was extended and vigorous. Some speakers resented his criticisms of sects and his derogation of denominational colleges. Others did not like his comparison of states and standards. Other critics wandered back to Eliot's Elmira speech and hurled a few more condemnations upon his opposition to governmental support of higher education. The chairman read a letter from Eliot in which he disclaimed responsibility for all ideas except opposition to the national university.

Ignoring or forgetting the fact that a standing committee already existed, the association reaffirmed its endorsement of the national university and appointed a new committee of thirteen with Hoyt as chairman.[11] Other prominent members of the committee were A. D. White,

[11] *Ibid.*, 138-139.

John Hancock, W. T. Harris, Mark Hopkins, Joseph Henry, J. P. Wickersham, W. F. Phelps, and Zalmon Richards.

Following these vigorous evidences of the association's interest in the national university, it is a matter for surprise that no further action was taken for more than a quarter of a century, except the passing of a resolution in 1875 to extend the life of the committee,[12] and listening, in 1889, to a lone speech on the subject by William A. Mowry, superintendent of schools, Salem, Massachusetts.[13] Possible explanations for this period of quietude are multiple. It might have been due to Hoyt's desire to broaden the base of popular support; it might have been considered strategic to let other organizations carry the burden of promotion; it might have been sheer weariness or discouragement.

Even though the National Educational Association drifted into a period of inactivity, there was only a short lull in the efforts of others. Hoyt continued his campaign of making speeches and contacting other organizations. President Hayes recommended the university in his messages of 1877 and 1878, and bills to effect its establishment were introduced in Congress in 1886, 1888, 1890, three in 1893, 1849, six in 1895, three in 1897, 1899, and two in 1900.

At length the National Educational Association, through its National Council of Education, renewed its interest in the national university. The cause would have been better served in this instance had the association continued its neglect. In July 1898, the council moved to appoint a committee of fifteen to "investigate the entire subject of the establishment of a national university and report to the Council."[14] President William R. Harper of the University of Chicago was appointed chairman; other prominent members were Angell of Michigan, Butler of Columbia, Canfield of Ohio State, Draper of Illinois, James of Chicago, Eliot of Harvard, and two superintendents, Soldan of St. Louis and Maxwell of New York.

According to its critics the procedure of this committee was tortuous and its report disingenuous. Prior to the first meeting various members prepared reports on different aspects of the proposed plan for establishing a national university. At the first meeting, November 1899, the twelve members present unanimously agreed (1) that the Federal government should aid but not control education, (2) that no satisfactory bill for establishing a university had ever been presented to Congress, and (3) that there was no need of a governmental university at the nation's capital.[15] Having reached such conclusions, the committee should

[12] NEA, *Proceedings, 1875*, 95.
[13] NEA, *Proceedings, 1889*, 189-202
[14] NEA, *Proceedings, 1898*, 497.
[15] NEA, *Proceedings, 1901*, 461.

logically have made its report to the Charleston convention in July 1900, but only "personal" remarks were made at that meeting by Harper and Butler.[16] Their failure to report was made glaring by the fact that B. A. Hinsdale, in his summary of the educational developments of the year, quoted the conclusions of the Committee of Fifteen, which rejected a national university and favored a plan to coordinate research in government offices and bureaus.[17] Unguided and officially uninformed by the committee itself, the council could do nothing but extend the life of the committee.

During the following year the committee, having decided against a national university, addressed itself to the problem of making the educational facilities of Washington available to advanced scholars. Having thus decided the major issue assigned to it, it proceeded to decide, for and in the name of the council, upon a substitute for the national university. It discovered the fact that Congress had, by a joint resolution of April 12, 1892, opened specified departments and bureaus to scientific investigators who were enrolled in educational institutions located in Washington, and had, on March 3, 1901, extended this privilege to qualified individuals from the several states and territories.

To coordinate research and facilitate the work of investigators, some of the members of the Committee of Fifteen joined with others to incorporate, on May 17, 1901, the Washington Memorial Institution. While this new organization was nominally a memorial to George Washington and made a pretense of carrying out his plan, it was in reality a mere makeshift for the broad and lofty institution which he visioned. Having fomulated and to some extent sponsored a substitute for the university on which it was instructed to report, the committee was finally ready in July 1901 to make its report to the council.

The report[18] disposed of the national university in summary fashion and devoted most attention to the problem of the coordination of research in Washington through the newly formed Washington Memorial Institution. The resolutions presented for action by the council do not even mention the national university. The report was signed by eleven members; Professor James and President Angell refused to sign, and the other two members did not attend the meetings of the committee.

The council was annoyed and resentful. President James H. Baker of Colorado and John W. Hoyt, who arose from a sickbed to attend the meeting, delivered stinging criticisms of the committee's activities and methods of operating. They questioned the motive behind such actions as releasing news of the decision against a national university just at

[16] NEA, *Proceedings, 1900,* 303.
[17] *Ibid.,* 320.
[18] NEA, *Proceedings, 1901,* 457-467; discussion, 468-474.

the time when a bill was likely to receive favorable consideration in Congress.

When the report of the Committee of Fifteen came before the business session of the council, President Swain of Indiana moved that the council reaffirm its support of a national university. After considerable discussion the motion was carried by a vote of 22 to 4.[19] When the subject came before the general association, President R. H. Jesse of Missouri moved that the NEA reaffirm its endorsement of the national university, and the resolution was adopted in spite of a vigorous appeal by Nicholas Murray Butler of Columbia to have it tabled.

The performance of the Committee of Fifteen constitutes a strange variation from the NEA's support of the national university. In view of past actions and the final disposal of the report, there is no doubt that it was a surprise and a disappointment to most members. One can only speculate as to what influence or arguments transformed several supporters of the university into opponents. Was it the status and dignity of the presidents of leading universities who constituted the majority of the committee? Was it the hope of appearing as objectively minded scholars capable of changing their minds? Could it be that the arguments against the university were actually convincing, or that the Washington Memorial Institution was accepted as a workable plan that met in part the functions of the proposed university? Whatever may have been the factors that convinced or influenced the members of the committee, they did not persuade the general membership of the council and the association.

The fact is, however, that the Committee of Fifteen won a great popular victory in spite of the censorious votes by the council and the association. The report brought incipient opposition into active maturity, emboldened timid opponents to express themselves, and coalesced scattered factions. The period of indifference and inarticulate acquiescence was ended. Never again did the opposition to the national university lack tongue and space. Following the report of the committee, there was another period of dormancy in the efforts of the NEA toward establishing a national university. Subsequent attention to the question was neither spirited nor energetic.

In November 1906 the National Association of State Universities appointed a permanent committee to work toward the establishment of a graduate university which would unify and coordinate research in Washington and called upon the National Educational Association to appoint a similar committee. At the Los Angeles meeting in July 1907, the association reaffirmed its endorsement of the national university, authorized the appointment of a committee to join with that of the National Association of State Universities, and appropriated $500 for the expenses

[19] *Ibid.*, 355.

of the committee. President Benjamin Ide Wheeler of California, President James B. Angell of Michigan, and President Charles Van Hise of Wisconsin were appointed. These two committees held a joint session in Washington and prepared a bill which was introduced in both the House and Senate.[20]

A general session of the Chicago meeting of 1912 was devoted to the issue of a national university. Edmund James, president of the University of Illinois, led off with a thorough analysis of the question. In a free society education must inevitably be a national issue. A state cannot survive half-literate and half-illiterate. People, literate and illiterate, by the thousands migrate from area to area, carrying the blessings of their training or the curse of their ignorance into all sections of the country. The question whether education should be paid by the district, county, state, or nation is a mere matter of expediency. If certain sources of wealth can be tapped best by the national government, let that be done. The Federal government has done a great deal; let it do more. Wisely it began at the top; it established colleges—not high schools or elementary schools, but colleges. Let it complete the task by erecting at the very top a graduate university to teach and train and investigate and experiment.[21]

Three others spoke on the same subject. President Charles R. Van Hise of Wisconsin listed some of the bureaus and offices in Washington which could contribute to research, and explained their low yield of scientific results as being due to the lack of teaching and directing. He endorsed the bill sponsored by the National Association of State Universities and the NEA, and saw the chief function as the coordination of research and not the granting of degrees. James H. Baker, president of the University of Colorado, saw the national university as providing a bond of unity between democracy and higher education; by upholding profound scholarship, creative power, and broad sympathies, it would promote high ideals and help to establish high standards in our national life. William O. Thompson, president of Ohio State University, decried the emphasis upon practical results. "It is easier to visualize the beneficent effects of two blades of grass or a large yield of corn and cotton than the effects of a revision of the scientific hypothesis concerning molecules, atoms, or electrons."[22] In spite of the great stress put upon research in Washington, none of the four speakers even referred to the Washington Memorial Institution, indicating that the council and association were justified in rejecting the recommendation of the Committee of Fifteen which proposed this institution in 1901 as a substitute for a national university.

[20] NEA, *Proceedings, 1907*, 40, 46, 47, 49, 52.
[21] NEA, *Proceedings, 1912*, 201-210, 45.
[22] *Ibid.*, 226.

It seems somewhat strange that this impressive program with its four prominent speakers did not evoke any action by the association, not even the formal reaffirmation of the general endorsement of a national university which it had passed so often since the initial resolution at Trenton in 1869. In fact, one more speech, that made by Congressman Simeon D. Fess of Ohio at the New York meeting in 1916, marks the end of efforts by the NEA to establish a national university.[23] Congressman Fess reported that two successive committees of the House had unanimously endorsed the bill to establish a national university. Thus, when the prospects were probably the best in the whole history of the movement, the association suspended further efforts.

While a history of the whole university movement would involve an extensive account of scores of articles and speeches, bills and hearings, resolutions and debates, it does seem desirable to list a few specific facts about the movement. The frequency and dates of bills introduced in Congress up to 1900 were noted above. Similar bills were introduced in the following years: two in 1900, two in 1901, 1902, three in 1905, 1907, 1911, 1914, 1917, 1919, 1921, 1923, 1925, 1927, 1929, and 1933. Bills to establish some kind of national academy, school, or university were introduced in 1935, 1936, and 1953.

Whether the national-university movement is dead or just sleeping is a question which the prophet rather than the historian would have to answer at this time.

[23] NEA, *Proceedings, 1916,* 189-194. Routine endorsements of the national university were made in the resolutions of 1914 (NEA, *Bulletin,* III, 22, September 1914) and 1918 (*Proceedings,* 26). In 1917, $25 was appropriated for the committee on the national university (NEA, *Bulletin,* VI, 7, September 1917). This paltry sum seems to epitomize the low status to which the movement had sunk.

19

The Simplified-Spelling Movement

1. Beginers ar advised to drop the final e of hav, giv, and liv.
2. Then they can try the eleven words of the Philological Association: ar, catalog, definit, gard, giv, hav, infinit, liv, tho, thru, wisht.
3. For the stronger in the faith there ar the five new rules.

These called for such spellings as hed, helth, alfabet, shal, clif, lasht, imprest.

The Chicago Tribune was the first to make the plunge. On the second day of September in the year of our Lord one thousand eight hundred and seventy-nine, this great progresiv representativ paper of the Northwest apeard in amended speling thruout.

The Missouri Pres Asociation, meeting at Sedalia in May, unanimously past the following resolutions:

Hweraz the iregyularitiz ov Inglish orthografi ar a great obstacl tu the progres ov the pepl, and . . .[1]

These excerpts from the record of the meeting of the Speling-Reform Asosiation at Chautauqua in 1880 illustrate the kind of changes which it advocated. The "asosiation" was organized at Philadelphia in 1876, and in the following year it met at Baltimore in connection with the American Philological Association. In 1878 it met in the White Mountains with the American Institute of Instruction, and in 1879 and 1880 at Philadelphia and Chautauqua in connection with the NEA.

The record of the Philadelphia sessions of the Spelling Reform Association of 1879 was printed in modified letters, blurred with diacritical marks and thinned into shadowy lines, giving the page the appearance of a very ancient or an obscure foreign language. Only a person with steady, unblinking eyes and a persistent patience can decipher it, and even then he needs the help of a puzzle-solving instinct and the skill of a conjurer. The use of this strange modification of English was a tactical

[1] NEA, *Proceedings, 1880,* 258-259.

blunder on the part of the spelling reformers,[2] and the retreat to the milder more legible version of 1880, from which the excerpts quoted above were taken, was the concession of the impatient progressives to the inertia of human nature.

The spelling-reform movement antedated by many years the formation of the society at Philadelphia in 1876. In fact, the natural evolutionary changes which occur in the growth of all languages have often been hastened by lexicographers, philologists, and grammarians. The movement in America was influenced by the deviations from English usage accepted by Noah Webster, by the publication in England in 1848 of Alexander J. Ellis's A Plea for Phonetic Spelling, and by numerous proposed schemes for new alphabets and simpler spellings.[3] The modifications made by Edwin Leigh were adopted by the St. Louis school system in 1866. According to Superintendent W. T. Harris, Leigh's system shortened markedly the time required to teach a child to read.[4] At the Hartford meeting of 1874 the American Philological Association devoted major attention to spelling reform, and annual reports on its progress were made by Professor Francis A. March of Lafayette College. In 1878 a number of state teachers' associations passed resolutions approving phonetic or simplified spelling. Thus it had become a somewhat popular cause by 1879, when the NEA welcomed the spelling association to its Philadelphia meeting.

The Spelling Reform Association was the articulate spearhead of an aggressive movement. It sponsored charts, bulletins, and books and carried on a campaign to induce editors, corporations, and institutions to use the simpler forms of specified words. It sponsored a bill, introduced in Congress in 1880, authorizing the use of simplified spelling in government documents and in the schools of the District of Columbia. At the meeting in 1880 a speaker urged the founding of a journal, the support of lecturers, and the employment of a secretary by the association.

In 1881 the Speling Reform Asoshiashun (spelled in the various ways indicated) met at Atlanta in conjunction with the NEA. T. R. Vickroy of St. Louis, editor of the Fonetic Techer, made a plea for the official endorsement of the spelling-reform movement by the NEA. He observed

[2] NEA, Proceedings, 1879, 249-283.

[3] Zalmon Richards, first president of the NEA, claimed the honor of having been the original spelling reformer. As early as 1844 he devised a phonetic alphabet that enabled him to teach reading in one-fourth the time previously required. He declared that "fonetic speling wud reduce it tu one-sixteenth ov the time usuali recwired for this end." NEA, Proceedings, 1880, 262. In 1876 an extensive paper on orthoëpy was given by Professor W. C. Sawyer of Wisconsin and a briefer one on phonetics by the Reverend E. Jones of Liverpool, England. See NEA, Proceedings, 1876, 134-140, 140-141.

[4] Francis A. March, The Spelling Reform, Bureau of Education, Circular of Information, No. 8, 1893, 7-8.

that the process of changes in language was going on constantly. He cited the 135 changes in spelling which had been made in the first chapter of Genesis between 1611 and 1879. He decried the needless labor and time involved in learning illogical spellings which often induced erroneous pronunciations. He quoted W. T. Harris as having said that consulting the dictionary for spelling and pronunciation had cost him five years of precious time. Vickroy predicted that the forthcoming phonetic edition of the New Testament (on which he was working) would provide a simple guide to pronounciation. "The new spelling will make readers. The time that is wasted in learning the merest *forms* can be concentrated upon learning the *substance*."[5]

Following the joint meeting in Atlanta in 1881, the NEA demonstrated no active interest in spelling reform for several years. In 1890 H. W. Brewster, on behalf of the Minnesota State Teachers' Association, presented a long, vigorous resolution at the St. Paul meeting, calling upon the NEA to approve the labors of the Spelling Reform Association; to appoint a committee of three to secure approval of the bill then pending in the House of Representatives, authorizing the use of simplified spelling in government documents; and to correspond with the spelling association respecting a dictionary of amended orthography.[6] The committee made its report at the Toronto meeting of 1891. It reviewed the spelling-reform movement, restated some of the arguments, invoked the weight of great names, praised the English language, and declared that the adoption of a phonetic alphabet would save the child two years of school time, would shorten written forms by 22 per cent and reduce the cost of books accordingly, and would give the English language a dominant prestige throughout the world.

In the discussion of this report H. H. Lincoln of Massachusetts said that he had been an advocate of reformed spelling as long ago as 1840. "I was called in those days a fanatic, while I was simply phonetic." Zalmon Richards recalled the speech which he had made to the NEA at Buffalo in 1860, advocating an amended and simplified alphabet. In fact, it was the first instance of the interest of the NEA in the simplification of language.[7]

Following the discussion of simplified spelling at Toronto in 1891, the NEA lapsed into inactivity. Then, in February 1897, the Department of Superintendence adopted a resolution to use simplified spellings in its record.[8] At its meeting in Chattanooga in February 1898, the department appointed a committee of five on spelling reform.[9]

[5] NEA, *Proceedings, 1881*, 88-93, 271-279.
[6] NEA, *Proceedings, 1890*, 38.
[7] NEA, *Proceedings, 1891*, 148-161.
[8] NEA, *Proceedings, 1897*, 196-197.
[9] NEA, *Proceedings, 1898*, 305-308.

These steps were overshadowed in importance by an action of the board of directors of the NEA at the summer meeting of 1898. After approving the wishes of the superintendents to use some simplified forms, the board then ordered the secretary by a vote of 18 to 17 to use henceforth the simplified spelling of the following twelve words in NEA publications, namely, *program, tho, altho, thoro, thorofare, thru, thruout, catalog, prolog, decalog, demagog,* and *pedagog.*[10] In the following year the resolution was amended to allow any author who so requested it to have his article printed with the standard spelling.[11]

In the spelling-reform movement three men stand out as aggressive proponents of a phonetic alphabet and amended spelling. Earliest in prominence was Professor Francis A. March of Lafayette College, who was president of the Spelling Reform Association in 1879. In 1881 he prepared a bulletin for the Bureau of Education, which was greatly expanded as *The Spelling Reform Circular No. 8, 1893.* It summarized the history of the movement and provided an extensive glossary of simplified words, thus serving as a sort of officially sponsored guide. March was hailed as "the Nestor, the Ulysses, and the Achilles"[12] of the movement and ridiculed as "that March hare from Lafayette."[13]

T. R. Vickroy of St. Louis edited the *Fonetic Teacher,* made fervent speeches, served on committees, and became the principal spokesman of the reform association in the central states. He was its secretary for a few years.

The third leader was E. O. Vaile of Oak Park, Illinois, editor of *Intelligence* and *The Week's Current.* For more than twenty years he used the minimum spelling list in his magazines and worked energetically for the appointment of committees and the promotion of the whole cause. He it was who provided the NEA with its original list of minimum revisions.[14] He was greatly interested in securing the adoption of a standard key of pronunciation and devoted several years to the undertaking.

Many others, besides these three, worked for spelling reform, but most of the educators were only mildly committed to the cause. Melvil Dewey, Zalmon Richards, J. M. Gregory, William H. Wells, F. A. P. Barnard, F. Louis Soldan, and W. T. Harris were a few of those who favored spelling reform. Harris, however, saw it as a general, not an educational, issue, and objected to the NEA taking any aggressive leadership in promoting language reform.

The opposition had a few spokesmen, such as John MacDonald of Topeka, editor of the *Western School Journal,* and Slosson Thompson of

[10] *Ibid.,* 37.
[11] NEA, *Proceedings, 1899,* 43.
[12] NEA, *Proceedings, 1902,* 130.
[13] NEA, *Proceedings, 1901,* 219.
[14] *Ibid.,* 223.

the Chicago *Times-Herald*. In general, however, the opposition needed no leadership, for custom and social inertia were on their side. Most adults, having struggled through the complications of spelling and learning to read, looked with no fervent sympathy toward the children who faced the same task. The success or failure of spelling reform was thus to be determined, not by active opposition, but by sheer indifference tinged with mild amusement.

The fullest, frankest, and most extensive discussion of spelling reform recorded in NEA publications took place in 1901 before the Department of Superintendence. E. O. Vaile prepared an elaborate resolution calling upon the department to support a request for an annual grant of $1000 from the NEA for five years in order to promote the spelling-reform "movement along moderate, reasonable, and practical lines." He had secured the consent of an impressive list of persons to serve as the supervising commission, not one of whom was a "zealot or even an enthusiast" in the cause. These twenty proposed members included William R. Harper, president of the University of Chicago; John Dewey, professor of pedagogy, and Ella F. Young, assistant professor of pedagogy, University of Chicago; Francis W. Parker, president of Chicago Institute; Melvil Dewey, librarian; Henry Holt, publisher; Thomas Wentworth Higginson, author; and the superintendents of the schools of Chicago, Cleveland, Cincinnati, Minneapolis, Philadelphia, and Boston.

Vaile took great pains to assure the audience that the proposed commission would proceed cautiously and judiciously. He wanted a "bureau of light and publicity," a moderate but authoritative voice that would inspire confidence. The very existence of such a commission would be a potent influence for reform and "would save the cause from its unwise friends." The supporters of the cause were scattered and unknown to one another; they needed the leadership of such a group of prominent educators as he had enlisted. The NEA had a fund of nearly $90,000; in what way could they more wisely spend a portion of it than by supporting the great cause of simplifying the task of children?

Then the opponents spoke. John MacDonald, editor of the *Western School Journal*, opened the rebuttal. "We read that in the beginning it was said 'Let there be light and there was light.' A few of the brethren met in Washington in 1898 and said, 'Let there be orthography' and there was orthography . . . eighteen men undertook to say to 150,000,000 people how they should spell twelve English words. . . . What effect has it had upon 76,000,000 of people in the United States? What effect upon the American press? . . . the reform is supported by two or three educational journals. Our reforming brethren might say to the people . . . 'We have piped unto you, but ye have not danced' . . . there is no demand for a reform of this kind. I am opposed to depredations on the English language and hope the depredators . . . may soon be 'clothed and in their right minds.' "

Principal E. B. Prettyman of Maryland: "Every time I have seen any of the twelve amended spellings in educational journals I have been greatly annoyed."[15]

Then came the long and spirited arraignment of Slosson Thompson of the Chicago *Times-Herald:*

> . . . the orthography of the English language needs no defense. It stands . . . glorious and unapproachable in its incongruity, matchless in the potency and picturesqueness of its irregularities. I revere it for its unmastered difficulties, its verbal snares and pitfalls, its inexplicable spelling, and its sweet unreasonableness. . . . English is not a perfect language. Heaven preserve it from the canker of perfection. The perfect languages are all dead. Regularity and reforms killed them. . . . But when the spelling reformers ask a representative body like this to expend $5,000 upon an undertaking to which the knight-errantry of Don Quixote was sanity, it is time the common-sense of the English-speaking multitude was heard in protest. . . . I would be the last man to rob Mr. Vaile of his rattle. Let him play with it. But when he asks a body of men devoted to teaching the English language to appropriate money to introduce scientific confusion of tongues into their teaching I submit that he is trespassing on hallowed grounds.[16]

Superintendent Charles R. Skinner of Albany, New York, was one of the seventeen directors of the NEA who had previously voted against the use of the revised spelling in the *Proceedings.* "I am still opposed to it . . . it would take 25,000 years to bring about the assimilation of the twelve amended spellings into our language."

William T. Harris, a speaker at nearly every NEA convention from 1870 to 1908, expressed himself on this occasion also. He said that from 1850 to the Civil War he had had hopes of the acceptance of a reformed alphabet each letter of which would represent only one sound, but he soon saw how difficult it was to change Anglo-Saxons whose genius is compromise rather than logic. He had favored the use of the twelve revised spellings, but he wanted nothing said about the change. He lamented Secretary Shepard's press release on the matter because he knew that the news would provoke opposition. "But we must not forget, any of us, that this is a National Educational Association, and that spelling reform, or temperance reform, or religious reform, or moral reform is not the special object of this association." He thought that the movement was "ill-timed and worse than useless" and regretted the initial step of two years ago since it was going to provoke ever-recurring discussions. He opposed Vaile's resolution and warned that its adoption

[15] *Ibid.*, 215.
[16] *Ibid.*, 216-220.

would divide the members into two opposing camps.[17]

Vaile closed the debate by forcing Editor Thompson to admit that Tennyson, Darwin, Howells, Eggleston, Brander Matthews, and other spelling reformers were also masters of English. Vaile then turned rather savagely on Harris and accused him of "misusing public funds" by publishing as United States commissioner of education a pamphlet on simplified spelling if such was not an educational matter. Vaile renewed his plea for the adoption of the resolution calling upon the NEA for the appropriation of $5,000 to promote the cause of simplified spelling for the sake of generations of school children. By a vote of 105 to 77 the resolution was postponed indefinitely.[18]

At the same convention in Detroit in 1901 a petition, signed by about thirty educators, called upon the board of directors to authorize the organization of a Department of Simplified Spelling. After some discussion the motion to create the department was laid on the table for a year.[19] In fact, the year was prolonged to this day.

Between 1901 and 1906 the spelling issue only simmered and the official flame under it burned low. The reform had started outside the NEA and the proclaimed protagonist of the cause was the Spelling Reform Association. Because of the presumed value for the pupil and time saved for the teacher, educators felt obligated, however, to approve and promote the cause in a restrained and dignified manner. During this period a request from teachers' associations in the Midwest led to the appointment of a committee in the Department of Superintendence. The reports of this committee won strong support in various quarters and the superintendents favored a permanent committee on simplified spelling by a vote of 1545 to 171. This apparent progress toward victory somehow failed to promote the cause. The complexities of procedures within the NEA might be blamed or the defeat might be explained in terms of the excessive caution of the educators with respect to giving formal approval and expending money in behalf of a movement which in real or imagined ways might be a threat to their conservative values.

Chancellor E. Benjamin Andrews of the University of Nebraska, a supporter of spelling reform, spoke to the superintendents at Louisville early in 1906 and touched on the nature of the problems to be faced. He said that progress was hindered by impatient demands for immediate emancipation from old practices. "Crudities in spelling must be laid aside a few at a time." If all crooked spelling was straightened out today, the devil of bad spelling would not be conquered; for the sounds of words, being liquid, tend to change, whereas the written forms tend

[17] *Ibid.*, 221-224.
[18] *Ibid.*, 224-227, 189.
[19] *Ibid.*, 36.

toward fixity. Slowness of progress is the only assurance of permanence, for it cannot be hastened by edict or stopped by jest. Just as the *k* has been dropped from *music* and *almanac,* so eventually other changes can be made. The influence of the NEA has greatly aided the spread of its minimum glossary of simplified spellings. In order to illustrate the folly of adhering to traditional practices, he quoted Sam Walter Foss's poem "The Calf-Path," a few lines of which are as follows:

> One day thru the primeval wood
> A calf walked home, as good calves should.
> But made a trail all bent askew,
> A crooked trail, as all calves do.
>
> This crooked lane became a road.
> The road became a village street.
> And men two centuries and a half
> Trod in the footsteps of that calf.
> A hundred thousand men were led
> By one calf near three centuries dead.
> For thus such reverence is lent
> To well-established precedent.
> For men are prone to go it blind
> Along the calf-paths of the mind.[20]

From 1901 to 1906 the indefatigable E. O. Vaile did not cease his efforts to secure the endorsement of a large national commission on simplified spelling and a grant of funds by the NEA. Each request contained the proviso than any sum granted would be matched by outside contributions; so it appears that Vaile hoped all along for some subsidy from outside sources. Nevertheless, it must have been annoying to run the maze of departments, boards, and councils that he encountered, and he must have been more than relieved when Andrew Carnegie agreed in 1906 to finance a national Spelling Reform Board. In view of the fact that the board grew out of his efforts before the NEA, Vaile was disposed to regard it as essentially a creation of the educators, even though financial support had come from an outside source.[21] Professor Brander Matthews of Columbia University became the temporary chairman of the spelling board and C. P. G. Scott its secretary. It enrolled distinguished persons in both England and the United States and proceeded to give dignity and importance to the movement. It issued a word list of 300 simplified spellings and set up agencies for further study and research.

Unfortunately for the eventual good of the cause, Matthews enlisted

[20] NEA, *Proceedings, 1906,* 148-153.
[21] NEA, *Proceedings, 1907,* 32. Vaile was emphatic that the Spelling Reform Board was "directly due to discussions and actions" of the NEA.

the aid and intended support of President Theodore Roosevelt, who forthwith ordered the public printer to use some of the revised spellings in certain designated government documents. This order aroused the punsters, latent opposers, and columnists, who proceeded to inform millions of people who had hitherto been unaware of the movement and of what Roosevelt had done. The issue simmered or seethed, depending upon personal reactions, until Congress met in the fall. Unimpressed by the arguments of the reformers and resentful of presidential power, Congress came to the rescue of traditional practices, and inserted provisos in various bills, specifying that the records should be printed with standardized spellings. Roosevelt retreated and left the movement to bear the opprobrium which he had aroused.[22]

While it is by no means certain that 1906 marked the high point of spelling reform, it is quite clear that subsequent to that date interest within the NEA became less vocal and that official endorsements became even more cautious. In fact, in the next year the spelling-reform movement actually moved in reverse.

When the new board of directors of the NEA assembled in Los Angeles in July 1907, Director John MacDonald, foe of reformed spelling, moved that the NEA return to the conventional spelling of *thorough, through,* and *though.* Nine years had passed since the simpler forms had been adopted, and they had, according to MacDonald, been spurned, ridiculed, and rejected. By a vote of 12 to 8, with thirteen directors not voting, the resolution was carried. MacDonald lost no time in passing information concerning this action on to the newspapers. On the following morning the spelling reformers were chagrined to learn of the retreat within their own household, and E. O. Vaile denounced the action of the board as "not only a defiance of fair play but in defiance of the well-known sentiment of a large majority of our members."[23]

In fact, the very day on which the retreat by the board of directors was announced, the association as a whole took an advanced step. The resolutions committee included not only a general blessing of the Simplified Spelling Board and its recommended list of 300 preferred spellings but also a proposed order for their use in future publications of the NEA. Director James M. Greenwood opposed that part of the resolution which directed the secretary to use the revisions in NEA publications, declaring that the board and not the association was empowered to make rulings on administrative matters.

This objection brought E. O. Vaile, fiery defender of simplified spelling, to his feet. He asserted that the order to the secretary requiring the use

[22] For information about Roosevelt and the spelling debacle, see Mark Sullivan, *Our Times* (New York, 1927), III, 163-164, 173-176, 184-190.

[23] NEA, *Proceedings, 1907,* 52, 32.

of the prescribed list was the vital point of the resolution and that it was not an administrative question. To defeat this resolution would bring discredit and ridicule upon the association. The NEA had sponsored the great national spelling board, even though it had been financed by an outside philanthropist. More than one hundred periodicals were using the twelve simpler forms, and now the whole movement was threatened in the house of its friends. The parliamentary issue was simply the question of whether a board of directors could countermand the will of the whole association. "You are the supreme court to settle this question."

Greenwood too was stubborn. "Now, if this mass meeting is to pass on matters of this kind, we could include 1,200 words just as well as 300. The point I make is, that it is the Board of Directors which should direct. . . . I want my objection to go on record, because this is a legal question."

A Miss Shirley supported the resolution. "If this reform spelling was good last year, it is good this year. I know of no higher tribunal than the teachers themselves. If our directors do not do as we wish, we will depose them and not be run by a clique."

The vote was taken. The resolution directing the use of the 300 simplified versions was carried, 209 to 23. The record of this meeting shows rather clearly by its footnotes and interpolations that Secretary Shepard was opposed to the motion and that he was recording evidence that would justify his refusal to follow the instructions. Thus it happened that the one apparently unequivocal resolution by the NEA endorsing the spelling-reform movement was nullified by the controversy over jurisdiction.[24]

At the Cleveland meeting in the following year (1908) a member reported that the secretary of the association did not feel bound by the resolution passed at the preceding meeting. In order to settle the matter the speaker "Resolved: That the Secretary is hereby directed to use in the publications of this Association the simplified spellings recommended by the Simplified Spelling Board in its circular of March 21, 1906."

"It was moved, seconded, and carried, that the resolution be laid on the table."[25]

In 1909 the Simplified Spelling Board appointed a committee of three to promote greater use of revised spelling in normal schools and invited the cooperation of the Department of Normal Schools of the NEA. Since the board had chosen three normal-school presidents to constitute the committee of three—Homer H. Seerley of Cedar Falls, David Felmly of Normal, Illinois, and Charles McKenny of the Milwaukee Normal School—it was easy for the Normal Department to assent to the proposed

24 *Ibid.*, 30-34.
25 NEA, *Proceedings, 1908,* 39.

cooperation and to regard the group as also a committee of the department.[26]

The committee made enthusiastic and optimistic reports to the department, blessing the work of the Simplified Spelling Board as "the greatest endeavor of the kind that civilization has seen." But in the matter of obtaining further NEA support for revised spellings, this committee's efforts met the usual fate. The completeness of its failure can be guessed by the fact that in the summer of 1921 the NEA withdrew its endorsement of the Simplified Spelling Board.

Like many other movements, spelling reform was neither simple nor unified. And like many other causes, it enlisted not only the NEA and at least four of its subdivisions but also numerous state associations and a few learned societies. One aspect of language reform that enlisted early and vigorous support was the attempt to standardize the keys to pronunciation. At the Cincinnati meeting of the Department of Superintendence in February 1903, E. O. Vaile introduced a resolution calling for the appointment of a committee of five to cooperate with similar committees from the Modern Language Association and the American Philological Association "to consider the need and possibility of a universal system of key notation for indicating pronunciation" and "a simple, practical phonetic alphabet." The motion also called for the appropriation of $100 toward the expenses of the joint committee. The motion carried and Vaile found himself chairman of a new committee.[27]

At the Milwaukee meeting of the superintendents in February 1905, Vaile reported that his joint committee had prepared a complete alphabet of forty-two letters, based upon the work of a committee of 1877. He asserted that the recommended plan was "a rational and scientific substitute for our present cumbersome and complicated system of diacritics." Professor Calvin Thomas of Columbia University and George Hempl of Michigan had prepared the report, which was ready for distribution to those present. Vaile urged all to give it an open mind and a receptive reading.[28]

The committee to prepare a standardized key to pronunciation, appointed in 1903, made its final report to the superintendents at Mobile in 1911. In the meantime it had submitted interim reports,[29] had publicized the new alphabet, and had argued the issues in the press and on platforms. Although the final report did not carry the endorsement of the two cooperating bodies, the Modern Language Association and the American Philological Association, it had the approval of experts and

[26] *Ibid.*, 548.
[27] NEA, *Proceedings, 1903*, 140-141; *1904*, 39, 175-176, 339. For a clear account of the difference between simplified spelling and a phonetic alphabet, see *1906*, 192-197.
[28] NEA, *Proceedings, 1905*, 158.
[29] NEA, *Proceedings, 1909*, 163-164.

scholars and seemed well designed to effect uniformity in cyclopedias, dictionaries, gazetteers, textbooks, and other references. The report called for the official adoption of the proposed pronouncing alphabet and presumably for its subsequent use in NEA publications.[30]

When the proposal came before the summer session of the NEA in San Francisco in July 1911, it was sidetracked by an amendment calling for further experiment, testing, and research at various universities.[31] In the following year the association voted down a motion to take it from the table and vote upon the issue.[32] This same year the Department of Superintendence tabled the Simplified Spelling Board's recommendation for revised spellings, and even the harmless resolution of E. O. Vaile calling merely for "appreciation" of the efforts of various organizations to effect spelling reform was tabled by a viva-voce vote.[33] Thus ended the long struggle to secure the active support of spelling reform by the NEA.

Since 1912 the NEA has demonstrated no interest in spelling reform, although its publications continue to use the minimum list of revised words. Even though the NEA lost its concern for spelling reform, the movement continued for a few years. The Simplified Spelling Board, generously supported by Andrew Carnegie, was active until 1924. After that date it issued occasional numbers of a small magazine called *Spelling*. At the height of the movement the Board said that 556 newspapers and periodicals were using the 300 recommended spellings, and that 460 colleges, normal schools, and universities used them in their catalogues or approved their use by students.[34] The movement provoked many extreme versions, such as *laff, vodvil, shobiz, nuf sed, izzatso,* and *slax,* and doubtless influenced scores of original spellings and eye-catching changes used in advertisements. A few widely separated individuals and periodicals doggedly persevered in their idiosyncrasies, but the last issue of *Spelling* in 1931 may be regarded as the demise of organized spelling reform in the United States.

Perhaps the anticlimax of the whole movement was reached in August 1955, when the Chicago *Tribune* announced its abandonment of most of the revisions which it had been a pioneer in adopting in 1879.[35]

---

[30] NEA, *Proceedings, 1911,* 323-329, 163-164. A long discussion of simplified spelling was held in the Department of Secondary Education. See *Ibid.,* 645-657.

[31] *Ibid.,* 35-36.

[32] NEA, *Proceedings, 1912,* 45-46.

[33] NEA, *Proceedings, 1912,* 332.

[34] H. L. Mencken, *The American Language* (New York, 1947), 399-403.

[35] *Time,* August 29, 1955, p. 51.

20

Teachers and Temperance

The Golden Rule is God's straight line of rectitude let down from worlds invisible into the mists of everybody's daily life; and reform is simply the endeavor, in the plane of morality, to bring the dark and tangled threads of all our lives into parallel with that bright plummet line. . . .

Blindly often, with step awkward and unwieldly as that of the primeval mastodon, yet with tremendous force and stern persistence, humanity moves on, impelled by an instinct immortal and divine, toward the gleaming, golden plummet line let down from God. . . . And the teacher . . . has it in his power to utter line upon line, precept upon precept, and to enforce these by gentle and considerate exmaple . . . and who yet fails to do so, is not worthy to stand in a life-barque freshly launched, with his hand upon the helm of an untaught human soul. . . .

What then is our most insidious and powerful foe? Where is the rendezvous of the low, the vulgar, the irresponsible members of our complex society? Whence comes the noisy horde . . . ? To all these questions, ominous and sad, there is but one reply—*the rum shops!*

This strange mixture of fact and fantasy, piety and rhetoric, determination and color, was a declaration of war and a call to arms written by Frances E. Willard.[1] Never was a human being more in earnest and never did one pursue a purpose with more courage and persistence than this ex-schoolteacher, dean of women, future president of the Woman's Christian Temperance Union, and reformer extraordinary. She had more to say in this declaration, which she sent to be read to the teachers assembled at Minneapolis in 1875, including some basic statistics designed to motivate her colaborers in the cause of temperance.

Of these cess-pools of vice America has, today, ten times as many as she has churches and school-houses combined. . . . Fifty per cent of the insanity in our country comes of strong drink. Sixty-five per cent of the poverty and pauperism have been traced to the same cause. Seventy-five per cent of all the murders grow out of drunken brawls. Eighty-six per cent of all our crimi-

[1] For some colorful lights on Frances E. Willard, see Jim Marshall, *Swinging Doors* (Seattle, 1949), Chapter VIII.

nals become such while crazed by alcohol. Ninety-five per cent of our vicious youth emerge from drunkard's homes. Each year, one hundred thousand of our citizens reel out into Eternity through the awful doorway of a drunkard's death.

At each election in our native land, a million drunkards stagger up to the polls and deposit their blurred and muddled ballots. From seeds like these what fruit might we expect? Just what we have—Crédit Mobilier, Salary Grabs, stuffed ballot-boxes, fraudulent returns, and corruption from the base to the apex of our grand pyramid of government.

As allies in the fight against rum sellers Miss Willard welcomed the Bird Defenders, the Juvenile Temperance Union, the Cold-Water Brigade, the Sisters of the Regiment, and the Look Up Legion with its slogan:

> Look up and not down;
> Look out and not in;
> Look forward and not back
> And lend a hand.

And her message to the NEA summoned teachers to join the crusade.

Miss Willard was emphatic as to the duties of teachers and of "the influential body here convened" (NEA) with respect to the reforms of the day. "Every teacher is bound to interest and instruct his pupils concerning all true reforms . . . the press is indifferent and the church drowsy." The teacher "moulds in clay while the temperance agitators are pounding away on marble. He *forms* while they almost vainly endeavor to reform."[2]

The assembled teachers were sympathetic. Superintendent John Hancock of Dayton thought that the schoolmaster was the true reformer. "When a true schoolmaster is let loose in a community, let vice beware." One speaker "recognized the propriety and the necessity of such suggestions before such an Association, and the appropriateness of such a paper on such an occasion." Another agreed that the public school was the place to teach young people the dangers of taking poison into the human body.[3]

Teachers had long been sympathetic to reforms, particularly temperance movements. In 1857 the teachers of Cambria County, Pennsylvania, resolved "That any person addicted to the use of intoxicating beverages is unfit to perform the duties of a Teacher or to have children under his charge; that while his precepts go unheeded his example leads many to ruin."[4] In Centre County of the same state they were even more determined. "Pledges were given by teachers to watch and guard each other's moral actions and characters and to denounce and disown all unworthy

[2] NEA, *Proceedings, 1875,* 181-186.
[3] *Ibid.,* 186-187.
[4] *Pennsylvania School Journal,* VI, 213, January 1858.

members of their sacred profession. And ladies enlisted particularly in aid of the Superintendent to suppress indulgence by teachers in alcoholic drinks."[5]

The teacher had long been regarded as an upholder of morality and religion, as a protagonist of loyalty and civic virtue, and as a purveyor of culture and enlightenment. Popular sentiment required him to be a sort of unordained minister, a person whose conduct should serve as an example to pupils and parents. Acquiescing to the expectations, the teacher was often an upholder of causes, a promoter of improvements, a forthright reformer. Responding to these varied demands, he sometimes failed to distinguish between teaching and preaching, teaching and advocating, teaching and promoting. In transmitting the social heritage he felt impelled to alter and improve it before passing it on to the pupils. Objectivity and detachment were professional ideals scarcely envisioned before the rise of the scientific movement in education in the early part of the twentieth century. The profession expected the teacher to be a moralist; the public required him to be a partisan in favor of good causes; so it is not surprising that crusaders and reformers rushed to teachers' conventions, institutes, and assemblies, and that these heralds of a new day found responsive chords in the hearts of many teachers.

The temperance movement had achieved considerable momentum before Miss Willard arrived on the scene. Thousands of local temperance societies were organized after 1830. While most of the early efforts were directed against "the abuse and not the use of alcohol," many reformers advocated complete abstinence and circulated pledge cards calling for teetotalism. The crusaders made use of booklets, charts, and fear-inspiring drawings of the human body showing the devastating effects of alcohol. Temperance lecturers, including some reformed drunkards, were accorded receptive hearings. Effective help came from Timothy S. Arthur's booklets and broadsides and particularly from his *Ten Nights in a Barroom* (1854), from the writings of Elihu Burritt, and from sermons by earnest preachers. Under the guidance of Neal S. Dow, Maine adopted prohibition in 1851, and within four years all the New England states, New York, Delaware, and Iowa had passed laws to curb and regulate the sale of intoxicating beverages.

All these antebellum efforts were surpassed by those of the postwar decades. The National Temperance Society, with William E. Dodge, merchant, philanthropist, and reformer as president, was organized in 1865 and began the publication of temperance materials, some of which were suitable for use in the schools. In 1869 the National Prohibition Party was organized, exemplifying the political approach to the problem of intemperance. In these years Miss Julia Colman prepared her *Cate-*

[5] *Ibid.*, VI, 261, March 1858.

chism on Alcohol.[6] Mrs. Mary H. Hunt of Boston, Mrs. J. Ellen Foster of Iowa, and many other women were promoting the cause by writing, lecturing, and organizing local societies. Most important of all was the organization of the Woman's Christian Temperance Union in Cleveland in 1874. Aided by all these developments, the Union set out on a crusade to secure the enforced teaching of the evil effects of alcohol upon the human body.

The Union was remarkably successful. Between 1882 and 1887 thirty-two states passed laws requiring the teaching of the dangers of alcohol and narcotics. Congress passed a similar law applying to the territories, the District of Columbia, Indian schools, and the military and naval academies. These crusading women wrote model statutes and used all known tactics to secure their prompt enactment. They inspired an avalanche of letters, circulated petitions, sent delegations to legislative halls, and sat through long sessions to see that their supporters carried out their promises. In Pennsylvania they used a petition signed by one hundred saloonkeepers of Germantown as proof that even the dispensers of liquor wanted their children protected against the evils of strong drink.[7]

The NEA continued to give some attention to the temperance movement. To the great educational show at Madison in 1884 came Frances E. Willard to plead for healthy bodies and clear brains and to decry the use of alcohol, which injured "the tissues of the body and the temper of the soul."[8] President Thomas W. Bicknell blessed the movement. "With a sagacity born of true philosophy and a holy purpose born of women's enthusiasm, the bravest knights have begun a great crusade which is as certain to drive intemperance, with its deadly hosts, from the land as is the light of day to chase away the fast-fleeing clouds of darkness."[9]

In 1885 the NEA approved "the effort to create a strong public sentiment in favor of temperance" and heartily endorsed "legislative action looking toward the healthfulness, happiness, and purity of the people."[10] At the Topeka meeting of 1886 two major addresses were devoted to temperance. Mrs. Foster gave a long review of the movement from the publication of Dr. Benjamin Rush's essay on the effects of alcohol, pub-

[6] The *Indiana School Journal*, XXI, 88, February 1876, cites a resolution of the state teachers' association endorsing such instruction and experiments as will show the nature of alcohol and "its dire effects on the human system." Samples from the *Catechism on Alcohol* are quoted, one of which reads: "Ques. Why do people grow fat that drink ale, porter, and beer? Ans. Because the alcohol puts so much impurity into the blood that it cannot all be worked off, and so it is tucked away in the corners as dead matter or fat."

[7] NEA, *Proceedings, 1886*, 85-103; *1887*, 655-657.

[8] NEA, *Proceedings, 1884*, 161-168. By resolution the association approved the legislation sponsored by the WCTU.

[9] *Ibid.*, 71.

[10] NEA, *Proceedings, 1885*, 21.

lished in 1785, to the passage of the latest compulsory-hygiene law. Professor A. C. Boyden of Bridgewater, Massachusetts, described thirteen simple experiments which teachers could perform in order to reveal the nature of alcohol and how it impaired digestion, destroyed blood corpuscles, ruined blood vessels, and paralyzed nerve matter. He declared repeatedly that the teaching of mere information was insufficient. "It is conviction that we are to bring to the minds and to the wills of these pupils."[11]

At the Chicago meeting of 1887 Mary H. Hunt, superintendent of scientific instruction of the WCTU, laid down the requirements for an acceptable textbook on the temperance question. Such a book must teach "(1) That alcohol is a dangerous and seductive poison. (2) That beer, wine, and cider contain this same alcohol. (3) That a little alcohol creates an uncontrollable appetite for more; therefore the pupils must be warned against taking that little. (4) That, since this is a temperance movement, the physiology should be only what is sufficient to make the temperance lesson intelligible." At this meeting the association adopted a resolution calling upon the states to pass laws requiring the teaching of physiology and hygiene with special reference to the injurious effects of alcohol and narcotics.[12]

For a few years after the Chicago meeting the NEA demonstrated no active interest in the organized temperance movement. It did, however, listen to a few speeches on the subject. For instance, at St. Paul in 1890 it heard a vigorous blast at the saloons, delivered by the colorful individualist, Rufus C. Burleson, president of Baylor University. "Two hundred thousand licensed saloons with their twin sisters, the gambling houses and houses of ill-fame, are pouring liquid, devouring streams of crime, death, and ruin over our land. These two hundred thousand saloons, licensed by law, murder sixty thousand fathers, brothers, and sons every year and clothe three hundred thousand helpless women and children in rags and shame. Indeed, this government is fast becoming a government of saloon-keepers, by saloon-keepers, for saloon-keepers."[13]

In 1894 the board of directors rejected a petition to create a department of temperance within the NEA.[14] Following this long period of relative inactivity—a bombshell!

A bombshell which scattered and divided the faithful and believing and distressed the well-wishers was dropped by an innocent professor at the Charleston meeting in 1900. W. O. Atwater of Wesleyan University carried on some experiments concerning the effects of alcohol on the human body and came to the conclusion that many statements made by

[11] NEA, *Proceedings, 1886,* 108-115.
[12] NEA, *Proceedings, 1887,* 655-657, 47.
[13] NEA, *Proceedings, 1890,* 678.
[14] NEA, *Proceedings, 1894,* 41-42.

the WCTU speakers and in the hygiene textbooks were unscientific, misleading, erroneous, false. He criticized such assertions as:

1. Alcohol is a poison.
2. Alcohol is never a food.
3. Even in small quantities and in the diluted forms in which it appears in wine and beer, alcohol is a poison.
4. One drink creates an irresistible appetite for more.
5. Physiologists, chemists, physicians, and toxicologists are agreed that alcohol is a poison.
6. In any quantity and in any mixture alcohol is not only a poison but a narcotic poison.

With reasonableness and at great length Professor Atwater explained his position. He was in favor of temperance and of teaching temperance, but he wanted the statements to be true. "The foundation of morality is the truth." He did not agree with a temperance worker who exclaimed, "But can't we fool the boys until their characters are formed?" He felt that exaggerations were detrimental to the cause. He approved the purpose but objected to the method of the temperance workers. "I protest against the dogmatic teaching of scientific theories which still lack demonstrative proof." He cited the instance of a teacher on the East Side of New York who was doing harm to true temperance. "The teacher asked, 'What is beer?,' the answer came in a chorus, 'Beer is poison.' Now, those little chaps knew that that was a lie. Their fathers and mothers drank beer every day. Such children are not fooled by any such teaching."[15]

Another instance of the hollow teaching of the enforced "truths" was reported by an observer in the schools of Baltimore. "In one class where they were having physiology, in answer to the question 'What is the effect of alcohol on the system?' I heard a ten-year old cry out at the top of his voice, and at the rate of a hundred miles an hour, 'It-dwarfs-the-body-mind-and-soul, -weakens-the-heart-and-enfeebles-the-memory.' "[16]

Professor Atwater closed his paper by saying, "In the great effort to make men better, there is one thing that we must always seek, one thing we need never fear—the truth." An eager audience was ready to pour forth spirited rejoinders. They fell into two groups: those who endorsed his findings enthusiastically because they had already objected to the required laws for various reasons, and those who sorrowfully conceded the necessity of taking account of the new evidence.

The superintendent from Brookline, Massachusetts, overflowed with resentment against the temperance groups that tried to specify the amount of space devoted to temperance in the textbooks, the number of

[15] NEA, *Proceedings, 1900,* 229-250.
[16] J. M. Rice, *The Public School System in the United States* (New York, 1893), 60.

lessons per week, the grades in which the lessons should be taught, the required reports to the legislature, and the heavy penalties prescribed for deviation from the required course. He regarded the whole plan as a reflection upon the honesty and capabilities of school boards, an assault upon the freedom of the teacher, and a violation of sound pedagogy. These coercive features were obnoxious to teachers and undermined their integrity. In spite of the opposition of teachers, college officials, and prominent clergymen, New York had passed such a law in 1895. If obeyed, the law was bound to result in unsound instruction, and if ignored, it made lawbreakers out of honest teachers. One senator, pressed to justify his vote in favor of such a law, smilingly replied, *"We did it to please the ladies."* The author of one of the required textbooks on hygiene, when asked to justify some unscientific statement, replied with irritation, "I have studied physiology, and I do not wish you to suppose that I have fallen so low as to believe all the things I have to put into those books."

Superintendent Richard G. Boone of Cincinnati thought that the attempt to teach temperance by stressing intemperance was psychologically unsound, and compared it to the folly of teaching spelling by using lists of incorrectly spelled words, of teaching English with specimen selections filled with inaccuracies, and teaching good manners by observing boorish behavior. The law did not require a particular interpretation of history, or endorsement of a particular school of literary criticism, or any exclusive hypothesis in science. Why then should these hygiene laws be so specific? They really compelled the acceptance of a creed; they required not teaching but indoctrination.

Superintendent C. F. Carroll of Worcester proclaimed his respect for the WCTU and his support of the temperance movement, but "This little company of leaders has covered the land with a network of legislation. They have done this without consulting the teachers. . . ." In fact, they have spurned counsel and cooperation in framing the legislation. He said that the writers were ashamed of their "so-called temperance books" bearing the approval of the WCTU. "If they are invited to engage in conversation upon this subject, they smile, look above or below, and as soon as possible pass to some other subject and leave you to draw your own conclusions."

D. L. Kiehle, state superintendent of Minnesota schools, was aggressively hostile to the WCTU because it had opposed the requirement of the state committee that the adopted books be "indorsed by responsible scientific authority." One book was approved by the WCTU and Kiehle and his associates were threatened unless they chose it for adoption in the schools. By prescribing time, methods, book, and pages he felt that the WCTU was guilty of "an unwarrantable intrusion upon the province of the teacher." He referred to "the crooked methods practiced in the effort to secure the adoption of the approved series."

Others spoke. The WCTU was lambasted and criticized. Was there danger of a one-sided discussion? No, for Henry Sabin of Iowa was there, and Mary H. Hunt of the WCTU.

Sabin begun slowly: "I am deeply moved. I am astonished that in all this great audience there is not a man of strength and power who dares stand up here and face you in spite of your applause, and defend that great organization—the Woman's Christian Temperance Union. I have known these women for more than a score of years; I have been in their confidence; I have counseled with them; and for sincerity of purpose, for purity of heart, for keen appreciation of moral questions, they are peerless." He pleaded for the teaching of temperance in the light of *experience* as well as the light of *science*.

Superintendent Joseph Carter of Champaign said that the temperance laws, even if they did violate some principles of pedagogy, were an effort in the right direction and that their effects were beneficial. Others spoke kind words, and then Mrs. Hunt herself took the floor.

With sarcasm and humor she disowned the woman who wanted untruths taught for the sake of promoting temperance. She arraigned Professor Atwater for the premature publicity concerning his experiments and accused him of misreading some of his own statistics. She acknowledged the compulsory features of the laws and ridiculed the idea that the promoters should have ceased their efforts because a few school men object to their methods. The textbooks were "submitted to the best scientific authorities" and inaccuracies were corrected. She closed her speech by referring to "the paths martyrs have trod."

In accordance with an oft-observed custom at NEA conventions, the opening speaker was given the opportunity for a last rejoinder. Professor Atwater answered a number of questions, reviewed his major points, and blessed the cause of scientific temperance.[17]

Before the close of the convention the president of the Department of Superintendence appointed a committee on temperance instruction.[18] In the following year it reported that the question whether alcohol was a food or a poison was a technical matter for experts, but that everyone recognized it was not a food in the ordinary meaning of the word; therefore the teacher should center his attention upon teaching the injurious effects of alcohol when used as a beverage.[19] Thus the problem of

[17] NEA, *Proceedings, 1900*, 250-266. Mrs. Jesse Willard Bolte, a kinswoman of Frances E. Willard, objecting to the time devoted to alcoholic physiology, characterized the textbooks as inartistic and unscientific, and concluded by praising self-control and temperance in all things, "not forgetting that where the whisky bottle has slain its thousands the frying-pan has slain its tens of thousands."

[18] NEA, *Proceedings, 1900*, 187.

[19] NEA, *Proceedings, 1901*, 193.

temperance instruction was, for practical purposes, in about the same situation as it was before Professor Atwater delivered his disturbing report at Charleston.

Following the spirited debate of 1900, the question of temperance was again relatively neglected by the NEA for a few years. Schools continued to teach from the approved hygiene books and temperance workers were busy on the political as well as the educational front. At the Los Angeles meeting of 1907 the local unit of the WCTU presented President Nathan C. Schaeffer of the NEA with a unique gavel made of eleven kinds of wood.[20]

The next evidence of interest in the temperance movement was the extended and spirited paper on "Temperance and Society" by David Starr Jordan, president of Stanford University, read before the San Francisco convention in 1911. Jordan dealt with the effects of alcohol (1) upon the human body, (2) upon the character of the individual, and (3) upon the society which sponsors its sale and consumption. His indictment was colorful, vigorous, and severe enough to win the approval of the WCTU and scientific enough to satisfy the cautious educators.[21]

Since Jordan's paper of 1911 the NEA has heard no speech, report, or discussion on the temperance question. The official position of the association was made clear, however, by resolutions and statements of principle. In 1918 it urged states to approve the prohibition amendment,[22] and in 1920 and 1930 it endorsed the Eighteenth Amendment and called for " the impartial and fearless enforcement of the Volstead Act."[23] In 1927 it urged "that reemphasis be given to the teaching of the evil effects of narcotic drugs and of alcoholic beverages."[24] In 1931 it declared that the "schools should continue to emphasize the evil effects" of alcohol, tobacco, and other narcotics.[25] In the following year the association and the Department of Superintendence renewed their approval of the Eighteenth Amendment and called for law enforcement.[26] Beginning in 1932, the NEA put its permanent policies into a platform, which was supplemented by annual resolutions. The platform included some pronouncement on temperance in nearly every year from 1933 to 1955.[27]

[20] NEA, *Proceedings, 1907,* 28. At the meeting in Los Angeles in 1899 the local unit of the WCTU had presented a large silk flag to the NEA. *Proceedings, 1899,* 35.

[21] NEA, *Proceedings, 1911,* 75-82.

[22] NEA, *Proceedings, 1918,* 25.

[23] NEA, *Proceedings, 1920,* 27; *1930,* 192. A separate resolution of 1920 was devoted to the evils of cigarette smoking, which was "not only a cause for alarm but a call to arms."

[24] NEA, *Proceedings, 1927,* 1158.

[25] NEA, *Proceedings, 1931,* 271.

[26] NEA, *Proceedings, 1932,* 219, 673.

[27] NEA, *Proceedings, 1933,* 221; *1934,* 182; *1935,* 211; *1936,* 891; *1937,* 894; *1938,* 877; *1939,* 913; *1940,* 903; *1941,* 908; *1942,* 512; *1943,* 312; *1944,* 351; *1945-46,* 213; *1948,* 401; *1949,* 353; *1950,* 372; *1951,* 117; *1955,* 117.

Thus it appears that the policy of the NEA was one of temperance instruction, leaving the political and legal aspects to the Anti-Saloon League and other groups. In fact, some educators lamented the fact that crusaders for temperance were so intrigued by the possibilities of immediate results through legal compulsion that they abandoned the slow, unspectacular process of achieving temperance through persuasion and education. When this program of compulsion failed, as evidenced by the repeal of the Eighteenth Amendment, the educative process assumed a new importance.

Instruction in temperance was carried on by means of a variety of methods and materials. Textbooks, courses of study, and bulletins issued by state departments of education dealt extensively with alcohol, tobacco, and other narcotics. They were frequently revised in the light of new knowledge and became increasingly objective and scientific. By emphasizing the dangers of alcoholic beverages, these new materials faithfully reflected the intent of the original hygiene laws; by incorporating recent findings, they avoided the errors and dogmatism of the early textbooks. Educators were probably justified in assuming that the program of temperance instruction was well organized, and that it was accomplishing all that could be reasonably expected of it.

On the other hand, it seems that the controversial issue of controlling alcoholic drinks which agitated the public during the past half-century is not reflected proportionally in NEA programs. During this period the Anti-Saloon League was aggressively pursuing its campaign of prohibition; the movement for the adoption of the Eighteenth Amendment commanded a degree of public interest amounting to fanaticism; the frightful period of bootlegging and crime following the First World War enlisted all the agencies for law enforcement and stirred the public to anxiety and alarm; the repeal of prohibition and the return of the saloons ushered in another period of uncertainty and perplexity. Were the educators alert to the educational implications of all these developments? Or were these issues so largely infused with politics and public policies as to fall outside the province of instruction in the schools?

During the past fifty years the NEA has devoted many speeches and resolutions to Americanization, citizenship, thrift, child labor, character education, law observance, and other problems that reflect changing social conditions. It is difficult to cite a convincing instance of a lag between social change and educational adjustment. So it seems that the relative neglect of prohibition and all its problems by the NEA is simply an instance of a clear-eyed perception of the distinction between public action and public education. Teachers deliberately chose to remain at their desks, and as teachers to let public issues be decided by the public.

21

Other Lost Causes

A PENNY SAVED

IN MARCH 1885, John Henry Thiry, commissioner of the Third Ward School of Long Island City, persuaded the principal to establish a school savings bank as an experiment. It succeeded. Within a year similar systems had been established in about fifty cities. By 1893, 317 schools in 78 cities had opened savings accounts for 33,810 pupils who had on deposit in their own names the sum of $345,634.52.

At the International Congress of Education at Chicago in 1893, Thiry made a report on the school savings plan and presented arguments for its greater adoption. He lamented the large number of criminals, paupers, insane, bedridden, homeless, aged, and infirm who had become public charges. These classes would increase and the only preventive, as he saw the situation, was to educate the children in the ways of thrift. He visualized the school savings bank as an ideal to the study of all subjects, an incentive to good citizenship, and a developer of vocational competence.[1]

At Minneapolis in 1902 the Department of School Administration appointed a committee to investigate the desirability of establishing penny savings banks in the schools in order to restrain the children from spending their surplus change for injurious articles and thus cultivating habits of excess and extravagance.[2] When the report of this committee was presented at Boston in the following year, one of the discussants was J. H. Thiry, who was identified in the record as "the father of the school savings bank system in the United States." The report that was adopted called for the establishment of the penny savings bank system in the schools.[3]

By 1913 the school savings plan had spread to thirty states and about 150 cities with about 1,500 participating schools. Pennsylvania was first

[1] NEA, *Proceedings, 1893*, 286-287.
[2] NEA, *Proceedings, 1902*, 791.
[3] NEA, *Proceedings, 1903*, 897.

with the plan in operation in fifty-one school systems. While the system was most frequent in the elementary schools, it was found in a few high schools. Plans for depositing and keeping records varied from city to city, but all endeavored to keep strict accounts and encourage frequent deposits by the children. Some claimed that the system was as educative as a course in arithmetic.[4]

All previous interest in school savings banks and thrift pales into insignificance when contrasted with the outburst at the 1916 sessions of the National Council of Education. At the February meeting eight and at the July meeting four papers on thrift were read. Thrift as an educational necessity, and in its relation to home, country living, industry, banking, health, character, normal schools, conservation, and various organizations, was discussed at length. Among the influences cited as promotive of thrift were the establishment in 1910 of postal savings accounts, the work of the Woman's Christian Temperance Union in promoting school savings banks, and the work of the American Society for Thrift, whose president, S. W. Straus, spoke at both the February and July meetings. Thrift was extolled as a virtue, a discipline and an exercise of the will, a developer of moral stamina, and a protection against the temptation to waste and squander.[5]

After the declaration of war against Germany in 1917, President Wilson and various government agencies admonished the people to avoid waste and practice thrift. S. W. Straus appeared before the National Council again and echoed official admonitions and added his own exhortations, proclaiming that "tomorrow the man who is not thrifty will be a social outcast . . . the spendthrift is a public menace." Another speaker sarcastically observed that no one was urging economy in the use of tobacco, and a suggestion of economy in drinking beer had provoked hysterical outbursts from the newspapers. She called for thrift that would provide a balanced diet, one that would maintain the health growth of children.[6]

In contrast with the general preachments of many speakers, Superintendent M. P. Shawkey of West Virginia made dozens of concrete suggestions concerning the practice of thrift to aid the war effort. Cut down on commencement expenditures; buy less candy; cut out the use of chewing gum; eliminate the lavish high-school annual; use school supplies sparingly; take care of clothes and shoes. In order to earn money and promote national thrift, he made several suggestions: gather and sell berries, nuts, waste paper, scrap iron; plant a vegetable garden. He quoted one of his associates as advising young people to buy War Savings Stamps by catching furs, selling a rabbit, testing seed corn, cutting wood,

[4] NEA, *Proceedings, 1915,* 904-908.
[5] NEA, *Proceedings, 1916,* 196-221, 274-285.
[6] NEA, *Proceedings, 1917,* 130, 145-161.

building fires, killing rats, and saving grease to make soap.[7]

The end of the war brought little if any diminution in the efforts to promote thrift. At Salt Lake City in 1920 the Committee on Thrift Education of the National Council of Education made a report in the form of a round-table conference. Chairman Arthur H. Chamberlain commended the zealous work of the members of the committee and scolded the universities and teacher-training institutes for failing to offer courses in thrift teaching. Another speaker declared that the teacher should ask each pupil the critical question, "Has your bank balance increased or diminished?" Other speakers reported that at Hyrum, Utah, each pupil had a thrift adviser and that in several Utah counties the teachers checked accounts and inspected pupils during their summer work periods. A representative from the Treasury Department at Washington reported the preparation of thrift outlines for the various grades.[8]

In 1921 Chairman Chamberlain made two reports and reviewed the work of his committee from its original appointment in 1915 to the summer of 1921. He insisted that thrift involved earning and spending as well as saving and investing; that conservation and the avoidance of waste were fundamental in any educational program. He said that the need for thrift had never been greater and urged its study in every grade from 1 to 12. The superintendent from Dallas reported that "an eleven-year-old bank president and a nine-year-old teller" had explained their savings plan to a mothers' congress and a service club. A speaker from Pittsburgh presented that city's outline of "civics-thrift" for the first three grades, with a recurring consideration of thrift of time, talent, energy, effort, material, food, health, and money in each grade.[9]

In 1923 a representative of the General Federation of Women's Clubs called upon the NEA to see that household budgeting and account keeping were introduced into the schools in order "to save waste, worry, illness, broken homes, and child ruin caused by ignorant choices in money spending."[10]

Chamberlain and his committee sponsored the National Conference on Thrift Education in Washington on June 27–28, 1924. Representatives from 150 national organizations and a dozen government bureaus attended the sessions. The results were reported in an eighty-page booklet, published by the NEA, which had a wide distribution.[11]

Chamberlain made annual reports to the association until 1925, when the committee on thrift, which had functioned since its creation at Oakland in 1915, was abolished and its functions assigned to the curricu-

[7] NEA, *Proceedings, 1918,* 589-592.
[8] NEA, *Proceedings, 1920,* 117-135.
[9] NEA, *Proceedings, 1921,* 167-169, 315-331.
[10] NEA, *Proceedings, 1923,* 147-148.
[11] NEA, *Proceedings, 1924,* 338-341; *1925,* 188-190.

lum committee of the Department of Superintendence. In reviewing his work, Chamberlain observed that the American people were well on the way toward establishing thrift habits by the end of the war. Unfortunately, a period of reckless and lavish spending followed and much of the value of the lessons of the war years was rapidly dissipated. He viewed thrift as a long-term curriculum problem and recommended that it be infused into every subject. His ambitious plan of setting up an international committee on thrift education was interrupted when the NEA terminated his committee on thrift.[12]

With the abolition of Chamberlain's committee in 1925, thrift drops out of the NEA *Proceedings* as completely as though it had never been on the educational scene. The topic had won its way into various parts of the curriculum, however, and probably needed no further attention from the association. During the depression years it was less appropriate, and during the Second World War the need for economizing assumed other forms. In addition, the topic was always potentially associated with banking, with parsimony, or with a mild form of the deprivation of children of harmless little expenditures. In all probability many persons believed or suspected what Charles H. Judd said about the matter in 1933: "The organized bankers of this country have carried on for years a persistent campaign to extend the school curriculum by the teaching of thrift. Their definition of thrift is to save money and deposit it in banks."[13] In 1956 the American Bankers Association reported that school children had $156,600,000 in bank savings accounts. If the accumulation of a bank balance is the major purpose of thrift education, the movement has been eminently successful. However, since thrift education, according to many of its proponents, was the cure for a multitude of ills ranging from wasteful spending to criminality, it is a lost cause.

One is led to speculate upon the educative value of carrying on campaigns which almost inevitably tend to overemphasize a particular topic or problem. An aggressive chairman who becomes sincerely convinced of the importance of his assignment can distort perspective and prolong attention beyond the period of maximum value. Whether thrift education needs redefining and reemphasizing is for some future group, committee, or association to decide.

CABINET STATUS FOR EDUCATION

"In many sections of the country the average rural school house . . . is not as well kept or as healthful as a good stable, dairy barn, pigpen, or chicken house. . . . But what more could be expected of a government that creates a cabinet department for animals but fails to recognize

[12] NEA, *Proceedings, 1923*, 393-396; *1924*, 338-341; *1925*, 188-190.
[13] NEA, *Proceedings, 1933*, 69.

one for man . . . ?" This stinging observation was made before the NEA at Salt Lake City in 1913 by Dr. R. W. Corwin of the University of Colorado.[14]

The crusade for a secretary of education with cabinet rank was only a relatively brief episode in the long struggle to secure Federal aid for the schools and generous support for the Bureau of Education. From its second meeting in Cincinnati in 1858 to the latest convention at Portland in 1956, the NEA passed resolutions, appointed committees, and conducted campaigns to secure Federal aid for education—for the freedmen, for the South, for illiterates, for a national university, for mechanical and agricultural colleges, for vocational education, for federally controlled areas, for emergencies, and, most frequently and consistently, for the support of the Bureau, and later the Office, of Education. The NEA followed a consistent policy of favoring Federal aid and opposing Federal control of education. The high-water marks of efforts to secure Federal aid were registered in the 1880's, when funds derived from the sale of public lands were to be distributed on the basis of illiteracy, and in the 1920's, when Federal aid was sorely needed to replenish a waning profession and bolster lagging schools. In spite of the urgency of both situations the NEA failed to convince a reluctant Congress or arouse a lethargic nation.

The crusade to secure a secretary of education with cabinet status had its remote origin in the original bill to create a bureau of education in 1867. Unfortunately such words as bureau, office, department, and division were quite unstandardized in 1867, and so the law that created a Department of Education gave rise to subsequent misunderstandings, although the term was not misconstrued at that time. Henry Barnard, the first incumbent, knew full well that he was not to have cabinet status. He said that the new office was called a "department" in order to free it from the control of existing departments, to give it dignity, and to protect its holder against partisan changes.[15] In 1869 Congress reduced the "department" to a bureau in the Department of the Interior and lowered the commissioner's salary from $4,000 to $3,000. In spite of the fact that the "department" of 1867 had never had cabinet status, some educators persisted in misreading history and entertaining the vain hope that it would be "restored" to a status that it had never had.

Most educators, however, knew that the Bureau of Education had never been a real department. In 1889 a committee of the NEA urged that "the Bureau of Education should be restored to its original position as an independent department." The report referred to the lack of "dignity" caused by the low salary, but it did not even imply cabinet

---

[14] NEA, *Proceedings, 1913,* 418-419.
[15] American Institute of Instruction, NTA, *Proceedings, 1867,* 41.

status for the commissioner.[16] A report by a committee of 1903 is quite unequivocal; it called for the restoration of the bureau "to the status which it had at the time of its formation, namely, that of an independent department—a status which the Departments of Agriculture and Labor had before they were raised to cabinet rank." The report referred to the enhanced dignity of a separate organization over its present lowly status as a bureau of a department.[17] A resolution of the NEA, passed in 1908, called for better support of the Bureau and concluded, "We are of the opinion that the importance of the subject under its control, and the dignity of this country require that this Bureau be maintained as an independent department of the government."[18] This resolution still indicates no plan or desire for a department with cabinet status.

Further proof that the NEA did not wage an early campaign for a secretary of education in the President's cabinet is supplied by the silence of the two early commissioners, who had long tenure, undoubted courage, and an intense interest in the position. John Eaton, commissioner from 1870 to 1886, attended and spoke at ten sessions of the NEA during his term of office and was active in the association until 1898. He was exceedingly frank in complaining about the inadequate support of the bureau and called upon the association for help. W. T. Harris, active in the association from 1870 to his death in 1909 and commissioner from 1889 to 1906, spoke many times and participated in committees that were appointed to secure larger appropriations for the bureau. Neither Eaton nor Harris are on record as favoring cabinet status for the commissioner.

Increasing solicitude for the Bureau of Education and plans for its greater usefulness were shown by the NEA resolutions of 1911 and 1914, which called for larger grants for research and dissemination of information, for an increase in salary for the commissioner, and for a committee to help the bureau to obtain the additional appropriations. Still no hint, however, of any change in status for the office. Such a hint, almost a declaration, was given in the resolutions of 1915, prepared by a committee of which Elwood P. Cubberley was chairman. The association called upon Congress to increase the allowance for the bureau and to place it in a position to render service to those engaged in the care and education of children analogous to the service which it had long provided for those engaged in the care of fishes, hogs, cattle, and crops.[19] In 1916 there was only an incidental reference to the bureau.

Then, in 1917, came a resolution that can almost be interpreted as a bugle call to a crusade to secure cabinet status for a secretary of educa-

[16] NEA, *Proceedings, 1889*, 39-40.
[17] NEA, *Proceedings, 1903*, 36-37, 307, 309. Nicholas Murray Butler was chairman of this committee.
[18] NEA, *Proceedings, 1908*, 37.
[19] NEA, *Proceedings, 1915*, 30.

tion. "We reaffirm the previous recommendations of this Association . . . the creation of a national department of education under the direction of a secretary of education."[20] This resolution opens with an erroneous statement, which can be condoned because of its loyalty to principle in spite of its deviation from fact. At last the NEA had almost pronounced in favor of a secretary of education with cabinet status, but not quite. The first unequivocal and indisputable pronouncement in favor of a secretary of education with a place in the President's cabinet was made in 1918 by the Commission on the Emergency in Education and confirmed by the NEA resolution of 1919.[21]

The vague wishes, ambitious hopes, nebulous notions, unformulated ideas, and half-expressed purposes that had hovered over the teaching profession for more than fifty years were at last coalesced into a definitive statement and promulgated as a tangible plan by the Emergency Commission. It was, in fact, the commission, rather than the NEA itself, that assumed leadership and directed the crusade to secure the establishment of a department of education with a secretary in the President's cabinet.

Appointed early in 1918 by Mary C. C. Bradford, president of the NEA, and Thomas E. Finegan, president of the Department of Superintendence, the Emergency Commission entered upon its aggressive career. Its chairman, George D. Strayer, played a large role in NEA affairs during the 1920's and 1930's—chairman of the Emergency Commission, 1918-1920, and of its successor the Legislative Commission, 1920-1927; president of the NEA in 1919; chairman of the Resolutions Committee in 1926 and 1927; chairman of other committees; and a frequent speaker on various topics. He was aided by a large group of prominent educators who deserved respect and commanded attention.

The arguments for a secretary of education with cabinet status were impressive. The post would facilitate Federal appropriations for education; it would coordinate the educational activities of the federal government; it would symbolize the assumption of an obligation that had often been evaded; it would coordinate the educational efforts of the states and of national organizations; it would provide educational leadership; it would facilitate the study and solution of international educational problems; it would dignify and elevate education; it would facilitate the teaching and practice of democracy. Education had become a national responsibility and it required a national agency of power and dignity to discharge that responsibility.

Not all educators were convinced by the arguments. At Pittsburgh in 1918 Nathan C. Shaeffer, state superintendent of public instruction of Pennsylvania and a former president (1907) of the NEA, referred with

[20] NEA, *Proceedings, 1917*, 27.
[21] NEA, *Proceedings, 1919*, 23-24.

apparent disapproval to to "a lobby to secure a secretary of education in the cabinet." Twice he declared his willingness to accept "Federal aid with or without a secretary in the President's cabinet."[22] Schaeffer was not opposing or criticizing an official policy, because the NEA had not yet adopted the Emergency Commission's proposals.

A more forceful opponent with a prophetic substitute plan appeared at the Cleveland meeting of the Department of Superintendence in February 1920. Dean W. P. Burris of the University of Cincinnati was opposed to a secretary of education with cabinet status. Cabinet officers, he said, were necessarily political and would inevitably change with the election of a new President. It was idle to suppose that Federal funds would be or could be granted without Federal control. He opposed the fifty-fifty matched grants because such a plan really involved the control of state education funds by Congress. Instead of a secretary of education appointed by the President, he proposed a commissioner, elected by a Federal board of education, whose tenure and overlapping terms of nine years would place them and the commissoner beyond political control.[23]

In spite of Schaeffer's skepticism, Burris's opposition, and the indifference of other educators, the Emergency Commission and its successor, the Legislative Commission, waged a vigorous campaign for a secretary of education with cabinet rank and for generous grants for educational purposes. Every device of publicity available was used—traveling field agents, local speakers, bulletins, articles, and conferences. The crusade for the cabinet position was interwoven with the campaign for higher salaries for teachers, democratization of educational administration, Americanization of immigrants, and a bigger NEA. The program proved that a call that involved action was more appealing than one that merely promised rewards. The morale of the teaching profession was unquestionably raised, and at various times success seemed to be in sight.

To clarify the issues and focus the entire effort upon one purpose, the bill before Congress was simplified in 1925. All appropriations were dropped and the sole objective of the new measure, known as the Curtis-Reed Bill, was to establish a Department of Education with a secretary in the President's cabinet. It received the vigorous endorsement of dozens of national organizations and evoked the enthusiastic labors of the secretary of the legislative commission, Charl O. Williams, who made scores of speeches and sent out thousands of pages of materials. She made optimistic reports, and the NEA passed vigorous resolutions.[24] In 1930

[22] NEA, *Proceedings, 1918,* 38-41.
[23] NEA, *Proceedings, 1920,* 444-449.
[24] NEA, *Proceedings, 1919,* 79-81; *1920,* 41-48; *1921,* 159-163; *1922,* 305-312; *1923,* 397-399; *1924,* 254-256, 1033-1040; *1925,* 244-248; *1926,* 1101, 1137; *1927,* 1157, 152-156.

Thomas E. Finegan, who had become chairman of the Legislative Commission, reported as optimistically as ever upon the prospects of securing cabinet rank for a secretary of education. Yet, inconsistently enough, Finegan reported in 1931 that no efforts had been made to secure legislation by Congress on any aspect of education, pending the report of the National Advisory Committee appointed by Secretary of the Interior Ray L. Wilbur in May 1929. He asked the association to pass a resolution reaffirming its stand in favor of a secretary of education, and the association did so. In fact, it passed such a resolution every year until 1944.[25] In that year it pronounced the final plea: "A Department of Education with a Secretary in the President's Cabinet should be established."[26]

In 1947 the NEA resolved, "Until the Congress establishes a Department of Education . . . " It is difficult to say whether this phrase reveals hope, persistence, petulance, resignation, or despair.[27] There is no doubt whatever concerning the resolution of 1951, for it emphatically called for a National Board of Education, with long overlapping terms, whose principal duty would be to elect a nonpartisan commissioner.[28] Thus in 1951 the association adopted the very plan which it had rejected in 1920. If any lingering hope that a secretaryship of education with cabinet status would be achieved, it was effectively dispelled in 1953, when the new Federal Department of Health, Education, and Welfare was established.

The crusade was over. Starting with an accumulated tradition of support for a strong Federal bureau, the NEA in 1915 and 1917 issued unclear calls for enlistments in an undeclared campaign. Came the Emergency Commission in 1918 and issued clear, unequivocal calls for an unrestrained crusade in favor of a Federal department of education with cabinet status. Frustrated and discouraged, the forces halted in 1929, renounced even the proclaimed purpose during the Second World War, and changed the objective completely in 1951. What defeated a plan that had been vigorously pursued for more than a decade, and one that was endorsed by so many and varied groups?

Federal aid and a department of education were defeated by a variety of forces. President Harding had a plan for reorganizing the Federal government; President Coolidge had another one; neither of these provided for a separate department of education. Some private schools

---

[25] NEA, *Proceedings, 1928*, 190-195; *1930*, 188-191; *1931*, 253-256, 273. The *Proceedings* after 1941 are so abbreviated, so confusing, and so poorly indexed that one cannot be sure of even an official resolution or the continuing platform.

[26] NEA, *Proceedings, 1944*, 353.

[27] NEA, *Proceedings, 1947*, 301. Almost the same phrase was used once before, *1931*, 273.

[28] NEA, *Proceedings, 1951*, 120.

and colleges, particularly those maintained by the Catholic Church, were opposed to the various bills that provided for Federal aid. Many public schools were indifferent or opposed; congressmen, however well disposed, felt no great pressures from their constituents to vote for such a measure. The philosophy of localism and states' rights, fear of Federal encroachments, and the belief of some southerners that Federal aid would enhance the status of the Negro were effective arguments against increasing the educational functions of the Federal government. Finally, the appointment in 1929 of a National Advisory Committee on Education by the new secretary of the interior, Ray Lyman Wilbur, to study and reexamine the whole question of the role of the Federal government in education, seemed to indicate the postponement if not the complete defeat of a new cabinet position for education.

By 1930 the crusade was over. No formidable citadels had been stormed and no fundamental principles had been established. But the crusaders had been unified, their numbers increased, their morale established, their dignity enhanced, their consciousness of power realized, and their profession strengthened and recognized.

THE CHILD-LABOR AMENDMENT

There are "three people interested in getting the child out of school: the parent, the child, and the employer. The parent wants the child's wages; the child wants to be independent; the employer wants cheap labor." Nevertheless, Congress enacted the Keating-Owen Bill into law on September 1, 1916. The act forbade the shipment in interstate commerce of products made by persons under fourteen years of age. President Wilson said, "I want to say that with real emotion I sign this bill because I know how long the struggle has been to secure legislation of this sort, and what it is going to mean to the health and to the vigor of this country."[29]

Notwithstanding the long struggle and the health and vigor of the country, the Supreme Court declared the law unconstitutional in 1918. Within weeks after this decision the NEA called for the enactment of a more inclusive law, one that would meet the objection of the Court.[30] In February 1919, Congress passed a new law, levying a tax of 10 per cent on the entire net profits of any establishment that employed persons under fourteen years of age. In 1924 this law too was overthrown by the Supreme Court.

Even before this decision, the NEA called for a child-labor amendment, giving Congress power to enact laws to regulate the employment

[29] NEA, *Proceedings, 1917*, 830-831.
[30] NEA, *Proceedings, 1918*, 25.

of children.[31] In the following year, 1924, the association called upon the states to ratify the child-labor amendment that Congress had proposed.[32] This call was repeated in varying forms by every convention from 1925 to 1956. The NEA was by no means the only proponent of the child-labor amendment. Scores of civic, fraternal, educational, and religious groups approved it. In fact, support for it assumed something of the nature of a crusade, and opposition was branded as gross selfishness or moral blindness.

In the meantime progress of the amendment in the state legislatures was disturbingly slow. Nine years after its recommendation by Congress only six states had ratified it. Then in 1933, during the enthusiasm of the beginning of the New Deal, fourteen more added their approval. Success seemed near. But the movement came to a virtual halt; only a few more states ever ratified it.

How did it happen that the child-labor amendment, approved by almost countless organizations and popularly regarded as a matter of simple justice, nevertheless became a lost cause?

A few manufacturers openly opposed the amendment and a few upholders of states' rights voiced their opposition; some influential religious organizations also opposed it; but the greatest opponent was latent indifference. To placate the opponents of increased Federal power, the authors of the amendment tacked on the absurdly redundant and self-contradictory provision that "the power of the several states is unimpaired by this article except that the operation of state laws shall be suspended to the extent necessary to give effect to legislation enacted by Congress," which is equivalent to saying that "states' rights remain the same except as they are appropriated by Congress." Naturally such an obvious display of tautology did not reassure those who opposed the amendment on the principle of restricted Federal powers.

Millions of farmers opposed the amendment because they feared that Congress would forbid them to utilize the labor of their own children. The tribal survivals on this point were well exposed before the NEA in 1934. "It is almost amazing how tenaciously the human mind has clung to the fiction of parent ownership of children . . . and to another fancied right, the privilege of parents to profit by the labor of children . . . the right to appropriate the child's earnings."[33]

The defeat of the child-labor amendment was brought about not by its opponents but by social developments. During the depression years, when young people could not find employment, thousands continued in school. State after state raised compulsory-school-attendance require-

[31] NEA, *Proceedings, 1923*, 56.
[32] NEA, *Proceedings, 1924*, 56.
[33] NEA, *Proceedings, 1934*, 133.

ments to high-school graduation or to eighteen, whichever came first, and granted control over work permits to school officials. These measures gave educators virtual control of child labor in most states. Economic aids in the form of mothers' pensions, unemployment compensation, and disability allowances lessened the need of child labor and consequently the need of laws to restrict it. With the opening of war in Europe in 1939 and our subsequent entry, wages and salaries rose markedly; the problem of child labor became less critical.

In spite of the changing status of child labor, the NEA repeated year after year its request for the ratification of the proposed amendment. In the face of changed conditions such an amendment was no longer a national issue; hence this NEA resolution was not only ineffectual but probably lessened the association's influence on other public issues. It is obvious that the child-labor amendment is, if not a lost cause, at least a lost method.

PART V

The NEA Builds a Profession

22

The Greatest Educational Show on Earth

One cold Saturday forenoon during the winter of 1883-84, there rushed into my office a large, well-dressed man, wearing a high silk hat, and an elegant blue-caped overcoat. He spoke in a stentorian voice, saying: "I am Mr. Thomas W. Bicknell, Boston, Mass., editor of the *New England Journal of Education,* president of the National Association. I have been told that you are a live man, and I want you to read a paper before the Association next July in Madison. I am travelling at my own expense . . . working up a general interest in the cause of education throughout the entire country. When do the Sunday schools meet tomorrow? I want to speak about ten minutes at each one, and tell your Sunday-school people who I am, and what I am endeavoring to do. Now, can you supply me with some stationery, as I must write a number of letters?"

James M. Greenwood, superintendent of schools in Kansas City, Missouri, arose from his chair, shook hands with the hearty stranger, and proceeded to do just as he was told.[1] In fact, people generally did what Thomas W. Bicknell told them to do, not because he was dictatorial, but because he sensed and undertook what everyone wanted done

Back in 1869, when Bicknell was commissioner of schools in Rhode Island, he took over the dying *Rhode Island Schoolmaster* and ran it until 1875, when it and other state journals were merged into the *Journals of Education,* the *New England* and the *National,* which the editor proclaimed as "the leading weekly educational papers in America; the largest in the world." He obtained some outstanding educators as associate editors—A. D. Mayo, Anna D. Brackett, W. T. Harris, John Swett, and William H. Ruffner—and boosted his circulation by awarding pictures of Louis Agassiz, George Peabody, Horace Mann, and Emma Willard to new subscribers.[2]

In 1877 Bicknell was president of the American Institute of Instruction and arranged the program for the Montpelier meeting. Even more significant was the fact that, contrary to precedent, he was reelected president,

[1] NEA, *Proceedings,* 1912, 153.
[2] NEA, *Proceedings,* 1893, 814, 819-820; *1912,* 153; advertisement in American Institute of Instruction, *Proceedings,* 1877.

and signalized his second term by staging the greatest meeting the Institute ever held, the one at Fabyan's Hotel in the White Mountains of New Hampshire. The hotel erected a large pavilion for holding the sessions and provided good food and accommodations at remarkably low prices. In addition, Bicknell secured the cooperation of the railroads by having them grant reduced rates to members only. The result was a gathering of more than 3,000 people from twenty-eight states. Through his *Journals of Education* he provided great publicity, and the Institute was projected into its most flourishing financial condition.[3] Bicknell was not silent about his contribution to this great success.

Leaders in the NEA, seeing what Bicknell had done for the American Institute, decided that he was the man to put new vigor into the national association. Their hopes were speedily realized. In September 1883, following his election as president at Saratoga Springs in July, Bicknell set out to choose the meeting place for the next convention. He visited White Sulphur Springs, West Virginia, and Madison, Wisconsin, and was welcomed in both places, but the officers, advised by Bicknell, unanimously chose Madison. Speakers were engaged, the railroads alerted, and the campaign of publicity began. In December Bicknell made a second trip to Madison, including talks and conferences with educators and editors in Minnesota, Kansas, Missouri, Illinois, Indiana, and Michigan. In May 1884, he was in Madison again, warning the little city of 12,000 to expect at least 3,000 and possibly as many as 5,000 visitors.[4]

In the meantime Bicknell was busy, for "the greatest educational show on earth" was no accident; it was the result of imaginative planning and bold, aggressive action. Week after week the *New England Journal of Education* and other publications carried numerous items about the forthcoming convention: the varied programs, the prominent speakers, the educational exhibits, the charm of Madison and the beauties of the lake region, the special railroad rates, and the numerous excursions in connection with the meetings—to Oregon, Alaska, Colorado, Yellowstone, California.

Bicknell knew the value of helpers. He appointed a general manager for every state and region; he designated an eastern and western transportation manager; he persuaded the railroads to publish folders with maps showing the various routes to Madison. Several editions were printed and the state managers distributed over 75,000 copies. In addition, Bicknell inspired five of the major railroads to publish and distribute 100,000 copies of a sixteen-page booklet describing the NEA and the Madison convention. Altogether he estimated that the railroads and other

---

[3] *Report of the Commissioner of Education, 1878*, 297; American Institute of Instruction, *Proceedings, 1877, 1878, passim.*

[4] NEA, *Proceedings, 1884,* 66-69.

corporations paid for nearly 250,000 pamphlets, circulars, and cards. Not the least of his achievements was the agreement by which the railroads collected the $2 membership fees and turned the money into the NEA treasury.[5]

Almost equal in drawing power to the program of great speakers was the widely proclaimed and carefully prepared exhibit of educational materials. President James H. Smart of Purdue University, assisted by an active committee, managed the exhibit and induced public schools, private schools, and colleges, museums, publishers, and supply houses to send a variety of materials for display. "The exhibition rooms were thronged from the very beginning" and the exhibit surpassed "anything attempted in the Philadelphia exposition of education." It "formed a very important feature in the greatest educational gathering ever held in this country." Such were the remarks of the restrained, cautious, and none-too-generous educator, W. T. Harris.[6]

And how did the teachers and educators react to these persuasive blandishments of the outgoing Bicknell? They came—nearly 3,000 members, 2,000 nonmembers, and uncounted visitors who merely saw a bargain in the reduced rates.[7] Regardless of the exact number, the visitors were numerous enough to fill the hotels, rooming and boarding houses, many private residences, and a number of tents pitched on the nearby lawns. One teacher "was lodged in a little hotel on the corner of Capitol Square; his cot was one of a dozen in a big room on the top floor."[8] The strain on the local-arrangements committee was frankly expressed in the welcoming address of ex-Governor Lucius Fairchild. "We have searched the town with a fine rake for beds for you. We have searched Chicago for cots for you. We have searched other towns for blankets for you. We have stretched out hospitality to its utmost extent, but as our Mayor has truly said, our welcome has not been stretched at all."[9]

A few days ahead of the greatest crowds came the members of the exclusive National Council of Education, with its limited membership of fifty-one. Seeking to escape the distractions of the multitude, it met for some quiet sessions in the senate chamber. Even so, this dignified gathering of educational venerables was invaded by the young and uninitiated who did not know that there was such a thing in the educational world as a closed discussion group. Young, inexperienced, well-meaning Super-

[5] *Ibid.*, 68-69.
[6] *Ibid.*, 83; NEA, *Proceedings, 1909*, 30-31.
[7] Observers and records are at a variance. Estimates of members were 1,729 (NEA, *Proceedings, 1906*, 932); 2,729 (*NEA Handbook, 1954-55*, 27); 2,739 and 2,778 (NEA, *Proceedings, 1934*, 247, 238).
[8] NEA, *Proceedings, 1934*, 248.
[9] NEA, *Proceedings, 1884*, 20.

intendent James M. Greenwood walked in, never suspecting that he was an intruder. Even worse, one of his principals accompanied him. To Greenwood's consternation, the chairman's surprise, the audience's astonishment, and the guests' amusement, the principal addressed the chair and made a five-minute speech, endured, as Greenwood assumed, because the principal was a Negro.[10]

Another first-timer, Carroll G. Pearse, subsequently president of the NEA in 1912, "did not know that these Council meetings were supposed to be for members only, and that the *profanum vulgum* was not invited; and so, having arrived to attend the convention, he blundered into this select gathering." The great debaters were tolerant, however, and allowed the brash young visitor to remain and to return, for he sat through four morning, three afternoon, and two evening sessions.[11]

Came the opening day of the general sessions, Tuesday, July 15. The crowds had arrived. No auditorium could hold them. The senate chamber was filled; the assembly hall was crowded; a third audience assembled in the Congregational church. Some speakers repeated their speeches before the second group, and other persons were drafted as impromptu orators in order that the teachers not be disappointed. But Bicknell had wisely planned many sessions and had enlisted many speakers.

The speakers as well as the crowds were there. Never before was there so complete a roll call of American educators as assembled in Madison for this conventon, some to speak and some to hear others speak. Former presidents of the NEA were there: Zalmon Richards, 1858; Andrew J. Rickoff, 1859; D. B. Hagar, 1870; J. L. Pickard, 1871; E. E. White, 1872; B. G. Northrup, 1873; W. T. Harris, 1875; William F. Phelps, 1876; M. A. Newell, 1877; John Hancock, 1879; J. Ormond Wilson, 1880; James H. Smart, 1881; Eli T. Tappan, 1883. Future presidents of the NEA were there: F. Louis Soldan, 1885; W. E. Sheldon, 1887; Aaron Gove, 1888; Albert P. Marble, 1889; James H. Canfield, 1890; W. R. Garrett, 1891; J. M. Greenwood, 1898; Carroll G. Pearse, 1912; and in all probability others.

Governor Jeremiah Rusk, "a towering figure with his wide shoulders, rugged features, and a heavy mane of gray hair,"[12] welcomed the visitors. Others seconded the sentiments. Not least among all the speakers was the great showman himself, Thomas W. Bicknell. He arose, "majestic, over six feet tall, straight as a ship's mast, with full beard, a bald strip running back over the top of his head, two wisps of iron-gray hair standing out on the sides after the fashion of two horns, and with the voice of Stentor."[13] He gave the longest (forty-three pages) and most inclusive

[10] NEA, *Proceedings, 1912,* 154.
[11] NEA, *Proceedings, 1934,* 242.
[12] *Ibid.,* 250.
[13] *Ibid.,* 249.

presidential address ever delivered to the NEA, covering everything from the Northwest Ordinance to the current educational bills then before Congress.

William T. Harris, superintendent, philosopher, author, editor, and ubiquitous speaker, was there to give one of the 145 speeches that he was destined to make at NEA conventions; F. Louis Soldan from St. Louis, with his blond mustache and German accent; Alexander Graham Bell, huge Scotsman with splendid full beard, majestic as President Bicknell, student of oral methods of teaching the deaf, who, "searching for some device to enable his wife, who had lost her hearing, to communicate with her friends, [had] developed the principles which made him the inventor of the telephone"; John W. Dickinson, "slender, cultured, ascetic Yankee," a successor of Horace Mann as secretary of the Massachusetts state board of education;[14] C. M. Woodward of St. Louis, the most forceful expounder of the educational values of manual training that America ever produced; and not least in prominence was John Eaton, United States commissioner of education, urging Congress to assume more responsibility for educating its people.

Scholars were there: B. A. Hinsdale of Cleveland, destined for a professorship at Michigan; G. Stanley Hall, Ph.D., just rising to fame; Professor W. H. Payne, fairly launched on a career of scholarly productivity; W. W. Folwell, incisive, frank-spoken president of the rising University of Minnesota; President John Bascom of Wisconsin, greeting the teachers with grace and cordiality; Dr. Felix Adler of New York, founder of a school of unique distinction.

The South and southern problems were well, even overly, represented on the program. There was Jabez Lamar Munroe Curry of Alabama and Virginia, diplomatic molder of southern opinion and creator of state school systems, astute handler of the Peabody and Slater funds, lordly in manner but quietly determined to secure opportunities for all southern citizens, white and black.[15] From Massachusetts came the Reverend A. D. Mayo, traveling missioner of education and enlightenment, declaring that women teachers were the hope of a new day in southern education. Major Robert Bingham of North Carolina, who had been with Lee at Appomattox, was there to plead for Federal aid. Sensitive, dogmatic, he insisted upon dual school systems and declared that there was less racial prejudice in the South than in the North. Good will and peace could not prevail until "the leprosy of illiteracy" was removed from the white people.[16] In colorful and eloquent language Albert Salisbury told what the missionary societies were doing for the South. General S. C. Armstrong of Hampton

[14] *Ibid.*, 250.
[15] NEA, *Proceedings, 1903*, 365-368.
[16] NEA, *Proceedings, 1884*, 76-95.

was there, pleading for further help in educating the Indian.

The Negro himself was eloquently represented by Booker T. Washington, exuding humor, common sense, and good will. No wonder Bicknell took pride in having given this great leader a national platform. William H. Crogman of Georgia was even more forceful than his Alabama colleague. Crogman ridiculed the idea of colonization. "No, gentlemen, colonization will not do." "No, gentlemen, we are not going anywhere . . . the more you educate men the more sensitive you make them to bad treatment." He marveled over the progress made by a race that twenty-two years ago "did not own itself."[17]

Women. Women delegates and women speakers. Fifty-four per cent of the delegates were women. President Bicknell had planned it that way, saying that "the large opportunity granted to women at the present meeting may be regarded as confession and penance for past shortcomings."[18] Frances E. Willard, "with her wonderful speaking voice, and her charming, earnest, persuasive personality"; Clara Conway of Tennessee, "the visible impersonation of the graceful, gracious woman of the South"; May Wright Sewall of Indiana, suffragist, crusader, "brilliant, attractive"; Sarah E. Doyle of Rhode Island; Louisa P. Hopkins of Massachusetts—all of them on the program.[19] Women were there. They had arrived in Madison; they had arrived in the profession.

A convention is not given wholly to speeches and discussions. Those teachers at Madison, eager for instruction, wanted also some entertainment. They joyfully attended Governor Rusk's reception, they visited and revisited the exhibits, and they took frequent strolls along the shore of Lake Mendota.

Subsequent writers have provided a few sidelights on some of the prominent persons attending this memorable meeting. Eager young Carroll G. Pearse reported what he saw on the campus one day: "two well-dressed, fine looking men, with iron gray hair and neatly trimmed beards were seen lying in the shade on the lawn, smoking cigars." Since school men did not smoke, the observer assumed that these two reclining and relaxed gentlemen were local politicians. He was greatly surprised to discover that they were superintendents of schools, John Hancock of Toledo and Andrew J. Rickoff of Yonkers.[20]

On the opening day of the convention, "[my] attention was attracted to a spanking top buggy coming down the street drawn by a high-headed, high-stepping sorrel horse. The driver, a slender gentleman in the early forties, with dark eyes and a heavy dark mustache that might have been dyed, was dressed in an elegant white wool suit, cut Prince Albert style,

[17] *Ibid.*, 106-116, 125-130.
[18] *Ibid.*, 40.
[19] NEA, *Proceedings, 1934*, 249-250.
[20] *Ibid.*, 249.

with a white stovepipe hat, tilted jauntily over one eye, and was smoking a long cigar. Surely some local sporting gentleman"—but no, it was Aaron Gove, superintendent of schools in Denver.[21]

"A few minutes later applause broke out back at the door. Looking around, he saw the crowd . . . part and a big fat man with a round head, a big walrus mustache, little eyes squinting, dark complexion, a bullet scar on his thick neck, smiling and bowing his acknowledgements as he came down the aisle. His seatmate told the new man, 'why, that is Col. Francis W. Parker.' "[22]

A mass meeting in Capitol Square on Friday evening closed the great convention. By Saturday night the visiting throngs were on their way home or on the various excursions. How did the meeting look in retrospect? Was it merely a great show or was it a great contribution to the educational development of America?

There is no question of the opinion of the participants themselves. The nominating committee, headed by the conservative W. T. Harris, brought in an unprecedented and unanimous report for the reelection of Thomas W. Bicknell to succeed himself. He declined the honor. The assembly passed a resolution which went far beyond the perfunctory, praising the quality of the program and giving all credit to the president. Bicknell never minimized his part nor belittled the importance of the meeting. In fact, years later, in 1912, he gave a paper, "The Rebirth of the Association in 1884,"[23] in which he said that the Madison meeting was the first one of truly national proportions.

From the standpoint of the NEA there is no question of the importance of the 1884 meeting. After paying all expenses, the treasurer had over $3,000. The board boldly consigned the money to the permanent fund and faced the coming year with a balance of $5.28. While the membership declined in the following year, it never again sank to previous lows. In fact, three years later, at Chicago in 1887, it reached a high-water mark not again equaled until 1918. The "greatest educational show on earth" was not only a show but a permanent gain for the whole profession of education.

[21] *Ibid.*, 249.
[22] *Ibid.*, 248-249.
[23] NEA, *Proceedings, 1912*, 139-145.

23

The Guardians of Correct Thinking

"THE National Council of Education shall have for its object the consideration and discussion of educational questions of general interest and public importance, and the presentation, through printed reports, of the substance of the discussions and the conclusions formulated. It shall be its object to reach and disseminate correct thinking on educational questions."[1] So read the first part of the preamble to the constitution of the National Council of Education, adopted in 1884.

Further clarification of the thinking of the founders of the council is afforded by the remarks of D. B. Hagar of Massachusetts, a former president of the NEA. He advocated "the formation of a national council . . . as a means of establishing correct opinions on educational questions and of combating and overthrowing heresies and false notions of education. Of course it must be so constituted as to command the confidence and respect of the great body of teachers, but it is not necessary that it should be a large body."[2]

The original suggestion for the formation of a council was made by editor Thomas W. Bicknell in his *New England Journal of Education* of July 24, 1879. Subsequent issues carried elaborations of the proposal, letters of endorsement appeared in other magazines,[3] and some state associations passed resolutions in favor of such a council. In February 1880, Bicknell appeared before the Department of Superintendence at its meeting in Washington and expanded his arguments for the organization of a council.[4] He urged the desirability of having some national authority, a court of last resort to which educators could appeal, a body competent to formulate principles and courses of study.

A number of educators spoke. One proposed that the Department of Superintendence, rather than the National Educational Association, be

[1] NEA, *Proceedings, 1884,* 64.
[2] NEA, *Proceedings, 1880,* 17.
[3] *Indiana School Journal,* XXV, 156, March 1880.
[4] NEA, *Fiftieth Anniversary Volume, 1906,* 607.

the sponsoring parent. W. T. Harris thought that the council would run into difficulties if it were invested with "any conclusive power." J. P. Wickersham thought that such a body of educators would attain the necessary power by virtue of their status and wisdom. Aaron Gove of Denver feared that the taint of exclusiveness would thwart the ultimate purpose. The question of organizing a council was referred to a committee,[5] which reported favorably to the NEA at Chautauqua in July 1880, and the association approved the organization of the council. It was to consist of fifty-one members, chosen by the five departments, by the board of directors of the association, and by the council itself. The report of the organizing committee and the original constitution are almost cryptically silent as to the purpose of the council. It was "to consider educational questions of general interest and public importance."

The first roster of members is a roll call of prominent educators: T. W. Bicknell, W. T. Harris, John Eaton, James McCosh, E. E. White, A. J. Rickoff, W. W. Folwell, Henry Barnard, D. B. Hagar, Daniel C. Gilman, W. F. Phelps, J. L. Pickard, Aaron Gove, and thirty-eight others of varying degrees of prominence.[6]

The energetic Bicknell, who forty years later identified himself as "Founder and First President of the National Council of Education," lost no time in launching the new organization. Its first annual meeting was held at Lookout Mountain in July 1881, with "members only" in attendance. "The general body of educational people was not invited and for fostering the philosophical type of thought was not wanted."[7] The location was chosen to convenience those who wished to go on to the general meeting of the NEA in Atlanta. And so this advisory organization, a select group of eminent educators, was launched upon its strange career. What kind of thinking led to the formation of such a council?

Educators of the nineteenth century, like Americans generally, had a naïve faith in the value of intellectual exchange and the efficacy of discussion. That wisdom would evolve from debate and unity from diversity were major articles of the national creed. Organizations for the interchange of ideas and the promotion of discussion were regarded as necessary forums for the solving of educational problems. The numerous variations in educational practices that were inevitable among so many diverse districts and states provided a realistic situation for testing the validity of this widespread faith.

This faith led teachers to attend conventions and engage in endless discussions and debates. While the custom of the period required them

[5] NEA, *Proceedings, 1880*, 15-19; *1882*, 77-87.
[6] NEA, *Proceedings, 1880*, 93-94.
[7] NEA, *Proceedings, 1920*, 110-111.

to listen patiently and respectfully to long lectures on object teaching, the proper program for normal schools, and the mental values of manual training, it did not require acquiescence nor forbid subsequent pronouncements upon the speakers and their ideas. In fact, some of the bitterest criticisms were directed at the speakers who did not allow time for discussion. They were accused, or at least suspected, of trying to evade the testing of their ideas in the caldron of discussion.

The NEA and its departments provided extensive opportunities for speaking and debating. In addition, there were the state-association meetings, scores of local conventions, and hundreds of institutes. At all these gatherings the teachers hoped for a chance to express their opinions and to hear the clash of conflicting ideas.

The problems crying for solution were indeed numerous: the education of the freedmen, illiteracy, Federal aid to education, the function of the superintendent, mental discipline, the decline of the classics, compulsory school attendance, curriculum changes, methods, textbooks, and, above all in importance, the training of teachers. These and dozens of other issues, inevitable in a nation that was trying to evolve state systems and a national policy, arose to trouble the educators.

These issues evoked a spate of opinions and proposals. The jaunty and sanguine doctrine of the values of diversity in educational practice and the alleged wisdom that emerges from discussion was being sorely tried in the forum of reality. Confusion and dissension, rather than wisdom and unity, followed all too often. Educational leaders as well as typical teachers were disheartened and bewildered in the face of conflicting assertions and competing doctrines. Thomas W. Bicknell described many of the conventions as being "the stamping ground of furious pedagogic partisans, bringing out the worst instead of the best side of the disputants."[8]

The trend of thinking seemed to point, however, not to a loss of faith in the value of discussion but to its failure when carried on in large, popular audiences, composed of untrained teachers and persons uninformed about the issues under consideration. The discussion process was valid, but it could operate successfully only within a small, select body. This faith is emphatically reflected in the preamble to the constitution and in all the discussion incident to the founding of the National Council. Different views were to be precisely defined, fully stated, freely debated, and recorded for consideration. There was no question of the right to disagree, and such disagreements were not only tolerated but respected.

The National Council of Education was an incongruous creation, a combination of popular and aristocratic elements, of authority and

[8] NEA, *Proceedings, 1882,* 77-87; *1880,* 15-19.

humility. It adopted the popular procedure of discussion and tried to restrict its operation to a select group. Its conclusions, recommendations, and pronouncements were to serve as the guidance of a wise parent, but it lacked authority to take any parental action. Perhaps most of the members expected the council to have only such power, authority, and influence as it merited in the minds of thoughtful educators; they recognized that its decisions had to prove their validity in the arena of experience; its conclusions were to be advisory and not mandatory. A few, however, thought otherwise. S. H. White of Illinois Normal University said, "There should be authority, else the council can do no more than present organizations. It seems that it can only be advisory,—and here lies the weakness of our educational and of our political system: there is need of a spinal column somewhere." W. F. Phelps of Winona Normal School, with characteristic dogmatism, declared that "the authority of the council at first would be only such as the *character* of its members and the *wisdom and justice* of its conclusions would give it. The time may come when legal sanction could be given to its conclusions."[9]

The council, then, was founded to a considerable degree upon a belief in authority and also upon a widespread and persistent faith in eternal verities. The prevailing assumption was that there were such entities as good taste, truth, correct thinking, right answers, and "the best that has been thought and said." From Aristotle to W. T. Harris there was an almost unbroken line of believers in intellectual authority, exercised by church, state, institution, association, or a unique individual. Nothing is more natural, when perplexed in the face of competing alternatives, than to turn to a parent, prophet, king, senate, committee, or organization. Since popular discussion had not seemed to result in correct thinking, it was natural to turn to a select few who presumably could do for the multitude what it could not do for itself. Since no such group existed, the National Council of Education was created to meet the felt need.

In action the council did not work as its founders had hoped. Its functions were altered in unpredicted ways, and much of its history is a direct repudiation of the ideas of its founders. None of these developments and deviations from the original plans in the direction of democratization, however, negate the fact that the council was conceived in authority and born in exclusiveness. In spite of protestations to the contrary, it stressed opinion rather than fact, judgments rather than evidence, assertion rather than demonstration, tradition rather than experimentation, and general impressions rather than research.

It would be a historical error and a gross injustice to the founders of the council to accuse them of unprofessional attitudes. While various individuals may have had their share of vanity and conceit, the group as

[9] NEA, *Proceedings, 1882,* 80.

a whole was remarkably objective in visualizing the council and its functions. While any chosen individual may have derived a little self-conscious smugness from belonging to a select little group of chosen leaders, the general atmosphere revealed a degree of humility, a sense of obligation, a profound realization of the seriousness of the tasks which they undertook to perform for the NEA and the public.

The council had great difficulty in maintaining its original exclusiveness. Twenty-two years after its first session Bicknell, attending the Boston sessions of 1903, was annoyed "that the meetings were open to all comers," and he "felt called upon" to remind them of the more decorous custom of earlier years.[10] In 1908 the council resolved that its meetings should be held in a hall with a capacity of only five hundred and that one hundred seats be reserved for members, no one else being "permitted to occupy them at any time."[11] In 1916 it decided the hall should seat only two hundred.[12] In 1910 and again in 1917 it was resolved that the president designate some sessions as open to members only.

The council had even greater difficulty in maintaining the original plan of a small, select membership. Occasional references to snobbishness, aristocracy, and exclusiveness made persons both inside and outside the council somewhat self-conscious, and the idea of democratizing it by securing representatives of various fields and levels of the teaching profession became recurrent and persistent. By 1920 the president of the council, Homer H. Seerley, was misinterpreting the original nature of the council in order to give it the flavor of contemporary ideas by referring to it as a "delegate organization," whereas the original qualification was professional attainment and presumed capacity to contribute to the purposes of the council. The choice of members by various subdivisions of the NEA was a mere convenience and in no sense was the appointee beholden to the body which chose him.[13]

While Seerley was mistaken about some aspects of the past, he was entirely correct as to the contemporary nature of the council in 1920. It had become a delegate organization with an inevitable lessening of pride in membership. One of the steps which marked this shift from the original plan and purpose of the council was a motion, passed in 1908 in the general business meeting, amending the NEA constitution to increase the membership of the National Council to 120. The argument was that the growth of the NEA should be reflected in an enlarged council.[14] Members of the council had no choice and they supported the motion in a lukewarm fashion. Further changes in membership followed

[10] NEA, *Proceedings, 1920,* 110.
[11] NEA, *Proceedings, 1908,* 322.
[12] NEA, *Proceedings, 1916,* 247.
[13] NEA, *Proceedings, 1920,* 112.
[14] NEA, *Proceedings, 1908,* 33, 7, 321.

and by 1940 the total was 178 council members. The NEA constitution, with seeming impatience over all the changes, decreed that the number should be more than 120 and less than 200.[15]

During its active career of more than sixty years, from 1880 to 1943, the National Council of Education rendered four major and several minor services to American education with varying degrees of success. The *first* of these was to provide a dignified forum for discussion, whose conclusions were similar to the decisions of a court of high opinion. The *second* service of the council was the long series of reports which it prepared or sponsored. These reports and discussions were the major portions of all council programs. For example, some of the topics and problems they dealt with in the early years were licensure of teachers, opportunities of the rural population for education, the educational value of manual training, what statistics should be collected, the practical culture of the moral virtues, and promotions in city schools.[16]

The *third* undertaking of the council was the directing of investigation and research. Beginning in 1898, it became the agent of the NEA "to initiate, conduct, and guide the thoro investigation of important educational questions. . . ."[17] It also received recommendations concerning research and made the decisions concerning appropriations for such purposes.

The *fourth,* and doubtless the greatest, service of the National Council was its sponsorship of hundreds of convention programs. Year after year the program makers chose timely topics, some of them highly controversial, secured prominent speakers, and often fanned platform differences into lively debates. Four or five sessions with three to eight speakers were typical. In 1911 it was reported that attendance was falling off because many members had to stay at home to teach in summer schools. The council decided upon a strange remedy, namely, to double the number of sessions by establishing a winter as well as a summer convention.[18] Attendance at both series increased. The roll call of speakers would include nearly all leading American educators from 1885 to 1943. If the council could claim credit for all that was said under its auspices and for all the achievements of its speakers, it would be an impressive record.

Among the minor and temporary services which the council rendered to the NEA and to the public, a few are worthy of mention: annual reports on educational developments in the United States; the passing of resolutions, thus providing the profession and the public with an index of educational thinking; recording, through its committees on necrology,

[15] NEA, *Proceedings, 1940,* 174, 691.
[16] NEA, *Proceedings, 1889,* 352-353; *1892,* 749-750.
[17] NEA, *Proceedings, 1898,* 495.
[18] NEA, *Proceedings, 1911,* 341; *1912,* 504-507, 575-577.

brief statements of the careers and achievements of some leading educators; sponsoring joint conferences with various groups and organizations; making recommendations to the NEA and to any of the departments which requested such help.

These varied services might seem to indicate strength and vitality, but in reality they evidence variability, uncertainty, and confusion. In the early years the selectness of the membership gave an aura of authority to its conclusions and recommendations. In varying degrees the council continued the function of appraising theories and practices, of synthesizing and, if possible, reconciling conflicting doctrines. But as the years passed its status and influence declined, and what was said in the council had no more effect than what was said in a dozen other conventions. It early became evident that as a director of research the council was ineffective. Such activities as could properly be called research were carried on in connection with the work of committees. In 1925 Jesse H. Newlon, president of the NEA, declared that it was "a useless duplication for the Council to undertake research or the direction of research."[19] The changing policies with respect to investigation and research, to the sponsorship of meetings, and to the relationships with other organizations, as well as shifts in the number of members and the exclusiveness of the sessions, all indicate the lack of a clear and definite program.

As the council wavered, its members became less faithful. They became lax in participating in discussion and suffered the indignity of listening to exhortations on their duties. "Opportunity was given for general discussion, but no questions were raised on the points brought out in the address."[20] "There was no time for a discussion of this report."[21] The president hurled such bromides as "Any organization needs to be active to maintain an effective service," and admonished the members to suggest problems for study, to be more active workers, to complete their studies, and to push their deliberations to a conclusion.[22] In 1936 it was resolved to ask the NEA "to change the National Council in a way that will give it a significant function."[23] In 1940 the membership committee scolded the council and advised that membership be restricted "to contributors, to faithful attendants, to those who take active part in voting and in responding to council communications."

The members of the council became gradually aware that dissolution by the NEA was a real threat. In 1912 the constitution of the NEA (Article IV, Section 8) was changed to read, "The powers and duties of the Council may be changed or the Council abolished upon a two-thirds

[19] NEA, *Proceedings, 1925,* 273.
[20] NEA, *Proceedings, 1927,* 291.
[21] NEA, *Proceedings, 1919,* 149.
[22] NEA, *Proceedings, 1920,* 111-113.
[23] NEA, *Proceedings, 1936,* 154.

vote of the Association. . . ."[24] That redundant provision, containing the harsh word "abolished," must have had a disquieting effect upon the members of the council, for it showed that some persons already had murder in their hearts. And how could a sensitive and fearful member escape a feeling of concern over the opening sentence of a former president of the council who was called upon to help celebrate the fortieth anniversary of its founding? He said, "I am happy indeed that this is not an obituary or a memorial service."[25]

In 1925 the president of the NEA, speaking to the council, said: "A generation ago the National Council of Education was a body of great importance. Membership was highly coveted and carried with it great distinction. . . . I am sure that membership in the Council is still regarded as an honor." The past tense and the fact that he felt impelled to mention the matter awaken some doubts as to the actuality of the honor. The speaker continued by saying that the council had been overshadowed by other organizations, that its programs had been no different from those of other groups, and that there were other research agencies; and he ended by declaring that if the council was only duplicating the functions of other organizations, "then it ought to go out of business." Here was a combination of threatened murder and suggested suicide.[26]

In 1937 Henry Lester Smith, president of the council, devoted a part of his address to the topic "Points to be considered regarding the advisability of continuing the National Council."[27] At the same meeting the committee on resolutions declared: "In view of the fact that the National Council has become an outmoded division of the National Education Association, with its original functions substantially served by the Educational Policies Commission and its consultants . . . That the National Council declare itself dissolved at the close of the forthcoming Detroit meeting. . . ." At Detroit, however, the council members unanimously declined to commit suicide, and so the council was given a further reprieve.[28]

In spite of the enthusiasm generated by a recoil from self-destruction, the crisis was merely postponed. At Buffalo in 1946 the Representative Assembly of the NEA decided that the work for which the council was created was then being performed by the Research Division and the Policies Commission, and that it was "the opinion of those who studied the matter . . . that it should be discontinued." At the Cincinnati meeting in 1947 the proposed amendment came up for a final vote. "Is there any discussion? (Question called for.) All those in favor of . . ." And so

[24] NEA, *Proceedings*, 1912, 8.
[25] NEA, *Proceedings*, 1920, 144.
[26] NEA, *Proceedings*, 1925, 271-275.
[27] NEA, *Proceedings*, 1937, 165-167.
[28] NEA, *Proceedings*, 1937, 167-168.

without any discussion the council that had been organized for discussion was abolished.[29]

Here the story of the National Council of Education would appear to be complete. The shifting purposes and functions and the changing personnel seem to explain its decline and demise. Such a view would, however, be quite incomplete and an opportunity for gaining insight into a basic change in educational attitudes would be lost if no reference was made to the external developments which wrote the death warrant for the National Council with much more certainty than did any of the internal difficulties. The council would have died from external pressures had all internal matters been managed differently.

Several interrelated factors were operating to nullify the easygoing assumption that discussion, debate, logic, and reason would settle educational problems. The rising and spreading sense of democracy ran counter to the exclusiveness and authoritativeness of the council. The freeing of the slaves, the development of coeducation, the entrance of women into teaching, and the growth of respect for children were trends that undermined the separatism of the council. While one teacher or one professor was not necessarily as good as another, the feeling that he should not be stigmatized by exclusion from the inner council was slowly evolving. The yearly meetings of the NEA were occasions for mild displays of dignity and elegance. The Prince Albert coats, flowing beards, and vigorous mustaches of the speakers and officers naturally awed and impressed the audiences. While these badges of formalism and style were relatively harmless, they did induce a mild degree of self-consciousness that found its outlet in colorful words and emphatic pronouncements. The spirit operating against these vanities may be called leveling rather than democratic; but, however it be identified, the eventual urge toward an equality that effaced acknowledged differences between rural teachers, city superintendents, college professors, men teachers, and women teachers was overwhelming. Whether the council was alien or friendly to this growth of equality within the profession, it seemed to many contemporaries to be an obstacle to democracy in education. It had to go.

Educational reforms, derived from the experience of teachers, were antithetical to the council's stress upon discussion as the method of ascertaining professional truths. Object teaching, grounded upon the basic principle that one learns through sense experiences, was immediately accepted by thousands of teachers, some of whom carried it to extremes. Object teaching and the kindergarten movement made progress whether they were blessed or condemned by the council.

Another reform was the child-study movement, which bounded into

[29] NEA, *Proceedings, 1946*, 135, 232; *1947*, 69-70.

popularity in the early 1890's. By 1894 it had a department within the NEA and numerous state societies. The idea of learning about children by observing them was a novel idea to those who thought that they already understood children.

Other reforms and developments, such as the manual-training movement, the establishment of mechanical and agricultural colleges under the Morrill Act of 1862, the growth of biological study under Agassiz and geology under Nathaniel Shaler, and the slow spread of Darwinism, were calculated to increase scientific objectivity and lessen reliance upon philosophizing, discussing, and arguing. Agassiz' warning to his students on Penikese Island not to read and promising never to ask them what they had been told, only what they had seen, and Shaler's scorn of textbooks and lectures,[30] stand out in contrast with the typical professor's injunction to read, study, memorize, and recite. Such developments were slowly changing the intellectual climate of America, and the members of the National Council of Education saw tradition and authority crumble under the impact of observation and evidence.

The status of the council was eventually jarred by another development, the quantification of the results of teaching. Educators were accustomed to debating the questions of how much time should be devoted to arithmetic or spelling, and what results should be expected. Along in the 1890's came J. M. Rice, who asked the much simpler question, "What results are actually obtained within a given period?" His studies showed that children who devoted ten minutes a day to spelling could spell as well as those who devoted forty minutes a day to the subject. Rice computed the results in arithmetic and language and concluded that it was practicable to compare the efficiency of school systems in various cities. His strictures upon the schools of St. Louis, Baltimore, and other cities provoked a great deal of discussion. There is no question that his studies had great influence in hastening the whole scientific movement in education.[31]

Another factor in the disintegration of the council was pragmatism. While the word was new, having been popularized by William James in the late 1890's, the idea was old. In 1857 Horace Greeley, speaking at an academy in Pennsylvania, said: "That son is not truly educated who cannot grow more corn on an acre than his unlearned father, and grow it with less labor. That educated daughter has received a mistaken and superficial training if she cannot excel her mother in making soap or

---

[30] NEA, *Proceedings, 1872,* 233.

[31] Rice's studies appeared in *The Forum* from 1892 to 1897. Most of them were subsequently published in his *The Public School System of the United States* (New York, 1893) and *Scientific Management in Education* (New York, 1913). His indictment was broad, including criticisms of administration, supervision, teacher competence, the curriculum, and many other elements.

cheese or butter."[32] Pragmatism was an idea that could be applied to evaluating a subject, a school system, and an organization. It was eventually applied to the National Council of Education, and the results proved fatal to that organization.

Further use of quantification as part of a growing scientific movement in education contributed to the outmoding of the council. The measurement of intelligence, started by Alfred Binet in 1905, was developed and refined by research and experimentation. The idea of using specific tests spread rapidly and scores of achievement tests to measure pupil performance were made. Surveys of school systems took on the aura of specificity, and by 1930 everything was being tested, measured, evaluated, and appraised, including administration and administrators, supervision and supervisors, teaching and teachers. Last to be affected were the curriculum and purposes, but these too were finally quantified. In the face of this impressive, scientific, and objective movement, the old debating procedure of the council seemed antiquated. "I think," "I believe," and "I am convinced" appeared quaint when contrasted with tables of figures.

The further growth of research and experimentation also served to contravene the assumptions and procedures of the National Council. While the council itself had sponsored investigations in the form of questionnaires and informal inquiries, it had not reached a high level of objectivity, and its function of advising the NEA on needed studies was little more than an official pretense. In the meantime universities, agricultural experiment stations, state departments, city school systems, and other agencies established research bureaus or divisions which developed techniques of gathering, studying, and presenting statistical data. By 1912 one writer proclaimed that education had become an "expermental science."[33] In 1923 William A. McCall published his *How to Experiment in Education*. The American Educational Research Association, organized in 1915 under a slightly different name, became a department of the NEA in 1930. In the meantime (1922) the NEA established its Research Division and began publication of its *Research Bulletin*. All these developments made the so-called research activities of the council seem obsolete.

The last of the external factors that made the council into an anachronism was the formation in 1935 of the Educational Policies Commission, established under joint auspices of the NEA and the Department of Superintendence. During the educational crisis brought on by the depression of the early 1930's, the NEA and the department had appointed an emergency commission whose work was so successful in

---

[32] *Pennsylvania School Journal*, VI, 158-160, November 1857.
[33] Quoted in Walter S. Monroe, *Teacher-Learning Theory and Teacher Education, 1890 to 1950* (Urbana, 1952), 63.

planning and in arousing popular interest that it was decided to transform the temporary agency into a standng commission and give it a trial period of at least five years.[34] The Educational Policies Commission was an immediate success. Its early publications were at once timely and influential. Its distinguished membership and the attention given its published statements indicated that by better procedures the commission was succeeding where the National Council had often failed.

[34] NEA, *Proceedings, 1936,* 463-467.

24

Departments of the NEA

THE National Education Association of the United States is a variegated organization, apparently changing its form as one changes his viewpoint. To the casual layman it is a centralized agency with impressive headquarters in Washington from which issue bulletins, pronouncements, and propaganda in favor of Federal aid for public education. To a delegate from West Virginia the Representative Assembly is the NEA. To the president of the board of education at Cedartown, Georgia, the NEA is a great national ally, ready to provide statistics and information. To a member of the Educational Policies Commission the NEA is a sponsor, patron, and supporter. To the superintendent at Faith, South Dakota, the American Association of School Administrators is the NEA. To the seventh-grade teacher at Tulare, California, the Department of Classroom Teachers is the NEA. To the biology teacher at Aspen, Colorado, the Department of Science Teachers is the NEA.

Within the NEA a large number of members think of the department to which they belong as the essence and core of the association. In truth, the departments do provide for many teachers the publications, the conventions, and the professional contacts that give reality and vitality to what otherwise might seem to them to be a remote, nebulous, and perhaps too inclusive organization.

Departments! Departments for various purposes—to improve the teaching of science, to promote the use of audio-visual materials, to build a better curriculum. Departments for various people—for teachers, superintendents, researchers, principals, supervisors, secretaries. Departments of all sizes—the Classoom Teachers with more than half a million members, the Secondary-School Principals with about 15,000, and the National Association of Journalism Directors with 1,450 members. Departments, past and present—the Department of Education of the Deaf, the Blind, and the Feeble-minded of 1897, the Department of Indian Education of 1899, the Department of Secondary Education that was in and out, and the thirty departments of 1957.

Departments originated in various ways. A group of kindergarteners belonged to the Froebel Institute of America. Seeing the advantages of affiliation with a larger organization, the institute asked for admission into the NEA; at Madison in 1884 it was reorganized as the Department of Kindergarten Instruction. The Department of Home Economics, founded in 1930, grew out of earlier organizations of cooking and sewing teachers and to some extent from the American Home Economics Association. The NEA occasionally sponsored a small group in a new subject in order to build up a department. Combinations of four regional associations joined the Department of Art Education in 1948, assuming the name of National Art Education Association. Thus departments grew or emerged from the fusion of existing councils and associations, or were adopted by the NEA, or were organized in response to its request.

The naming of departments was usually a matter of little consequence. The Journalism Directors, Elementary Principals, and Council of Teachers of Mathematics have revealing and accurate names. Since several departments started as independent organizations, they tended to keep their original name and simply add the designation "Department of the NEA." Eighteen departments use the word "association" in their names, thirteen use "national," four use "council," and four use "American." Occasionally a department changes its name because of shifts in purpose or changes in conditions. For example, the Department of Immigrant Education seemed somewhat out of date after the establishment of restricted immigration quotas in the 1920's; so the department changed its name to Adult Education and enlarged its functions. With the changes in educational thinking the name Manual Training seemed too restricted and so it became Industrial Arts. A few names were not apt or revealing. For example, one could not tell from the name that the former Department of School Administration was for school-board members, nor could one know that the former Department of School Patrons was composed essentially of women's organizations that sought to strengthen public education. In general, however, the names are apt and accurately indicate the function or area of endeavor.

The departments have somewhat similar policies and practices. With the exception of the classroom teachers and higher education, each department has separate membership fees and maintains a budget separate from that of the parent association. Most departments elect a president, vice-president, and a secretary, called an executive secretary if he is a full-time employee. Each department appoints numerous committees, whose reports are discussed and sometimes published. Many departments have state and local affiliates that sustain and in turn are sustained by the national department. Most departments hold meetings in connection with the summer convention, and some also meet in February at the convention of superintendents. In addition, several hold separate conventions. For example, the music teachers meet in the spring and the social-studies teachers hold their annual convention at Thanksgiving.

The departments are exceedingly active in providing materials for their members and the public. Most of them publish a magazine, a yearbook, series of books on particular issues, bulletins, and service booklets. The departments pass resolutions and carry on programs of public relations. In a sense, each department is a miniature edition of the National Education Association, trying to promote educational progress, extend popular understanding, and increase public support of education. Departments are independent and yet they are also part of a great, inclusive national organization. The NEA as a whole is literally one organization and many organizations, each of which is, like a child within a family, both independent and dependent.

The parent organization provides offices in the NEA Center in Washington for the twenty-one departments that have chosen to maintain headquarters and staffs there. Most of the other nine departments, with headquarters elsewhere than in Washington, have part-time secretaries. Some departments receive financial assistance from the NEA treasury, but most are self-supporting. All that maintain headquarters offices in the NEA Center receive the *de facto* subsidy of free office space, furniture, phone, and custodial service. They also receive aid from the NEA in publicizing their activities, in selling their publications, and in joint purchase of supplies, printing, and various services.

The departments, on their part, make substantial contributions to the parent association. Their individual and collective services to better teaching, supervision, administration, welfare, and public relations are great indeed. While some activities are carried on under formal arrangements for joint sponsorship by the NEA and one or more of its departments, varied patterns of informal cooperation are more numerous and significant. For example, departmental staff members in Washington are in continual contact with members of the staff of the NEA proper.

The combined annual expenditures of the thirty departments are only slightly less than the annual budget of the NEA itself. Most of this money, amounting to nearly three million dollars a year, is collected in the form of departmental dues from persons who also pay dues to the parent association. Although the NEA bylaws require that department members shall also be members of the NEA, this regulation is not rigidly enforced.

There are many who find places for their special interests and for participation in an NEA department who would never find such opportunities in the parent association alone. For some of these, their major loyalty is to the department rather than to the NEA, because of their interest in the publications, conventions, and other activities of their favorite specialty group. It sometimes happens that such departmental members fail to understand the connection between departments and parent organization and the substantial benefits that departments derive as a result of that connection.

The separateness of the departments has troubled many NEA officials, and several attempts have been made to bring about a degree of uniformity in their relationships with the parent body. In 1903, when Charles W. Eliot was president of the NEA, he called a meeting of department presidents "to consult together concerning the preparation of programs for the convention. . . ."[1] To bring about better integration of the departments with the NEA among other duties, Lyle W. Ashby, long a member of the NEA staff, was appointed assistant secretary for professional relations in 1949. A 1951 statement of guiding principles for departments spoke of "the strength, initiative, and honest differences which spring from diversity. . . . Freedom on the part of NEA units to act in their respective areas is one of the great sources of strength in the Association." In 1954 an annual two-day conference of the presidents and secretaries of the departments was started. In spite of the autonomy of the departments and their diversity of interests, the NEA seems to be evolving a policy of cooperative integration.

The conditions under which a department of the NEA is authorized are stated in the bylaws. The revision of 1924, which is still effective, requires that 250 members signify an interest in the proposed department and that the group hold successful meetings for three successive years. It is recommended but not required that the proposed department be self-supporting. In 1924 it was expected that a service, such as supervision or classroom teaching, rather than subject matter, such as history or science, should be the basis for the organization of a department,[2] but the expectation has not been realized in practice.

Several petitions for the establishment of departments have been postponed or refused. For example, in 1904 the board turned down the request to establish a department of mathematical education.[3] Director J. M. Green argued that the increase in departments lessened interest in those which already existed, and that mathematics already received ample attention. Another director referred to "the rather chaotic condition of the teaching of mathematics" and favored the establishment of the department. Nevertheless, the board rejected the petition and a department for mathematics was not authorized until 1950.

The board of directors has been willing to abolish departments as well

[1] NEA, *Proceedings, 1903*, 38.
[2] NEA, *Proceedings, 1924*, 92; *1925*, 941.
[3] NEA, *Proceedings, 1904*, 33.

as create them. In 1924, for example, it abolished the Department of Elementary Education, the Department of the Wider Use of School-houses, the Department of Higher Education, and the Department of School Administration. It also merged the Departments of Child Health and Physical Education into the Department of School Health and Physical Education.[4] The Department of Adult Education voted its own dissolution in 1951 after it had participated with other groups in the field of adult education in establishing a new, more inclusive, independent organization—the Adult Education Association. The NEA board of directors cooperated by agreeing to discontinue the department.

In spite of the great similarities of the departments, each has evolved out of widely different circumstances and conditions; each has developed unique characteristics and methods of operation. Each has effected changes and exerted influence for professional betterment in the area of its interests. In addition to the rise and decline of departments, many have changed their names from time to time to indicate a change of scope or to identify former organizations incorporated by merger. Past and present there have been about fifty departments of the NEA. At present the thirty departments fall into four groups or categories: (1) administrative, (2) curriculum, (3) the nature or level of those instructed, and (4) service. In the lists that follow the departments are identified by their 1957 names, and the date given for each is the year in which it became a department (although it should be remembered that many had existed independently for some years prior to that date).

ADMINISTRATION

1. American Association of School Administrators, 1870
2. Department of Elementary School Principals, 1921
3. National Association of Women Deans and Counselors, 1918
4. National Association of Secondary-School Principals, 1927
5. National Council of Administrative Women in Education, 1932

CURRICULUM AREAS

1. American Association for Health, Physical Education and Recreation, 1937
2. American Industrial Arts Association, 1939
3. Association for Supervision and Curriculum Development, 1929
4. Department of Home Economics, 1930
5. Department of Vocational Education, 1875
6. Music Educators National Conference, 1940
7. National Art Education Association, 1933
8. National Association of Journalism Directors, 1939
9. National Council for the Social Studies, 1925

[4] NEA, *Proceedings, 1924,* 92, 96.

10. National Council of Teachers of Mathematics, 1950
11. National Science Teachers Association, 1895
12. Speech Association of America, 1939
13. United Business Education Association, 1892

INSTRUCTION OF SELECTED GROUPS OR CLASSES

1. American Association of Colleges for Teacher Education, 1948
2. Association for Higher Education, 1942
3. Department of Kindergarten-Primary Education, 1884
4. Department of Rural Education, 1907
5. International Council for Exceptional Children, 1941
6. National Association of Public School Adult Educators, 1955

SERVICE

1. American Educational Research Association, 1930
2. Department of Audio-Visual Instruction, 1923
3. Department of Classroom Teachers, 1913
4. National Association of Educational Secretaries, 1946
5. National Retired Teachers Association, 1951
6. National School Public Relations Association, 1950

To identify a typical department of the NEA is somewhat like trying to name a normal year. It is easy, however, to name a department that illustrates many of the characteristics and generalizations described above. The typical, or at least the modal, department will be concerned with the curriculum, since the number in that category is largest of the four groups. For purpose of illustration the National Council for the Social Studies may be cited, although the science, mathematics, art, or music department would be equally revealing and typical. A calendar of the development of the chosen department is illustrative of the evolution and activities of many other departments.

THE NATIONAL COUNCIL FOR THE SOCIAL STUDIES

1. Was organized at Atlantic City in 1921.
2. Became a department of the NEA in 1925.
3. Published its first yearbook in 1931.
4. Held its first independent convention, in New York, in 1935.
5. Started its own magazine, *Social Education,* in 1937.
6. Was incorporated under the laws of Illinois in 1939.
7. Established headquarters at the NEA building in Washington in 1940 with a full-time executive secretary.
8. Published a joint report, with the cooperation of historical associations, on American history in 1944.
9. Holds joint meetings with the historical, geographic, and political-science organizations as well as the NEA and American Association of School Administrators.
10. Started in various years a series of bulletins, a curriculum series, a "how

to do it" series, and booklets published in cooperation with other organizations.

11. Appointed more and more active committees as the Council grew in size.
12. Held bigger and better conventions with more programs and speakers as it gained experience.
13. Sponsored and nourished regional, state, city, and local affiliated councils.

Largest and least typical of the departments is that of Classroom Teachers. In fact, it is so unlike the others that it is almost misleading to call it a department at all. It has no roll of membership and no income of its own, depending entirely upon the parent body (the NEA) for support. Every NEA member who is a classroom teacher below the college level is, by definition, a member of this department, but thousands are unaware of the fact.

In its state and regional branches, as well as in its national organization, the DCT trains classroom teachers for positions of leadership in the NEA and other parts of the organized profession. Of the several classroom teachers who have served as presidents of the NEA during the past quarter-century, nearly all had previously been officers in the Department of Classroom Teachers.

The department issues publications of practical value to teachers; it sponsors national and regional conferences; and it speaks for the teaching with a commanding voice. The prominence and influnce of the classroom teachers in the NEA of the mid-twentieth century is symptomatic of the basic change in the nature of the national association that has taken place since the latter decades of the nineteenth century (see Chapter 27).

The Department of Classroom Teachers was, indeed, late in emerging. One explanation for the delay is obvious. The majority of classroom teachers were women; and in the days before the Nineteenth Amendment (1920), women were regarded as not quite full-feathered citizens or full-plumaged members of the profession. So the story of the classroom teachers' department is part of the story of the transformation of women from passive recipients to active participants; it is also part of the story of the democratization of the NEA and the profession.

While the NEA passed innocuous resolutions in 1863, 1885, 1898, 1911, and at other times in favor of better salaries for teachers, for more than half a century it did little to secure them. The educational leaders assumed that the building of a profession took precedence over problems of the personal welfare of teachers; that once the profession was established, teachers would naturally achieve status, security, and dignity. Time has not proved that they were wrong. In the meantime, however, teachers were not nourished by future prospects or solaced by the higher status of educational administrators. Even though they accepted the philosophy of "eventually," they decided to hurry the inevitable. In short, they resolved to organize and nudge destiny into a faster pace.

At Chicago in 1912 the NEA endorsed woman suffrage; appropriated money for a further study of salaries, tenure, and pensions; and received a petition to create the Department of Classroom Teachers. At Salt Lake City in the following year the petition was approved, and the first program of the department was presented at St. Paul in 1914. The first president was Florence Rood,[5] mild in manner, but determined in spirit; other persons of similar nature assumed leadership and demonstrated that the new department was going to pronounce and act, not wait decorously for time and chance to solve the problems of teachers. In fact, the first few meetings remind one of a broken dam releasing long-pent pressures.

Even though dignitaries—such as Joseph Swain, president of the NEA; J. W. Crabtree, president of River Falls Normal College; Superintendent Ella F. Young of Chicago; and various professors—were present at the early meetings, the members lost no time in airing their grievances and proclaiming their demands. Led by Margaret Haley, experienced organizer of Chicago teachers, Mary O'Connor of Buffalo, and other outspoken teachers, the department adopted vigorous resolutions denouncing "arbitrary or perfunctory" teacher-rating scales and calling for the establishment of advisory councils of teachers to give expert professional advice to superintendents and school boards. One teacher characterized standardized rating scales as a "pernicious system" and "fundamentally wrong." He saw no more sense in trying to standardize teachers than in standardizing lawyers, doctors, and preachers, and no more justice in discharging a teacher than in discharging a missionary or a minister.[6] Salary, tenure, and pensions were discussed without disdain or apology, for the classroom teachers saw no antithesis between these factors and President Swain's admonition to keep "the interests of the children" in view.

During the First World War speakers at the meetings of the Department of Classroom Teachers discussed vocational guidance, preparedness, democracy, teacher shortage, and salaries, and one speaker demonstrated the use of the phonograph. At Pittsburgh in 1918 the department resolved to start "a nation-wide campaign for increased salaries for teachers in order to avert the most serious menace that public education in the United States has ever had to meet. . . ." W. C. Bagley of Teachers College, Columbia University, lamented the lack of status of the classroom teacher and saw some hope if the public would distinguish between administrative details, which lay boards could carry out, and educational policy, which only educators could formulate. In 1919 President Lotus D. Coffman of the University of Minnesota scolded the teachers because

---

[5] NEA, *Proceedings, 1912*, 43; *1914*, 909-916.
[6] NEA, *Proceedings, 1915*, 1161-1177.

he had heard that some of them wanted to eliminate supervision, because some demagogue had declared that school administrators were mediocre, and because he feared that class dictation might evolve from class consciousness. Other speakers discussed teacher shortage, salaries, democracy, and citizenship.[7]

At Salt Lake City in 1920 appeared A. E. Winship, circuit-riding educator, editor, optimist, and ubiquitous speaker, declaring, "There will be no democracy in education that does not come to and thru and by the classroom teachers." Sara H. Fahey, president of the department from 1917 to 1922, showed how salary schedules established caste and how the great reservoir of teacher knowledge was unused by architects and administrators.[8]

At Boston in 1922 the department adopted a constitution that provided for sectional representation on an executive committee. It asked for and received a grant of $5,000 from the NEA as an annual budget. A spirited and prolonged contest finally resulted in the election of Effie MacGregor of Minneapolis as president. Activities increased. The first yearbook was issued in 1926. A *News Bulletin,* appearing three times a year, began in 1928. Pamphlets on tenure, retirement, ethics, taxation, credit unions, and other topics were also published. The program and influence of the department expanded greatly after 1942, when it employed its first full-time executive secretary, Hilda Maehling, prior to that date a junior-high-school teacher in Terre Haute, Indiana, and since 1955 an assistant executive secretary of the NEA.

In addition to meetings and publications the department has cooperated with other departments, commissions, and committees and has played an important part in the over-all program of the NEA. It was influential in securing the creation of the National Commission for the Defense of Democracy Through Education in 1941 and the National Commission on Teacher Education and Professional Standards in 1946. It stimulated contributions to the DuShane Memorial Defense Fund, and it originated the idea for the Overseas Teacher-Relief Fund. Accomplishments inspired confidence and built morale. By 1955 the annual budget reached $100,000. In view of the enormous growth in total NEA membership (of which an estimated 85 per cent are classroom teachers), it is clear that the destinies of the Department of Classroom Teachers and of the NEA are closely identified.

Second oldest, and in some respects the most influential of all NEA departments, past and present, is the American Association of School

---

[7] NEA, *Proceedings, 1916,* 637-652; *1917,* 615-622; *1918,* 381-387; *1919,* 376-377.
[8] NEA, *Proceedings, 1920,* 343-355. For J. W. Crabtree's forceful and beautiful tribute to Winship, see NEA, *Proceedings, 1933,* 175-176.

Administrators. Out of educational chaos it evolved procedures and built a profession of school administration. Known until 1937 as the Department of Superintendence, it was a charter member or an original component of the National Educational Association that was formed at Cleveland in 1870. In fact, the organization of the National Association of School Superintendents was started at Harrisburg in 1865 and completed at Washington in February 1866. As an association it held meetings in connection with the National Teachers' Association at Indianapolis in 1866 and at Nashville in 1868, and it also met in Washington every winter. It met in the nation's capital in order to promote the creation of the Federal Bureau of Education and to forward Federal aid for the South. Thus, since 1870, the superintendents have maintained the dual role of being an independent association and also being a cooperative unit of the more inclusive NEA.

From 1866 to 1890 the Department of Superintendence held its annual business meeting at the time of the summer convention, electing superintendents to office and placing a great variety of educators on its programs. In 1890 it shifted its business meeting to the February session. Other groups began to meet concurrently with the superintendents, and the winter meeting became a great convention with multiple interests.

The programs during these early years, at both the summer and winter sessions, constituted a mirror of evolving principles and practices. When recorded in the *Proceedings* they became a guiding textbook for those who tried to keep abreast of the fast-developing profession known as school administration. The four greatest problems which the superintendents considered in successive conventions during these years were (1) taxation and school support; (2) the functions of the superintendent and his relations to the board of education, particularly the question of the superintendent's control of the business aspects of managing schools; (3) the making of the curriculum; and (4) supervision of teachers and programs. District organization was slowly replaced by consolidated, township and county units, and the percentage of funds that was handled by state departments of education gradually increased. Step by step superintendents won ascendancy over business managers and gained a clearer acceptance of their prerogatives as administrators. Supervisors, principals, and eventually teachers came to assume the major role in curriculum-making, and, contrary to the ideas of the nineteenth century, supervision finally emerged as a function quite separated from administration.

In all these changes, trends, and movements, the Department of Superintendence played a prominent part. Starting in a period when educational principles were general to the point of vagueness, and practices so individualized as to provide few generalizations, the department served as an annual clearinghouse of evolving theories and practices. While school men cheerfully accepted the great variations among states and cities and fiercely maintained the principle of local autonomy in educational matters, they nevertheless unwittingly began the creation of a nationwide policy even though there could not be a national educational system. The contributions of the Department of Superintendence, both the spoken words and the printed *Proceedings*, were especially influential in the first fifty years (1857-1907), when educational communication was still in an embryonic stage.

In addition to sustaining their own department of administration, the superintendents were mainstays of the National Council of Education, appeared frequently on the general programs and at the meetings of other departments, and conducted the exhibits at the winter conventions.

The superintendents provided a galaxy of devoted leaders who contributed to the development of education in general as well as to the superintendency in particular. Andrew J. Rickoff (1824-1899), second president of the National Teachers' Association, superintendent in Cincinnati and in Cleveland from 1867 to 1882, was sometimes called "the father of the graded school system."[9] James P. Wickersham (1825-1891), state superintendent of public instruction of Pennsylvania, advocated Federal aid for the South, promoted normal schools, and devised uniform systems of reporting educational statistics. John D. Philbrick (1818-1886), associate of Henry Barnard, superintendent of Boston, 1856-1874 and 1875-1878, author of textbooks, and director of educational exhibits at Paris and Vienna, spoke on industrial education, advocated compulsory-school-attendance laws, and presented detailed plans for school buildings.[10] John Hancock (1825-1891), principal, editor, superintendent at Cincinnati and Dayton, and state commissioner of Ohio, managed educational exhibits, spoke on a variety of topics, and sustained the association "in the times that tried men's pockets."[11] Emerson E. White of Ohio (1829-1902), next to W. T. Harris the most frequent speaker at NEA conventions, talked about finances, rural schools, and courses of study. He was known as the author of *The Art of Teaching, School Management*, and other professional books, as state commissioner, as editor of the *Ohio Educational Monthly*, and best as "a dignified, courtly, Christian gentleman, whose motives were pure and whose path was straight."[12] James M. Greenwood (1837-1914) was almost unique in his long tenure in one position, superintendent at Kansas City, Missouri, for forty years, from 1874 to 1914. He held every high office in the association and served

[9] NEA, *Proceedings, 1899*, 247-248.
[10] NEA, *Proceedings, 1886*, 246-250, 318-331.
[11] NEA, *Proceedings, 1891*, 44-48.
[12] NEA, *Proceedings, 1902*, 369.

on ten important committees. Although conservative and cautious, he promoted changes; he practically eliminated corporal punishment from his schools, he developed supervision to a fine art, and he led a community as well as a school system.[13] William H. Maxwell, superintendent of New York City, objected to Latin in the elementary grades, believed that examinations were a part of teaching, discussed the textbooks of Comenius, and proved that a superintendent could be a public figure as well as an educator. Aaron Gove, superintendent at Denver, talked about medical inspection, curvature of the spine, uses of schoolhouses, and the teaching of drawing.[14] Charles H. Judd (1873-1950), although a professor rather than a superintendent, showed how to steer school surveys into useful channels; he argued that secondary schools should have a six-year program, that school buildings should be made so as to facilitate instruction, and that supervision was the hopeful means toward improved teaching. Susan Dorsey of Los Angeles demonstrated that a woman could be a great superintendent.

Much of the credit for the growth and influence of the superintendents' department during recent decades belongs to its able staff at NEA headquarters in Washington. Heading the staff as executive secretary, S. D. Shankland served from 1922 to 1946 and Worth McClure from 1946 to 1956.

As the years passed school administration became more complex and inclusive. In 1939 George D. Strayer of Teachers College, Columbia University, summarized the functions of an administrator. A superintendent had to be a student of society, of taxation, of government, a social philosopher, a coordinator, and an upholder of democratic ideals. He had to recognize that the high school had become universal; that the life work of the graduate was as important as college life. Whereas external affairs had formerly engaged the major share of the superintendent's time, the internal problems of curriculum, teaching guidance, and health now called for major attention. He had to expand his vision and his plans to encompass the kindergarten and nursery and also the junior college and adult education. In brief, he had to keep an educational system abreast of a rapidly changing society.[15]

A view of what the superintendents were doing in 1950 is provided by condensed statements which appear in the *Proceedings* of that year. At the Atlantic City meeting, "Over 13,000 persons heard lay speakers of national and international distinction; took part in 64 group discussions of current school problems; exchanged ideas; viewed the School Building Architectural Exhibit and the most comprehensive exhibit of school

[13] NEA, *Proceedings, 1915*, 533-539.
[14] NEA, *Proceedings, 1895*, 230; *1900*, 216.
[15] NEA, *Proceedings, 1939*, 238-247.

supplies and equipment ever displayed. There are now 779 subscribers to the Educational Research Service . . . including city, county, and state school systems, colleges and universities, and educational organizations," who "received more than 100 publications in addition to special services furnished in response to requests. . . ."[16]

In 1952 the department's Thirtieth Yearbook, *The American School Superintendency*, presented a picture of the status of the profession as it presented itself in various types of communities. Its size, complexity, and maturity cast a shadow of inferiority over the bungling, unformulated superintendency of 1870, but its functions were just as simple, its purposes just as clear, and its lines of procedure just as direct as they were in the earlier year. The position had demonstrated its ability to adjust, to change as conditions changed, and to enlist men of courage and resourcefulness.[17]

The principles and procedures of departments are also illustrated by those that are no longer in existence. The rise and decline of some of them illuminate past educational conditions as well as the nature of departmental activities.

Closely related in the nature of its topics and discussions to the Department of Superintendence was the work of the organization of school-board members, which assumed the rather unrevealing, if not actually misleading, name of Department of School Administration. Authorized in 1895, the department held its first sessions at Detroit in 1896. The first speaker, William G. Bruce, editor of the *American School Board Journal*, expressed the purpose of the department: "to elevate the standards of school boards, to increase their efficiency and dignify their labors." The superintendents welcomed the new department and participated in its deliberations. While its membership was composed of school-board members, thus expanding the number of persons interested in education, its program dealt with the same topics and issues that were considered by the superintendents, by speakers at the general sessions of the NEA, and at the meetings of the National Council of Education. Because of overlapping and duplication, the executive committee of the NEA voted in 1924 to abolish the Department of School Administration. It is interesting to note that William G. Bruce, who made the first speech at the first session of the department in 1896, served as secretary of the last session in 1924.[18]

[16] NEA, *Proceedings, 1950,* 245.
[17] NEA, *Proceedings, 1952,* 266.
[18] NEA, *Proceedings, 1895,* 46; *1896,* 968-970; *1924,* 96, 739. The intervening volumes of the *Proceedings* contain extensive reports of the papers and discussions of the Department of School Administration.

A unique department, unique in membership, in structure, and in purpose, was authorized by the NEA in 1907. Representatives of six organizations of women—the General Federation of Women's Clubs, the National Congress of Mothers, the Association of Collegiate Alumnae, the Woman's Christian Temperance Union, the National Council of Jewish Women, and the Southern Association of College Women—met with NEA officers and drew up a petition for the creation of the Educational Department of National Organizations of Women. Among the thirty-one signers were Commissioner E. E. Brown, C. G. Pearse, James H. Baker, Nathan C. Schaeffer, E. O. Vaile, Ella Flagg Young, and Henry Suzzallo.[19]

The new department was an amazing development. Without apparent effort the educators had received the unselfish and wholehearted cooperation of five national organizations of women, offering to concentrate upon the problems and issues which the educators would select. The general purpose of "bringing the home and the school into more helpful relations" was acceptable to all educators, as were also its announced principles: to work for compulsory attendance laws, restrictions on child labor, better buildings and equipment, better pay and better-prepared teachers, an expanded and enriched curriculum, more supervision, and the objectives of knowledge, efficiency, and character for all students. No wonder Commissioner Brown and other educators were delighted and gave their hearty approval to a lay group that could achieve many results totally beyond the educators themselves.[20]

Proud of the fact that they were "the first lay members ever admitted" to the NEA,[21] the department, which changed its name in 1910 to School Patrons, entered upon an active career. Speakers discussed the ideal school board, juvenile delinquency, home study, child growth, the schools as community centers, rural schools, public schools in the Philippines, Americanization, and child study. In 1909 a member from Colorado reported, "Already the parent-teacher associations under the Congress of Mothers are actively working in thirty-two states and we shall before long see the home and the school in warmest cooperation all over the land." In the following year a member urged the School Patrons "to increase the speed with which the progressive movement passes from the National Education Association mountain-top to the valley and the plains." In 1912 William H. Allen and Luther H. Gulick discussed the question of how outside agencies could help without interfering with

---

[19] NEA, *Proceedings, 1907,* 51.

[20] NEA, *Proceedings, 1908,* 1217-1219; Marion Talbot and Lois Rosenberry, *The History of the American Association of University Women, 1881-1931* (Boston, 1931), 297-299.

[21] Under present (1957) rules laymen are not eligible to become "active members" in the NEA.

schools. One speaker of 1914 summed up his suggestions by saying, "To grow better children in individual homes is unquestionably the first responsibility of the school patron. . . ."[22]

The session at Des Moines in 1921 was the last one for the Department of School Patrons. At the Boston meeting of 1922 the board of directors of the NEA passed a resolution to drop the department because "it was the belief that the work for which the Department was created was being cared for by the National Congress of Mothers and the Parent-Teachers Association. . . ."[23] From 1908 to 1921 the department rendered a great service to the NEA and to the schools by agitating for specific improvements and by building a wider, more sympathetic support for public education.

The history of the Department of the Wider Use of Schoolhouses illustrates the fact that even a good idea sometimes leads to the creation of an unnecessary organization. Authorized in 1915, the department presented its first program in 1918 and its last one in 1922. Raymond F. Crist of the Bureau of Naturalization was the prime mover in the organization, serving as secretary or president during most of its duration. In line with Crist's interest, the department concentrated upon Americanizing immigrants and teaching illiterate adults in evening classes which were conducted in schoolhouses. Thus the department, in spite of its name, demonstrated a rather narrow interpretation of "the wider use of schoolhouses." The creation of the Department of Immigrant Education in 1921 led to such an obvious duplication by the two departments that the Board of Directors abolished the Department of the Wider Use of Schoolhouses in 1924.[24]

The Department of Secondary Education, authorized at Topeka in 1886, presented its first program at Chicago the following year. The department resolved that English be given a place in high-school programs equal to the classics and science.[25] Annually, the Department of Secondary Education presented ambitious programs at the conventions. Many papers were concerned with the various subjects, such as English, Latin, history, science, and modern languages. Other papers and reports dealt with college-entrance requirements, moral instruction, teacher training, and other pertinent topics. Unquestionably the greatest

[22] NEA, *Proceedings, 1909,* 993-1016; *1910,* 1078; *1911,* 1093-1116; *1912,* 1323-1363.

[23] NEA, *Proceedings, 1922,* 88.

[24] NEA, *Proceedings, 1918,* 471; *1919,* 443, 471-482; *1920,* 403-405; *1921,* 460; *1922,* 905; *1924,* 96.

[25] NEA, *Proceedings, 1886,* 21; *1887,* 395-442; *1888,* 403-433; *1889,* 501-533; *1890,* 615.

achievement of the department was its sponsorship of the highly successful Commission on the Reorganization of Secondary Education, which was started in 1913 and made its remarkable report on the Seven Cardinal Principles of Secondary Education in 1918.[26] However, in 1924, the department was discontinued.[27]

In 1931 the Representative Assembly authorized the revival of the Department of Secondary Education.[28] Under the leadership of Ernest D. Lewis of Childs High School, New York, as president and then as executive secretary, the department began a period of considerable activity. The change in name in 1939 to Department of Secondary Teachers helped to clarify its status and function. The department sponsored the publication *Secondary Education* that appeared four times a year, and set up large national committees on citizenship, motion pictures, consumer education, inter-American relations, and other problems.[29] In spite of all these efforts, however, the department did not prosper. Its members never exceeded a thousand. In 1951 the department voted to merge with the Department of Classroom Teachers, a step that was consummated at the Detroit meeting of 1952.[30]

Long before the organization of a Department of Indian Education in 1899, the NEA had demonstrated its interest in the area repeatedly, and in the case of Alaskan education it assumed almost a major role. At the Saratoga Springs meeting of 1883 and at the Madison meeting of 1884, General S. C. Armstrong, principal of Hampton Institute, described his project of bringing seventy-five Indian boys from various tribes to Hampton in order to give them practical training in mechanical and agricultural arts.[31] The adviser and sponsor of this group was Booker T. Washington, who had recently been graduated from Hampton. In his autobiography he tells some amusing incidents about this mingling of two submerged races.[32]

Indian education presented a series of tangled problems, including enormous variations among the tribes, a primitive disinclination to learn the ways of civilization, the bad influence of frontier traders and exploiters, the venal selfishness of Indian agents, the incompetence of many teachers, the unkept treaties that promised schools, the virtual withdrawal of the churches after the government assumed control of Indian

[26] NEA, *Proceedings, 1913,* 489-491; *1914,* 481-488; *1921,* 163-167.
[27] NEA, *Proceedings, 1924,* 775.
[28] NEA, *Proceedings, 1932,* 482.
[29] NEA, *Proceedings, 1939,* 620; *1941,* 597-599.
[30] NEA, *Proceedings, 1951,* 165, 249; *1952,* 98-99.
[31] NEA, *Proceedings, 1883,* 59-63, 63-64; *1884,* 177-180.
[32] Booker T. Washington, *Up From Slavery* (New York, 1901), Chapter VI.

education, and varied theories as to how the natives could best be taught to become self-supporting. One theory held that reservation schools, operating among the Indians, would train the young and civilize the old. Another theory required the removal of the young men to distant places where they would become immersed in modern ways and ideas; when trained, these young men would, in theory, return to the tribes and civilize their kinsmen. Some doubted that the Indian could be civilized at all and were disposed to abandon all efforts to do so. All these theories were tried and none was entirely satisfactory. The fact that the Bureau of Indian Affairs reported in 1954 that its 104,470 Indian students were scattered among Federal, public, private, and mission schools indicates that no one system ever proved to be satisfactory.

The NEA also demonstrated an early interest in educating the natives of Alaska. Speaking at the Saratoga Springs meeting of 1882, the Reverend Sheldon Jackson gave a long description of Alaska and lamented the shameful neglect of education in that newly acquired territory. The schools maintained by the fur company were closed at the time of the purchase in 1867, and only two of those supported by Russian priests remained. For ten years the area slipped back into ignorance, until only 400 out of 8,000 could read in any language. Jackson had made two trips to Alaska as a missionary for the Presbyterian Church, and established schools at Sitka and Fort Wrangell. He introduced a resolution calling upon Congress to appropriate $50,000 for education in Alaska. The association adopted this resolution unanimously.[33]

In view of the long duration of the problem of Indian education and the NEA's interest in it, the organization of the Department of Indian Education in 1899 seems somewhat belated. The number of Indian schools was constantly increasing, however, and consequently so was the number of teachers interested in such a department. The creation of the department was in response to a petition signed by twenty-five members, including Nicholas Murray Butler, W. T. Harris, and several teachers from Indian schools.[34]

"Our reservation system separates the Indian from the white man; it pauperizes him by giving him rations." "Slavery under favorable conditions was a much more successful school for training of a barbarous race than is the reservation." This striking indictment was made by H. B. Frissell, principal of Hampton Institute, at the first meeting of the Department of Indian Education in Charleston in 1900. He continued his castigation by saying that many Americans preferred annihilation of the Indian to his assimilation. "It is because the Indian problem is so much

---

[33] NEA, *Proceedings, 1882*, 61-75. This charming article is accompanied by a map and five full-page pictures.

[34] NEA, *Proceedings, 1899*, 35-36.

the problem of educating the white man and lifting him out of his barbarism that it is so discouraging."[35]

While the Department of Indian Education was maintained for only nine years, from 1899 to 1908, it showed a surprising vitality during its brief career. Speakers and teachers came from nearly all the states that had Indian schools and discussed every pertinent topic from government policies to sanitation for the dormitories at reservation boarding schools. Again and again the teachers denounced the reservation, the ration system, and the meddling, graft-loving agent, all of which interfered with the building of an effective, self-respecting school. The names of the Indian schools sound like a roll call of the frontier: Haskell Institute, Kansas; Tomah, Wisconsin; Tulalip, Washington; Truxton Canyon, Arizona; Chilcoco, Oklahoma; Little Eagle, South Dakota; Standing Rock, North Dakota; Chemawa, Oregon; Fort Shaw, Montana; and Wild Rice River, Minnesota.

The department had some notables on its programs: Commissioner W. T. Harris, Nicholas Murray Butler, Michael E. Sadler of England, Archbishops John Ireland and John J. Glennon, Edward Everett Hale, G. Stanley Hall, Judge Ben Lindsey, various governors, well-known superintendents, and professors. While no one would claim that the Department of Indian Education, in its brief period of nine years, made a major contribution, it did provide a spirited forum for the exchange of experiences and ideas during a critical period in the development of educational methods for Indian education.

The changing pattern of departmental structure within the NEA has been accompanied by a steady expansion of departmental functions and activities. This expansion has, in general, been more in the direction of improving the quality of educational administration and instruction than of improving members' status and welfare. In the meantime, the NEA itself has greatly increased its activities in the welfare field. While no clear-cut distinction can be made between these two types of functions, and while no division of labor between the NEA and its departments has ever been explicitly defined, it is interesting to note the pattern that has in fact been developed as the NEA of 1957 fulfills the dual purpose declared in 1857: "To elevate the character and advance the interests of the profession of teaching and to promote the cause of popular education in the United States." It is an oversimplification, with a core of truth, to say that the NEA proper is today primarily devoted to advancing "the interests of the profession of teaching," while the departments are mainly concerned with "promoting the cause of popular education."

[35] NEA, *Proceedings, 1900,* 683-684. The first two sentences are slightly abbreviated and repunctuated; they faithfully preserve the author's point, however.

25

Committees and Commissions

FRANCIS W. Parker was disappointed. "I shall accept this report respectfully; I shall take it home and study it prayerfully; but I move that a committee of fifteen be appointed to revise it."[1]

Colonel Parker was neither the first nor the last member of the NEA to call for the appointment of a committee, wait eagerly for its report, and then move for the appointment of another committee to revise the report of the first committee. Committees were popular because they were convenient, time-consuming, inexpensive, often helpful, and sometimes fundamental.

Committees and subcommittees, commissions, and councils—special, standing, temporary, joint, advisory, cooperative, and emergency. Committees of every part of the NEA—of the Representative Assembly, of the board of directors, of the executive committee, of the National Council of Education, of the Department of Superintendence, of all the other departments. Committees for every purpose, problem, and topic—committees on citizenship, ethics, credit unions, international relations, tenure, academic freedom, professional standards, health, publicity—everything. No limit to the number, purpose, and duration of committees.

Why appoint a committee? Because it stops the debate. Because it postpones the issue. Because it seems like a solution. Because it provides time for consideration. Because it shifts responsibility from the whole group to designated individuals. Because some persons want to be appointed. Because it is a way of yoking proponents and opponents. Because it is a way of securing free service. Because more information might help. Because it is a kind of representative democracy. Because . . .

At the earliest meetings of the NEA the members knew all about committees. They used them from the beginnning. At its first annual meeting, in Cincinnati in 1858, the National Teachers' Association authorized the appointment of three committees. One was to recommend a course of

[1] NEA, *Proceedings, 1895*, 344.

study for high schools, one to prepare an ideal program for the education of youth, and the third to report on school registers and annual reports. None of these committees took its responsibilities seriously, and when the association met in Washington the following year, President A. J. Rickoff scolded the members severely for neglecting their assignments. But it is difficult to see how the scattered members could in one year prepare tangible reports on such vague and general topics.[2]

The unpromising results of the first committees seem not to have lessened faith in their efficacy, for at the same meeting the association authorized a committee of three to advise the secretary of the interior as to the kinds of educational statistics that should be collected in the forthcoming census of 1860. The same committee was also charged with the responsibility of memorializing Congress to establish a national agency for collecting and disseminating educational statistics.[3] Other committees were subsequently appointed to urge the establishment of a National Bureau of Education; the committee appointed in 1864 consisted of E. E. White of Ohio, Henry Barnard, and Zalmon Richards.[4] Still other committees were appointed for the purpose in 1865 and 1866. In 1867 Congress met the wishes of the educators by establishing the Department of Education.[5]

One of the first committees in the history of the NEA that can properly be regarded as approaching a high standard in purpose, procedure, and result was the one on object teaching, appointed by President W. H. Wells at Ogdensburg in 1864. This committee of seven exchanged ideas by correspondence, solicited the help of President Thomas Hill of Harvard, and at least two of the members, S. S. Greene, who wrote the report, and David N. Camp, superintendent of schools in Connecticut, visited Oswego, the great center of object teaching, and observed lessons taught by that method. With some reservations on the part of two members, the report was favorable to object teaching. The procedure of the committee set a high standard for its time by (1) exchanging opinions, (2) securing expert opinion from outside the committee, (3) making direct observations, and (4) providing for dissenting opinions.[6]

At the Trenton meeting of 1869 the association authorized a committee on the establishment of a national university. The committee consisted of one member from each state, thus introducing the two ideas of wide representation and of enlisting widespread support. (This practice of appointing large committees was carried to extremes; in 1926 each of the committees on classroom teachers' problems, retirement allowance,

[2] NTA, *Proceedings, 1858,* 13.
[3] NTA, *Proceedings, 1859,* 4.
[4] NTA, *Proceedings, 1864,* 143.
[5] NTA, *Proceedings, 1865,* 220, 223-224; *1866,* 10, 74-76; *1868,* 36, 37.
[6] NTA, *Proceedings, 1865,* 245-270.

tenure, and rural teachers' problems numbered 100, and in 1931 the one on international relations consisted of more the 200 members.)[7] The committee on the national university was continued until 1876. While the issue was the storm center of many heated debates,[8] the committee was relatively inactive, leaving the task largely to the chairman, John W. Hoyt.

Committees to draw up suitable resolutions on the occasion of the death of prominent members were appointed at the earliest meetings of the NTA. In 1866 the custom of appointing a committee on necrology was started. In 1879 Zalmon Richards, chairman of the committee, urged the compiling of a permanent list of past members, and in the following year he mentioned some of the members who had died since the founding of the association—T. W. Valentine, one of the founders, William H. McGuffey, and President Daniel Read of the University of Missouri.[9] Still chaiman of the necrology committee in 1882, Richards reported the death of W. D. Henkle of Ohio, who had been secretary of the association from 1876 until his death in 1881.[10] The report of 1885 covers six pages and provides considerable information about some of the deceased, and in 1886 the memorial notices of John D. Philbrick were unusually extensive.[11] The report of 1894 contains sketches of several deceased members, including Elizabeth Peabody; Leland Stanford, who had been a life director of the NEA; and the notable California kindergartener, Emily Marwedel.[12] The report of 1895 was somewhat unusual because it included memorial sketches of Thomas Henry Huxley, James Anthony Froude, Hermann Helmholtz, and other Europeans who had had no connection with the NEA, although the death of a prominent American who had never been a member was occasionally recorded in the necrology reports. For example, Mark Hopkins, who was not a member of the association when he died and probably never had been, who demonstrated no leadership in public education, and whose reputation rested upon a quip by James A. Garfield, was given a three-page memorial when he died in 1887.[13]

The report of 1900 contains accounts of Henry Barnard, a faithful

[7] NEA, *Proceedings, 1926*, 1034-1039; *1933*, 1027-1030.

[8] See Chapter 18.

[9] NTA, *Proceedings, 1866*, 6-7, 9; NEA, *Proceedings, 1879*, 97-98.

[10] NEA, *Proceedings, 1882*, xv-xvii.

[11] NEA, *Proceedings, 1886*, 246-250, 318-331.

[12] NEA, *Proceedings, 1894*, 221-251.

[13] NEA, *Proceedings, 1887*, 661-664. "The ideal college is Mark Hopkins on one end of a log and a student on the other." According to the latest study, Hopkins was a straddler on current issues, deferential in the presence of wealth and position, ignorant of Kant, Hume, Darwin, and Huxley, mediocre as a philosopher, unsuccessful in maintaining enrollments at Williams, hostile toward curriculum reforms, and easygoing in his class requirements. Frederick Rudolph, *Mark Hopkins and the Log* (New Haven, 1956), 33, 31, 28, 249, 216, 43, 29.

member, and three former presidents of the association, W. E. Sheldon, James H. Smart, and the first president, Zalmon Richards.[14] After 1905 the space devoted to deceased members fell off almost to the vanishing point, except for rather extended accounts of W. T. Harris, who died in 1909.[15] While the bylaws adopted in 1912 provided for a necrology committee that would list deceased members "accompanied by memorial sketches whenever practicable," it was found "practicable" to list merely the names.[16] The necrology committee had difficulty in securing the names of deceased members, and so the work was necessarily done by the headquarters staff.[17] Finally, in 1953, the committee was abolished, but the custom of standing in conventions for a moment of silent tribute to deceased members and listing their names in the *Proceedings* has continued.[18]

A committee of fifty with a unique assignment was appointed at the Madison meeting of 1884. The members were asked to observe the educational exhibits at the World's Cotton Centennial Exposition at New Orleans and report to the association in 1885. Ten members made their reports, covering such exhibits as those by kindergarteners, by Negroes, by normal schools, and by the Christian Brothers.[19] Earlier committees had prepared exhibits for the expositions at Paris and Philadelphia, and subsequent committees did likewise for later exhibits.

The success of the association in persuading the secretary of the interior to enlarge the scope of the census and influencing Congress to establish the Bureau of Education demonstrated the value of committees. In view of the widely scattered membership, the small number of members, the brevity of conventions, and the lack of funds, it is not surprising that great reliance was placed upon committees. Most of the committees were given assignments that called for some kind of action—to memorialize Congress, stir up popular support, or secure some specific information. Only one committee appointed before 1885, the one of 1865 on object teaching, had studied an important educational problem, topic, or issue and made a report that served as a guide to educational practice.

The conception of what educational committees might accomplish was expanded by the work of the National Council of Education. This select group, operating within the NEA, established twelve standing committees to study continually the major areas, of education, namely, state and city systems, elementary, secondary, and higher education,

[14] NEA, *Proceedings*, 1900, 24, 712-717. For an extended account of Barnard, see 1901, 390-438.

[15] NEA, *Proceedings*, 1910, 185-198.

[16] NEA, *Proceedings*, 1912, 10, 114-115.

[17] NEA, *Proceedings*, 1925, 1058-1059.

[18] NEA, *Proceedings*, 1953, 126, 166-167.

[19] NEA, *Proceedings*, 1885, 512-551.

normal schools, hygiene, pedagogics, educational literature, statistics, and education of girls.[20] According to plan each committee was to make an annual report; in practice this did not prove to be feasible, but several reports were made on coeducation, moral instruction, pedagogy, practice teaching, rural schools, Herbartianism, technical training, formal discipline, and other topics of current interest and importance. For example, the report of 1884 and 1885 by the committee on hygiene dealt with the topic of "Recess or No Recess." The effects of the recess on health, discipline, progress in studies, and administration were asserted with vigor and denied with vehemence. Each side seemed to find evidence to confirm its practice of having or not having a recess period for the pupils.[21] Council reports were usually followed by spirited, almost uninhibited, discussion. W. T. Harris once remarked that those who could not follow the papers were instructed by the debates. In subsequent years more than one educator looked back with nostalgic affection upon these spirited exchanges of opinion.

Logical as was the plan of assigning every council member to a committee, it proved in time to be unsatisfactory. A particular member might have little interest in the assigned topic, and thus tend to neglect his duties, so the custom of enlisting outside specialists to carry on some of the investigations gradually became popular. However, the council's experience with committees enabled it to guide and direct even though its limited membership did not provide the personnel to carry out the undertakings. In the meantime it sponsored one of the truly remarkable reports in the history of American education, that of the Committee of Ten on Secondary School Studies[22] (see Chapter 6).

Even before the Committee of Ten had made its report in 1893, the Department of Superintendence set up a Committee of Fifteen on elementary education. This committee, unlike the one on secondary education, which was composed almost wholly of college and college-oriented people, was composed of persons directly concerned with the elementary schools. It consisted of thirteen city superintendents; one university president, Andrew S. Draper of Illinois and formerly state commissioner of New York; and Commissioner W. T. Harris. Its report dealt with the training of teachers, the program of studies, and the administrative organization of city schools. The report denounced the idea that teachers are born rather than made and called for a thorough training in academic content, child study, psychology, the history of education, and methods of teaching. An elementary teacher should have at least a high-school education and successful experience in practice teaching under expert

[20] NEA, *Proceedings, 1888*, 254-255.
[21] NEA, *Proceedings, 1884*, 8, 9-12; *1885*, 414-428.
[22] *Report of Committee of Ten on Secondary School Studies* (New York, 1894).

supervisors. The program of elementary studies should be logical, representative of all the major divisions of human knowledge, psychologically symmetrical, and realistically related to the child's social and natural environment. Language, arithmetic, geography, history, natural sciences, drawing, vocal music, physical culture, and physiology and hygiene as required by the state laws were the principal subjects. The report stressed the idea of correlation; in fact, the section dealing with the curriculum was called "Correlation of Studies." The recommendations were supported by extensive comments from educational specialists outside the committee.[23]

The reports on secondary and elementary education did not deal with country schools. To cover this portion of the educational system the National Council of Education at its meeting in Denver in 1895 appointed a Committee of Twelve on Rural Schools, with Henry Sabin, state superintendent of public instruction of Iowa, as chairman. The report pronounced the school district as "the most undesirable unit possible." It therefore called for the consolidation of districts into township or county units. This plan would involve transporting pupils at public expense, but it would enable the schools to employ better teachers, to offer a wider program, and to secure better buildings, equipment, and libraries. Above all these, it would make possible a system of supervision which had never been achieved in country schools.[24]

Other important and influential reports of the NEA followed. A Committee on College Entrance Requirements tried to bring order and understanding out of the "conflicting, incongruous, and unsatisfactory" condition that had been brought about by the varying requirements of the hundreds of colleges. By setting up specific books to be read, laboratory exercises to be performed, and subjects to be studied, the report, published in 1899, tended to standardize secondary courses and college requirements.[25]

A Committee on Normal Schools, reporting in 1899, laid down specifications as to admission standards, course requirements, and practice teaching. The report revealed the wide variations in normal-school practices and publicized desirable standards.[26] A Committee on the Relations of Public Libraries to Public Schools recommended library procedures and provided lists of suggested books.[27] The Committee of Seventeen on the Professional Preparation of High School Teachers made an extensive report in 1907 in which it called for broad academic preparation; courses in the history of education, the principles of education,

[23] *Report of the Committee of Fifteen on Elementary Education* (New York, 1895).
[24] *Report of the Committee of Twelve on Rural Schools* (Chicago, 1897).
[25] NEA, *Proceedings, 1899*, 625-817.
[26] *Ibid.*, 836-903.
[27] *Ibid.*, 452-529.

educational psychology with emphasis upon adolescence, special methods in the subjects that the student expected to teach; and observation and practice teaching with high-school students. Because of the reasonableness of the recommendations and the high status of the members of the committee, it set standards which in essence are still in effect fifty years after the report was given.[28]

The scope of other committees that reported around the turn of the century is indicated by their names: Committees on Salaries, Tenure of Office, and Pensions of Teachers (1903); Committee on Industrial Education in Rural Schools (1905); Committee on the National Bureau of Education (1904); Committee on Contemporary Education Doctrine (1903); and Committee on Instruction in Normal Schools in Library Administration (1906).

These reports demonstrate the vigor and resourcefulness of the NEA and its subdivisions. Some of the reports were published and republished and distributed by the thousands. They did not and were not intended to produce uniformity, but they were designed to reveal current practices and indicate desirable standards.

How committees could be used in educational controversies can be illustrated by two reports made in 1911. The Committee on the Articulation of High School and College cited the resolution of the Department of Secondary Education of the preceding year "requesting colleges to discontinue the entrance requirements of two foreign languages and to recognize as electives all subjects well taught in the high school." The committee argued for an enriched program for secondary schools, unhampered by college requirements. This report has something of a tone of defiance and reveals the growing resentment over the restrictive influences of the colleges. The Committee on College-Entrance Requirements of the Manual Training Department reported that 62 of 141 colleges that answered an inquiry had lessened the number of prescribed subjects, and that 26 institutions recognized shopwork, drawing, household science, and art as acceptable entrance subjects.[29]

One of the most influential committees ever appointed by the NEA was the Commission on the Reorganization of Secondary Education. Appointed in 1913 and continued until 1921,[30] this large commission, which eventually consisted of sixteen subcommittees with a total membership of over one hundred drawn from thirty states, made some notable reports. Among fifteen bulletins that the commission prepared, two stand out as still significant in 1957. The one on *Social Studies in Secondary Education,* published in 1916, recommended a course in problems of democracy for

[28] NEA, *Proceedings, 1907,* 523-668.
[29] NEA, *Proceedings, 1911,* 559-567; 729-739.
[30] NEA, *Proceedings, 1913,* 489-491; *1921,* 163-167.

the twelfth grade. This was the first time that a responsible agency had advocated the classroom study of contemporary issues as distinguished from formalized subjects. The recommendation was received with acclaim by teachers, and several state legislatures made this integrated study of American problems a required subject. Another bulletin, *Cardinal Principles of Secondary Education* (1918), was even more popular, influential, and enduring (see Chapter 6). The bulletins of the commission were published by the U.S. Bureau of Education and were in demand for more than a decade, reaching a total circulation of about 140,000.

Partly as a result of the popularity and influence of the seven cardinal principles and partly because of changed and changing conditions, two other committees returned to the problem and evolved statements of the objectives of education. Reflecting the discontent and perplexities of the depression years, the Committee on Social-Economic Goals for America formulated objectives in terms of the hopes and strivings of the American people. As the committee saw the situation, everyone desired:

1. Hereditary strength
2. Physical security
3. Skills and knowledge
4. Values and standards
5. Adjusted personality
6. Suitable occupation
7. Economic security
8. Mental security
9. Equality and opportunity
10. Freedom
11. Fair play

This statement aroused considerable discussion, and articles about it continued to appear for several years.

The other statement of objectives that met with general approval was the more philosophical and general one issued by the Educational Policies Commission in the volume called *The Purposes of Education in American Democracy,* issued in 1938. This volume grouped objectives under the headings Self-realization, Human Relationship, Economic Efficiency, and Civic Responsibility, with eight or ten specific qualities, abilities, or conditions under each.

A rather unusual committee with an unusual function was the one on Racial Well-Being, appointed in 1917 to promote the study of human improvement. An anonymous donor provided $4,000 for prizes for the senior classes in teacher-training institutions which made the best studies that would give support and meaning to the proposition: "It is as much the duty of educators to assure through educational procedures that individuals shall be well-born as that they shall be well-reared." In 1922 the committee still had $3,500 left for prizes and it continued to function until 1925, after which it became a lost cause.[31]

[31] NEA, *Bulletin* IV, 36-38, April 1916; *ibid.,* V, 22-24; *Proceedings, 1916,* 240-245, 248-254; *1921,* 362; *1922,* 562-564; *1923,* 24; *1924,* 39; *1925,* 966.

Another committee of major importance was the Commission on the Emergency in Education, appointed in 1918 and continued through the Legislative Commission of 1920. It was one of the most successful committees that ever served the NEA. It halted the decline in teachers' salaries, it prevented ruinous reductions in school taxes, it led to the Americanization of immigrants, it lectured the Federal government on its educational duties, it rallied the supporters of public education to its timely defense, it united a profession, and, possibly most important in the perspective of time, it brought thousands of teachers into the NEA.

The commission, appointed by Mary C. C. Bradford, President of NEA, consisted of twenty-nine prominent educators, including college presidents, professors, and superintendents, with Professor George D. Strayer of Columbia University as chairman and Lotus D. Coffman of the University of Minnesota as secretary. At the Pittsburgh meeting in July 1918 several members of the commission described the emergency and advanced suggestions as to how it should be met.

The emergency, which was characterized as a calamity and as the collapse of the teaching profession, was complex and inclusive; it was a condition revealed and aggravated by war rather than caused by it. The teacher shortage was acute; it grew constantly worse as thousands left the classrooms for better-paying positions. Those still in school were shamefully underpaid, more than half of them receiving less than $500 a year. Thousands of unprepared girls were teaching on emergency certificates, and crowded rooms and double shifts were becoming commonplace. Thousands of drafted men could not read and write, and rejections because of poor health and disabilities were alarmingly numerous. Many soldiers from immigrant groups could not understand English, thus demonstrating the failure of the melting-pot theory.

The remedy for all these ills was money. Since states and localities had failed, it seemed to the members of the commission that the Federal government must come to the rescue. In fact, some of the speakers boldly advocated the nationalization of education, for it had become a national concern. "Commerce and industry have long since been nationalized. Of all our collective enterprises education alone remains hampered and constrained by the narrow confines of an obsolete conception. . . . The golden hour of American education has struck. The opportunity is here and the need is compelling to employ the resources of the nation for the education of the nation's children."[32] Let the nation assume the responsibility for health, teacher training, adult illiteracy, and the rural problem, for local initiative has broken down and local resources are insufficient.[33]

[32] W. C. Bagley, NEA, *Proceedings, 1918,* 57.
[33] *Ibid.,* 55-58.

Many specific proposals were made by the commission speakers: appoint a secretary of education in the President's cabinet; let pupils in the elementary grades begin the study of trades, commerce, and industry; begin secondary work at twelve rather than fourteen years of age; adopt universal conscription in education; Americanize the immigrants; let the Federal government take over the normal schools and train teachers for national service; conscript women to teach; and pay teachers salaries that will keep them in the profession.[34]

Not all the educators at Pittsburgh agreed to all the statements about the emergency in education or to the proposed solution. Nathan C. Schaeffer, state superintendent of public instruction of Pennsylvania, spoke somewhat disapprovingly of a plan to increase the membership of the NEA to 250,000 "and inaugurate a lobby to secure a federal appropriation of one hundred million dollars to be distributed among the states for school purposes."[35] But Joseph Swain, president of Swarthmore College and chairman of the Committee on Salaries of the NEA, proposed that teachers should compel the nation to wake up and pay decent salaries by "the application of the principle of collective bargaining."[36]

The commission entered upon its aggressive career. It coordinated the contacts of the various government agencies and bureaus with the schools; published a report on teachers' salaries; campaigned for higher salaries; formulated plans for teacher participation in educational policies; induced teachers to join the NEA; secured the cooperation of dozens of organizations in support of the Smith-Towner Bill, which provided Federal aid for schools; prepared plans for the removal of illiteracy, the improvement of rural schools, and the improved training of teachers. While many of these objectives were more nearly achieved under the Legislative Commission and other later agencies, the Emergency Commission set the goals, devised the methods of publicity, and gave the NEA a great demonstration in the techniques of securing popular understanding and support.

The Joint Commission on the Emergency in Education, so called because it was jointly sponsored by the NEA and the Department of Superintendence, was appointed in 1933 to help the schools meet the adversities of the depression. The commission characterized itself as "a board of strategy" and gathered the facts about unpaid teachers, canceled courses, closed schools, and shortened terms and tried to combat the propaganda put out by tax-minded groups and hostile critics. It

[34] *Ibid.*, 62-68. Strayer made three speeches at Pittsburgh on the national-emergency question. See 129-131, 187-189, 205-207.
[35] NEA, *Proceedings, 1918*, 40-41.
[36] *Ibid.*, 49.

urged the Federal government to assist the states since their schools had
to depend so largely on local property taxes; it organized groups of consultants in every state to carry on campaigns for the support of public
education. In its final report the commission urged the establishment of
a permanent Educational Policies Commission.[37]

Among the committees of the last fifty years are some unusual ones
which show the great diversity of interests and sometimes the ingenuity
and imagination of their promoters. The Committee on Janitor Service
of 1913 was in essence a committee on health conditions for school buildings. In 1923 a Committee to Cooperate with the Federation of Women's
Clubs was designed to offset the loss of the Department of School
Patrons, which had been abolished the year before, and the Committee
to Cooperate with Conferences on the Limitation of Armaments of 1922
is unlikely to be duplicated for some years. In 1929 a National Commission on the Enrichment of Adult Life was appointed to provide not
vocational but avocational plans. The Committee on Equal Opportunity
of 1935 set out to eliminate discrimination because of race, sex, marital
status, and state of residence. The Hippocratic Oath Committee was appointed in 1952 to evolve a suitable oath for teachers.

After years and years of committees, a Committee on Committees in
1925. This committee felt that there were too many committees. It
recommended the abolition of a dozen, restraint in establishing new ones,
and time limits on those that were established. It saw no need of committees on health, citizenship, democracy, morals, and character building, because the whole association was committed to achieve such purposes. It laid down the principle that no committee should duplicate the
work of a department; for example, the Committee on Rural Problems
was a duplication of the whole program of the Department of Rural
Education and should be abolished.[38] In 1935, ten years after this report
by the Committee on Committees, the number of committees was
greater than ever—twenty-one committees, commissions, and councils.[39]
In 1942 the executive secretary reported: "During the school year 1941-42
the Association sponsored thirty-one committees, commissions, and councils. These were classified into five types as follows: convention, 8; standing, 4; special, 7; joint, 5; and commissions and councils, 7."[40]

In 1957 there are twenty-three continuing committees and commissions and one council—a total exactly equal to that of 1942 (excluding
the seven "special" committees of that year). Today's twenty-four may be
classified into four groups with six in each group, as follows:

[37] NEA, *Proceedings, 1933*, 182-191; *1934*, 30-47; *1935*, 166-167.
[38] NEA, *Proceedings, 1926*, 270-274.
[39] NEA, *Proceedings, 1935*, 777-792.
[40] NEA, *Proceedings, 1942*, 504.

COMMISSIONS AND COUNCIL

1. Educational Policies Commission
2. Legislative Commission
3. National Commission for the Defense of Democracy Through Education
4. National Commission on Safety Education
5. National Commission on Teacher Education and Professional Standards
6. National Council on Teacher Retirement

STANDING COMMITTEES

1. Citizenship
2. Credit Unions
3. International Relations
4. Professional Ethics
5. Tax Education and School Finance
6. Tenure and Academic Freedom

JOINT COMMITTEES

1. American Legion
2. American Library Association
3. American Medical Association
4. American Teachers Association
5. Magazine Publishers Association
6. National Congress of Parents and Teachers

CONVENTION COMMITTEES

1. Auditing
2. Budget
3. Bylaws and Rules
4. Credentials
5. Elections
6. Resolutions

There are not so many special committees as formerly, but one special commission—scheduled to terminate its work at the end of 1957—merits mention. This is the NEA Centennial Celebration Commission of twenty-three members (including both educators and laymen), appointed in 1954 to plan the 1957 observance of the NEA's centennial. At its first meeting the commission selected the centennial theme: "An educated people moves freedom forward." By mid-1956 the chairman of this commission was able to report to the representative assembly at Portland: "We have assigned some 28 different projects, which constitute the fundamental core of our program, but by no means all of it, to as many committees drawn from the NEA and its various departmental staffs, with some from the field. These committees are now at work."[41]

The continuing commissions will be reviewed in subsequent pages of this chapter. The six joint committees will be considered in the chapter

[41] NEA, *Proceedings, 1956,* 122.

following. The standing committees, whose fields of activity are well indicated by their names, are described in the 1956-1957 *NEA Handbook* in these words: "This type of committee carries on a continuous program of study, interpretation, and action. Each standing committee consists of five members appointed by the NEA president for terms of three years each on a rotating basis, no member to serve more than two terms in succession. Each committee has a nationwide advisory group usually consisting of the chairmen of similar committees in the state and local associations."

It is clear that a fundamental change has taken place with respect to the nature and procedures of NEA committees. Instead of *ad hoc* groups with widely scattered members who could confer only by mail or in hasty sessions in the weary hours of conventions, each major committee now has continuity, a grant of funds to finance meetings, and assistance from one or more designated members of the headquarters staff.

The five continuing commissions differ from the six standing committees in that they have larger memberships and larger budgets, and each commission is served by a full-time staff of several persons. (Staff service for committees is part time, except in the case of the Committee on International Relations.) The one council—National Council on Teacher Retirement—is usually classed with the commissions, but it differs from them in two important respects: it has no full-time staff, and its constituent members are not individuals but state and local retirement systems.

LEGISLATIVE COMMISSION

Oldest of the continuing agencies of the NEA is the Legislative Commission, established in 1920 with George D. Strayer of Columbia University as chairman. The commission launched an aggressive campaign to secure Federal aid for schools and the establishment of a Department of Education with a secretary in the President's cabinet.[42] The commission sponsored and supported a succession of omnibus bills to provide funds to remove illiteracy, to Americanize the foreign-born, train teachers, provide health services, and equalize educational opportunities among the states, as well as to establish a department of education with a secretary in the President's cabinet. The bills to achieve all these purposes

[42] The Legislative Commission was in essence a continuation of the Commission on the Emergency in Education, established in 1917 by joint appointments by Mary C. C. Bradford, president of the NEA, and Thomas E. Finegan, president of the Department of Superintendence. The two commissions had the same chairman and the same secretary, and pursued the same aggressive tactics to carry out the same policies. Finegan afterward (NEA, *Proceedings, 1930*, 188-191) mistakenly referred to his appointees as having been made to "the Legislative Commission in 1917."

were successively called the Smith-Towner, the Towner-Sterling, and the Sterling-Reed bills. To overcome the confusion caused by the frequent changes in name, Strayer and other advocates referred to the current bill, no matter what name it bore, as the Education Bill.

Aided by the field secretary of the NEA, Hugh Magill (and later Charl Ormond Williams), the commission set out to convince Congress and the American public that Federal aid was necessary to save the schools from deterioration and to solve postwar problems. Illustrative of the activities of the commission, in 1926 Miss Williams reported that she had sent out 93,193 booklets and information sheets, had interviewed 69 congressmen, and had spoken in ten states before such groups as the General Federation of Women's Clubs, the Conference of Southern Governors, and the Woman's Christian Temperance Union. She reported that the Education Bill was endorsed by thirty national organizations, thirty Protestant denominations, and a host of individuals.[43] The efforts of the commission to secure a secretary of education with cabinet status are recounted elsewhere (see Chapter 21).

After the Legislative Commission suspended its efforts to secure a Department of Education, it turned its attention to Federal educational activities. While education was the primary responsibility of the states, the Federal government had evolved extensive and complicated practices even though it had no clear or unified educational policy. It had made land grants for schools, authorized agricultural and mechanical colleges, supported vocational programs, conducted academies for the armed forces, maintained schools in Federally affected areas, and promoted research and graduate study in a score of its bureaus and divisions. In 1950 the Federal government spent three and a half billion dollars on education. The decline in veteran attendance at colleges lessened this amount somewhat during the succeeding years. Thus the Federal government is interested in education, supports it, and performs hundreds of educational functions.

In 1930 Willis A. Sutton, president of the NEA, proposed a reexamination of the association's legislative policy. To study, advise, and interpret Federal activities became one of the major undertakings of the Legislative Commission. Just as the state teachers' associations assumed the responsibility of watching and guiding state legislation on educational matters, so the NEA through its Legislative Commission assumed a similar responsibility in the Federal area. The increasing participation in educational matters had involved an increasing expansion in the functons of the commission.[44]

[43] NEA, *Proceedings, 1921*, 159-163; *1922*, 117-120, 305-312; *1923*, 397-399; *1924*, 254-265; *1925*, 244-248; *1926*, 1135-1140.
[44] NEA, *Proceedings, 1931*, 254-255.

During the depression years the Legislative Commission favored but did not aggressively campaign for a Federal department of education. It helped to secure emergency grants to the states, loans to build schools and pay teachers' salaries that were in arrears, and keep rural schools open. It conferred with the committees appointed by President Roosevelt to plan the reorganization of Federal agencies. The commission also cooperated with the Joint Commission on the Emergency in Education of the NEA and with other emergency committees. To support bills for Federal aid the commission assembled persons to testify before Congressional committees and published several booklets explaining the case for general Federal aid to education. It set up a legislative reference service for state associations and published booklets on teachers' contracts, oath laws, minimum-salary laws, and other issues vital to teachers.[45]

Perhaps the part that the Legislative Commission took in securing the repeal of the "Red Rider" was one of its most gratifying achievements. In appropriating funds for the District of Columbia in 1935 Congress required teachers to take an oath that they had not taught or advocated communism. The law was interpreted to require an oath each time the teacher received a pay check.[46] The Legislative Commission, aided by Theodore D. Martin and others of the NEA staff, pressed the case for repeal, which was achieved in May 1937. The commission was also influential in securing a modification of the Hatch Act in such a manner as to exempt teachers from the ban on political activity.[47] The Commission, at the request of the NEA Committee on Induction into Citizenship, secured the enactment of a joint resolution by Congress authorizing the President to proclaim the third Sunday in May as Citizenship Day (later changed to September 17).[48]

In 1937 President Roosevelt appointed the Advisory Committee on Education, with Professor Floyd W. Reeves of Chicago as chairman. The report of this committee so nearly agreed with the policies of the NEA that the Legislative Commission devoted a great deal of time and effort to promoting the report as it was embodied in a succession of Congressional bills. The Reeves committee recommended general Federal aid for education, aid for teacher training, for school construction,

[45] NEA, *Proceedings, 1933*, 195-198; *1934*, 215-219; *1935*, 168-172; *1936*, 873-876.

[46] This requirement of repeated oaths recalls the complaint of a county commissioner in Kentucky, who wrote in 1871: "Trustees are under the necessity of riding from five to twenty miles to make a special oath to each report. It is difficult to see why a trustee should swear to every separate act. One good, strong oath well phrased and well administered ought to last a man of ordinary conscience at least one year." *Report of Commissioner of Education*, 1871, 188.

[47] NEA, *Proceedings, 1943*, 50. The chairman of the Defense Commission said that Donald DuShane was largely responsible for the Brown Amendment to the Hatch Act.

[48] NEA, *Proceedings, 1940*, 897-898.

for state departments of education, for adult education, for rural libraries, for research, and for pupils in Federally controlled areas.[49]

Over the years the Legislative Commission has developed its policies from resolutions and the platform of the NEA. The commission reports annually to the NEA representative assembly, and from that body it receives its general directives. As new issues arise between conventions, the commission looks to the NEA executive committee for further guidance. The three-year terms of the members and the services of a continuing staff of specialists (some of whom are registered as "lobbyists" with the U.S. Congress) facilitates a continuity of policies and efforts. The importance of the NEA's legislative activities, and the need for coordinating the efforts of the national association with those of the affiliated state associations, were signalized in October 1956 by the appointment of James L. McCaskill (who for several years had served as executive secretary of the Legislative Commission) to a newly created NEA post: assistant executive secretary for state and Federal relations.

Success enabled the commission to write off some objectives as achieved. For example, in 1950 Congress established the National Science Foundation, which the commission had advocated;[50] and in 1954 Congress provided, in line with the commission's program, a tax exemption for retirement incomes.[51] The objectives of the commission changed as the NEA developed or changed its policies. The major objectives in 1955 were to secure Federal aid for school construction, vocational education, and school lunches. The area of Federal responsibility grows larger, and the work of the Legislative Commission shows no prospect of becoming less important with the passing of time.

EDUCATIONAL POLICIES COMMISSION

"Discouragement, pessimism, and defeatism regarding public education were widespread." Such was the situation in 1933, according to Dean J. B. Edmonson of the University of Michigan. The NEA, acting jointly with the Department of Superintendence, appointed an emergency commission to try to offset the drastic retrenchments in school funds, stay the petty restrictions being imposed upon teachers, and give new directions to educational planning. This commission, consisting of ten prominent educators and nine hundred consultants, was remarkably successful in arresting some of the unfavorable trends. In fact, it was so successful in securing public attention and in answering unfriendly critics that the NEA decided to establish a planning commission and give it at least a five-year tenure. The result was the Educational Policies Commission,

[49] NEA, *Proceedings, 1938*, 871-880.
[50] NEA, *Proceedings, 1950*, 122.
[51] NEA, *Proceedings, 1955*, 305.

appointed in 1935 by the NEA and the Department of Superintendence, and supported by a grant from the General Education Board.

The new commission, which held its first meeting in January 1936, was at first an emergency commission, the fourth since 1917.[52] In another sense it was the inheritor of the policy-making National Council of Education, with fundamental differences. Whereas the council was expected to evolve policies from discussion by selected members, the new commission was expected to make recomendations upon the basis of careful research and widespread surveys of fact and opinions. Like the council, its recommendations were to have such force as scholarship and leadership could provide, but they were to have no official status. Subsequent action by the representative assembly or other agency of the NEA was necessary to give them such status.

During the depression years in the 1930's national and state planning boards became numerous and popular. In the depth of disaster, men turned to analyze and explain and to project measures that might avoid the errors of the past. Educators entered fully into the spirit of this movement. New materials and new methods were tried, and visions of a new society evolved out of a new education were glimpsed. Restrained by realistic factors and mindful of practical obstacles, the Educational Policies Commission nevertheless tried to formulate plans for a better educational program.

The Educational Policies Commission took all education as its province and proceeded in a manner that inspired confidence and enlisted support. It appointed 1,200 consultants, employed expert advisers and helpers, and proceeded to study the basic problems of American education. The needs of the period were numerous, and the necessity of leadership was recognized. The personnel of the commission won respect, and its early publications more than met expectations.

Among its first publications was a series of five policy statements devoted to a reexamination of the role of education in a democracy. The volume entitled *Learning the Ways of Democracy* (1940) consisted of case studies of outstanding programs of civic education in high schools. Two subsequent volumes, *Education for ALL American Youth* (1944) and *Education for ALL American Children* (1948), proposed an extension and improvements in secondary and elementary education. Other studies dealt with such varied topics as the nature of educational organizations, gifted children, Federal-state relations in education, education and peace, military training, health services, school athletics, moral and spiritual values in the public schools, and manpower.

[52] NEA, *Proceedings, 1936,* 463-467. The emergency background of the commission was emphasized by John A. Sexson, one of the original members. After 1940 the EPC became a continuing body, with rotating membership, financed by the sponsoring associations.

In 1947 the commission was reorganized, with four of its twenty members to be named by specified NEA departments and the majority of its members to be named, as before, by joint action of the NEA executive committee and the executive committee of the American Association of School Administrators. Its function was condensed into one sentence: "The Educational Policies Commission shall prepare, publish, and disseminate, from time to time statements of proposed policy regarding the conduct of education in the United States, and the international relationships of American education." The commission emphasized fundamental values and stressed long-range planning.[53]

Adequately financed, comprised of representative members, and directed by capable secretaries, the commission has made an enviable record in issuing timely, pertinent, and influential reports. Under the guidance of Secretary William G. Carr (1935-1952), and since 1953 of Secretary Howard E. Wilson, the commission in recent years has explored new areas of educational thinking. No longer regarded as an experiment, the Educational Policies Commisson is answering the continuing need of reviewing the past, analyzing the present, and charting the future.

THE DEFENSE COMMISSION

In 1941 Donald DuShane, president of the NEA, vigorously advocated the creation of the National Commission for the Defense of Democracy Through Education. The situation, he said, was serious: "classes overcrowded . . . criticism rampant . . . when charges are made, there is no method to meet them . . . there is no one to speak for the profession . . . it is just as important to defend democracy thru the schools as it is to defend democracy thru the army or armament"[54]

The commission was established. It became the protagonist of schools, the defender of teachers, the upholder of academic freedom, and the castigator of unfriendly critics and avowed enemies of public education. With a membership of fifteen, including Alonzo F. Myers, Frank P. Graham, and Ernest O. Melby, aided by forty-four widely scattered advisers, the commission set out upon its aggressive course. In its first year it helped manage school campaigns in Omaha and Kenosha, investigated individuals and organizations who were critical of public schools, conducted regional conferences, set up local defense committees, and campaigned for increased salaries for teachers.[55] In the second year it worried about child labor and teacher shortage and advocated the estab-

[53] NEA, *Proceedings, 1955*, 303-305. See summaries in the *Proceedings* after 1936 and the numerous publications of the commission.
[54] NEA, *Proceedings, 1941*, 767-768.
[55] NEA, *Proceedings, 1942*, 531.

lishment of an international office of education. And, more in line with its subsequent activities, it conducted a vigorous defense of three teachers who were discharged by the school board of Muskogee, Oklahoma. This defense led to the establishment of the Kate Frank Fund, so named in honor of one of the discharged teachers, who was subsequently reinstated.[56] Because of this case the commission set out to campaign for better tenure laws and called upon teachers to join the NEA and support its policies. This was at least one factor in causing the membership of the association to rise from 219,334 in 1943 to 271,847 in 1944. In fact, subsequent instances of defending teachers unquestionably explain, to some extent, the phenomenal growth of the NEA, which reached a total membership of 659,190 in 1956.

Other cases in which the NEA came to the defense of teachers, schools, and educational standards followed. In 1944 the commission rebuked Mayor F. H. La Guardia for illegally interfering with the Board of Education of New York City. In 1945 it made a report on Chicago, which was "conceded to be the worst educational situation in the United States." The superintendent of schools was expelled from the NEA, and he and some of the school board resigned. Teachers all over the nation became aware of the growing power and influence of the NEA. Chairman Myers, in referring to Kate Frank's reemployment in Muskogee, observed that "the organized teachers of America . . . have effectively served notice . . . that they do not intend to permit capable members of the teaching profession to be dismissed without just cause."[57]

The Defense Commission investigated cases involving academic freedom and tenure only after it was invited to do so by a state or local association. Calls for help increased in frequency—from McCook, Nebraska; Las Vegas County, New Mexico; North College Hill, Ohio. In each case the investigating committee made an objective report; in some instances no immediate solution was found, but in the course of time the commission gained wide acceptance for its proclaimed principles—that a teacher deserved prior notice of his faults or shortcomings, written notice of impending discharge, a chance to answer charges in a public hearing, and the right to appeal. Such investigations served also to clarify the relationship between school boards and superintendents and between boards and the public. The commission defended school boards, superintendents, principals, and supervisors as well as teachers. It tried to establish principles regardless of the persons involved.

Donald DuShane, who had been secretary of the commission since 1941, died in 1947 and was succeeded by Richard B. Kennan. Chairman Myers was succeeded by Ernest O. Melby, who served for one year. Melby was

---

[56] NEA, *Proceedings, 1943,* 50-55; *1945,* 180.
[57] NEA, *Proceedings, 1944,* 59-63; *1945-1946,* 180-181.

followed by Harold Benjamin, whose colorful statement, "Free men cannot be taught properly by slaves; courageous citizens cannot be well educated by scared hired men," became a well-publicized slogan. Dr. DuShane's death was used as the occasion for renaming the defense fund in his honor and starting a campaign to enlarge it.

Changes in membership and leadership in no wise lessened the activities of the commission. Investigations continued. In response to local requests the commission alone, or in conjunction with the state association, set up a committee which made the study, and nearly everyone revealed some variation of educational malpractice. At Chandler, Arizona, there was no procedure for discharging teachers; at Grand Prairie, Texas, the board discharged teachers who had been active in a school election; at Oglesby, Illinois, some teachers were guilty of unprofessional conduct; in Pasadena a whole community suffered from nationwide propaganda directed against public education; at Mars Hill, North Carolina, political considerations interfered with the educational program; and in Utah the committee recommended changes in the state department of education. Other variations from desirable practice were found and recommendations were made to schools in Miami, Florida; Kelso, Washington; Newport, New Hampshire; Kansas City; Houston; and other cities.

Investigations were only a part of the commission's activities. It cooperated with the tenure, ethics, and citizenship committees of the NEA, with the Department of Justice in sponsoring citizenship conferences, and with many local and state committees. The commission was especially diligent in investigating the source, nature, objectives, and effects of capricious attacks and criticisms that seemed tinged with animosity. In the course of effecting this purpose it called off-record conferences and sent out semiconfidential reports. It opposed teacher-oath laws, censorship of textbooks, and officious investigations. It tried to offset attempts to sow distrust of the public schools and suspicion of the loyalty of teachers.[58] Through its bulletins and the pronouncements of its leaders the commission breathed a fierce spirit of loyalty to American traditions and assailed defamers of public education as the enemies of democracy. Its bulletin, *True Faith and Allegiance,* calling on education to combat prejudice against minority groups, attained an extensive circulation. Its reports of investigations achieved the status of textbooks of educational principles.

In 1955 the commission reported that "the trouble making was more subtle and more localized," arising from "magazine articles and books." The commission distributed materials designed to answer legitimate as well as evilly disposed critics. It continued its system of conferences, cooperated with state associations in studying school revenues, promised

[58] NEA, *Proceedings, 1949,* 150-152.

to investigate and expose teachers who might be guilty of subversive attitudes, and promoted unity and morale in the teaching profession.[59]

SAFETY COMMISSION

Safety for the school child is an old concept. In the latter years of the nineteenth century, educators who were mindful of safety emphasized fresh air and ventilating systems, fire escapes, and fire drills. One school board was reported as having been so admonished about safety that it ordered the contractor to erect the fire escape before starting on the building. The National Safety Council, organized in 1913, established demonstration centers where trained teachers showed how safety programs could be taught and carried out. By 1929 many well-developed safety programs had been established in the schools, and the number of school-age children killed by motor vehicles was on the decline, even though total deaths from this cause were on the increase. The programs of safety education in the schools unquestionably made the difference. A variety of methods were used—demonstrations of the right and wrong way, dramatized stories, safety games, posters, slides, and motion pictures.[60]

During the 1930's safety education was discussed in a number of sessions at NEA conventions. In 1937 Paul G. Hoffman of the Studebaker Corporation made a plea for the teaching of automotive safety in high schools. Various cities developed programs in which fire drills, contests, and discussions were utilized and school patrols were widely adopted.[61]

"There is today probably a greater chance for a citizen to be injured or killed by an automobile than there was for a citizen in colonial days to be scalped or shot by an Indian." So declared Henry H. Hill, chairman of the 1940 Yearbook, *Safety Education,* sponsored by the American Association of School Administrators.[62] The war increased the need of attention to safety education. In 1943, under the leadership of Frank W. Hubbard, director of the Research Division (which had for some years been active in the safety field), the NEA authorized the National Commission on Safety Education, which began its activities in 1944. Its first secretary, Robert W. Eaves, was succeeded in 1951 by Norman Key.

By 1948 the commission and the NEA had issued twenty-five bulletins and a series of leaflets. By 1956 its list included films, posters, and bulletins, the latter dealing with fire, home, bicycle, and bus safety and driver education. Part of the effectiveness of the safety commission was due to its cooperating with a large number of national organizations.

[59] NEA, *Proceedings, 1955,* 308.
[60] NEA, *Proceedings, 1921,* 623-630; *1924,* 949; *1929,* 557; *1930,* 520-522.
[61] NEA, *Proceedings, 1936,* 100-102; *1937,* 99-103, 371-372.
[62] NEA, *Proceedings, 1940,* 290.

While the statistics of automobile fatalities offer slight encouragement for general optimism, the death rate of school-age children from such accidents was only twenty per 100,000 in 1955 as contrasted with forty per 100,000 in 1925. Thus it appears that safety instruction was at least somewhat effective, and for this result the National Commission on Safety Education could justifiably claim some of the credit.

NATIONAL COMMISSION ON TEACHER EDUCATION AND PROFESSIONAL STANDARDS

At the Buffalo meeting in 1946 the representative assembly created the youngest of the NEA's five continuing commissions. The assembly action of that year charged the commission—the National Commission on Teacher Education and Professional Standards, commonly known as TEPS—with several responsibilities:

1. To give leadership to the movement for establishing higher, and more widely accepted, standards of teacher competence.
2. To develop improved standards for institutions that prepare teachers.
3. To seek the foregoing goals through study, conference, and action in the fields of teacher education, certification, in-service growth, and accreditation.
4. To encourage teacher recruitment.

Some of the things that have been done by the commission in meeting these responsibilities during the past decade are related elsewhere in this volume (see Chapters 7 and 29). In addition, it should be recorded that TEPS has, since 1950, published *The Journal of Teacher Education;* it holds an annual conference every year in June immediately preceding, and near, the NEA convention; it holds a series of regional conferences during the winter months; it has encouraged the establishment of TEPS units in the several states.

Early in its history the national commission initiated a series of basic studies to determine prevailing and prospective facts about demand and supply for teachers at various grade levels, in each subject field, and broken down by states and regions. These studies have proved enormously valuable to the profession and the public, and have helped to influence the decisions of countless young people in making specific plans for their own professional preparation. The studies are now continued annually by the NEA Research Division.

The commission also now sponsors the Future Teachers of America, an organization of high-school and college students. The FTA idea, originated in the mind of Joy Elmer Morgan, devoted disciple of Horace Mann and editor of the *NEA Journal* for more than thirty years. Dr. Morgan originally encouraged the formation of FTA chapters and clubs in connection with the national observance of the Horace Mann centennial in 1937.

Perhaps the most important single achievement of TEPS, to date, was the creation of the National Council for Accreditation of Teacher Education. Although the NCATE from the first, 1952, has been jointly sponsored by several cooperating groups, TEPS was the prime mover, having begun discussion of the idea at its 1948 national conference.[63]

[63] NEA, *Proceedings, 1952,* 125-127.

26

Friends and Allies

EVERY profession has to mend its fences, keep the people informed, and enlist support for its program. While the intimate and interdependent nature of society makes many contacts and joint endeavors among organizations inevitable, many interrelated interests go unrecognized, unacknowledged, and unorganized. Failure to formalize these joint interests often results in a loss to the organizations involved. Fortunately for the field of education, the NEA was sensitive to the situation and was in a position, because of its numbers and prestige, to assume the role of formal as well as actual leadership in forming alliances and capitalizing upon the joint interests that made natural allies out of several great national organizations. The NEA's mechanism for achieving such purposes has been the joint committee. Six such committees are currently active.

AMERICAN MEDICAL ASSOCIATION

For many years educators recognized the importance of health in education. Long before ventilation, lighting, and sanitation were understood and applied to school buildings, superintendents were concerned over the health of school children. School hygiene became an area of study and concern even before its basic principles were known. Fortunately, the leading school men called upon the doctors for help. In 1911 the NEA Committee on Health Problems in Education cooperated with a similar committee of the American Medical Association. Soon thereafter the two committees merged to become a joint committee of the two associations. It has sponsored more than twenty publications, including health manuals for teachers, health charts, health standards for rural schools, and made many suggestions as to how teachers might identify children with defective vision and hearing.

For many years, from 1911 to 1939, the joint committee had the advantages of the continuous chairmanship of Dr. Thomas D. Wood of Columbia University, who was both a doctor and a professor. Symposiums on school health problems were held at medical meetings, thus informing the doctors concerning the health programs of the schools. In 1955 the committee published several booklets and offered a number of suggestions. Among others it disapproved the use of oxygen for athletes and issued a list of precautions concerning the release of children from school. While no one would assign all the credit of advances in school health to the cooperative work of the two associations, it is clear that a formal understanding facilitated the exchange of information and promoted good will between these two important organizations.[1]

AMERICAN LEGION

The second alliance which the NEA formed was with the American Legion. The Legion was greatly concerned with the removal of illiteracy, the Americanization of aliens, and the teaching of history, citizenship, and patriotism. These objectives were also objectives of the NEA. In 1921 a joint committee was established to promote cooperation. Legion speakers have since then appeared regularly on NEA programs, and educators, in turn, have been invited to speak at national conventions of the Legion. The original joint committee sponsored a series of teaching booklets and arranged for the joint sponsorship of American Education Week, which rapidly became an annual occasion for emphasizing the role of the schools and securing good will and support for them. While the joint committee soon lapsed, the sponsorship of the week continued.[2] At the New York meeting of the NEA in 1938 it voted unanimously to renew the affiliation with the Legion and appointed another committee.[3] At the Milwaukee meeting in 1940 Raymond J. Kelly, national commander of the American Legion, declared that he was "proud of the fact that for twenty-one years it has been a flag-waving organization." He trembled to visualize the day when high-school youth would not want to visit at Mount Vernon or no longer yearned "to view the hallowed sepulcher of the immortal Abraham Lincoln. When patriotism ends our country dies." The Legion endorsed Federal aid for "equalizing opportunity for all children of the nation," although it attached the reservation of forbidding Federal control. Fifteen thousand teachers had been veterans of the First World War and so there was a degree of overlapping as well as joint interest in the cause of education. The Legion recommended the formation of Legionnaire Schoolmaster Clubs and asked the NEA to employ a full-time person to prepare a list of those eligible for such clubs.[4]

---

[1] NEA, *Proceedings, 1911,* 338; *1912,* 540-545; *1913,* 416-424; *1922,* 325-329; *1934,* 209-212; *1938,* 867-868; *1940,* 892-893; *1955,* 298-300.

[2] NEA, *Proceedings, 1922,* 303-305, 220-224; *1923,* 399-402; *1926,* 186-188.

[3] NEA, *Proceedings, 1939,* 874-875.

[4] NEA, *Proceedings, 1940,* 168-170, 881-882, 719; *1942,* 525.

In greeting the teachers at Boston in 1941, Milo J. Warner, national commander of the Legion, denounced the use of textbooks that preached "the glories of the collectivist society" and asked "that the child be given the same unerring training for a sound take-off that guides the bee in his flight toward honey-making blossoms." Charles F. Dienst, chairman of the joint committee, declared that "We are as much concerned about subversive material in the text as you are . . ." and agreed to work for its elimination.[5] The commander in 1942, Lynn U. Stambaugh, referred to the "lunatic fringe" that was inevitable in large organizations such as the educators and the veterans, and declared the intention of the Legion to oppose the fringes of pacificism and radicalism without interfering with the teaching profession.[6] In 1943 the Legion asserted its intention of enrolling returning veterans who were teachers in both the Legion and the NEA.[7] Over the years the committee supported Federal aid to education and sponsored oratorical contests, athletic events, youth clubs, and American Education Week. In 1949 the week was opened by a broadcast by President Andrew D. Holt, who spoke from the restored Lincoln-Berry grocery store at New Salem, Illinois.[8]

In 1952 discord threatened to disrupt the cooperative program of the association and the Legion. It was endangered by an article, "Your Child Is Their Target," that appeared in the June issue of the *American Legion Magazine*. The article asserted that a subversive movement had existed in the teaching profession for thirty years. Members of the NEA at the Detroit meeting in July denounced the article as "replete with misstatements," filled with errors of interpretation, and hostile to teachers and schools. One leading educator branded it as "a false and unprovoked attack upon the National Education Association." A strongly worded rebuke of the Legion was defeated by the argument that the president of the association, J. Cloyd Miller, had already answered the attack in a masterful manner. When the NEA submitted an answering article, the publication committee of the Legion refused to publish it, but agreed to prepare an article which it would submit to the NEA for criticisms. Time seems to have healed the wound, and the Legion and the NEA continue their cooperative committee, their sponsorship of American Education Week, and their joint endeavors to promote patriotism and citizenship.[9]

AMERICAN TEACHERS ASSOCIATION

While relationships with the American Legion involved some irritations, cooperation with the National Association of Teachers in Colored

[5] NEA, *Proceedings, 1941*, 35-37, 695, 763-764, 927-928.
[6] NEA, *Proceedings, 1942*, 26-38.
[7] NEA, *Proceedings, 1943*, 325.
[8] NEA, *Proceedings, 1950*, 313-314.
[9] NEA, *Proceedings, 1952*, 63, 120, 170, 236, 328; *1953*, 40, 223; *1955*, 295-297.

Schools evoked mostly appreciation and good will in spite of attendant complexities and embarrassments. The informal committee of the NEA, appointed in 1926 to study problems in Negro schools, soon grew into a joint committee of the two organizations. The committee had the good fortune to have chairmen who served year after year. N. C. Newbold, director of Negro education in North Carolina, was a member from 1926 until 1947 and chairman from 1928 to 1939; S. L. Smith of Peabody College was chairman in 1926 and from 1939 to 1946.

Beginning slowly and cautiously, the committee sponsored studies of the treatment of Negroes in textbooks, of the status of Negro education, and of discrimination in the use of Federal funds for education. It planned a motion picture that would portray Negro life and contributions, and prepared kits of materials on race relations for use in teacher-training institutions.

The textbook studies showed that Negroes were accorded more space as slaves than as citizens; that their contributions in the various wars went unmentioned; that Nat Turner received more attention as the leader of a slave insurrection than Booker T. Washington did for founding a unique college. Publishers were reluctant to use pictures of Negroes, and some authors were condescending in their treatment. In the course of a few years revisions were made, including some of the changes that the committee had recommended, and materials on Negro history became more plentiful.

Other changes occurred. In 1939 the Negroes adopted a new name for their organization, namely, American Teachers Association. It exchanged speakers with the NEA and cooperated in many efforts for Federal legislation and for other purposes. The original committee of four on problems of colored schools grew into a joint committee of eleven with more than a hundred advisers. Negroes and Negro education received more attention in textbooks and books, on the motion-picture screen, and over the radio, and state and local committees on racial relations were established.

In 1947 the joint committee called for the full integration of Negro teachers into the NEA. In the following year three states in the area of separate schools for Negroes sent Negro delegates to the NEA convention, being allowed representation in proportion to the number of members in the NEA. Although Negroes had, from the earliest years of the NEA, participated as individual members and delegates representing both all-Negro and mixed *local* associations at the annual convention, the innovation of the late 1940's consisted of direct affiliation of all-Negro *state* associations (such state associations being the constituent bodies of the American Teachers Association). At the Boston meeting in 1949 there were thirty-seven accredited Negro delegates from states with dual school systems, the largest delegation of thirteen coming from Tennessee, and in 1951 nine Negro state associations and four locals sent delegates to the NEA assembly.

This official integration of Negroes into the NEA in spite of local customs and legal difficulties led, of course, to other difficulties. Some hotels would not admit Negroes, and the Representative Assembly in 1943 adopted the policy of meeting only in those cities where "every NEA delegate could have equality of accommodation."

In the course of thirty years the committee on Negro education achieved some tangible results. Several teacher-training schools instituted courses on racial relations and minority problems; studies on the status of Negro education were widely circulated, thus tending to bring about a more even distribution of funds; the Negroes secured a status within the NEA that was denied them in the segregated states. With these and other achievements behind it, the joint committee announced in 1955 that it would work for the integration of the races in the schools in accordance with the Supreme Court decision of 1954.[10]

AMERICAN LIBRARY ASSOCIATION

The next formal alliance which the NEA made was with the American Library Association. In spite of the large and obvious area of overlapping interests of the two organizations, formal cooperation was not authorized until 1929 and was not started until two years later. This long delay in taking an obviously desirable step is readily explained, however, by the fact that there was an active Library Department of the NEA, which functioned from 1896 until 1923. In spite of its small membership, having only 181 in 1922, it provided the occasion for the presentation of many practical papers. In 1934, shortly after formal cooperation was initiated, the library committee recommended the reestablishment of the Library Department, explaining that the sponsorship of the NEA with its publication of articles in the *Proceedings* would enlist more support for libraries. This suggestion was not accepted by the NEA, and the joint committee started its program of service to both organizations.[11]

In fact, the joint committee soon convinced itself that the discussion of libraries and their utilization before mixed groups of educators and librarians was preferable to a library department in which librarians talked to one another.[12] The committee established exhibits at the annual conventions, distributed book lists and reprints of pertinent articles, and sponsored discussion groups. It started also to worry about the mutilation of books by young students who found that the enriched curriculum required the assembling of pictures and charts.

[10] NEA, *Proceedings, 1926-1954, passim.*
[11] NEA, *Proceedings, 1922,* 988; *1934,* 171-172.
[12] NEA, *Proceedings, 1935,* 153-155; *1937,* 862-864.

The committee issued bulletins on buying books for school libraries, on library standards and services, and on the planning of buildings with properly located libraries. It published annual lists of children's books, prepared bibliographies for the departments of the NEA, and compiled lists of audio-visual aids. The committee recommended that school librarians meet the educational standards required of teachers; thus they would be able to interest students in the content as well as to locate material for class assignments. In various ways the committee proved that the cooperation of the NEA and the American Library Association was of value to both organizations.

CONGRESS OF PARENTS AND TEACHERS

Parents are natural allies of teachers. This obvious fact was emphasized in 1929, when the NEA and the National Congress of Parents and Teachers made their first efforts at formal cooperation. "Education is in need of a well-conceived program of public relations, and progress in education is safe only as it carries with it public understanding and support."[13] This declaration by the joint committee of the two organizations stated the problem and implied a policy. In fact, the joint committee soon induced the Congress of Parents and Teachers to worry about the same problems that troubled the association—better teachers, better pay, better conditions, adequate school buildings, financial support, revising the curriculum, guidance programs, and the support that comes from public understanding.

To achieve the solution of these problems the joint committee planned for the exchange of speakers at national conventions, promoted discussion groups, secured cooperation between congresses and state teachers' associations, and sponsored the publication of booklets.[14] Over 500,000 copies of the 1951 leaflet, *Everybody's Schools,* were distributed, and several others also achieved a wide circulation. The congress was especially active in defending the schools against what it regarded as hostile and unjust attacks. It became one of the sponsors of American Education Week and in a variety of ways demonstrated its concern for the welfare of public education.[15]

MAGAZINE PUBLISHERS ASSOCIATION

The latest of the joint committees was the one appointed in 1954 to promote cooperation between the NEA and the Magazine Publishers Association. The joint committee sponsors an annual editor-educator conference, facilitates exchange of information between educators and lay

[13] NEA, *Proceedings, 1940,* 899.
[14] NEA, *Proceedings, 1931,* 263; *1932,* 199; *1936,* 872.
[15] NEA, *Proceedings, 1940,* 998-999; *1945-1946,* 448; *1952,* 333-334; *1955,* 302.

magazines, and assists in arranging for magazine editors and publishers to appear as speakers at educational meetings.

Stimulated by a proposal from this committee, the NEA undertook to prepare for circulation to some 10,000 educators at regular intervals summaries of articles about education appearing in general magazines. The joint committee in 1956 noted with satisfaction that "articles on education in magazines of national circulation increased from 220 in 1952 to 484 in 1955."[16]

These formal alliances do not indicate the full range of the cooperative endeavors of the NEA. At various times it has participated in programs, publications, or campaigns in cooperation with the National Council of Teachers of English, the Office of Education, and the American Association of Museums. Mindful of educational problems and devoid of organizational self-consciousness, the NEA has at times cooperated with potential rivals such as the Progressive Education Association and the American Federation of Teachers.[17]

Still another kind of cooperation was involved when the NEA became an institutional member of other organizations. For more than three decades it has been a member of the American Council on Education, and in 1952 it helped to organize and became a member of the World Confederation of Organizations of the Teaching Profession (see Chapter 30).

American Education Week is the result of cooperation by four national agencies. Sponsored originally by the NEA and the American Legion, the period of December 4-10, 1921, was set as the first education week. Its success was immediate, and in the course of time the Office of Education and the National Congress of Parents and Teachers joined in sponsoring the movement. Since 1926 the week that includes Veterans' Day (November 11) has been observed as education week. The sponsors select a theme, such as "Schools for a Strong America," distribute materials, and suggest programs of local activities, such as open house in schools, exhibits of pupil materials, and education sermons on the preceding Sunday. Presidential and gubernatorial proclamations announce the week, and the press, radio, and television give it wide publicity. Untainted by commercialism, American Education Week has served as an annual reminder of the role of the schools in American life.[18]

[16] *NEA Handbook, 1956-57*, 163. See also NEA, *Proceedings, 1956*, 317-318.

[17] NEA, *Proceedings, 1941*, 694-695.

[18] The origin of the week is somewhat involved. The original sponsor may have been the American Legion; other facts seem to point to the Bureau of Education as the prime mover, although in 1926 Commissioner John J. Tigert temporarily withheld the Bureau's sponsorship, NEA, *Proceedings, 1926*, 186. See Mildred S. Fenner, *The National Education Association, 1892-1942* (Ph.D. thesis, The George Washington University, 1942), 270-273.

27

Democratizing the Association

THE National Teachers' Association of 1857 was founded in part as a protest against lay leadership in education. Horace Mann, Henry Barnard, and other crusaders in the great public-school movement of the 1830's and 1840's wisely and properly had enlisted the help of public officials, lawyers, writers, preachers, and other popular leaders. The help of such men was timely and necessary. After a few years, however, the teachers came to feel that they should assume the active and prominent role in educational leadership. This new association, initiated by leaders of state teachers' associations, was an organized effort by practical teachers to gain control of their own profession. They succeeded. They restored education to the educators. In doing so, however, they failed to include women, who constituted a large percentage of the teachers, and they assigned too much power to the officers. In time the organization which had been founded in protest was the recipient of protests. The democratizing agency itself needed democratizing.

Democracy in management is not necessary in all organizations. Some societies may exist for purposes whose realization requires a concentration of authority. Economy or efficiency or expedition may under some circumstances be more important than general participation. An educational association, however, which operates within a democratic framework and undertakes to promote the teaching of democracy, cannot ignore the problem of democratic management. Within such an organization sovereignty must be dispersed and authority regulated.

The democratization of the NEA resulted from the same forces which operated upon all aspects of American society. Political democracy, with its doctrine of equality and opportunity, its stress upon citizenship and patriotism, affected the schools as well as other institutions. The growth of congregationalism in the churches was based in part upon the application of democratic thought to religion. The rising status of the child, as exemplified in the kindergarten and child-study movements, was both

322

a result and a cause of democratic ideas. Science and invention eventually exerted a great leveling, equalizing force which some interpreted as democratic in essence. The freeing of the slaves, the rise of labor unions, the extension of suffrage, and the growth of government regulation and services were all powerful factors in the spread of democratic ideas and practices.

All these influences and developments, national and regional, were utilized by the women, the members, and the classroom teachers to effect the democratization of the NEA. The major democratic reforms that were realized in the first century of the association were the achievement of equality for women within the profession and within the association, and the winning of status for members and their control of the association through the Representative Assembly. Related to these developments were the rise of the Department of Classroom Teachers (see pages 280-282) and increased attention by the association to promoting the personal as well as the professional welfare of its members (see Chapter 28).

The president of the New York State Teachers' Association in 1853 was asked why he had placed no females on the program or on committees. He explained: "Behold the beautiful pilaster of this superb hall; contemplate its pedestal, its shafts, its rich entablature, the crowning glory of the whole. Each and all the parts in their appropriate places contribute to its strength, symmetry, and beauty. Could I aid in taking down that entablature from its proud elevation and placing it in the dust and dirt of the pedestal?"

Susan B. Anthony, one of the teachers who heard this rhetoric, was not impressed. She resented all restrictions based upon sex and decided to defy the custom which forbade a woman teacher to speak even at meetings of the association to which she belonged. After the men had discussed at length the question of why teachers do not receive the respect accorded lawyers, doctors, and preachers, Miss Anthony arose and requested permission of the chairman to speak. With determination she remained standing while a prolonged discussion ensued among the startled officers. When the embarrassed chairman finally granted her recognition, she said: "It seems to me that you fail to comprehend the cause of the disrespect of which you complain. Do you not see that as long as society says that a woman has not brains enough to be a lawyer, doctor, or minister but has plenty to be a teacher, every one of you who condescends to teach tacitly admits before all Israel and the sun that he has no more brains than a woman."[1]

The New York State Teachers' Association immediately passed a resolu-

[1] D. Emma Hodge and Lamont F. Hodge, *A Century of Service to Public Education* (Albany, 1945), 197-198.

tion admitting women to all the privileges of the association, but several
years passed before it was fully effective. This pattern was followed in
the National Teachers' Association. The constitution of 1857 restricted
membership to "gentlemen." When the limitation was challenged at
Indianapolis in 1866, the association promptly changed the word "gentlemen" to "person." Having been accepted as members, the women had,
of course, to win the struggle for recognition, participation, and leadership, and convince their timid sisters as well as the men of the desirability
of their aims. In excluding and restricting women, the men were guilty
not so much of overt discrimination as of the unwitting acceptance of
conventional mores. When they faced the fact that women teachers outnumbered the men in many states,[2] they saw the absurdity, if not the
injustice, of their policy. But it was easier to remove official restrictions
than to change customs. The official change merely admitted women to
the field of battle.

The movement for equality for women was, of course, only an aspect
of the larger crusade for women's rights in society as a whole. The movement within the NEA was not merely a feminist but a democratic movement. It was interwoven with the rise of classroom teachers, the
recognition of the rights of members, and the democratization of management. All these causes were concurrent and interrelated; a discussion of
any one is therefore likely to impinge upon one or more of the other
movements.

The rise of women in teaching was rapid. As late as 1856 men teachers
in Indiana outnumbered women almost four to one (3,973 to 1,070).
During and after the Civil War the number and percentage of women
teachers rose rapidly. Anna C. Brackett triumphantly pointed out that
in 1870 women teachers outnumbered the men two to one, and that the
excess of women over men was greatest in the "states which are universally recognized as the leaders"—three to one in Michigan and New
York, five to one in Maine, and in Massachusetts, seven to one.[3] Alice E.
Brown of the Lafayette, Indiana, High School, claimed that women,
because of their restricted sphere, had developed the traits that make
good teachers—"personal magnetism, sympathy, quickness of resource,
ability to read character, attention to detail, and patience."[4] The men
seemed to accept the predominance of women with good grace. One
referred to the progress that had characterized education since women
had taken over the schools. Another reported that the final note of

[2] Elwood P. Cubberley, *Public Education in the United States* (rev. ed., Boston,
1934), 401. Remarkable in 1919 when it first appeared, this book maintains its unique
place in the history of American education.
[3] NEA, *Proceedings, 1872*, 184.
[4] *Indiana School Journal*, XXV, 71, February 1880.

encouragement from the South was the fact that women were assuming the major share of the positions.[5]

Women made other gains within the NEA. Following their admission to full membership in 1866, some ladies at the Trenton meeting of 1869 asked the nominating committee to name a woman as one of the vice-presidents and one as assistant secretary. J. L. Bulkley of New York objected, declaring that it was contrary to the constitution to nominate women, but E. E. White of Ohio corrected Bulkley.[6] In 1870 the list of officers included Della A. Lathrop, Mrs. M. A. Stone, and Kate S. French as vice-presidents and Amelia A. Rockfellow and Mrs. M. Whittington as members of the board of directors.

Women were chosen for office in several of the departments. They, as was quite natural, practically monopolized the offices of the Kindergarten Department. Of the thirty-four persons who served as president of the Elementary Department between 1871 and 1907, eleven were women. During this period the department had a total of 102 officers (president, vice-president, and secretary), forty of whom were women. Of the thirty-six officers of the Child-Study Department during 1895-1907, ten were women; of the 102 officers of the Normal Department, eighteen were women; of the sixty-six officers of the Art Department, thirty were women. Even the Department of Higher Education chose one woman, Alice E. Freeman of Wellesley College, as vice-president in 1888. Between 1880 and 1907, eighteen women were elected to the National Council of Education, and a few served on the board of directors.

While women did not achieve offices and recognition in proportion to their numbers, their status within the association was probably higher than in the profession; certainly it was better than the one which society accorded them. Consequently it is unjust to belabor the NEA for its tardiness in according women a status which society denied them, unless one insists, as he could with a degree of justification, that an educational organization should lead rather than follow popular practices.

The Madison meeting of 1884,[7] notable for many reasons, made an impressive contribution to the winning of equality for women within the association. President Bicknell arranged one general meeting at which four women spoke. One of the women speakers, Mrs. May Wright Sewall of Massachusetts, could not resist the opportunity of scolding the men. "Nothwithstanding the fluttering of fans and the fluttering of ribbons, and the gay waving of plumes, and the glancing smiles, and the eloquent blushes from the audience, speakers have persisted in addressing their audiences as 'gentlemen.' "[8] While Bicknell's enthusiasm for women's

[5] NEA, *Proceedings, 1884*, 123.
[6] NTA, *Proceedings, 1869*, 714, 723.
[7] See Chapter 22.
[8] NEA, *Proceedings, 1884*, 153.

rights was not shared by all his colleagues, no one could erase the effects of the Madison program or restore the custom of enshrining women on pedestals of chivalrous neglect.

The movement for women's rights in the NEA achieved a sudden and dramatic success with the election in 1910 of Ella Flagg Young as president. Beginning in 1862 as a primary teacher in the Chicago schools at the age of seventeen, Mrs. Young was successively a principal, district superintendent, professor of education in the University of Chicago, and superintendent of Chicago schools. She was democratic in policy as well as theory, courageous enough to oppose the board that elected her, and energetic enough to sponsor new practices and methods. One of the first women to become superintendent of a large school system, she enlisted an enthusiastic following and quickly achieved a national reputation.[9]

Soon after Mrs. Young's election as superintendent of the Chicago schools, some of her supporters conceived the plan of electing her president of the NEA. They wrote letters, enlisted supporters, and circulated the news of her candidacy for several months before the Boston convention. A. E. Winship, editor of the *Journal of Education;* Carroll G. Pearse, superintendent of Milwaukee; Francis G. Blair of Illinois; and other prominent and influential leaders favored Mrs. Young's election. Even more important in securing her election were Grace Strachan and Katherine D. Blake of New York and Margaret Haley of Chicago, who rallied supporters and took charge of the campaign.

When the nominating committee of forty-nine members met to choose a candidate for the presidency, it voted overwhelmingly in favor of Z. X. Snyder, president of the Normal School at Greeley, Colorado. Miss Blake and Winship were the only members of the committee who favored the nomination of Mrs. Young. After the nominating committee made its report, Miss Blake obtained the floor and moved to substitute the minority report, which proposed the name of Ella Flagg Young for president. The convention then voted 617 to 376 in favor of substituting the minority for the majority report, and so Mrs. Young became the first woman president of the NEA.[10]

This unprecedented election gave rise to disputes and rumors. Mrs. Young's supporters declared that they favored her, not because she was

[9] NEA, *Proceedings, 1918,* 685.

[10] In her motion Miss Blake said, "As a member of the nominating committee in which the vote for nominee for President was comparatively close . . ." (NEA *Proceedings, 1910,* 33). Years later Miss Blake gave a different account. In a letter to Mildred S. Fenner, February 25, 1942, she said that Mrs. Young received only two votes in the nominating committee, hers and Winship's. Mildred S. Fenner, *The National Education Association, 1892-1942* (Ph.D. thesis, The George Washington University, 1942), pp. 138-139. Dr. Fenner gives a detailed account of the election of Mrs. Young.

a woman, but because she was the "human being" best qualified for the position. Her opponents said that their opposition was based, not upon the fact that she was a woman, but upon the objectionable tactics that had been used to secure her election. The use of badges, the letter-writing campaign, the attendance of members primarily for the purpose of voting for Mrs. Young—these and other criticisms and charges were made. It was said that some persons voted who were not entitled to vote. Some conservative members regretted the breaking of traditions; they felt that the association had lost dignity and that the presidency had been degraded. In spite of all protests and charges, everyone regarded Mrs. Young's election as a feminist victory.

The efforts to elect another woman as president in 1912 did not turn out to be as successful or as promotive of women's rights as the election of 1910. As a president Mrs. Young evoked some criticism because of her suspicion of the officers in charge of the permanent funds of the NEA, and while she was an entirely satisfactory president, she did not meet the expectations of some of her supporters. When she failed to help Grace C. Strachan, a district superintendent in Brooklyn, to become president in 1912, she alienated many of her eastern admirers.

Katherine D. Blake, who had successfully promoted Mrs. Young's election at Boston, tried at Chicago in 1912 to perform a similar service for Miss Strachan. When the nominating committee brought in the name of Edward T. Fairchild, Miss Blake moved that Miss Strachan's name be substituted. A lengthy discussion ensued which became in essence an unseemly wrangle between the New York and Chicago delegates. Miss Strachan made a rambling, untactful speech in which she chided the Chicago teachers for failing to repay the help which they had received at Boston and for being so cowed by the Chicago Principals' Club, which had decided to support the regular nominee, that they were afraid to vote for her. She reviewed charges and countercharges, and Miss Blake carried them to even further extremes. When the votes were counted Fairchild had won by an unquestioned majority.[11]

The wrangle among the women delegates made an unfavorable impression on some of the spectators and explains, in part at least, why another woman was not elected president until 1917. After that the custom of electing a woman every other year was faithfully observed. (From 1917 until 1945, a woman was elected in every odd-numbered year, and a man was elected in every even-numbered year. No election was held in 1945. Since then a woman has been elected in every even-numbered year, a man in every odd-numbered year.) A. E. Winship expressed his admiration for the generosity of the women, who consti-

[11] NEA, *Proceedings, 1912,* 32-42.

tute an overwhelming majority of the members of the NEA, for allowing a man to be president one-half of the time.[12]

In the meantime the classroom teachers organized a department,[13] and devoted much attention to salary, tenure, pensions, and other welfare matters. The establishment of women's complete equality with respect to the presidency was indicative of similar changes in other official matters. With the help of an inclusive movement in behalf of women outside of the association, custom itself had been changed within the NEA. Women had won the crusade to be accepted as teachers, members, and persons, and not merely as women.

The second major achievement in the democratization of the NEA was the slow rise in the status of members and the establishment of the representative assembly in 1920, effective at the Des Moines meeting in the following year. This reorganization was the culmination of a long struggle, the solution to the problem of democratizing a national organization with widely scattered members, the answer to the question of how to secure the participation of members and the responsibility of officers.

From its inception in 1857 until 1921 the association was officially and actually in the hands of the members who were present at the annual summer meetings. This town-meeting type of direct democracy worked well for many years. A fairly large percentage of the members came regularly and thus provided a continuity for the work of the association. They learned to work together harmoniously on programs, in committees, and in publishing the annual proceedings. The nominating committees named men for office who had won the respect of their fellow members, and their recommendations were tantamount to election. No person announced his candidacy for an office; had he done so it would have been construed as evidence of his unfitness. The tradition of dignity and aloofness was firmly established and rigidly respected.

Why then was a system that seemed to work so well and give such general satisfaction eventually overthrown? Many factors were involved. As the association grew in size and importance, its honors were more coveted. Ambitious newcomers saw the professional value of participating in its activities. The older members who had built the association and established its procedures and traditions naturally assumed a possessive and proprietary attitude. For a time newcomers felt a degree of respect, even awe; then they became impatient at being kept on probation; and finally they resented the control of the association by a small, even though worthy and capable, group. As the years passed, criticisms be-

[12] Fenner, *op. cit.*, 152.
[13] See Chapter 24.

came harsher and more frequent. It was said that the NEA was run by a self-perpetuating clique, that an inner group of mutual admirers held all the offices, and that a small circle of administrators and professors made all decisions and determined all policies. While such criticisms were mixtures of truth, errors, misconceptions, and injustices, they sounded plausible to those who were eager to participate and ambitious to gain recognition. Most probationers consider the probationary period too long, and persons of ability and spirit resent the slowness with which others perceive their high qualities. Thus the leaders of the NEA, especially those of long service and high station, inevitably became the objects of envy and suspicion. Guilty or innocent of the faults and frailties assigned to them, they came to be regarded as upholders of outmoded ideas and practices, opponents of reform, and road blocks in the path of progress.

In defense of the orthodox leaders it should be said that they demonstrated an impersonal concern for the welfare of the association. There is no instance of rewarded self-seeking. Group judgment rather than personal ambition determined elections. While choices tended to fall upon older members with a record of faithful attendance and service, there is no evidence of favoritism or any instance of the incompetence of officers chosen under the system. The leaders can be charged with failing to realize that the wisdom of all the members was greater than that of a part of them, even though that part consisted of experienced leaders.

While leadership was predominantly in the hands of superintendents and college presidents, membership was open to all practical educators. Presumably each had his chance to serve and rise to leadership if judged worthy of such honor. In the Department of Higher Education, where exclusiveness and class consciousness would have been manifest, if it existed anywhere in the association, there was apparently no such attitude. In fact the members were divided into three approximately equal groups —college, university, and secondary teachers. While high-school teachers were assigned to the department when it was organized in 1870, some doubts arose as to their status or welcome. To settle the matter, a resolution was adopted by the department in 1885 declaring that it included "the University, the College, the Academy, and the High School" and inviting workers in such institutions to enroll themselves as members. The list of members for that year includes several secondary-school teachers, two editors, some unidentified persons, and one superintendent.[14] While the programs were weighted with college topics, a few papers dealt with problems of secondary education. The multiplicity and diversity of interests and the rapid increase in the number of high schools, rather than any class consciousness as to status, led in 1887 to the organization of a separate department of secondary education.

[14] NEA, *Proceedings, 1885,* 192-193.

By the 1890's some dissatisfaction with the management of the NEA found expression in attempts to curb the power of the president to name the nominating committee. Some critics expressed the fear that the president by this power could virtually choose his successor. It is difficult to understand the basis of this fear, because the nominating committee, by an old and strictly observed custom, starting as early as 1865, was composed of members from various states. In 1866 it consisted of seven members, in 1870 it numbered twenty-three,[15] and additional members were added as new states were represented at the conventions. In 1895, when Nicholas Murray Butler was president, the nominating committee consisted of forty-eight members.[16] Nevertheless, proposals for a restrictive amendment were made at Denver in 1895 and rejected as unsound by the board of directors. At Milwaukee in 1897 Superintendent Robert E. Denfeld of Duluth proposed that the members of the nominating committee be chosen by the delegations from each state. This proposal was well received, and E. E. White of Ohio, a member of the board, revised the proposal to the extent of authorizing the president to fill vacancies that might arise when states failed to select nominees. White, representing the board, then introduced the amendment and it was adopted.[17]

This slight restriction upon the president's power did not alter the results of the elections. It was significant, however, for two reasons. It was a step in increasing the role of the members in association affairs, and it demonstrated that the leaders were sensitive to the criticisms of the members and responsive to their wishes when convinced of the practicality of the proposed changes.

This effort to curb the prerogatives of the president was evidence of an evolving attitude of opposition to customary policies and procedures. The decision in 1905 to ask Congress for a charter to replace the old one, granted under the laws of the District of Columbia, which expired in 1906, was the occasion for objections and wrangles over the status of the National Council of Education within the association and over the control of the permanent fund. Margaret Haley of Chicago and S. Y. Gillan of Milwaukee objected to the semi-independent status of the council and to the control of the fund by the board of trustees. They argued that association money should be at the disposal of the members rather than in the hands of a small board. Miss Haley appeared before a congressional committee and registered her opposition to the proposed charter. In spite of her opposition the new charter was granted by act of Congress and signed by President Roosevelt on June 30, 1906.

[15] NTA, Proceedings, 1865, 200; 1866, 6; NEA, Proceedings, 1870, 96.
[16] NEA, Proceedings, 1895, 21.
[17] NEA, Proceedings, 1897, 27-28.

Perhaps the most effective argument for shifting the control of the NEA from the business meeting of members to a system of nationally elected representatives was the constant fear that the meetings would be overwhelmed by the local members, who would break precedents, change policies, and elect their own candidates. The likelihood of such an outcome was real, because the host state for the convention made strenuous, and generally successful, efforts to enroll a large number of new members. In fact, one of the reasons for moving the convention from region to region was to increase the membership. This advantage was gained at the risk of the continuity of leadership. So the officers and leaders, who had patiently endeavored to make the association national, were haunted by the fear that it might be degraded by sudden seizure of control by a local or regional group.

Those who feared partisan and local control cited the attendance at the Boston meeting of 1910 of a large number of women who came for the sole purpose of voting for Mrs. Young. The New York teachers who tried to select Grace Strachan at Chicago in 1912 cited the bloc voting by Chicago teachers as an example of local control. Later it was said that the Chicago teachers went to Milwaukee in 1919 primarily to defeat the proposed establishment of a representative assembly.

The idea of establishing a representative assembly grew in favor. It was the answer to the danger of regional or local control, and it was also a promising means for establishing a direct connection between the state and local associations and the NEA. At the Oakland meeting of 1915 a committee was appointed to work out a plan of representation that would establish such an organic relationship. William B. Owen, principal of the Chicago Normal School, was chairman of the committee that reported first at Pittsburgh in 1918 and then at Milwaukee in the following year. At Pittsburgh the proponents of reorganization feared defeat and so did not present the matter for a vote.

At Milwaukee the proposed reorganization could not be effected for two reasons. It was discovered that the change of control from the convention to a representative assembly would require a change in the congressional charter. The executive committee was authorized to secure the necessary amendment from Congress. The second difficulty was the opposition of many teachers from New York, Chicago, and Milwaukee. Led by Margaret Haley, they defeated the reorganization plan. By thus defeating national sentiment, they demonstrated the need for the very measure which they opposed.

One necessary step was taken at Milwaukee. Howard R. Driggs of Utah gave notice of an amendment, to be voted on at the next meeting, to the effect that any reorganization accepted in 1920 could go into effect at once. Salt Lake City was chosen as the meeting place in 1920, in the belief that the teachers of that area would favor the reorganization plan and in order to escape "the packed meetings of recent years," as the *School Review* expressed it.[18] In May 1920, Congress approved the amended charter, and everyone looked to Salt Lake City with the expectation that reorganization would at last be effected.

The plans were all made. President Josephine Preston was ready to speed the progress of the committee report, and rather harshly refused to recognize Margaret Haley and other opponents of the plan. Howard R. Driggs piloted his amendment through the parliamentary procedure. Seeing that the refusal to let the opposition speak was creating an unfavorable impression, he moved that Miss Haley be recognized. Her opposition speech was ineffective, and the convention voted for the reorganization by a large majority. Thus, the proponents of the new plan used some of the same tactics to effect it that it was designed to prevent.[19]

The assembly plan was successful immediately. Local and state associations affiliated at once with the NEA, and when the first Representative Assembly met in Des Moines in 1921, 463 local and all but four state associations (South Carolina, Rhode Island, Wisconsin, and Minnesota) sent delegates. The number of affiliates increased rapidly; and by 1955, 66 state and 5,542 local associations sent representatives to the national convention.

While the Representative Assembly solved some basic problems, it occasioned the rise of others. It soon became obvious that discussion and deliberation were difficult in an assembly that by 1955 numbered more than five thousand persons. While caucuses of state delegations offset this defect to some extent, the problem remains. The election of state and local delegates results in some overlapping of representation. Some have proposed that the locals be made subsidiary to the states and that they be represented in the national body only through state delegations. Even though the basing of representation upon affiliates unites all associations into an integrated unit, it results in the disfranchisement of individuals who are not members of either state or local associations; such persons are not represented. To be represented one must have membership in a state or local as well as in the national association. There is thus no possibility of direct membership in the NEA that carries with it the democratic prerogatives of participation and representation. The delegates to the assembly are not uniformly chosen on the basis of qualifications. Some are chosen because they are to be in the vicinity of the convention city; some are chosen because they can afford the expense of attending the convention; some are chosen because they are admin-

---

[18] *School Review*, XXVIII, 481-482, September 1920.
[19] Howard R. Driggs, *Some Closing Scenes in the Old NEA* (typed Ms.).

istrators. The payment of part of the expenses of the delegates by the NEA tends to correct some of these weaknesses. An assembly composed of a changing personnel is naturally less effective than one which consists of experienced delegates. Some affiliates have established the practice of sending the same person year after year. A possible improvement would be to lengthen the term of the delegate to three or four years. Thus the old problem of securing continuity in the formulation of policies remains to challenge the affiliates as well as the national association. There is also the danger that an association will fail to maintain affiliation, for it can secede by the simple act of not paying its affiliation fee.[20]

In spite of all these and other problems, the NEA faces the future with equanimity because it has the machinery for resolving difficulties. It is a national body; it is composed of numerous and widely scattered units; it is permeated by a professional spirit. The leader, spokesman, and proponent of American education, it is mindful of its responsibilities and proceeds with dignity and decorum to discharge them.

[20] Erwin Stevenson Selle, *The Organization and Activities of the National Education Association* (New York, 1932). Selle discussed some of these problems as they appeared in the period 1918–1928. His analysis is now somewhat outdated, of course.

28

The NEA and Teacher Welfare

THE National Education Association, during its first half-century (1857-1907), was not greatly concerned with the personal welfare of either administrators or teachers. The lofty impersonal detachment that characterized the leaders was not a pose or a revelation of indifference, but a deliberately adopted philosophy. They were mindful of the difficulties of evolving an educational system that would fit an emerging society. They believed that all educators, including classroom teachers, should seek first to establish a profession. Hence they regarded attention to salary, tenure, and status as premature, as entirely secondary to the growth of the profession. So it is pointless and possibly unjust to belabor the early leaders of the NEA for neglecting teacher welfare; they also neglected administrator welfare. Their attitude toward the rank and file of teachers may be described as aristocratic aloofness or indifference, but such a description, however merited, is quite unrevealing of their basic philosophy.

The record of the association's efforts in behalf of teachers during the first fifty years is not blank. At the first meeting in Philadelphia in 1857, when the National Teachers' Association was founded, T. W. Valentine spoke of the need for more adequate remuneration as one reason why the profession should organize. He cited the instance of a county superintendent of schools who was paid only $300 per year. Six years later the president of the association, John D. Philbrick, insisted that "the situation of the teacher must be made desirable, by adequate compensation." Apparently in response to Philbrick's address, the association at that meeting (1863) passed its first resolution on salaries. There was, indeed, relatively more concern for teacher status and welfare in the meetings of the first ten years or so than there was in the last three decades of the nineteenth century, when such "higher" matters as national policy, educational philosophy, and curriculum were exalted and debated by the professors, college presidents, and superintendents who dominated convention programs. In this respect the National Education Association of 1907-1957 is more like the National Teachers' Association of 1857-1870 than it is like the National Educational Association of 1870-1907. However, in the early years the concern could be expressed, but there was little that the association could *do* to influence actual practices, whereas since 1907 the NEA has had the strength and power and machinery to wield enormous influence for the improvement of teacher welfare. And, especially since 1920, it has done so.

Even in the years when lofty ideas seemed to matter much more than mundane considerations of money and status, practical matters were not ignored. A notable instance was the Madison meeting of 1884, at which were assembled more classroom teachers than had ever before been brought together in one place in the history of the United States (see Chapter 22). The audience applauded when President Thomas W. Bicknell made an eloquent plea for higher salaries for all professional workers in education. At the same meeting Bicknell appointed a committee on salaries—the first such in NEA history. The following year, 1885, the convention called for appointment of another committee to study teacher tenure.

The association in these years also tried to improve employment practices for its members. It was customary at some of the conventions to provide a teachers' exchange. An announcement was made of a time and place where administrators in search of teachers and teachers in search of positions could meet and discuss their respective needs. Sometimes this informal teachers' agency was handled by a committee. It is not known how many teachers benefited from this service, but at least it had the virtue of direct action.

With the minor exception of the teacher-exchange service, the record of the association for its first forty-eight years was almost entirely one of words—devoid of action. Then in 1905 came the monumental factual report on teachers' salaries, a document of 466 pages, based on questionnaire returns from more than 400 cities of 8,000 or more population and from representative rural school districts in twenty-three states. The report revealed that annual salaries averaged $661 for urban elementary-school teachers and $1,046 for urban high-school teachers, with rural salaries considerably lower.[1]

The 1905 salary study demonstrated the efficacy of facts as weapons in the campaign for convincing the public and the profession itself of the need for remedial action. Other such studies followed. Their reports

[1] The Bureau of Labor of the Federal government took note of these facts with the comment: "In a majority of cities the minimum salary for regular teachers in their first year is below a fair living standard and therefore too low to attract to the profession the best material. . . . The increases are, as a rule, too small, too slow, and continued for too short a period." *NEA Journal,* XLIV, 342, September 1955.

included additional data to help interpret the salary figures—cost-of-living statistics, comparisons with remuneration in other occupations, trends from year to year, the effects of establishing salary schedules. This experience of the years following 1905, coupled with the rising demand of the membership for more effective action in the welfare field and the growth of teacher influence in the association, led to the establishment in 1922 of the Research Division at NEA headquarters, which for thirty-five years has issued nationwide salary studies biennially.

When one recalls the hopes of Valentine and other founders and rereads their words in the 1857 preamble ("To . . . advance the interests of the profession of teaching"), and when one notes that the massive efforts and achievements of the association toward improvement of teacher welfare have actually come about only in relatively recent years (approximately the past four decades), he may well ask: Why was the association so seemingly tardy in this area of activity? The question is partially answered by the opening paragraph of this chapter, which interprets the philosophy of the association's early leaders. But that alone does not fully explain the facts, for the membership at large seems to have acquiesced in the leaders' views.

To be sure, convention speakers and annual resolutions from 1857 on did from time to time make pronouncements in favor of better pay, status, working conditions, pensions, and tenure. But such pronouncements during the first half-century were mild and relatively infrequent. They were not really designed to bring definite results. They were educative and admonitory rather than proclamations of intended action. Perhaps the most tangible outcome of these pleas was the cumulative effect they had upon the teachers. Eventually they began to take seriously what they once considered as ritualistic routine.

Even though teachers received few tangible benefits and little recognition from the association, they were neither scorned nor ignored. They were assumed to be as professionally minded, as devoid of self-seeking, as the leaders appeared to be. The fact that the teachers stood in greater need of help with respect to salary, tenure, and status did not produce any change in the basic philosophy of giving professional development priority over personal welfare. In fact, it is doubtful if direct action by the association would have produced beneficial results for teachers much before the twentieth century. Even the labor unions were slow to adopt direct action, and when they did they failed as often as they succeeded. The educators seem to have been exasperatingly consistent in believing that teacher welfare would result from education rather than direct action. In achieving lasting and satisfactory results this policy may have validity even today.

During its first half-century few classroom teachers belonged to the

NEA or attended its meetings. The salary, tenure, and general prospects of the typical teacher scarcely warranted his joining a professional organization. Moreover, annual meetings were the principal activity of the NEA in those years, and the typical teacher could rarely afford the cost of attending. So it was more the absence of the teacher, rather than discrimination against him, that explains his lowly part in the NEA during its early years. The association, which was itself struggling for existence, had neither the disposition nor the resources to wage campaigns for the benefit of unprepared, temporary, young, and underpaid teachers who had demonstrated no professional interests. Such conditions explain, even though they may not justify, the long neglect of teacher welfare by the association. Even those who dominated the association in the nineteenth century—superintendents, principals, college professors, and college presidents—paid little attention to considerations of their own personal welfare. It was the welfare of all educators, and not just teacher welfare, that was neglected.

During the NEA's second half-century the story changed dramatically. Teachers, administrators, professors, and all other educators came to look to the NEA and its state and local affiliates as the principal means through which they could help themselves to gain recognition and status, tenure and freedom, better conditions of work, increased remuneration, and security for old age. By 1910 the NEA was demonstrating some interest in teacher welfare; in the 1920's it was vigorously advocating higher salaries and tenure laws; in the 1940's it became almost militant in its defense of teachers and their rights; and in the 1950's the NEA was leading the teachers' demands for professional standards and for more reasonable work loads as well as for continued improvement in economic status.

During the past fifty years average annual salaries for elementary- and secondary-school teachers in the United States have increased about sixfold—from less than $700 in 1907 to approximately $4,000 in 1957.

In 1920 only five states recognized by law the principle of permanent tenure for public-school teachers. By 1955 there were thirty-two states with tenure laws.

Until 1917 no state had a statewide joint-contributory retirement plan for teachers. Today such plans are operating in forty-five states.

Fifty years ago a teacher or a principal or a superintendent could be discharged at the whim of a school board, without recourse. Today the more than a million professional personnel of the nation's schools know that in the event of unjust dismissal they can call for help from the NEA's Defense Commission or its Committee on Tenure and Academic Freedom or the similar agencies of the several state teachers' associations that are affiliated with the NEA.

A generation ago it was a matter of opinion whether or not unethical actions of teachers or superintendents merited condemnation. Today such actions can be labeled and exposed by reference to the code of ethics drafted by the NEA Ethics Committee and approved by the NEA representative assembly in 1952.

In 1927 scarcely half the city school systems in the country granted any sick leave with full pay, and only 7 per cent of them provided for accumulating sick leave from year to year. In 1951 the corresponding percentages were 95 and 84, respectively.

In 1938 there were 474 credit unions for teachers. By 1955 the number had nearly doubled.[2]

The NEA, of course, is not wholly responsible for all these gains. But the NEA and its affiliated state and local associations undoubtedly deserve much more credit than they usually receive, because the historical record is too little known by either teachers or laymen in 1957.

Changes in teacher welfare since 1907, both as causes and effects, were closely related to the democratization of the NEA (see Chapter 27). Teachers' consciousness of their goals and rights and the realization that they could wield their latent power to effect such ends were stimulated in part by the climate of social reform that pervaded the United States in the first two decades of the present century, in part by their fuller opportunities for professional education in teachers' colleges and universities, and in part by dissemination of the democratic educational philosophy of John Dewey, William H. Kilpatrick, and others.

Teacher consciousness was also aroused, in part, by the concomitant rise in status and influence of educational administrators. As the superintendent won status and rewards faster than the classroom teacher, the distance between them became greater. The increase in the number of principals, supervisors, and special teachers tended to relegate the classroom teacher to a still lower status. Having long been accorded a low status on the social scale, he was embittered to think that he was being consigned to a relatively similar position within his own profession. He resolved to change his position even if it involved battles within and beyond the profession. The injustices within were more recent and easier to understand, and their apparent perpetrators were nearer; so administrators became the objects of envy and distrust; they were blamed for low salaries and uncertain prospects. Since they were prominent in

---

[2] For a compact summary of twentieth-century gains in teacher welfare, see the series of nine articles that appeared monthly in the *NEA Journal* from September 1955 through May 1956. From this series it is evident that substantial advances have been registered in all aspects of welfare *except* "teacher load." The problem of load, aggravated by recent high-level birth rates and shortages of teachers and school buildings, is perhaps the most widespread cause of complaint within the teaching profession at the present time.

the management of the NEA, it too had to bear some of the reproaches for the teachers' situation.

The emergence of the teacher from passivity to activity, from relative silence to articulate remonstrance, from relative obscurity to professional prominence, naturally produced changes in the NEA as well as the profession. His status rose with his courage, and he enlisted many allies. In 1907 Ella F. Young, principal of the Chicago Normal School, asserted that "the isolation of the great body of teachers from the administration of the school must be overcome."[3] Within a few years teachers' federations, the Emergency Commission of the NEA, Secretary J. W. Crabtree, and an occasional administrator were advocating the recognition of the teacher and the utilization of his abilities in the solution not only of classroom problems but also of educational policies and principles. In 1920 a superintendent bewailed the rift between administrators and teachers; a high-school teacher referred to the stultifying effects of being told what to do; a normal-school teacher deplored the practice of appointing committees of teachers and then ignoring their recommendations;[4] a superintendent approved teacher participation in administration; a member of the American Federation of Teachers called for the election of teachers to boards of education;[5] and the dean of a teachers' college advocated faculty participation in appointing and discharging professors.[6] These and similar sentiments became so frequent by 1930 as to sound axiomatic.

These developments in educational theory and practice soon had their effect upon NEA policies. The formulation of a policy of teacher welfare was a growth; it consisted of a series of steps rather than any one spectacular change in policy. Unquestionably one of the most important of these steps was the succession of salary studies, referred to above. The Emergency Commission of 1918 gathered data that enabled Field Secretary Hugh S. Magill[7] and subsequently Charl O. Williams to present the situation effectively to the public and even more specifically to the superintendents. Evidence that the publicity and the pleas were effective is quite convincing.

In addition to the salary surveys the attitude of James W. Crabtree, the secretary of the NEA from 1917 to 1935, was very influential in changing official policy. He saw the great benefits to the profession and to the NEA of utilizing the abilities and influence of the hitherto somewhat-neglected teacher. With only lukewarm support from some educators and the mild indifference of others, Crabtree pursued an aggressive

[3] NEA, *Proceedings, 1907,* 403.
[4] NEA, *Proceedings, 1920,* 93-99.
[5] *Ibid.,* 176-184.
[6] *Ibid.,* 244-247.
[7] NEA, *Bulletin,* VII, 19, April 1919.

policy of cultivating the teacher and giving him all possible help in his efforts to secure tenure and status.[8]

The creation of the representative assembly in 1920 convinced teachers that the NEA had broadened its outlook and democratized its structure. They joined local and state associations, as well as the NEA, in increasing numbers. Thus this constitutional change became one of the steps in the development of the policy of increased concern for teacher welfare.

The policy has been made effective through increased member participation in continuing committees as well as in the annual assembly, through development of a network of cooperation between the national association and its expanding roll of state and local affiliates, and through increased activities by the enlarged headquarters staff in Washington.

How all three of these factors can, and do, work together to achieve tangible results is illustrated by a recent incident reported by the chairman of the NEA Committee on Tenure and Academic Freedom.[9] Members of an affiliated teachers' association in a certain state were working to persuade their state legislature to enact a "fair-dismissal or tenure bill" for teachers. They wanted a "model" draft for such a bill and wired their request to NEA headquarters. The staff member responsible for the work of the national tenure committee sent in reply not a "model" bill but a previously prepared report of the Research Division analyzing existing state tenure laws together with a report of the tenure committee listing desirable characteristics of tenure legislation.

Specialists from the NEA staff are constantly available to individual members and affiliated associations to help, by correspondence and by consultation, on such practical welfare problems as how to set up good salary schedules, how to wage local campaigns for school bond issues, how to protect teachers against unjust dismissal or unfair attack, how to organize a credit union for members of a local teachers' club, how to develop a sound system for teacher retirement, how to determine criteria for promotion of teachers and administrators, how to deal with unethical conduct within the profession, how to frame an equitable formula for sick leave, how to . . . Very practical problems! And the problems usually become manageable, if not always solvable, by the practical help which some 700 thousand NEA members know is theirs for the asking from 1201 Sixteenth Street, Northwest, in Washington, D.C. The help is forthcoming in 1957 only because a generation of teachers, year by year, built the machinery for providing it: committees on salaries, tenure, academic freedom, credit unions, school finance; commissions on legislation, defense, standards; a council on retirement; policy directives from annual meetings and auxiliary deliberative bodies; facts and more facts,

[8] NEA, *Proceedings, 1927,* 1184-1185.
[9] Theodore J. Jenson, in *NEA Journal,* XLIV, 407, October 1955.

case studies and examples, memoranda, bibliographies, statistics, charts, and graphs from the Research Division; flyers, broadsides, throwaways, recordings, and films from the Division of Press and Radio Relations; a headquarters center in the nation's capital with expert personnel, excellent library resources, and the means for answering questions on this and questions on that.

This useful—and much used—machinery is available because American teachers in ever-increasing numbers have *bought it to serve themselves,* as well as to express their pride and to serve American children through improved education. They bought it with their NEA dues. When two-dollar annual dues wouldn't buy all they wanted, they voted to charge themselves three dollars. When that still wouldn't buy enough, they raised the figure to five dollars. And already they have served notice that they want to raise it again!

Thousands have joined the NEA because they see it as a mechanism for enhancing their welfare. Its effectiveness for doing so, on the other hand, has been made possible only because other thousands had joined on faith. Growth in numbers and growth in strength have, of course, been inseparable and reciprocal concomitants.

Thus, step by step, as the NEA accepted increased responsibility for teacher welfare, it also attracted more and more teachers. The enrollment of the NEA grew from 10,104 in 1918 to 52,850 in 1920, and on to 220,149 by 1931. During the depression years it faltered and slipped back to 165,448 in 1936. After that year it rose again, year by year, increasing phenomenally near the end of the Second World War. By 1957 its membership approached 700,000, which is considerably more than half of all teachers in the United States.

The great growth in the NEA can be attributed to its changed policies and to the revolution in the attitude of classroom teachers. They had at last found a defender, and curiously enough that great defender was themselves, united in action through their own voluntary professional association.

29

Advances Toward a Profession

In 1870 Eli T. Tappan, president of Kenyon College, referred with vigorous scorn to those ignorant persons "who do not know that education is a science and that teaching is a learned profession."[1] The remarkable aspect of this statement is its unreality. In 1870 education was not a science, and teaching was not a profession except in the minds of those who chose to regard it as such. Educators saw the necessity of a profession of teaching and boldly proclaimed its advent nearly a hundred years before its actual arrival.

Consider some of the basic facts about teaching in the period following the Civil War: 40 per cent of the teachers were new each year; the professional expectancy was only about three years; the sessions lasted only three, five, or seven months; the pay was less than $50 a month; the teacher had to take an examination every year and was engaged for only one session; the majority of teachers were young women who hoped to teach for only a few sessions; and half the teachers were less than twenty-two years of age. How could a profession evolve from such conditions? The answer is clear that it could not, but the educators kept right on talking and thinking and planning for a profession. Eventually, after nearly a hundred years, their hopes were realized to a considerable extent. Who will say that their ideals and dreams were not a factor in achieving this result?

At various times teaching was designated as a high, noble, or sacred calling, a vocation, a trade, a business, a temporary occupation, a craft, a skill, a science, and an art. Most frequently, however, it ws called a profession. Earnest speakers made hundreds of speeches in which they examined, defined, described, and reexamined, the meaning of the word profession. Often they came to the satisfying conclusion that teaching was already, or would at least soon become, a profession.

One discouraged speaker declared that law, medicine, and divinity

[1] NEA, *Proceedings, 1870,* Part II, 6.

conferred gratuitous importance upon their members, but that a teacher had no sight draft to recognition. Some teachers gained high places, not because they were teachers, but in spite of being teachers. Teachers might claim high status, but the claim was not allowed, or if it was it was a favor to the individual and not a recognition of the profession. The speaker went further and declared that the majority of teachers were quacks, because the majority were mechanics, farmers, loafers, and ramblers, and not teachers. Charlatanry, he said, predominated, and the empiric drove out the teacher.[2]

Efforts to achieve professional status involved opposition to the educational pretensions of preachers, lawyers, and other public figures. Even at educational meetings these presumptuous laymen occupied the center of the stage and crowded the principal or superintendent into the background. At the dedication of a particular school building the principal was recognized by one oblique reference. The resentment over lay pretensions was instanced by the editor of the *Illinois Teacher*, who quoted the following from an Ohio publication: "M. F. Cowdery, for many years Superintendent of Schools at Sandusky, has resigned his position and is succeeded by Rev. T. Hildreth." The editor then adds in vengeful mood, "We don't know Mr. H.; but we wonder if there was no practical teacher in Ohio who could have been induced to superintend the schools of Sandusky. Most likely, if there was, he has just been called to Mr. Hildreth's vacant pulpit!"[3] The same editor had previously admonished: "Let the physician stick to his physic, the clergyman to his divinity and the lawyer to his law books," but only persons trained in education should be placed in charge of school systems.

The use of the phrase "practical teachers" in the original call of 1857, and the subsequent requirement of an educational position as a prerequisite to membership in the National Teachers' Association and the Department of Superintendence, were designed in part to exclude the officious laymen who hung on as vestiges of a former day in which they knew almost as much about teaching as anyone else. Their day had passed and the educators justly grew weary of their prominence.

Some popular prejudices operated against the evolving of a profession of teaching. The idea that teachers are born and not made instanced the vitality of error and the longevity of superstition. In spite of the obvious fact that the number of nature's teachers would be hopelessly short of the demand, each school presumed that it could secure such a teacher. Even teachers unwittingly fell into the error. In reporting to the normal department of the NEA concerning the desired characteristics of teachers, a committee of 1889 used such phrases as "natural fitness," "native

[2] *Ohio Journal of Education*, V, 358-361, December 1856.
[3] *Illinois Teacher*, X, 281, July 1864; X, 203, May 1864.

ability," "natural aptitude," "intuitive knowledge," and high-mindedness" as though teachers were born and needed only to be identified.[4] Even though normal schools existed because nature produced no teachers, the notion that a poet wrote with divine fire, a preacher preached with divine inspiration, and a teacher taught by means of innate powers would not die.

A closely related fallacy was the misleading and pernicious assertion that he who knows can teach. It is pernicious because it rests upon the unrecognized blunder that the transmission of information is the essence of teaching. The scholar does not necessarily know how to teach a child to read and the scientist may not know how to make a theory intelligible. In fact, there are so many exceptions to the assertion that it should be labeled misleading if not actually erroneous.

Another derisive bromide, calculated to belittle teachers, was the once-clever quip that "Those who can do; those who can't teach." The popularity of this saying rests upon the assumed superiority of the man of action over the man of ideas. It is as true as the parallel saying that "The critic criticizes because he can not create." Such quips are admired by those who belittle theory, scoff at professors, and denounce eggheads. As civilization advances it reviews and sloughs off the wise saws of superficial and primitive thinking.

In spite of the actuality of low status, mean pay, and dim prospects, the teacher was accorded an unctuous recognition in sermons and orations. The idea of the teacher was enshrined with respect, and the idea of education drew adulation and approbation. Only after long years did the public become aware of the discrepancy between sentimental ideals and actual practices. In the meantime teachers did have the recognition that fine words could bestow.

The importance of the teacher was recognized and iterated. Bishop John L. Spalding's sentiments of 1896, "The teacher is the school. . . . The question of education is a question of teachers,"[5] were uttered in varying combinations on all fitting occasions. Such recognition was intended in part as a compliment as well as an assertion of basic truth. Speakers were fond of magnifying the sacredness, nobility, and dignity of the teacher's work. The traits and characteristics of the good teacher constituted the main content of numerous homilies. At Saratoga Springs in 1885 a speaker described the good teacher as manly, forceful, dignified, and practical; a philanthropist, patriot, prophet, scholar, philosopher, creator, artist, and a Christian, though not necessarily a preacher.[6]

Soothed and comforted as long as the laudations and encomiums lasted,

---

[4] NEA *Proceedings, 1899,* 839-840.
[5] NEA, *Proceedings, 1896,* 169.
[6] NEA, *Proceedings, 1885,* 69-80.

teachers quickly recovered from such orations. When they came to them-selves they reviewed the facts and proceeded in a flagellating mood to pour ridicule and scorn upon themselves and their so-called profession. Emma McRae of Muncie reported that some people thought "that any one can teach, especially if he happens to have been so unfortunate as to lose a limb, become blind in one eye, or in some way has become unfit for anything except a teacher. I know of no other business which has seemed to be so dependent on a bodily infirmity. An ailment of some sort has been really a necessity to the typical school teacher."[7] She added that teaching was used as a method of reforming wayward sons, of caring for doctors when health prevailed and lawyers when litigation was scarce. Another referred to teaching as a form of charity for Miss Goody Misfortune or Widow Oldtime and as a waiting room for Embryo Blackstone.[8]

A disheartened Illinois teacher reported that the popular idea of a teacher was "somebody that can parse and cipher; has little brains and less money; feeble-minded, unable to grapple with real men and women in the stirring employments of life, but on that account admirably fitted to associate with childish intellects, as being somewhat akin to them . . . a crabbed old bachelor, or despairing old maid."[9]

Stories of poor pay, degrading experiences, indignities, and professional humiliations were numerous. In 1867 teachers in a suburb of Boston re-ceived $2.50 a week and Negro cooks $3.[10] Ten year later a speaker declared that adequate pay would never be achieved "anterior to the millennium" and that any one who became a teacher was deliberately selecting the poorhouse for his old age.[11] As late as 1920 a speaker referred to teachers as "Marms" and "Ichabods," and another complained that architects and administrators provided no restrooms for teachers or lunchrooms for pupils.[12]

Another ignominy that teachers long endured was the taking of ex-aminations, which one sufferer referred to as "annual tortures." The humiliation was heightened by the fact that the examiner was generally an ignorant layman who asked tricky questions in arithmetic and required the applicant to read tongue-twisting passages. Rarely did the examiner ask a relevant question, and when he did, he did not know how to evaluate the applicant's answer. According to one sufferer, "It is even

[7] Emma McRae, "Teaching as a Profession," *Indiana School Journal*, XXV, 167-168, April 1880. The quotation has been slightly abbreviated.
[8] NEA, *Proceedings, 1882*, Part II, 30.
[9] *Illinois Teacher*, X, 289, August 1864.
[10] American Institute of Instruction, *Proceedings, 1867*, 131.
[11] NEA, *Proceedings, 1876*, 31.
[12] NEA, *Proceedings, 1920*, 424, 351.

whispered that it makes a material difference with a man's chances whether he believes in Cotton Mather or in Darwin."[13]

Perhaps the acme of ignobility of the teacher's status was revealed in the report of the school commissioner of Ballard County, Kentucky, who wrote to the state superintendent that the law should authorize him to report to the grand jury "every person who goes to the school house to whip or insult a teacher. If any one desire to whip a teacher, let him wait until Saturday."[14]

Many explanations were given for the lowly status of teachers—short tenure, poor pay, petty controls, low standards of certification. In 1874 James H. Hoose of the Cortland, New York, normal school complained that teaching was not a profession because educators scorned other educators, because thories and practices were so unstable, because there were few mature educators, because there was no educational terminology, because there was no uniformity of practice.[15]

Contemporary with these derogatory and discouraging analyses of the status of teaching in America, there were also numerous speeches, committee reports, and legal enactments designed to move teaching toward a professional level. Year after year educators discussed better training programs for teachers, higher standards of certification, and the good effects of higher pay and tenure. A report of 1887 declared that tenure was for the sake of enhancing the function of teaching and not merely for the convenience of the teacher. It stressed the profession's obligation to help schools get rid of incompetent teachers.[16] In 1895 New York passed a law requiring at least one year of professional training for all teachers.[17] Many speakers stressed the matter of salary, and some were inclined to say that the securing of good teachers was merely a matter of money; that when salaries were high enough the schools would be filled with competent teachers.[18] Occasionally a speaker saw the growth of professional standards as primarily a problem of attitude. The enthusiastic educational exhorter, A. E. Winship, declared that teachers could elevate their profession by buoyant faith and joyous relish in their work.[19] Unquestionably these admonitions helped to build professional morale.

The NEA committee report of 1905 on tenure and salaries showed that the annual salaries of elementary teachers in six large, widely separated cities in 1903 was about $700, for principals about $1,800,

[13] NEA, *Proceedings, 1872*, 77.
[14] *Report of Commissioner of Education, 1872.* 188.
[15] NEA, *Proceedings, 1874*, 214-216.
[16] NEA, *Proceedings, 1887*, 307-313.
[17] NEA, *Proceedings, 1895*, 191.
[18] NEA, *Proceedings, 1894*, 759.
[19] NEA, *Proceedings, 1899*, 229-231.

for high-school teachers about $1,200, and for superintendents about $5,000. In general, men received about 20 per cent higher salaries than women. Salaries in the smaller cities and rural districts were markedly lower than in the large cities.[20]

In 1907 the Committee of Seventeen on the Professional Preparation of High School Teachers recommended great attention to psychology and its application to education, stressed the importance of a scholarly knowledge of the subjects, underscored with vehemence the necessity of recasting the content in terms of student interest and capacity, restated the importance of practice teaching, recommended a course in reading materials for pupils, advised careful attention to the teaching of character, and urged that the teacher be at least conversant with school administration, the history of education, and the competing claims of vocational and cultural studies.[21]

Speaking to the National Council of Education in 1913, Professor Henry Suzzalo of Teachers College proposed a thoroughgoing reorganization of educational associations in order to raise teaching to the status of a profession. He redefined a profession and proposed that the organized teachers raise their standards, increase their services, and secure the necessary legal enactments. The discussants warmly endorsed the proposals and called for tenure of position, adequate pay, better selection of trainees, and more professional preparation. These aspects they labeled as the business side of teaching. One speaker said, "Potentially we are a giant but kinetically we are a pigmy." The discussion involved plans for the reorganization of the NEA, which finally resulted in the establishment of the representative assembly in 1920.[22]

After 1920 committees, reports, and speeches on teacher welfare and professional advancement became more numerous and frequent. State and local associations, as well as the NEA, devoted time and attention to the development of the profession. Great progress was made in the 1920's, and after the Second World War even greater advances were made.

Several developments in American life contributed to the growth of the NEA and to the advancement of teaching as a profession. Population increased rapidly and school enrollment, particularly in the high schools, even faster. Drives and campaigns during two world wars and organized efforts to meet the depression of the 1930's demonstrated the advantages of cooperation. Nearly all organizations grew in numbers and most of them became units in networks of organizational federations that tried to solve social and economic problems. The Nineteenth Amendment,

[20] NEA, *Proceedings, 1904*, 370-377.
[21] NEA, *Proceedings, 1907*, 523-538.
[22] NEA, *Proceedings, 1913*, 362-379.

which transformed women into full citizens, strengthened their position as teachers and as members of the community. The League of Nations and the United Nations dramatized the inevitable growth of intenational responsibilities. Willingly or unwillingly, the American people slowly accepted membership in a larger, more intimate world. At the same time they developed a corresponding awareness of nationalism and a more tolerant understanding of their fellow countrymen. These and other trends affected education.

The tribulations of teachers slowly aroused them from their propensity toward individualism. Oath laws singled them out as potentially important, but stigmatized them as naïve and gullible, prone to embrace error. Restrictions on freedom of movement, behavior, and dress, which were especially numerous and vexatious during the depression, showed teachers that they had not quite arrived as citizens, or as members of an accepted profession. The privations of living on stationary salaries in periods of rising prices finally forced them to emerge from bitter contemplation and muttering discontent to aggressive action. Both as a means and as a result of fighting for status, teachers became citizens of the community and members of a profession. In accordance with the admonition of a speaker at the NEA convention of 1920, teachers began to look at and deal with doctors and bankers and businessmen without self-consciousness or apologies for their profession.[23]

Within the profession the teacher also slowly gained recognition and acquired status. As he gradually took over the making of the curriculum, he gained assurance in meeting the needs of pupils and an accompanying sense of growing professional competence. As he participated in educational organizations and conventions, he developed a wider and stronger sense of professional competence. As he participated in educational organizations and conventions, he developed a wider and stronger sense of professional unity. As the number of educational publications increased, more and more teachers discovered the value of reporting their professional experiences. Outside and inside the profession forces were operating to free educators from traditional restrictions and to open the possibilities of action on a national scale.

The NEA itself was changing. Women had won their rights within the association and were slowly but surely winning their status in the family and community. The creation of the Representative Assembly in 1920 was incontrovertible proof that teachers could actually control the policies of their association. The series of reports on tenure, salaries, pensions, and other welfare matters convinced them that the NEA was their champion

[23] NEA, *Proceedings, 1920*, 100-103. The speaker was Edward Sisson, president of the University of Montana.

and that it could become more effective as it grew in size.[24]

The decision to make the NEA the inclusive educational organization for American teachers and the protagonist of the new profession entailed consquences which some individuals deplored. An organization cannot attract and hold large numbers of members unless it adopts policies that meet the wishes of the vast majority of them. In becoming the spokesman for the majority, in meeting the needs of the typical teacher, the association sacrificed some degree of freedom and inevitably developed a degree of caution in making pronouncements and promoting changes. A majority is usually less wieldy than a minority, and the majority of a large organization is less flexible, less sensitive to new proposals, than the majority of a smaller organization. Consequently the decision to leave to individuals and to smaller, more homogeneous organizations the advocacy of advanced ideas, the trying out of new policies, the implementation of revolutionary reforms, and the sponsoring of forthright resolutions on controversial matters. These limitations, however, may be more than offset by the capacity to effect improvements within the range of popular acceptance. Bringing all schools up to the level of accepted practices is the natural work of a large inclusive organization. By centering its major efforts upon the implementation of proven practices, the NEA may be pursuing not only the wisest policy from the popular standpoint but the method of securing the most lasting gains. Whether it was the wisest policy or not, the fact remains that such was the inevitable result when the NEA committed itself to the policy of the eventual enrollment of every member of the teaching profession.

The consequences of this policy of bigness can be easily overstated and overstressed, for the inclusiveness of the NEA enables it to tolerate a wide range in the philosophy and practices of its various subdivisions. In fact, it would be difficult to cite a group that has moved with more wisdom, courage, and success than the National Commission for the Defense of Democracy Through Education. Tactful, careful, judicious, it has nevertheless proved that the NEA can and does move with commendable courage and forthrightness. It is also difficult to see how bigness can hamper research or affect its findings. The very size of the NEA lends weight and significance to its pronouncements and policies and has facilitated its efforts to transform teaching into a profession.

Out of the extensive and prolonged discussions of education as a profession a degree of consensus emerged. A profession consists of members who:

1. Have acquired by training and experience some specialized techniques, basically intellectual in nature.

[24] NEA, *Proceedings, 1922,* 94, 105; *1923,* 87-88; *1924,* 97; *1927,* 1184-1191.

2. Form associations as a means of promoting the purposes of the profession.
3. Establish a degree of unity in purpose and procedure.
4. Oversee and set the standards of the training of recruits and guarantee the competence of the new members.
5. Establish and enforce standards of practice, usually embodied in a proclaimed code of ethics.
6. Have a large degree of individual autonomy in the practice of the profession.
7. Place altruism, service, and social welfare ahead of personal gain.
8. Promote the personal welfare of its own members.
9. Counsel the government with respect to the necessary legal regulations.
10. Inform the public and guide its expectations concerning the profession.
11. Cooperate with other professions in adjusting related and overlapping functions.

Out of the discussions also emerged a clearer conception of the educator as a member of a profession. Professional functions and activities needed to be differentiated from those of the typical citizen or worker. Any person might read a weekly newsmagazine, teach a Sunday-school class, and participate in a community welfare drive. Obviously these were not professional activities.

As members of a profession, educators:

1. Study and analyze the contemporary culture; they are students of society in order that they may serve it effectively.
2. Make the curriculum; from their study of society they select portions for instructional purposes.
3. Study the learner and the way he learns; they thus try to understand children and the learning process.
4. Direct learning; they are instructors and guides for classes, groups, and individuals.
5. Interpret education to the community; they serve as links between the school and the community, between education and society.
6. Engage in professional activities; they join educational associations, attend conventions, participate in programs, and some engage in experiments, research, and publications.

Thus the educator is, professionally speaking, (1) an analyzer of society, (2) a curriculum-maker, (3) an expert on child nature and the learning process, (4) a director of learning, (5) a liaison betweeen education and society, and (6) an active member of the teaching profession. These are the distinguishing marks of an educator.

In order to make education into a profession it was necessary to define and refine these professional activities of the teacher in such a way as to give him professional status. Because of the active role of the NEA and its various agencies this process of professionalization has been greatly advanced since 1920 and enormously accelerated since the organization of the National Commission on Teacher Education and Professional Standards in 1946. For years the American Association of Teachers Colleges (merged into the American Association of Colleges for Teacher Education in 1948) had labored to raise the standards of professional preparation. This new commission, designated by its letters as TEPS, under the vigorous direction first of Secretary Ralph McDonald and then of Secretary T. M. Stinnett, called upon the educators in each state to establish similar TEPS commissions; by 1955 all but two states had done so. The commission utilized a statement by Joy Elmer Morgan as a sort of challenge: "It is not possible for society to guarantee to every child a devoted mother and a wise provident father, but society can guarantee to every child a competent, well-prepared, and adequately paid teacher." To effect this ideal standard the commission proclaimed its goals: discriminating selection of those admitted to teacher preparation, and adjusted supply of qualified teachers, thorough preparation of teachers, certification requirements of four college years for beginning and five years for fully qualified teachers, continuous professional growth of teachers in service, professional accreditation of all teacher-training institutions, a professional concept of teaching, and adequate provision for teacher welfare.[25]

As a result of persistent efforts by the American Association of Colleges for Teacher Education and the national TEPS commission of the NEA, professional standards were advanced greatly between 1946 and 1955. In the former year fifteen states required a degree for elementary teachers; in 1955, thirty-five states had such a requirement. In 1946 there were 123,000 emergency, substandard certificates; in 1955, only 71,589. In 1946 only 41,000 degree-holding teachers were trained; in 1955, 86,696. In 1946 only 45 per cent of elementary teachers held a degree; in 1955 the percentage was 68. In 1946, 882,980 teachers belonged to their state associations; in 1955, 1,026,932. In 1946, 340,973 teachers belonged to the NEA; in 1957 the number reached about 700,000. In 1946, 78 per cent of teachers had some kind of legal tenure; in 1955, 82 per cent. In fact, it appeared that education was at last almost a profession.

In spite of these advances O. Meredith Wilson, president of the University of Oregon, declared at the Chicago meeting of the Association for Higher Education in March 1956 that "teaching at all levels, during the past thirty years, has suffered a decline in status."[26] In contrast with this pessimistic judgment Superintendent Martin Essex of Akron said at Portland in July 1956 that "the present professionalization of teaching

[25] NEA, *Manual for State and Local TEPS Commissions* (Washington, 1955), *passim.*
[26] Association for Higher Education, *Proceedings, 1956,* 171.

is an achievement. The teacher's social status has risen far beyond the expectations of 1920."[27]

In 1952 the various groups interested in the improvement of teacher education formed the National Council for Accreditation of Teacher Education, for which the NEA provides the major share of financial support. The council includes representatives from teachers' colleges, state departments of education, school boards, and the NEA. This unity of effort augurs for success. Already the council has examined and accredited a large percentage of the institutions engaged in training teachers.

Within recent years educators under the leadership of the NEA have identified and described the professional techniques of a teacher; in great numbers they have joined associations for the purpose of promoting professional objectives; by cooperation they have achieved a great degree of unity; they have raised the standards of trainees for the teaching profession and devised more effective programs of training; they have established codes of professional ethics; they have placed pupils, patrons, and country ahead of personal gain; they have won higher salaries, tenure, pensions, leaves of absence, sick leaves, and other welfare benefits; they have cooperated with legislatures and state departments of education to secure legal safeguards for the profession; they have cooperated extensively with other organizations; they have, through numerous and effective publications of the NEA, informed the public concerning the schools and educational procedures. In fact, education has become a profession.

[27] Associated Press, Portland, Oregon, July 5, 1956.

30

Reaching Toward World Horizons

"RESOLVED, That a committee be appointed to correspond with leading educators throughout the world . . . upon the feasibility of calling a World's Educational Convention. . . ." The National Teachers' Association assembled in convention at Harrisburg in 1865 considered this proposal, and at Indianapolis in the following year a committee proposed "greetings to all Educators under whatsoever name, title, or dignity, and wherever found."[1] Even though the plan of a world conference was not adopted, the proposed resolutions demonstrate the breadth of the educational vision of some of the early leaders.

Other evidences of an international outlook on the part of the NEA followed in every decade. Speeches, resolutions, and exchanges of greetings between the educational associations of different countries were so frequent and numerous as to become almost routine. Interest in world affairs, educational conferences, and school exhibits was continuous, and official participation by the association was frequent. Educators from foreign lands were frequent visitors and speakers at NEA meetings.

A few instances of these worldwide interests will show that American educators were not professionally isolated. In 1873 the association resolved that the United States should repay the excess indemnities which it had collected from China and Japan because of some slight damage that American ships had suffered during the Civil War period.[2] Committees were appointed to cooperate with the Bureau of Education to prepare exhibits at successive world's fairs in this country and in Europe. In addition to the exhibits the congresses on education were quite notable at the world's fairs or expositions of 1876, 1893, and 1904. At the Madison convention of 1884 the members debated a proposal to establish a permanent international council of education. A similar resolution was debated and adopted at Boston in 1910. United States Commissioner of Education E. E. Brown was made chairman of a large committee on the

[1] NTA, *Proceedings, 1865,* 222; *1866,* 13.
[2] NEA, *Proceedings, 1873,* 92-93.

353

formation of an international council of education, consisting of the ex-presidents of the NEA and the presidents of several universities. In 1911 Brown reported that it had not been feasible to organize in time to call a meeting of the council in 1911.[3] No further entry concerning the proposed council appears in the *Proceedings*. Brown's relinquishment of the commissionership in 1911 may explain the inactivity of the committee.

Other instances of the international outlook of the NEA can be cited. In 1898, during the Spanish-American War, the association considered a recommendation that called for the increased teaching of Spanish in the schools.[4] In 1899 the association sent a telegram of congratulations to Andrew D. White, the American representative at the Hague Conference,[5] and in 1907 it recommended that teachers use the work of the peace conferences to inculcate attitudes of good will toward foreign countries.[6]

Any recital of the interests and actions of the NEA on international matters would closely parallel the history of developments in that area. In 1900 it resolved that the common-school system be extended to Cuba, Puerto Rico, and the Philippines.[7] In 1908 it commended the use of the Boxer indemnity to bring Chinese students to America. In 1909 it praised the American School Peace League for its materials on peace and citizenship. In 1915 it endorsed the League to Enforce Peace, of which William Howard Taft was president. It blessed the efforts toward greater friendship with Latin America. It endorsed the League of Nations and called on the Senate to ratify the treaty, including the covenant of the League. It rejoiced over the disarmament conference of 1921, and a few years later recommended the classroom study of the Kellogg-Briand Pact. Subsequent developments on the world front elicited corresponding efforts on the part of educational organizations.

The members of the NEA were not impractical visionaries or sentimental idealists who assumed that mere good will would overcome all obstacles to international peace. They were keenly mindful of the obstacles. The International Congress on Education which met in San Francisco in 1915 passed resolutions lamenting the overemphasis of nationalism, the hero worship of "killers of men," the smug recital of national achievements, the talk about national honor, and the neglect of national obligations. To offset these faults the resolutions called for the establishment of good will; the rewriting of school histories and geographies; a shift from emphasis upon war to peace; surveys of the

3 NEA, *Proceedings, 1884*, 8-9; *1910*, 36; *1911*, 39-40.
4 NEA, *Proceedings, 1898*, 26.
5 NEA, *Proceedings, 1899*, 28.
6 NEA, *Proceedings, 1907*, 31.
7 NEA, *Proceedings, 1900*, 31.

biologic, economic, and human waste of war; and the subordination of the love of dominion.[8]

This brief review of the early international interests of the NEA shows clearly that the educators of those years saw no conflict between American education and international pedagogy. Enthusiasm for our native public schools and pride in their progress did not obscure the potential lessons that might be learned from foreign systems. American educators seemed to regard knowledge as international, psychology as non-partisan, methods as impersonal, and childhood as nonracial. Pestalozzi was a Swiss, but his object teaching was a universal for teachers; Froebel was a German, but the kindergarten was a timeless gift to childhood; Lancaster was an Englishman, but his monitorial system knew no national boundaries. In fact, the early educators, while prone to extravagant statements about our public schools and their unique contributions to America, seem to have been quite free from prejudice, respecting foreign systems and willing to import ideas, methods, plans, materials, and procedures from any and all countries.

Education for world understanding was not the work of educators alone. Long before they were mindful of the problem, the representatives of government and business carried on a kind of educational process. Diplomats tried to achieve a degree of understanding, and commerce pursued its age-old purpose of promoting the interchange of goods. In addition to government and business there were scientists, scholars, missionaries, and travelers who served as cultural ambassadors, as cross-pollinators of ideas and customs. So the educators appeared not to occupy an unoccupied area, but to modify, strengthen, and redirect some of the forces and influences that were already operating to bring about world understanding.

Events played their part in promoting the dissemination of international information which was not always synonymous with understanding. As a result of the emergence of the United States as a world power in 1898, its great advance after the First World War, and its phenomenal preeminence since the Second World War, the American public has been forced to learn more and more about the races, countries, and problems of the world. In line with this trend the newspapers, magazines, radio, television, and other information agencies have gradually increased the space and attention devoted to foreign affairs. All available means have been pressed into the cause of educating a people for world leadership.

Curriculum-makers were mindful of the changing situation. Current events, units on Latin America, booklets on world trade, courses in international relations, and guides to the United Nations and the UN's

[8] NEA, *Proceedings*, 1915, 25-30.

specialized agencies were introduced into the schools. Attention to international relations was doubled and quadrupled within a generation. In fact, American schools probably included more in their programs about other areas of the world than did the schools of any other country. In spite of this achievement, however, many serious students of the curriculum insist that international problems do not yet receive the attention in the schools to which their importance entitles them. They hold that Americans must be the best-informed and most internationally minded of all the citizens of the world. So government, business, communication media, and the curriculum are all world-conscious. The educator comes onto the scene, not to create an interest in world affairs, but to promote good will and understanding, and to make progress toward the goal of universal peace.

In seeking to elevate international relations, educators encounter inertia and apathy. People of all countries are hemmed in by national sanctions, racial preferences, social conventions, and cultural limitations. Even when there are no overt obstacles to the cultivation of a world viewpoint, indifference and boredom can become barriers almost as formidable as prejudice and hostility. World understanding requires effort; it involves questioning accepted beliefs, reexamining conventional attitudes, and acquiring new information. Inertia favors a degree of national self-sufficiency, a group complacency, and a kind of isolated provincialism.

In addition to inertia, the advocate of international understanding frequently encounters misunderstanding and opposition. Even though motivated by the noble ideals of peace and brotherhood, the person who proclaims that manhood is more inclusive than citizenship, that character is a higher ideal than patriotism, and that humanity takes precedence over nationality may be suspected of disloyalty to his own country.

Fortunately for the cause of international understanding, its advocates in the NEA have been realists as well as idealists. Again and again they have proclaimed the association's support of America's basic principles and doctrines. The origin of the public schools was almost a guarantee that they would sustain the author of their being. The NEA helped to weld the scattered state systems into an integrated national policy with respect to education. Repeatedly the NEA stood by the principle of local and state control when circumstances seemed to call for some degree of Federal control. By resolutions, committee activities, and campaigns the NEA supported the government in all of its wars and by its pronouncements helped to build and sustain public morale. The leaders were a unit in declaring that international understanding comes not to replace but to expand and enrich national citizenship and patriotism.

Education for international understanding involves both *objective* and *content.* The *objective* is clearly revealed by such words and phrases as "peace," "good will," "understanding," "justice," "intercultural relations," "racial harmony," "cooperation," "friendship," "neighborliness," "interdependence," "arbitration," "conciliation," "brotherhood," and "fraternity." The *content* consists of the whole stock of culture—ideals, knowledge, techniques—which spreads from country to country. This cultural pluralism is enriched by each country as it spreads around the globe. Thus education for international understanding in its broadest sense becomes the process of participating completely in worldwide, contemporary civilization. From the standpoint of educators, education for international understanding means the interchange of whole cultures and the exchange of curriculums, methods, and educational practices. The professional content for teachers is indicated by such titles as the history of education and comparative education, and for pupils content consists in the subjects that are common to the various countries.

The subjects which are most emphasized because of their social content are history, geography, literature, and comparative government. Every promoter of international good will laments the consequences of chauvinistic national history, of smug, self-congratulatory geography, of a self-contained literature, and of a proclaimed superiority in governmental organization. He hopes by revisions and deletions to effect a somewhat objective treatment of all these subjects.

The techniques and procedures for achieving international understanding are numerous and time-tested—student exchanges; traveling fellowships; exchange professorships; correspondence among the youth of all countries; promotion of friendships; oratorical and essay contests; observance of special days; the holding of conferences; promotion of games, singing, and dancing; the exchange of toys, cultural objects, stories, and printed materials; the sending of money and needed supplies to teachers and pupils; and the maintenance of international federations and associations. The NEA, some of its committees, and various organizations for promoting international understanding and good will have used all these and other techniques.

Since 1920, much of the NEA's interest in world affairs has been expressed through its Committee on International Relations, although it was called by other names at various times. At its 1920 convention the association endorsed, as it had several times before, the formation of an international bureau of education, and it also authorized the appointment of a committee on "international education relations."[9] Within a year this committee became very active and has continued throughout the years to work aggressively for international understanding and good

[9] NEA, *Proceedings, 1920,* 26.

will. Under the leadership of Augustus O. Thomas, state commissioner of education in Maine; William F. Russell of Teachers College; Annie C. Woodward of Somerville, Massachusetts; Ben M. Cherrington of Denver; Howard E. Wilson of New York; Earl J. McGrath of Kansas City; and others, the committee carried on a variety of activities. It sponsored international conferences, prepared curriculum materials, encouraged the appointment of state committees on world affairs, promoted the study of Latin American relations, prepared materials for teachers, distributed thousands of kits of information about Unesco, sponsored tours by foreign educators, conducted exhibits, promoted the observance of United Nations Week, provided information for study clubs, and distributed pamphlets and books for use by teachers and students. The committee also published newsletters, booklets, and an annual *Box Score on the United Nations,* showing the achievements of that organization. For a time it sustained a clearinghouse of information about the United Nations and its specialized agencies.

In 1948, in cooperation with two NEA departments (the Association for Supervision and Curriculum Development and the National Council for the Social Studies), the committee published *Education for International Understanding in American Schools.* In this book were first set forth the oft-quoted "ten marks of the world-minded American," thus providing tangible objectives for teachers and pupils.

The Committee on International Relations has promoted the good-neighbor policy toward Latin America. In 1929 Uel W. Lamkin, president of the NEA, called an Inter-American Conference on Education, which met in Atlanta following the regular convention of the association.[10] In 1940 and 1941 the NEA commended inter-American friendship, and in the latter year the Educational Policies Commission urged the schools to develop programs to further hemispheric understanding. Throughout the 1940's and 1950's the Research Division and the Press and Radio Division, as well as the Committee on International Relations, promoted the development of inter-American understanding.

After the Second World War, American teachers became much concerned over the impoverishment of schools and the plight of teachers in countries that had been devastated by the war. At its summer conference in 1947 the Department of Classroom Teachers expressed the sentiment that teachers in the United States would like to give material help to their fellow teachers in war-torn lands and proposed that the NEA set up machinery for transmitting such aid. So, in the fall of 1947, the NEA's Overseas Teacher-Relief Fund (later called the Overseas Teacher Fund) was established. More than half a million dollars was collected, consisting

[10] NEA, *Proceedings, 1929,* 974.

entirely of voluntary donations—nearly all of which came in small contributions from thousands of NEA members. The money was expended for books, study grants, medical supplies, food, and clothing for teachers in more than twenty foreign countries. The fund was reactivated in 1952-1953 to send aid to teachers and schools in war-stricken Korea. Thus the worldwide sympathies of American teachers were tangibly demonstrated.

The NEA has played a consistent role of world leadership in bringing together the voluntary teachers' associations of different countries. The association was host to a series of educational conferences held in connection with the world's fairs in Philadelphia in 1876, Chicago in 1893, St. Louis in 1904, and San Francisco in 1915. The 1915 conference, held in connection with the Panama-Pacific International Exposition, was attended by delegates from thirty countries and visitors and speakers from a dozen others, including some of the warring nations of Europe. But a later meeting in San Francisco, in 1923, was unique in that it led to the organization of a permanent federation.

In 1921 the president of Czechoslovakia suggested that the NEA sponsor a world conference on education. The association accepted the suggestion, and Augustus O. Thomas, chairman of the NEA committee that later became the Committee on International Relations, made the plans. President Harding invited other countries to send delegates, and about fifty responded favorably. The conference met at San Francisco a week in advance of the NEA convention in Oakland and held a series of meetings on such topics as world health, international ideals, the dissemination of educational information, and rural life. The conference approved the formation of the World Federation of Education Associations (WFEA), whose membership was composed of the teachers' associations of the various countries. Thomas was chosen the first president of the federation.[11]

The San Fransisco conference evolved a statement of objectives that remains valid in spite of subsequent developments in procedures and techniques:

1. To promote friendship, justice, and good will among the nations of the world.
2. To bring about a worldwide tolerance of the rights and privileges of all nations regardless of race or creed.
3. To develop an appreciation of the value of inherited gifts of nations and races.
4. To secure more satisfying information and more adequate statements of fact for textbooks used in the schools of the different countries.

[11] The articles of incorporation and the platform of principles are in NEA, *Proceedings, 1927*, 1009-1016.

5. To foster a national comradeship and confidence which will produce a more sympathetic appreciation among all nations.
6. To develop the consciousness of an international morality in the minds and hearts of the rising generation.
7. Finally, throughout the world, in all schools, to emphasize the essential unity of mankind and the evils of war and to develop a psychology of peace, together with a true patriotism based upon love of country rather than upon hatred of other peoples and countries.[12]

In earnest and colorful language Augustus O. Thomas, president of WFEA from its inception until 1931 and secretary-general until his death in 1933, explained the program of the federation. "Ignorance," he said, "causes misunderstandings. Misunderstandings cause hatreds and hatreds cause war. War therefore becomes an intellectual problem." He was insistent that the federation use education and not propaganda to effect its purpose. He saw no conflict between patriotism and love of humanity. He declared that the federation came, not to supplant politics and diplomacy, but to provide educational bases that ensure the treaties and agreements that diplomats made. Since, however, they had failed to achieve peace, it was the obligation of teachers to cultivate the moral conscience of the world and bring about the reign of peace and wood will. He visualized peace as basically a problem of education. He wrote: "So long as there is hatred or malice or jealousy or revenge in the human heart, we shall find it in the heart of nations."[13]

The World Federation of Education Associations entered upon a useful program. The first biennial meeting was held in 1925 at Edinburgh and was attended by 1,400 delegates and hundreds of visitors.

The federation adopted the educational plan proposed by David S. Jordan former NEA president, in his prize-winning essay on how to promote peace through education. Following the San Francisco conference, Raphael Herman had offered a prize of $25,000 for the best plan to promote peace. The jury, consisting of outstanding educators, awarded the prize to Jordan. At Edinburgh the federation accepted the Jordan plan in principle and appointed committees on the teaching of history, military training in the schools, athletic sports, and other aspects of international relations.

At two-year intervals the federation held its conventions: at Toronto, 1927; Geneva, 1929; Denver, 1931; Dublin, 1933; Oxford, 1935; and Tokyo, 1937. The eighth meeting, which was scheduled for Rio de Janeiro, was canceled by the Brazilian government.[14] The delegates substituted a good-will tour of South America. During the Second World War the

[12] NEA, *Proceedings, 1926*, 1000.
[13] NEA, *Proceedings, 1927*, 85-87; *1929*, 96-102; *NEA Journal*, XII, 261, September 1933.
[14] NEA, *Proceedings, 1941*, 637, 824.

federation was unable to continue its regular meetings, but the organization was kept alive by the acting secretary general, Henry L. Smith of Indiana. In addition to the persons already mentioned, Paul Monroe, Uel W. Lamkin, and Charles H. Williams were other NEA members who served as president or secretary general of WFEA.

In 1946 the NEA sponsored the World Conference of the Teaching Profession, which met at Endicott, New York. It effected the formation of the World Organization of the Teaching Profession (WOTP), which held successive annual meetings at Glasgow, London, Berne, Ottawa, and Malta. At Malta in 1951 a new constitution was drawn up in an effort to satisfy the demands for recognition of the separate associations of elementary and secondary teachers that flourished in some countries. The new organization was initiated at Copenhagen in 1952. It was a union of WOTP, the federation of elementary teachers' associations, and the federation of secondary teachers' associations. The new name was the World Confederation of Organizations of the Teaching Profession (WCOTP). The new organization was much more inclusive than its predecessors and could speak more effectively for the teachers all over the world. The confederation met at Oxford in 1953, Oslo in 1954, Istanbul in 1955, and Manila in 1956, and it will meet in the United States in 1957. Since 1946, William G. Carr of the NEA staff has served as secretary general of WOTP and WCOTP, successively. William F Russell of the United States was president of WOTP, 1946-1952.

These successive organizations—WFEA, WOTP, and WCOPT—were organized attempts to promote a reciprocity of ideas and understanding among teachers of the various countries. Indirectly, of course, the results were calculated to affect peoples and governments.

Another aspect of NEA efforts to promote international understanding consisted of a veritable network of cooperation with other organizations. In fact, the NEA worked jointly with or supplemented the efforts of nearly every organization that had for its purpose the broadening of sympathies and the promotion of understanding and peace. Prominent among these organizations were the Pan-American Union, which was a semiofficial association of countries; various agencies connected with the League of Nations; the Institute of International Education, which promoted the exchange of teachers and students; and the Carnegie Endowment for International Peace, which provided intellectual leadership by issuing a number of studies. The NEA has also cooperated with the Department of State and the specialized agencies of the United Nations in carrying out their various programs of cultural relations and assistance to other countries.

It is probable, however, that none of these efforts toward cooperation equaled in significance the services that the NEA rendered in connection with the organization of the United Nations and Unesco (United Nations Educational, Scientific, and Cultural Organization). Unesco was anticipated in *Education and the People's Peace* (published in 1943 by the Educational Policies Commission), which outlined plans for a postwar intergovernmental agency in the field of education.

When the American delegation to the San Francisco conference of 1945 appointed consultants from various organizations, it opened the door to the educators. Representatives of American educational organizations, including the NEA, were instrumental in securing specific recognition for education in the United Nations Charter. One of the provisions so secured led to the subsequent organization of Unesco as a specialized agency of the United Nations. The NEA and several of its departments have been represented on the United States National Commission for Unesco; and one of these representatives, Williard E. Givens, served as chairman of the commission during 1955-1956, after retiring as executive secretary of the NEA. Mr. Givens' experience with the two educational missions to Japan in 1946 and 1950, his worldwide knowledge of educational conditions, and his experience as a delegate to meetings of WOTP and WCOTP enabled him to exercise great influence in the field of international educational cooperation.

The NEA and its several subdivisions have been consistent supporters of the United Nations and Unesco. The constitution of Unesco seems to appeal for help: "Since wars begin in the minds of men, it is in the minds of men that the defences of peace must be constructed." The NEA and other organizations of educators are endeavoring to answer this call; they are trying through education to build "the defences of peace."

31

Resolved: That . . .

"RESOLVED: That the thanks of this Association are due and are hereby tendered to the citizens of Cincinnati for their kindness and attention on this occasion. Adopted."[1] Thus did the National Teachers' Association express its feelings at the close of the meeting of 1858.

"Youth should be given an international understanding which will encourage friendly relations among nations and serve as basic preparation to face the problems of living in an interdependent world." This plank in the platform of the National Education Association was reaffirmed at the Portland, Oregon, meeting of 1956.

During the century 1857-1957, the NEA issued hundreds of resolutions, dealing with ephemeral happenings, routine procedures, appreciation and thanks, public affairs, and professional matters. The nature of these resolutions and their influence upon education are to some extent the measure of the effectiveness of the NEA.

For several years the offering and passing of resolutions was a very informal matter. Members made them on all kinds of subjects at almost any time of the convention. As early as 1865 the president appointed a committee on resolutions, but that did not prevent others from introducing them. In 1877 the association resolved that all resolutions be presented to the designated committee,[2] but in subsequent meetings this regulation was forgotten or ignored. A review of those passed at some early meetings will illustrate their range and type. The meeting of 1858 and three subsequent ones, at seven-year intervals, are selected for this purpose.

At the first anniversary meeting in Cincinnati in 1858 it was resolved that the thanks of the association be extended "to Mr. Philbrick for his able and truly excellent address upon that most important of all subjects 'Moral Culture,' and that a copy of the same be solicited for publication";

[1] NTA, *Proceedings, 1858*, 12.
[2] NEA, *Proceedings, 1877*, 23.

that all teachers, whether in colleges, academies, public, private or parochial schools, be regarded as brethren and fellow laborers; that it was the great duty of the state to provide full and free education for all youth within its borders; that the first meeting was an earnest of a glorious future for the association; that the association tendered its thanks to Zalmon Richards, the retiring president; that a committee prepare a paper on "The Combination of the Mental, Mechanical, Ideal, and Positive in the Education of Youth"; that the association hail women teachers as honored colaborers; that Barnard's *American Journal of Education* deserved the support of all teachers; that a committee report at the next meeting on a course of study for high schools; that a committee report at the next meeting on school registers and annual reports; that thanks be extended to the newspapers of Cincinnati for reporting the meeting and to the railroads for giving free return tickets.[3]

At Harrisburg in 1865 resolutions were passed providing for a correspondence committee on school costs; lamenting the death of Bishop Alonzo Potter; calling upon Congress to promote the establishment of public-school systems in the South and to establish a Federal bureau of education; providing for a committee to explore the feasibility of a world convention on education; recommending the postponement of excursions until the close of the convention; memorializing Congress to establish competitive examinations for choosing students for the military and naval academies; recommending that future programs provide for discussions of each topic; and expressing thanks to railroads, local committees, and hosts.[4]

At Boston in 1872 the resolutions committee gave a systematic report. The association endorsed the use of funds from the sale of public lands for education and their allocation on the basis of illiteracy; thanked Senator Hoar and Congressman Perce for their support of the bill before Congress; recommended the teaching of art in the schools; stressed the importance of normal schools and teachers' institutes; urged greater attention to the teaching of science; asked for more generous support of the Bureau of Education; and expressed thanks and appreciation to various persons and groups.[5]

At Philadelphia in 1879 resolutions were passed at four sessions, three of them on the motions of individuals. These resolutions endorsed graduating exercises in country schools, provided for the publication of a speech given by Superintendent John D. Philbrick, and called upon Congress to establish at least one institution in each state for the higher

[3] NTA, *Proceedings, 1858, passim.*
[4] NTA, *Proceedings, 1865, passim.* The overlapping and duplication are probably more apparent to the reader than they were to the members at Harrisburg.
[5] NEA, *Proceedings, 1872,* 107-109.

education of women. The resolutions reported by the committee and adopted by the association asked Congress to provide for the enlarging of the pedagogical museum of the Bureau of Education, commended Congress and the President for their efforts in behalf of education, and thanked railroads, hotels, local committees and institutions, program performers, and association officers.[6]

These resolutions, passed at four early meetings, are interesting mixtures of the significant and the insignificant. Those concerned with national policies, congressional activities, and the Bureau of Education demonstrate an early concern with matters of high import. Those dealing with subjects, courses of study, and teacher preparation reveal the serious professional interests of the members. Those which express appreciation for courtesies and services are routine and necessary, but those which hail all teachers as fellow laborers, assign unintelligible tasks to committees, and commend a speaker now appear as rather unimportant. The process of arriving at a dignified level on which only matters of serious import were treated in resolutions was slow and long. In fact, no such level was fully reached in the history of the NEA until 1932.

A resolution was regarded as an expression of good will and concurrence and was in part a matter of politeness and custom. It is a curious fact that the first resolution ever passed by the NEA concerning teachers' salaries was obviously passed as a compliment to President Philbrick, who had mentioned the matter in his opening address in Chicago in 1863.[7] In 1873 President Charles W. Eliot of Harvard asserted that some resolutions were approved "through easy good nature"; others were passed precipitately in the inevitable haste of transacting business in a large assembly.[8] Evidence that even the secretary was not always impressed with the importance of resolutions is afforded by the uncertainty in the record of the Chautauqua meeting of 1880 as to whether the resolutions which were recorded were actually adopted by the association.[9]

From these casual and informal practices of early days the passing of resolutions slowly assumed a more formal procedure. While the development was gradual, it is possible to perceive three stages. The first period of relative informality extended from 1858 to 1896. It is characterized

[6] NEA, *Proceedings, 1879,* 18, 56, 96, 98, 99.
[7] NTA, *Proceedings, 1863,* 297-322.
[8] NEA, *Proceedings, 1873,* 110.
[9] NEA, *Proceedings, 1880,* 157. Further evidence of the slight importance attached to resolutions is the varying and unsystematic manner in which they are presented in the *Proceedings* and cited in the indexes. The resolutions of 1913 and 1914 were omitted altogether. In various indexes resolutions are cited under "Resolutions," "Report of Committees on . . . ," "Committee on . . . ," "National Education Association," "Declaration," "Principles," and "Platform." In a considerable number of indexes the resolutions are not cited at all. These editorial vagaries are more pronounced in the period since 1941 than before that date.

by an easygoing lack of system in which anyone could introduce a resolution on almost any topic at any convenient time during the convention. Although a so-called resolutions committee was appointed, its function was to see that there were resolutions rather than to serve as a channel through which all of them were sent. In 1870, 1871, and 1882, for example, the committee introduced resolutions which dealt only with expressions of thanks and appreciation. Many resolutions of this haphazard period were trivial, but they nevertheless served to promote good will and the growth of group consciousness and solidarity.

The second stage in the development of resolutions, extending from 1896 to 1932, was characterized by an increasing awareness of their importance and an increasing effort to differentiate between routine matters and important policies. The second stage was inaugurated by Professor B. A. Hinsdale of the University of Michigan, who was chairman of the resolutions committee in 1896. His report referred to "our annual declaration of facts, principles, and sentiments." It carefully expressed thanks to local persons, committees, and organizations, and then in a separate category it presented "the more general declarations." This differentiation was made even clearer by Nicholas Murray Butler, who was chairman of the resolutions committee from 1897 to 1900 and in 1903. In 1898 the "declaration of principles" was presented as the report of the committee. Expressions of thanks and appreciation were introduced in separate resolutions.[10] The practice of separating principles and routine expressions continued. In subsequent years some sets of resolutions were classified into categories, such as finances, curriculum, teacher welfare, Federal relations. Thus the systematizing of resolutions made steady progress.

During the third period in the history of NEA resolutions, extending from 1932 to the present, those which expressed a more or less permanent policy were collected into a declaration known as the platform. The platform has been supplemented by annual resolutions that deal with current and evolving issues. When a resolution was endorsed in three successive years, it usually became a part of the platform. Thus the members and the public had a full statement of the continuing principles and the current pronouncements of the NEA.[11] Unfortunately, the *Proceedings* do not always include the platform, and in some years it is fragmented among resolutions, amendments, and motions; but in spite of these editorial derelictions, the procedure of passing resolutions and building a platform is clearly established.

Regardless of the informal manner of early years and the routinized procedure of recent decades, the passing of resolutions had some definite

[10] NEA, *Proceedings, 1896,* 27-30; *1897,* 28-29; *1898,* 34-36.
[11] NEA, *Proceedings, 1931,* 270-273; *1932,* 212-220.

values and tangible outcomes. (1) In the first place, the practice disclosed articulate leaders who could voice the opinions of the assembly. (2) The process of discussing, amending, and passing resolutions clarified ideas and purposes. (3) By promoting acquaintance among widely separated educators, the discussions led to the growth of nationwide harmony and unity in educational matters. (4) Fourth, and possibly most important, the passing of resolutions promoted loyalty to the association among those who read as well as those who heard them. (5) The resolutions served to inform the public as to the purposes, functions, and plans of the association. (6) The resolutions set the goals, directed action, and provided a tangible measure of achievement.

Because of the varying forms in which resolutions were stated, numbered, and recorded, and because some of them were multiple in ideas, it is next to impossible to count those devoted to particular topics. In spite of this difficulty, it is easy to identify the topics which received most attention, thus revealing something of the changing purposes and emphases of the NEA in the various periods.

At the early meetings the topic which occasioned the greatest number of resolutions was the role of the Federal government in education. Some aspect of this issue was the subject of one or more resolutions in nearly every meeting of the NEA from 1865 to the present. Surpassing in frequency all other aspects of Federal participation in education were the resolutions calling first for the creation and then for the support of the Bureau of Education. Year after year the association asked Congress to increase its appropriation in order that the Bureau might make more studies and present fuller reports. It repeatedly called attention to the shamefully low salary of the United States commissioner of education. This recommendation was renewed from time to time, and in 1919 the creation of a department of education with a secretary in the President's cabinet became a major purpose. A resolution endorsing this plan was passed at almost every convention until 1944. Then the former request for a more liberal appropriation for the bureau was renewed. Beginning in 1951 the NEA asked for a national board of education that would elect and direct the commissioner of education.[12]

Next in frequency to the plea for support of the Bureau and the creation of a department was the request for Federal aid to education. The most popular plan called for the use of money from the sale of public lands and its appropriation on the basis of illiteracy. This plan was designed to provide most liberally for the South, and it had the support of most educators. Its principles were embodied in a succession of bills, the most promising of success being the one introduced by Senator Henry W. Blair of New Hampshire in 1884. It and similar bills were approved

[12] NEA, *Proceedings, 1951*, 120.

by numerous resolutions of the NEA during the 1880's, although Congress passed none.

The movement to secure Federal appropriations for the aid of education continued throughout the entire century of the NEA, appearing to be nearly successful right after the First World War and in 1948, 1949, and 1956. Proposed Federal appropriations for school buildings gained the support of President Eisenhower in the 1950's, but this specific plan and all efforts to secure Federal aid of a general nature were unsuccessful.

The NEA also passed many resolutions approving Federal appropriations for special purposes. Its efforts probably helped to gain support for the land-grant institutions; the establishment of experiment stations in 1887; the passing of the second Morrill Act in 1890; the Smith-Lever Act of 1914, which provided support for the teaching of agriculture and home economics at the secondary level; and the Smith-Hughes Act of 1917, which enabled the Federal government to pay the salaries of high-school teachers of vocational courses. Resolutions have advocated changes in regulations concerning vocational rehabilitation and expressed anxieties lest the Federal government duplicate and interfere with the control of education by the states. In many pronouncements and resolutions the NEA has advocated Federal aid without Federal control.

One other area of Federal responsibility deserves mention. The NEA pointedly reminded Congress again and again of its direct responsibility for education among the Indians, in the territories, in Alaska, and on Federal reservations.[13] During the world wars the number of children who became essentially educational wards of the Federal government increased enormously.

Second in frequency to the area of Federal participation are those resolutions which dealt with the teacher—his training, standards of certification, and personal welfare. The NEA has shown a consistent solicitude for the establishment and maintenance of normal schools, teachers' colleges, schools of education within universities, and other institutions that train teachers. Many resolutions called for more professional courses and stricter certification requirements. As the schools increased in size and the curriculum in complexity, the necessity of training in content and methods became more apparent. In many resolutions the NEA proclaimed minimum standards. In 1898, for example, a high-school education plus one year of professional training was set as the desirable standard.[14] As the years passed the standards rose, and the NEA was pronouncedly in favor of such progress.

The NEA was slow to develop a program of teacher welfare. Mild pronouncements in favor of better pay and tenure were passed in 1863,

[13] NEA, *Proceedings, 1905,* 43.
[14] NEA, *Proceedings, 1898,* 35.

1885, 1894, 1898, 1904, 1911, and in other years, but no really vigorous program of teacher welfare was inaugurated until after the First World War. Since that period the NEA has proclaimed repeatedly, and usually in the name of and for the sake of the pupils, in favor of higher salaries, tenure, retirement pensions, reasonable teaching loads, community status, and freedom for the teacher.

Next in frequency to those dealing with the teacher, NEA resolutions dealt with administrative and financial matters and the improvement of supervision. The evolution of the kindergarten evoked many resolutions of approval and calls for its integration into the school system. Similar resolutions were passed concerning the emerging junior high schools, junior colleges, nursery schools, and various kinds of technical schools and schools for specialized groups. In the early years of the NEA the leaders were clear-eyed as to the necessity of state support for all kinds of schools, the desirability of developing a specialized profession of administration and supervision, and the importance of sound fiscal policies. All these were recommended in a series of successive resolutions.

Regardless of frequency, the resolutions on some other issues are also of interest and importance. A number of resolutions and prefatory remarks reveal something of the social and educational philosophy of the members of the NEA. The following were selected to illustrate this area.

1875. Ignorance is a curse to any people and a menacing danger to republican institutions.

1876. Resolved, That next to liberty, education has been the great cause of the marvelous prosperity of the Republic in the first century of its history, and is the sure and only hope of its future.

1889. Universal suffrage without universal education is a national peril.

The aim of the school is not training of the mind alone, but *the training of the man.*

1892. The American public school is distinctly the product of American soil.

1894. Education is the inalienable right of every child of our Republic.

1898. A sound and intelligent public opinion must be in the future, as it has been in the past, the support of every movement to elevate the ideals and to strengthen the efficiency of our schools. . . .

1901. Legislation with respect to public education must not wait for public sentiment. It should lead public sentiment when necessary.

A free people must be developed by free schools.

1905. The association regrets the revival in some quarters of the idea that the common school is a place for teaching nothing but reading, spelling, writing, and ciphering . . . biography, history, ethics, natural history, music, and manual arts [are also necessary].

1910. We affirm our faith in the schools of the Republic, believing that it is impossible for the citizens of a great democracy to develop power and efficiency without the public schools, owned and controlled by the people.

The National Education Association reaffirms its unalterable opposition to any division of the public school funds among private or sectarian schools. . . .

1915. The people of each and every nation need to sink their nationalism in a larger internationalism. . . .

1918. The schools of a modern, efficient democracy must necessarily be socialized schools. They must train for the whole life of all the people.

1920. . . . general or cultural education must not be overshadowed by vocational training.

1932. No nation can afford to entrust its children to incompetent teachers.

1944. Education should prepare each generation to meet the social, economic, and political problems of an ever changing world.[15]

Many resolutions reflect the interests of the association in national and world affairs. In 1870 it recommended the adoption of the metric system and its early introduction into school programs as a means of securing its general use.[16] Three years later it resolved that the large indemnities collected from Japan and China in excess of the actual damages suffered by American ships in 1863 be returned to those countries.[17] In 1884 the association expressed gratitude that Lieutenant A. W. Greely and a few companions were preserved from starvation on the polar ice and were "elated by the fact that an American has added so much to our geographical knowledge, and planted the American flag nearer the North Pole than any other explorers."[18] In 1890 a resolution called for the abolition of tariffs on books, maps, charts, and art products.[19] In 1894 the association denounced riots, insurrections, and violence, and commended President Cleveland for his wisdom and firmness in enforcing law and restoring order in connection with the Pullman strike. It also pronounced that "Riot, incendiarism and conspiracy are not native growths, but have come among us by importation."[20] In 1898 the association deplored war but endorsed "the present struggle" because it was started "in the most unselfish spirit, and from the loftiest motives."[21] In 1900 a resolution called for the extension of the public-school system to Cuba, Puerto Rico, and the Philippine Islands.[22]

In 1911, in spite of vigorous opposition by a member who characterized the resolution as "political," the association declared that the admission of Arizona and New Mexico to statehood would greatly enhance edu-

[15] NEA, Proceedings, 1875, 96; 1876, 73; 1889, 37; 1892, 247-248; 1894, 35; 1898, 34; 1901, 28; 1905, 43; 1908, 39; 1910, 35-36; 1915, 26; 1918, 25; 1920, 25; 1932, 214; 1944, 354.

[16] NEA, Proceedings, 1870, 143, 151-152.

[17] NEA, Proceedings, 1873, 8-15, 92.

[18] NEA, Proceedings, 1884, 15.

[19] NEA, Proceedings, 1890, 39.

[20] NEA, Proceedings, 1894, 34-35.

[21] NEA, Proceedings, 1898, 34-35.

[22] NEA, Proceedings, 1900, 31-32.

cational conditions in those territories.[23] In 1912 a resolution called for a constitutional amendment to provide for uniform marriage and divorce laws, because "children are often innocent victims of our present unequal and unjust laws." At the same session the association asked for the granting of suffrage to women, and in 1919 asked the states to call special sessions of the legislatures in order to approve the proposed amendment.[24] In 1914 the NEA commended President Wilson for his "moral self-restraint" in dealing with Mexico and endorsed his aim of no "territorial aggrandizement." It called for the celebration of the hundred years of peace with Great Britain which followed the signing of the Treaty of Ghent in 1814.[25] In 1918 a resolution called upon the states to ratify the Eighteenth Amendment.[26] Following the First World War the association was outspoken in calling for compulsory Americanization and the exclusive use of the English language in instruction. In 1919 the association endorsed the League of Nations, an international bureau of education, and a bureau of international study under whose auspices 300 young men and women would be sent abroad annually for higher education, at government expense.[27] In 1933 it approved the World Federation of Education Associations.[28] In 1944 a resolution voiced vigorous opposition to a proposed amendment that would limit Federal income, inheritance, and gift taxes. Again and again the NEA proclaimed its support of international good will, worldwide education, national defense, and peace.

The element of commendation and approval loomed large in many sets of resolutions. Assertions concerning educational progress were numerous, and credit for such results was assigned to a loyal public as well as to the faithful profession.[29] Frequently the association praised the President, commended Congress, and congratulated officers and legislatures for performing noteworthy acts.[30]

In general NEA resolutions avoided criticism and faultfinding, but on occasions they could be caustic and critical. In 1897, for example, the association denounced the label of "fads" as applied to nonacademic instruction. In 1907 and 1909 it condemned high-school fraternities and sororities as "inimical to the best interests of schools and pupils."

One of the most forceful and merited rebukes in the whole history of the NEA was the following given in 1927: "The growing tendency of

[23] NEA, *Proceedings, 1911,* 34-35.
[24] NEA, *Proceedings, 1912,* 43; *1919,* 27.
[25] NEA, *Bulletin,* III, 21, September 1914.
[26] NEA, *Proceedings, 1918,* 25-26.
[27] NEA, *Proceedings, 1919,* 22-28.
[28] NEA, *Proceedings, 1933,* 351.
[29] NEA, *Proceedings, 1896,* 28-30.
[30] NEA, *Proceedings, 1918,* 26.

state legislatures to pass laws compelling or forbidding the teaching of particular subjects or topics in the public schools is an unwise and dangerous practice which if continued will transform our educational institutions, now consecrated to the teaching of the truth, into prejudiced schools devoted to the interests of special propaganda." In 1930 the NEA deplored the fraudulent advertising of cigarettes, the commercialization of athletics, and the sale and interstate transportation of obscene literature and pictures. In 1932 the NEA severely condemned the spasms of retrenchment that resulted in bigger classes, shorter terms, unqualified teachers, and curtailed health and recreational services. Two years later it condemned motion pictures that ridiculed sacred institutions, glorified lawlessness, and jested about juvenile delinquency; it included a pronouncement against block booking in motion-picture distribution as a wholesale evil. In 1940 it condemned subversive propaganda and asked the schools "to turn the searchlight of truth on alien ideologies." In various years it denounced political interference with education in Chicago, in Pennsylvania, in New York City, and in various other specified systems.[31]

Some resolutions were devoted to personal messages of commendation, congratulations, solicitude, and sympathy. The first of this kind was sent from Washington in 1859 to Mrs. Horace Mann, in honor of her famous husband, who had died a few weeks before the meeting. In 1927 the NEA congratulated Mrs. Evangeline Lindbergh, a fellow teacher, upon the achievement of her son. Greetings to distinguished educators and public officials were numerous.[32]

A number of resolutions called upon the states to prohibit the publication and sale of "impure" or "evil and corrupting literature of all descriptions," and in 1925 upon Congress to prohibit the interstate transportation of such literature, pictures, and tokens as were denied the use of the mails. In 1918 the NEA urged that "all teachers, as soldiers of the common good, take the oath of allegiance," and made the sweeping pronouncement that "In the emergency that now exists, the Association urges that all the manhood and womanhood of the United States be conscripted for selective service."[33] In the following year it made the astounding proposal that the Federal government provide a full year's training in "civic responsibility and vocational efficiency" for every boy and girl between the ages of seventeen and twenty. The government was to "bear the entire expenses of this undertaking, including adequate maintenance allowance for dependents of such students in training."

[31] NEA, *Proceedings, 1897*, 29; *1907*, 30; *1909*, 35; *1918*, 26; *1927*, 1159; *1930*, 192-193; *1932*, 218-219; *1934*, 181-182; *1940*, 901.

[32] NEA, *Proceedings, 1873*, 15-19, 93; *1874*, 137; *1885*, 22; *1890*, 546; *1892*, 248; *1927*, 1159; *1941*, 907-908.

[33] NEA, *Proceedings, 1885*, 21; *1887*, 47; *1925*, 1010; *1918*, 25-26.

In contrast with these recommendations of restrictions, restraints, and regimentation, the NEA at subsequent dates changed some of its policies. In 1934 it condemned the "singling out of teachers to take an oath of allegiance" as a form of intimidation designed to destroy academic freedom, and two years later the Department of Classroom Teachers demanded the repeal of such laws, characterizing them as "totalitarian" and "a first step in restricting freedom." In 1935 it charged its committee on academic freedom to investigate and report upon cases in which teachers had been discharged in violation of such principles. It repeatedly demanded that the teacher be free to present all points of view, to join organizations of his own choice, and be free from intimidation. It labeled academic freedom as the "child's right to unfettered teaching." In 1949 it condemned "the careless, incorrect, and unjust use of such words as 'Red' and 'Communist' to attack teachers. . . ." In 1936 the association condemned the "Red Rider" which restricted freedom of teaching in the District of Columbia and demanded that Congress repeal the provision. In the following year the association had the pleasure of expressing its appreciation to the newspapers and other agencies which protested the rider and to Congress for repealing it.[34]

In recent years the NEA has pronounced upon a great variety of issues. It endorsed the United Nations and Unesco, statehood for Alaska and Hawaii, Federal aid for worthy college students, and the creation of a national board of education. It condemned cigarettes and narcotics, book burnings, communism, and racial discrimination in the selection of teachers. It called for higher professional standards for teachers, lower income taxes for retirement allowances, higher salaries for teachers, educational opportunities for the children of migrant workers, Federal assistance for schools in federally affected areas, an improved civil defense for the nation, and reduced postal rates on educational materials. The association demanded that criticism of the public schools be "constructive" and "honest," that the separation of church and state "be vigorously and zealously safeguarded," that the issue of racial integration in the schools be approached with a spirit of "fair play and good will," and that voting privileges be granted at the age of eighteen.

This concludes the review of the resolutions of the first century of the NEA. Had it included the resolutions of all the subdivisions, they would have been counted by thousands rather than hundreds. In order to provide a detailed statement of the contemporary policies of the NEA, the latest platform, adopted at Portland, Oregon, in July 1956, is presented as Appendix C on pages 398-403.

[34] NEA, *Proceedings, 1934*, 185; *1935*, 208; *1936*, 211, 888; *1937*, 892; *1940*, 904; *1951*, 122.

32

Headquarters and Staff

ON SATURDAY, July 9, 1898, in the Grand Opera House at Washington, D.C., Nicholas Murray Butler, professor at Columbia University and former president of the NEA, arose to address the "annual business meeting of the active members" of the National Educational Association. He proposed that the constitution of the association be amended. He presented his proposal with evident awareness of its historic significance:

The amendment is, in my judgment, one not only of high importance, but of vital interest to the future development of the association, if it is to go forward on the lines that it has recently pursued. I refer to its greatly increased size, to the succession of large and well-attended meetings, and to the increasing complexity of its business administration, involving time, labor, and special knowledge that but very few of us have in our possession or, having it in our possession, would be able to give. It is an amendment to except hereafter from the list of officers to be annually elected by the association the office of Secretary, and to make that officer a paid and permanent servant of the association. By paid and permanent I mean suitably compensated for his services and elected for a term of years.

This proposition is not new in any sense. It has been before the Board of Directors for many years. It has always been favorably considered in principle, but the moment of its adoption has been postponed. . . . The time, however, has now come when, as I shall show in a moment, our financial development has put us in a position to sustain this charge, and to sustain it to our own ultimate profit. In addition, the time has come (and I say this on my own responsibility) when I am entirely confident that we shall be able to secure, as our Secretary, the one man whose years of service and whose distinguished fidelity to the interests of this association have put his name upon every lip.[1]

The "one man" alluded to by Butler was Irwin Shepard, president of the normal school at Winona, Minnesota, and since 1893 the part-time secretary of the association. He was an able administrator and a genial diplomat. He had kept the association records in orderly fashion, had

[1] NEA, *Proceedings, 1898,* 27.

won the confidence of members and officers, and by astute management had brought unprecedented income into the association's treasury from sale of back numbers of the *Proceedings* and from collection of back dues from lapsed members.

The constitution was amended as had been proposed.[2] Mr. Shepard was thereupon elected as first full-time secretary of the NEA,[3] at an annual salary of $4,000. He resigned as president of the normal school and set up NEA headquarters in his home in Winona.

For the first time the hitherto roving, incorporeal, ubiquitous NEA was anchored to a particular person and place. Prior to this time the business of the association—between conventions—was dispersed among the several officers and was handled from whatever location was theirs at the time. This meant that mailing addresses usually shifted every year, as the officers were usually changed every summer. Although most incumbents of the secretaryship, like other officers, had served only one-year terms prior to the 1890's, there were some exceptions: William E. Sheldon of Massachusetts, who had served for one day as secretary of the organizational meeting of the National Teachers' Association (August 26, 1857), was secretary in 1864-1865, 1882-1883, and 1884-1886; William D. Henkle of Ohio, 1875-1881; and James H. Canfield of Kansas, 1886-1889.[4]

The moving of the secretaryship from person to person and from place to place had many disadvantages that came to be well recognized. Files of correspondence, reports, and other papers—except as they were published in the *Proceedings*—simply were not kept. J. H. Canfield saved a file of papers from his three-year term as secretary, but, he reported later, "nearly all the correspondence was afterwards burned by instuction of the Executive Committee, as they thought it was not worth preserving."[5] The growing accumulation of volumes of the *Proceedings*—virtually the only tangible property that the association owned in the nineteenth century—had been scattered in different parts of the country until placed in a depository in Washington shortly before 1880 (and subsequently shipped to Winona in 1902).

Secretary Shepard resigned in 1912 and was succeeded by Durand W.

[2] *Ibid.*, 29-30.

[3] His election was an action of the board of trustees rather than of the convention as a whole. This procedure was provided for by the constitutional amendments introduced by Butler, who had told the members that they should give up their power to elect the secretary and transfer it to the five trustees, since the board of trustees was the only legally responsible body corporate in the association. The 1898 amendment on this point, which has remained in force ever since, further provided that the trustees should fix the salary of the secretary and should set his term of office, for a period not to exceed four years.

[4] *NEA Handbook, 1956-57*, 114-115.

[5] Letter from Canfield to Shepard, May 5, 1893, quoted in Mildred S. Fenner, *The National Education Association, 1892-1942* (Ph.D. thesis, The George Washington University, 1942), 31.

Springer, certified public accountant, high-school principal, and former treasurer of the NEA. Because Mr. Springer lived in Ann Arbor, Michigan, that city became the seat of the association's national headquarters for the five years of his secretaryship (1912-1917).

James W. Crabtree served as NEA secretary for seventeen years and four months (1917-1935) and was followed by Willard E. Givens, who served for seventeen years and seven months (1935-1952). These thirty-five years witnessed spectacular growth of the NEA in membership, phenomenal multiplication of its activities, and vast expansion of its influence, as has been recounted in the earlier chapters of this book. They were also marked by the stabilizing of location for national headquarters and the assembling of a large and able staff of men and women to take care of the work of the association.

While the great growth in the association after 1918 was in part the result of national conditions and trends, and while the success of the committees and commissions was due to popular support from the members, the fact remains that behind all these developments were devoted individuals who planned and to some extent directed the forces which appear to have been impersonal and inevitable. Outstanding among the many individuals who served the association in the period of its great growth from the First World War to the 1950's were James W. Crabtree, Willard E. Givens, and Joy Elmer Morgan.

When J. W. Crabtree opened the NEA headquarters in Washington in 1917, he brought a background of extensive experience as a teacher, superintendent, and normal-school president in Nebraska and Wisconsin. He had been an active NEA member, having held several positions in the association. He had the reputation of being an organizer, an administrator, and, most important, a believer in teachers. Principle and policy guided Crabtree as he worked toward the dual goal of strengthening and democratizing the NEA. During his tenure as secretary, services were expanded, the Research Division was started, the *Journal* began its impressive career (1920), and the membership rose from about 8,000 to nearly 200,000.

Willard E. Givens, formerly superintendent of schools for the Territory of Hawaii and the city of Oakland, became executive secretary on January 1, 1935. During the next seventeen years, new commissions were created, additional departments were started or affiliated with the parent association and several established headquarters in the NEA building, activities designed to improve the welfare of teachers and administrators were intensified, attempts to secure desirable educational legislation were implemented with increased staff and budgets, the NEA led the organized teaching profession in meeting the challenges presented by the Second World War and the peace that followed, the

NEA became active in international relations, and membership grew to 490,000 by the time he retired in 1952.

Overlapping the tenure of both Crabtree and Givens was that of Joy Elmer Morgan, editor, author, publicist, inventor, inspirer, and exhorter. As editor of the *NEA Journal* for more than thirty years, he proclaimed his messages to a large audience. He was active in promoting American Education Week, Citizenship Day, Personal Growth Leaflets, the Horace Mann League, the Future Teachers of America, and the Centennial Action Program of the NEA. His resourceful aggressiveness and his optimistic outlook were reflected in spirited editorials that contributed greatly toward the growth and the integration of the NEA.

Crabtree's first task after assuming the secretaryship on September 1, 1917, was to establish headquarters offices in Washington, D.C., pursuant to action taken at the NEA convention in July. At first the secretary and his staff of three began work in two rented rooms, but in a short time the work to be done demanded more space and more staff.

At the Milwaukee convention, on July 4, 1919, members voted unanimously to authorize the board of trustees to expend money from the permanent fund to purchase a building in Washington to be used for headquarters offices. The trustees selected a four-story mansion five blocks north of the White House that had once been the home of Senator Guggenheim of Colorado and later of Robert Bacon, secretary of state in the administration of President Theodore Roosevelt.[6] The purchase price was $98,000.

The new quarters, first occupied by Secretary Crabtree and his staff in the summer of 1920, had the address 1201 Sixteenth Street, Northwest. This soon became the best-known address in the educational world. Ready identification of location was an important factor in making the NEA as well known as it has become during the past thirty-seven years. It has unquestionably contributed to growth in membership and to sale of publications.

As the number of NEA members increased, so also did the staff employed to assist Secretary Crabtree and his successors at 1201 Sixteenth Street. By 1922 there were fifty; and by 1956 there were 660. The latter figure includes the approximately 220 employees of the twenty-one NEA departments that maintain Washington headquarters as well as the 440 employees of the NEA proper.

The building was soon outgrown. So adjacent buildings were purchased and connected with the original mansion. In 1930 a new seven-story addition was completed. In 1954-1956 the seven-story addition was

[6] NEA, *Proceedings, 1919*, 13.

completely remodeled; the mansion and other adjacent buildings were razed to be replaced by new structures. As the NEA approached its hundredth birthday, an impressive five-million-dollar modern edifice was nearing completion at 1201 Sixteenth Street: the NEA Educational Center in the nation's capital.

The new Educational Center provides greatly expanded space and improved facilities for handling the increased headquarters activities of the association and its departments: plans for the annual conventions and other special meetings and conferences, prolific publishing enterprises, maintaining membership records and other mailing lists, bookkeeping, correspondence, research, and innumerable services to members and to the public at large. The nature of some of these activities is indicated by the work of departments, committees, and commissions, described in Chapters 24, 25, and 26; by the research studies and other "welfare" activities mentioned in Chapter 28; and by the over-all picture of present functions in Chapter 32. The nature of headquarters activities is further revealed by the names of the thirteen divisions into which a large part of the central staff of the NEA is grouped. These thirteen divisions are:

Accounts
Adult Education Service
Audio-Visual Service
Business
Legislation and Federal Relations
Membership
NEA Journal
Press and Radio Relations
Publications
Records
Research
Rural Service
Travel Service

The work of the divisions engages a majority of the members of the headquarters staff and a large share of the association's financial resources. It is possible, however, to give here only brief mention of a few examples to illustrate the role of the headquarters divisions.

About one-sixth of the annual budget of the NEA is allocated to publishing the *NEA Journal*. It is, of course, the one major service that goes to every member of the association. Editor of the *Journal* since December 1954 has been Mildred S. Fenner, who had served on its staff for many years under the preceding editorship of Joy Elmer Morgan.

The Division of Rural Service has had great influence in the movement for professionalization of the county superintendency and in the development of the concept of the "intermediate unit" of school administration.

The Division of Press and Radio Relations carries the story of education to an ever-widening audience through films, recordings, radio, and television as well as through releases to newspapers and aid to magazines. The Adult Education Service, with its National Training Laboratories, has made outstanding contributions to research and practice in the field of group development and leadership training.

The Research Division has the largest professional staff of any unit at NEA headquarters. In the thirty-five years of its existence the division has probably done more than any other agency in the United States to make the teaching profession conscious of the role of research as a means of improving education, and its studies and publications have had immeasurable influence on the actual improvement of educational practice. Educational research is the process of ascertaining relevant, pertinent facts to promote the cause of education. The movement for tenure would never have started if the *facts* of teacher turnover had not been assembled. The demand for higher salaries would never have materialized if some one had not gathered the *facts* about low salaries. The health of school children is better than formerly because the *facts* about effective methods of health education have been assembled and made known to teachers.

A research function for the association was foreseen at the time of its birth,[7] but it was not until 1922 that a division was established to serve this purpose, with John K. Norton as director. Its first bulletin was *Facts on the Cost of Public Education.*[8] By 1926, three state educational associations had also established divisions of research. In that year Dr. Norton optimistically asserted, "Teachers associations are destined to play an increasingly important role in contributing to the growing body of exact knowledge upon which the science of education is being built."[9]

The Research Division of the NEA grew steadily in functions, personnel, and output. In 1931 Norton was succeeded as director by William G. Carr, who served until 1940, to be followed by Frank W. Hubbard, who directed the division for the next sixteen years. In its thirty-five years the Research Division has distributed approximately three million copies of its *Bulletin* and has answered more than 200,000 letters of inquiry.

In addition to making studies and distributing materials the Research Division is a service bureau for all other divisions and departments of the NEA. As such, it is the upholder of the philosophy of operating, as far as possible, upon the basis of ascertainable facts.

William G. Carr, who became NEA executive secretary in August 1952,

[7] T. W. Valentine said in 1857 that one purpose of the National Teachers' Association should be "to gather and arrange educational statistics."

[8] NEA, *Proceedings, 1922,* 146-147.

[9] NEA, *Proceedings, 1926,* 1155.

asked the executive committee to authorize a staff reorganization to group and streamline complex and scattered staff activities, concentrating responsibilities in the posts of business manager and six assistant executive secretaries. Persons holding these seven positions, plus the secretary of the Educational Policies Commission, constitute the cabinet of the executive secretary. As of early 1957 they are:

Lyle W. Ashby, assistant executive secretary for educational services
Karl H. Berns, assistant executive secretary for field operations
Richard E. Carpenter, business manager
Frank W. Hubbard, assistant executive secretary for information services
James L. McCaskill, assistant executive secretary for state and Federal relations
Hilda Maehling, assistant executive secretary for professional development and
    welfare
Glenn E. Snow, assistant executive secretary for lay relations
Howard E. Wilson, secretary, Educational Policies Commission

Members of the headquarters staff have come to play an extremely important role in the NEA. One or more staff members usually participate in nearly every activity of every department, committee, commission, council, and board of the NEA. The staff's function is largely that of supplying management, information, services, and advice rather than in formulating policies and making decisions. Influential, indispensable, and irreplaceable, staff members nevertheless abstain from attempting to control either policies or the selection of elected officers. They recognize themselves as employees and prudently refuse to become involved in making decisions that might affect their status.

A large number of the staff are persons of extensive training and long experience in schools and colleges. A considerable number are able administrators; others specialize in research, publicity, and persuasion; others in writing and editing; and others in business management. A large percentage of the staff hold graduate degrees and are in every way on a par with the faculties of universities. As authors they have a large number of books to their credit; as editors, an impressive number of magazines under their editorship; and as speakers, a countless number of speeches behind them. By faithful attention to the affairs of the NEA, the staff has built an enviable reputation for competence, objectivity, and devotion. The staff never presumes to direct; neither does it affect any false humility; it does faithfully and effectively what it is supposed to do—promote the purposes and execute the program of the NEA.

33

The NEA Today

I~N~ 1875 Superintendent O. V. Tousley of Minneapolis characterized the NEA as "a Gigantic Educational Ganglion—a sort of pedagogical, cerebro-spinal centre." The person who tries to describe the NEA of 1957 needs the imagination of all seven of the blind men who examined the elephant; in fact, seven seeing men can scarcely perceive the organization in all its ramifications. It is indeed an enormous structure, a complicated mechanism, an involved growth, and a perplexing cluster of functions.

Yet the NEA is in essence as simple as its purpose: "To elevate the character and advance the interests of the profession of teaching, and to promote the cause of popular education in the United States." The profession takes precedence over the teacher, and the purpose determines the form.

The NEA is a many-sided organization with multiple functions. One glance reveals it as an association to promote educational progress; another shows it to be an upholder of the status quo; and still another reveals it as a many-handed disseminator of educational information. It is all these and more. Viewed from fourteen different standpoints, it appears to be fourteen different entities or else one composite organization performing fourteen varied functions.

1. *The NEA is an animated, functioning definition of education.* Its thirty departments include nearly every aspect of education. Each teacher or administrator may join the department which is pertinent to his work. The history teacher belongs to the National Council for the Social Studies, the high-school principal to the National Association of Secondary-School Principals, and the leader of the high-school band to the Music Educators National Conference. The sum total of these thirty departments is a mirror of American education. In 1870 there were four departments; in 1890 there were ten; in 1910, seventeen; in 1930, nineteen; and in 1957, thirty. The number, nature, and functions of the departments serve as indexes of the status of educational progress

in the various periods. The NEA correlates and integrates these varied specialties into one inclusive process.

2. *The NEA is a system of educational forums.* Speakers deliver their messages, committees make their reports, and the members discuss issues, consider proposals, and formulate plans. New theories, methods, programs, and materials are examined, sifted, criticized, and evaluated. The teachers attend these varied forums to receive ideas, exchange experiences, and renew contacts, personal and professional. Thus conventions are occasions when teachers become self-acknowledged learners, take short courses in professional stimulation, and store up morale for improved performance upon their return to the classroom. The forums are the nerve centers for the exchange of educational messages; meeting places for conflicting, competing, and congruent ideas; and the unifying center for reconciling differences and adopting plans for action.

3. *The NEA is an educational commonwealth.* It maintains permanent headquarters in Washington and sets up a temporary capital each year in the convention city. This movable and moving capital sooner or later is located in every large city in nearly every area of the United States. Thus, in the course of a few years, nearly every member is close to the convention city and has an opportunity to attend the sessions, where he meets colleagues who are working in his particular subject or field. The plan of a roving capital also increases the interest of editors and reporters, who inform the public of the policies and activities of the association. In this way the educational leaven works in various sections on citizens and educators to the advantage of the whole educational process.

4. *The NEA is a conserver.* It jealously treasures records of the past and carefully preserves the valuable lessons of experience. In fact, from one standpoint, its chief function is the preservation and transmission of the social heritage; it is an upholder of accumulated culture, a proponent of existing civilization. Until better ways of teaching arithmetic, making examinations, and classifying pupils are discovered, the NEA accepts current practices. Even after improvements have been made and adopted, the past should still be available. The set of annual *Proceedings,* the bound volumes of the *Journal* and the *Research Bulletin,* and the numerous yearbooks, magazines, and other publications issued by committees, commissions, and departments are vast storehouses of facts, theories, practices, and beliefs available to the historian and the researcher. The true conserver has no scorn for past errors, unsound theories, and erroneous practices but views them as necessary elements in the search for more successful procedures. In its records and reports, its principles and policies, the NEA conserves the past.

5. *The NEA is a proponent of progress.* Old practices sometimes fail, new situations call for new procedures, and the educator must look, to

a considerable extent, into the future. Respecting the past and treasuring its lessons, the NEA is nevertheless a promoter of experimentation, a seeker after better methods, an advocate of improved procedures, and a prophet of a new day. Through conventions and publications it disseminates information concerning new practices, promising proposals, and revised materials. It believes that teaching can be improved and that learning can be facilitated.

6. *The NEA is an aggressive defender.* It defends children, teachers, schools, democracy, freedom, civilization. For over fifty years it defended all these by words and resolutions; during the last generation it has defended them by investigations, reports, publicity, and persuasion. The teacher at Springfield and the superintendent at Greenville know that the NEA can and will help them to secure their rights. Erring school boards, willful administrators, and demogogic individuals have felt the sting of rebukes and the cold drafts of public disapproval when their unwarranted intrusions into educational affairs were exposed. The NEA defends teachers and tries to secure and maintain freedom of teaching in order that the pupils may have freedom to learn. Since freedom cannot be rationed, it must be free for all or denied to all.

7. *The NEA is an independent, voluntary organization.* Although chartered by Congress, it is neither supervised nor sustained by the government. And it is not dependent on, or organically related to, any other noneducational organization. It works with many other groups for the promotion of better schools, but it is beholden to none. Nearly 90 per cent of its annual budget of three and a third million dollars is derived from membership dues; the remainder comes largely from advertisements in the *NEA Journal* and from the sale of publications. Thus the association must depend for its support, as well as its effectiveness, upon the sustained enrollment of volunteers. Each teacher makes his annual decision as to whether he joins or continues his membership. This dependence upon dues is a source of continual concern to the officers, but it is also a source and an explanation of the vitality and energy of the organization. Being a voluntary organization, the NEA must be sensitive to the wishes of the members, circumspect in the management of its finances, and unselfish in its devotion to proclaimed educational purposes.

8. *The NEA is a national organization.* This fact involves a number of important consequences. Since education in the United States is primarily a responsibility of the states, with only supplementary help from the Federal government, the NEA exercises much of its influence through cooperating with state and local teachers' associations. With respect to the limited area of Federal action, the NEA can and does assume direct leadership; but in the larger area of state control, it must win, rather than

command, leadership. Its effectiveness within the states is determined largely by its help to state and local affiliates rather than directly. These constitutional and legal facts explain why the NEA is in part a combination of federated units as well as a simple-structured organization. Without authority to compel changes in educational practice or in the status of the teaching profession, the national organization nevertheless wields a nationwide influence through facilitating the cross-fertilization of ideas and the dissemination of information. Thus it contributes importantly to the phenomenon of unity amid diversity in American education—a phenomenon that is often baffling to foreign observers of the educational scene in the United States. The NEA helps to evolve *national policies* out of *state systems*. In spite of the resulting complexity and difficulty, the NEA opposes Federal control and vigorously upholds the existing arrangement for state control of education.

9. *The NEA is a research organization.* Facts about teachers' salaries, sick-leave practices, and school taxes must be gathered every year. These three examples indicate the varied kinds of data which the educational profession constantly needs. Since its establishment in 1922 the Division of Research of the NEA has made scores of studies and has answered thousands of inquiries. It concentrates upon gathering data that have immediate utility. It has grown from a one-man staff in 1922 to a division that employs fifty persons. The American Educational Research Association, a department of the NEA, encourages research and experimentation that have long-range possibilities. In addition to these two agencies of research, every division and department of the NEA carries on surveys and investigations. In fact, the whole association is permeated with the scientific spirit and bases most decisions upon the results of experimentation and research.

10. *The NEA is a vast publishing enterprise.* In 1955, for example, the NEA and its commissions, committees, departments, and divisions published 20 monthly magazines, 181 bulletins, 36 yearbooks and other books, and 1,070 miscellaneous publications. The annual *Proceedings*, which have been published since 1858, are complemented by the monthly *Journal* and scores of other publications. The aggregate output of educational materials exceeds that of any similar agency in the world. In 1956 a customer ordered all current publications, including yearbooks, films, and newsletters. The 36-page invoice amounted to about $2,000. While no one reader could possibly keep up with all of the publications, he can read those that deal with his position, subject, or area of interest. From the *Journal* all members can obtain monthly overviews of the entire association and its activities and of nationwide ideas and practices in education.

11. *The NEA is a promoter of American enterprise.* At its various conventions the NEA invites exhibitors to display professional books, text-

books for schools, school supplies, films, maps, school buses, and commercial products that have educational value. Through its publications, especially the *Journal,* it carries the message of advertisers to members of the profession. Thus educators are constantly informed of new products, improved equipment, and current materials which are supplied by American ingenuity. No educator apologizes because exhibitors and advertisers hope to benefit financially, for he recognizes them as contributors to educational progress.

12. *The NEA is an ardent advocate of education.* The NEA enthusiastically and repeatedly tells the American people that their schools and colleges are treasurers of great worth. It affirms and heralds the doctrine that the nation's schools constitute an essential means for preserving American liberties and maintaining democracy. Therefore, it advocates good school buildings, ample supplies, and well-paid teachers. In trying to effect these results it appeals to other organizations, state departments of education, state legislatures, the U.S. Office of Education, Congress, and the public. In its advocacy of education it utilizes magazines, the press, radio, television, and all other means of mass communication. Although public education receives, perhaps, the major share of the NEA's promotional attention, the association does not oppose nonpublic education; indeed, it has insisted on the right of private schools to be maintained and patronized, and much of the benefit of its advocacy of education flows to all kinds of educational enterprises.

13. *The NEA is a coordinator of educational efforts.* The NEA is itself a union of many different educational interests and it is also a leader in bringing other national organizations together for the purpose of promoting educational improvements. Through joint committees and other cooperative arrangements it secures wide support for better health services in the schools, more books in school libraries, larger appropriations for school buildings, and other such goals. In these efforts the NEA enlists the support of physicians, publishers, editors, librarians, parents, school-board members, and others. Each department similarly stimulates and coordinates the efforts of many other groups with related interests.

14. *The NEA of today is the teaching profession of tomorrow.* The teacher of today is not only developing the citizen of tomorrow; he is also building the profession for his successors in the classroom. The standards of a profession are set by its members, and in education they are determined by the voluntary associations of teachers. Since the NEA is the major educational organization of the United States, it determines to a considerable extent the quality of educational services and sets the standards for the future.

This review of fourteen roles of the NEA indicates something of its nature, spirit, and influence. The machinery that has evolved to carry out these roles—to serve the varied functions just enumerated—is necessarily complex. But it is rational, and it is relevant.

The central structure, that of the "NEA proper," is shown in the accompanying diagram. The nearly 700,000 members, operating through 66 state and approximately 6,000 local affiliates, choose from 4,000 to 5,000 delegates each year to constitute the representative assembly. Each year at the convention the assembly elects the officers, passes upon resolutions, recommendations, reports, bylaws, and amendments; it is the policy-determining body. The board of directors, consisting of at least one member from each state and certain specified officers, is the deliberating and action agency of the assembly. The executive committee, consisting of eleven persons, is the interim board of directors. The board of trustees cares for the permanent fund and elects the executive secretary, who serves the association and the executive committee and directs the headquarters staff.

The National Education Association, however, is more than its officers, directors, trustees, and executive committee. It is more than its executive secretary and staff. More than its many state and local affiliates. It is more, even, than its nearly 700,000 members and their annual representative assembly. It also is the thirty departments described above in Chapter 24 and the twenty-four committees and commissions described in Chapters 25 and 26. It is a "gigantic educational ganglion," indeed!

The National Education Association of the United States! Far-flung and scattered, yet unified and integrated. Big, and growing bigger, yet it engenders no fear because of its size. Its members trust it because they have the will and the procedure for controlling its policies and managing its activities.

The policies of the NEA originate with the members and are formalized by a vote of the representative assembly. The resolutions committee, large and representative, formulates tentative statements and presents them at open meetings of the committee. Criticisms and suggestions are numerous and spirited. The revised versions are then presented for action by the assembly. The resolutions that are adopted three years in succession are usually, although not always, placed in a continuing platform which is supplemented by annual resolutions. The platform and the current resolutions constitute the NEA's statement of policy (see Appendix C).

Commissions and committees, the officers and staff, the departments and affiliated associations, both suggest and undertake to carry out the announced policies. The interpretation and application of these policies are observed by a careful and sometimes jealous assembly, watching to

THE NEA

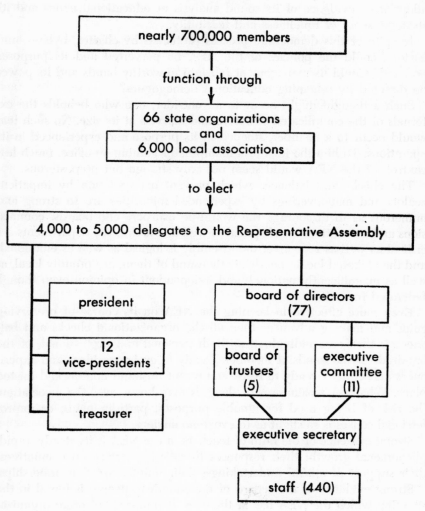

nearly 700,000 members

function through

66 state organizations
and
6,000 local associations

to elect

4,000 to 5,000 delegates to the Representative Assembly

president

12 vice-presidents

treasurer

board of directors (77)

board of trustees (5)

executive committee (11)

executive secretary

staff (440)

see that its agents have correctly interpreted its intentions. In case of uncertainty as to the meaning of a statement or its applicaion to a new situation, a commission or officer can call upon the executive committee for an interpretation of the NEA's policy. In emergencies the executive secretary is authorized to make tentative interpretations.

In addition to this formal procedure for developing and adopting policies, the NEA has set up a supplementary process. The Educational Policies Commission, established in 1935, is charged with the responsibility, not of making policies, but of proposing and advocating them.

The fact that many of its proposals have gained acceptance and official adoption is evidence of its sound analysis of educational issues and its strategic sense of timeliness and feasibility.

In spite of this democratic process protected by charter, bylaws, and custom, could the policies of the NEA be perverted and its purposes polluted? Could its management fall into unworthy hands and its power be directed by scheming educational demogogues?

Such a thought might occur to an outsider, one who beholds the externals of the complicated structure and marvels at its size. No such fear would occur to a member, steeped in its purpose and experienced in its operations. To him the idea of a manipulator gaining an office, much less control, of the NEA would seem not only strange but preposterous.

The checks and balances which prevent manipulation by impatient zealots and maneuverings by experienced minorities are so strong and numerous as to discourage the would-be usurper. The boards, commissions and committees are skeptical as well as trustful; the departments are critical as well as receptive; the assembly is logical as well as emotional; and the affiliated locals, nearly six thousand of them, are proudly local, as well as magnificently national, and independent in opinion even though federated for action.

Even more effective in keeping the NEA on its course of preserving gains and making advances than all the organizational checks and balances is the fierce individualism, both personal and professional, of the hundreds of thousands of members, ready to exchange ideas and experiences and equally ready to resist and resent unsound notions and foisted plans. Whatever weaknesses or dangers may hover over the association, the risk of being used for ignoble purposes, partisan plans, or unprofessional causes is so slight as to evoke no anxiety.

Strong evidence of the faith of teachers in the NEA is its steady, rapid, phenomenal growth; their responses to calls for service on committees; their support of official undertakings; their uninterrupted memberships.

Strong evidence of the regard of the American people is found in the standing which the NEA has in the eyes of hundreds of other organizations; in the numerous occasions on which it supplies information and data for government agencies; in its influence with state legislatures and state departments of education; in its cooperation with a succession of United States commissioners of education; in its objectivity and impartiality even in the eyes of those who have felt the force of its criticism.

All these testify to the integrity, disinterestedness, and uprightness of the NEA. Compounded of growths, revisions, amendments, and inventions, the association has flourished this hundred years. If past performance is an augury of the future, it will flourish even more creatively for another hundred years.

Appendixes

Appendix A

MEETINGS AND OFFICERS, 1857-1957

National Teachers' Association, 1857–1870

1857. Philadelphia, Pa. (Organized)
James L. Enos, Chairman
W. E. Sheldon, Secretary

1858. Cincinnati, Ohio
Z. Richards, President
J. W. Bulkley, Secretary
A. J. Rickoff, Treasurer

1859. Washington, D.C.
A. J. Rickoff, President
J. W. Bulkley, Secretary
C. S. Pennell, Treasurer

1860. Buffalo, N.Y.
J. W. Bulkley, President
Z. Richards, Secretary
O. C. Wight, Treasurer

1861, 1862. No session

1863. Chicago, Ill.
John D. Philbrick, President
James Cruickshank, Secretary
O. C. Wight, Treasurer

1864. Ogdensburg, N.Y.
W. H. Wells, President

David N. Camp, Secretary
Z. Richards, Treasurer

1865. Harrisburg, Pa.
S. S. Greene, President
W. E. Sheldon, Secretary
Z. Richards, Treasurer

1866. Indianapolis, Ind.
J. P. Wickersham, President
S. H. White, Secretary
S. P. Bates, Treasurer

1867. No session

1868. Nashville, Tenn.
J. M. Gregory, President
L. Van Bokkelen, Secretary
James Cruickshank, Treasurer

1869. Trenton, N.J.
L. Van Bokkelen, President
W. E. Crosby, Secretary
A. L. Barber, Treasurer

1870. Cleveland, Ohio
Daniel B. Hagar, President
A. P. Marble, Secretary
W. E. Crosby, Treasurer

National Educational Association, 1871–1907

1871. St. Louis, Mo.
J. L. Pickard, President
W. E. Crosby, Secretary
John Hancock, Treasurer

1872. Boston, Mass.
E. E. White, President
S. H. White, Secretary
John Hancock, Treasurer

1873. Elmira, N.Y.
B. G. Northrop, President
S. H. White, Secretary
John Hancock, Treasurer

1874. Detroit, Mich.
S. H. White, President
A. P. Marble, Secretary
John Hancock, Treasurer

1875. Minneapolis, Minn.
W. T. Harris, President
M. R. Abbott, Secretary
A. P. Marble, Treasurer

1876. Baltimore, Md.
W. F. Phelps, President
W. D. Henkle, Secretary
A. P. Marble, Treasurer

1877. Louisville, Ky.
M. A. Newell, President
W. D. Henkle, Secretary
J. Ormond Wilson, Treasurer

1878. No session

1879. Philadelphia, Pa.
John Hancock, President
W. D. Henkle, Secretary
J. Ormond Wilson, Treasurer

1880. Chautauqua, N.Y.
J. Ormond Wilson, President
W. D. Henkle, Secretary
E. T. Tappan, Treasurer

1881. Atlanta, Ga.
James H. Smart, President
W. D. Henkle, Secretary
E. T. Tappan, Treasurer

1882. Saratoga Springs, N.Y.
G. J. Orr, President
W. E. Sheldon, Secretary
H. S. Tarbell, Treasurer

1883. Saratoga Springs, N.Y.
E. T. Tappan, President
W. E. Sheldon, Secretary
N. A. Calkins, Treasurer

1884. Madison, Wis.
Thomas W. Bicknell, President
H. S. Tarbell, Secretary
N. A. Calkins, Treasurer

1885. Saratoga Springs, N.Y.
F. Louis Soldan, President
W. E. Sheldon, Secretary
N. A. Calkins, Treasurer

1886. Topeka, Kans.
N. A. Calkins, President
W. E. Sheldon, Secretary
E. C. Hewett, Treasurer

1887. Chicago, Ill.
W. E. Sheldon, President
J. H. Canfield, Secretary
E. C. Hewett, Treasurer

1888. San Francisco, Calif.
Aaron Gove, President
J. H. Canfield, Secretary
E. C. Hewett, Treasurer

1889. Nashville, Tenn.
Albert P. Marble, President
J. H. Canfield, Secretary
E. C. Hewett, Treasurer

1890. St. Paul, Minn.
J. H. Canfield, President
W. R. Garrett, Secretary
E. C. Hewett, Treasurer

1891. Toronto, Ont.
W. R. Garrett, President
E. H. Cook, Secretary
J. M. Greenwood, Treasurer

1892. Saratoga Springs, N.Y.
E. H. Cook, President
R. W. Stevenson, Secretary
J. M. Greenwood, Treasurer

1893. Chicago, Ill. (International
Congress of Education)
Albert G. Lane, President
Irwin Shepard, Secretary
J. M. Greenwood, Treasurer

1894. Asbury Park, N.J.
Albert G. Lane, President
Irwin Shepard, Secretary
J. M. Greenwood, Treasurer

1895. Denver, Colo.
Nicholas M. Butler, President
Irwin Shepard, Secretary
I. C. McNeill, Treasurer

1896. Buffalo, N.Y.
Newton C. Dougherty, President
Irwin Shepard, Secretary
I. C. McNeill, Treasurer

1897. Milwaukee, Wis.
Charles R. Skinner, President
Irwin Shepard, Secretary
I. C. McNeill, Treasurer

1898. Washington, D.C.
J. M. Greenwood, President
Irwin Shepard, Secretary
I. C. McNeill, Treasurer

1899. Los Angeles, Calif.
E. Oram Lyte, President
Irwin Shepard, Secretary
I. C. McNeill, Treasurer

1900. Charleston, S.C.
Oscar T. Corson, President
Irwin Shepard, Secretary
Carroll G. Pearse, Treasurer

1901. Detroit, Mich.
James M. Green, President
Irwin Shepard, Secretary
L. C. Greenlee, Treasurer

1902. Minneapolis, Minn.
William M. Beardshear, President
Irwin Shepard, Secretary
Charles H. Keyes, Treasurer

1903. Boston, Mass.
Charles W. Eliot, President
Irwin Shepard, Secretary
W. M. Davidson, Treasurer

1904. St. Louis, Mo.
John W. Cook, President
Irwin Shepard, Secretary
McHenry Rhodes, Treasurer

1905. Asbury Park and Ocean Grove, N.J.
William H. Maxwell, President
Irwin Shepard, Secretary
James W. Crabtree, Treasurer

1906. No session

1907. Los Angeles, Calif.
Nathan C. Schaeffer, President
Irwin Shepard, Secretary
J. N. Wilkinson, Treasurer

National Education Association of the United States, 1908——

1908. Cleveland, Ohio
Edwin C. Cooley, President
Irwin Shepard, Secretary
Arthur H. Chamberlain, Treasurer

1909. Denver, Colo.
Lorenzo D. Harvey, President
Irwin Shepard, Secretary
Arthur H. Chamberlain, Treasurer

1910. Boston, Mass.
James Y. Joyner, President
Irwin Shepard, Secretary
Arthur H. Chamberlain, Treasurer

1911. San Francisco, Calif.
Ella Flagg Young, President
Irwin Shepard, Secretary
Durand W. Springer, Treasurer

1912. Chicago, Ill.
Carroll G. Pearse, President
Irwin Shepard, Secretary
Katherine D. Blake, Treasurer

1913. Salt Lake City, Utah
Edward T. Fairchild, President
Durand W. Springer, Secretary
Grace M. Shepard, Treasurer

1914. St. Paul, Minn.
Joseph Swain, President
Durand W. Springer, Secretary
Grace M. Shepard, Treasurer

1915. Oakland, Calif.
David Starr Jordan, President
Durand W. Springer, Secretary
Grace M. Shepard, Treasurer

1916. New York, N.Y.
David B. Johnson, President
Durand W. Springer, Secretary
Grace M. Shepard, Treasurer

1917. Portland, Oreg.
Robert J. Aley, President
Durand W. Springer, Secretary
Thomas E. Finegan, Treasurer

1918. Pittsburgh, Pa.
Mary C. C. Bradford, President
J. W. Crabtree, Secretary
A. J. Matthews, Treasurer

1919. Milwaukee, Wis.
George D. Strayer, President
J. W. Crabtree, Secretary
A. J. Matthews, Treasurer

1920. Salt Lake City, Utah
Josephine Corliss Preston, President

1921. Des Moines, Iowa
Fred M. Hunter, President
J. W. Crabtree, Secretary
Cornelia S. Adair, Treasurer

1922. Boston, Mass.
Charl O. Williams, President
J. W. Crabtree, Secretary
Cornelia S. Adair, Treasurer

1923. Oakland, Calif.
William B. Owen, President
J. W. Crabtree, Secretary
Cornelia S. Adair, Treasurer

1924. Washington, D.C.
Olive M. Jones, President
J. W. Crabtree, Secretary
Cornelia S. Adair, Treasurer

1925. Indianapolis, Ind.
Jesse H. Newlon, President
J. W. Crabtree, Secretary
Cornelia S. Adair, Treasurer

1926. Philadelphia, Pa.
Mary McSkimmon, President
J. W. Crabtree, Secretary
Henry Lester Smith, Treasurer

1927. Seattle, Wash.
Francis G. Blair, President
J. W. Crabtree, Secretary
Henry L. Smith, Treasurer

1928. Minneapolis, Minn.
Cornelia S. Adair, President
J. W. Crabtree, Secretary
Henry L. Smith, Treasurer

1929. Atlanta, Ga.
Uel W. Lamkin, President
J. W. Crabtree, Secretary
Henry L. Smith, Treasurer

1930. Columbus, Ohio
E. Ruth Pyrtle, President
J. W. Crabtree, Secretary
Henry L. Smith, Treasurer

1931. Los Angeles, Calif.
Willis A. Sutton, President
J. W. Crabtree, Secretary
Henry L. Smith, Treasurer

1932. Atlantic City, N.J.
Florence Hale, President
J. W. Crabtree, Secretary
Henry L. Smith, Treasurer

1933. Chicago, Ill.
Joseph Rosier, President
J. W. Crabtree, Secretary
Henry L. Smith, Treasurer

1934. Washington, D.C.
Jessie Gray, President
J. W. Crabtree, Secretary
Henry L. Smith, Treasurer

1935. Denver, Colo.
Henry L. Smith, President
Willard E. Givens, Exec. Secty.
R. E. Offenhauer, Treasurer

1936. Portland, Oreg.
Agnes Samuelson, President
Willard E. Givens, Exec. Secty.
R. E. Offenhauer, Treasurer

1937. Detroit, Mich.
Orville C. Pratt, President
Willard E. Givens, Exec. Secty.
R. E. Offenhauer, Treasurer

1938. New York, N.Y.
Caroline S. Woodruff, President
Willard E. Givens, Exec. Secty.
R. E. Offenhauer, Treasurer

1939. San Francisco, Calif.
Reuben T. Shaw, President
Willard E. Givens, Exec. Secty.
B. F. Stanton, Treasurer

1940. Milwaukee, Wis.
Amy H. Hinrichs, President
Willard E. Givens, Exec. Secty.
B. F. Stanton, Treasurer

1941. Boston, Mass.
Donald DuShane, President
Willard E. Givens, Exec. Secty.
B. F. Stanton, Treasurer

1942. Denver, Colo.
Myrtle H. Dahl, President
Willard E. Givens, Exec. Secty.
B. F. Stanton, Treasurer

1943. Indianapolis, Ind. (Representative Assembly only)
A. C. Flora, President
Willard E. Givens, Exec. Secty.
B. F. Stanton, Treasurer

1944. Pittsburgh, Pa. (Representative Assembly only)
Edith B. Joynes, President
Willard E. Givens, Exec. Secty.
B. F. Stanton, Treasurer

1945. Chicago, Ill. (Meeting of Board of Directors only)
F. L. Schlagle, President
Willard E. Givens, Exec. Secty.
B. F. Stanton, Treasurer

1946. Buffalo, N.Y. (Representative Assembly only)
F. L. Schlagle, President
Willard E. Givens, Exec. Secty.
B. F. Stanton, Treasurer

1947. Cincinnati, Ohio (Representative Assembly only)
Pearl A. Wanamaker, President
Willard E. Givens, Exec. Secty.
B. F. Stanton, Treasurer

1948. Cleveland, Ohio (Representative Assembly only)
Glenn E. Snow, President
Willard E. Givens, Exec. Secty.
Gertrude E. McComb, Treasurer

1949. Boston, Mass. (Representative Assembly only)
Mabel Studebaker, President

Willard E. Givens, Exec. Secty.
Gertrude E. McComb, Treasurer

1950. St. Louis, Mo.
Andrew D. Holt, President
Willard E. Givens, Exec. Secty.
Gertrude E. McComb, Treasurer

1951. San Francisco, Calif.
Corma Mowrey, President
Willard E. Givens, Exec. Secty.
Gertrude E. McComb, Treasurer

1952. Detroit, Mich.
J. Cloyd Miller, President
Willard E. Givens, Exec. Secty.
Gertrude E. McComb, Treasurer

1953. Miami Beach, Fla.
Sarah C. Caldwell, President
William G. Carr, Exec. Secty.

Gertrude E. McComb, Treasurer

1954. New York, N. Y.
William A. Early, President
William G. Carr, Exec. Secty.
Gertrude E. McComb, Treasurer

1955. Chicago, Ill.
Waurine Walker, President
William G. Carr, Exec. Secty.
Gertrude E. McComb, Treasurer

1956. Portland, Oreg.
John L. Buford, President
William G. Carr, Exec. Secty.
Gertrude E. McComb, Treasurer

1957. Philadelphia, Pa.
Martha Shull, President
William G. Carr, Exec. Secty.
Gertrude E. McComb, Treasurer

Appendix B

NEA MEMBERSHIP, 1857–1957

Year	Membership	Year	Membership	Year	Membership
1857	43	1891	4,778	1925	158,103
1858	75	1892	3,360	1926	170,053
1859	—	1893	—	1927	181,350
1860	—	1894	5,915	1928	193,145
1861	—	1895	1,065	1929	205,678
1862	—	1896	1,579	1930	216,188
1863	187	1897	1,857	1931	220,149
1864	—	1898	1,963	1932	207,418
1865	173	1899	2,214	1933	189,173
1866	126	1900	2,332	1934	187,645
1867	—	1901	2,838	1935	190,944
1868	—	1902	3,215	1936	165,448
1869	—	1903	4,288	1937	181,228
1870	170	1904	4,541	1938	195,605
1871	—	1905	5,261	1939	201,682
1872	292	1906	5,168	1940	203,429
1873	380	1907	5,044	1941	211,191
1874	345	1908	—	1942	217,943
1875	355	1909	6,030	1943	219,334
1876	214	1910	6,909	1944	271,847
1877	160	1911	7,036	1945	331,605
1878	—	1912	7,865	1946	340,973
1879	256	1913	7,582	1947	386,643
1880	354	1914	7,063	1948	441,127
1881	247	1915	7,441	1949	427,527
1882	290	1916	7,878	1950	453,797
1883	253	1917	8,466	1951	465,266
1884	2,729	1918	10,104	1952	490,968
1885	625	1919	—	1953	516,463
1886	1,197	1920	52,850	1954	561,708
1887	9,115	1921	87,414	1955	612,716
1888	7,216	1922	118,032	1956	659,190
1889	1,984	1923	133,566	1957	
1890	5,474	1924	138,856		

Appendix C

THE NEA PLATFORM OF 1956

The National Education Association believes that our American system of free public schools is an indispensable foundation for our democratic way of life; that the public school is a chief source of national unity, common purpose, and equality of opportunity; and that the functions of the public school are enhanced by our traditional policy of the separation of church and state.

I. The Child

Every child should have the opportunity for full development in the attitudes, knowledges, habits, and skills essential for individual happiness and effective citizenship. To this end, the Association advocates:

A. Education for cultural, vocational, recreational, social, and civic responsibilities, adapted to individual interests, needs, and abilities.

B. Encouragement to all agencies that foster a stable, happy, and secure home and community life.

C. Physical fitness programs including instruction in the scientific bases of physical and mental health, and the effects of alcohol, narcotics, malnutrition, and nervous tension.

D. Amendment of the Constitution of the United States to provide for the prohibition of child labor.

E. Compulsory school attendance laws based on high school graduation or age 18 with provision for work permits at 16 where individually desirable.

F. The right to information concerning controversial issues.

G. Educational and vocational guidance, including vocational placement and followup.

H. Unified community recreational programs stressing physical and mental health, effective citizenship, and constructive use of leisure.

I. Continuous improvement of children's literature and of radio, motion pictures, and television programs.

II. The Teacher

Education is a major profession comprising classroom teachers, administrators, and specialists. The interests of the child require that these professional workers should have certain responsibilities, rights, and characteristics:

A. Sound character, good health, high civic ideals, and dynamic personality.

B. Preparation based on a rich cultural background, adequate professional education, thoro knowledge of subjectmatter, and a well-developed social consciousness.

C. Continued study of educational and professional problems.

398

D. Professional membership in local, state, and national education associations and conduct consistent with their Codes of Ethics.

E. Participation and leadership in local, state, and national professional and civic organizations, in community activities, and in interpreting the schools to the public.

F. Freedom of speech, worship, press, assembly, and thought subject only to such controls as those of other responsible citizens. Freedom to present all points of view without danger of reprisal, intimidation, loss of position, reduction of salary, loss of opportunities for advancement, or deprivation of their usual assignments and authorities. The right to organize and support organizations they consider to be in their own and the public interest.

G. Participation in determining and carrying out school policies to improve existing practices, teaching conditions, and teacher welfare.

H. Salary schedules adequate to attract and hold men and women of marked ability and thoro preparation developed in a professional way thru group discussion and action.

I. Effective tenure laws balanced by corresponding responsibility for continuing personal and professional growth.

J. Protection by credit unions and by sound retirement systems, including provision for disability.

III. The Adult

The adult furnishes to society leadership and vision. It is essential that he be prepared in the fundamentals of education, be cognizant of the demands upon him as a citizen, and be able to give guidance to youth. To this end, the Association advocates:

A. Adult education that enriches the cultural aspects of life, prepares for parenthood, provides opportunity to develop personal talents, and increases the effectiveness of citizenship.

B. Unified recreational programs that develop physical and mental health and worthy use of leisure.

C. Naturalization programs that encourage the development of ability to read and write the English language, develop general knowledge of government, instill a desire to exercise the right of suffrage, and lead to mental and economic competency.

IV. The School

The public school continues to be a major democratizing influence in our American way of life. The Association believes that a modern school program embodies these principles:

A. The traditional tools of learning, commonly known as the fundamentals, are basic in our instructional program.

B. Additional fundamentals, such as family living, physical and mental health, safety, economic and civic competence, and wholesome recreation are essential to meet modern needs.

C. Along with the home, the church, and the community, the school has a major responsibility for building fundamental moral and spiritual values into human behavior.

D. The educational program should include conservation of human and natural resources involving cooperative planning with industry, business, labor, agriculture, governmental and welfare agencies, and the general public.

E. America's growing international responsibilities call for thoro study and effective teaching of the role of our country in world affairs.

F. School athletics should be administered solely by school authorities as a part of a balanced educational program.

G. School staffs should constantly evaluate the curriculum, student activities, and the guidance program to insure optimum opportunity for all boys and girls to be prepared to participate in a democratic society, enjoy its freedoms, and willingly assume the corresponding responsibilities.

V. Organization and Administration

Effective public education requires efficient school districts, strong state and county departments of education, and able leadership by boards of education and school administrators. To this end, the Association advocates:

A. Provision by the state for a system of public education from nursery school thru the university including:

1. Education for children in rural and small communities comparable to that provided in larger communities.

2. Vocational education as an integral part of local school systems with part-time and evening classes as needed.

3. Adult education.

4. Educational opportunities for exceptional children, whether gifted or handicapped, with instruction, guidance, and care in terms of their respective needs.

5. A school year of 180 days or more.

6. Class enrolment of not more than 30 pupils.

B. State departments of education adequately staffed and financed with authority and responsibility for:

1. Administering the system of certification for teachers based upon professional standards.

2. Certifying local school programs as to adequacy in meeting state standards.

3. Presenting recommendations for educational improvements to the legislature and the people.

4. Providing specialized consultative services to schools.

5. Furnishing leadership for improved educational opportunity thru public education.

C. Reorganization of local school districts, wherever needed, into larger administrative units with sufficient resources and enrolment to provide a good educational program for all.

D. Selection at large of local, county, and state boards of education on a nonpartisan basis with overlapping terms of office.

E. Further professionalization of the superintendency of schools at local, county, and state levels thru:

1. Upward revision of standards of eligibility, preparation, and certification.

2. Appointment by nonpartisan boards.

F. The selection, promotion and payment of teachers on a professional basis:

1. Equal pay, regardless of sex or grade taught, for teachers of equivalent education and experience.

2. No discrimination because of race, color, residence, economic or marital status, sex, religion, or nonsubversive political beliefs.

G. Adherence to good standards of school administration:

1. Budget prepared by the school superintendent and his staff and presented to the board of education for adoption.

2. Board of education guided by the recommendations of professional educators.

H. Service to state and local schools by the federal government in the form of information, recommendation, and support.

I. Legislation to establish a National Board of Education, appointed for long overlapping terms by the President with the consent of the Senate, as an independent agency to administer the United States Office of Education.

The National Board should select a professionally qualified commissioner of education responsible to the Board for the performance of his duties.

VI. *Finance*

Educational opportunities thru combined liberal support from local, state, and national sources are essential to personal well-being and happiness and to national security and freedom. To this end, the Association advocates:

A. Coordination of the taxing policies of national, state, and local units of government.

B. Financial assistance from the federal government to the states and territories, possessions. Commonwealth of Puerto Rico, and District of Columbia for the support of public education:

1. Federal funds should be provided with the understanding that the expenditure of such funds and the shaping of educational policies be matters of state and local control.

2. Special federal funds should be made available without federal dictation to prevent the interruption of education in devastated areas when widespread disasters occur.

3. The federal government should reimburse local taxing bodies where federal acquisition of property and establishing of federal projects have distorted the tax base by loss of revenue or by increased population requiring extra school services.

C. Adequate appropriations to the Office of Education.

D. Provision by each state for a complete system of free public schools from public funds with a broadening of the tax base to include sources of revenue other than real and personal property taxes.

E. Freedom for each unit of government from constitutional limitations placed on taxation within the various states.

F. Financial autonomy for boards of education in order to fulfil their responsibilities.

G. Continuous exploration of fiscal policy and the dissemination of information concerning the best sources of revenue and efficient expenditures.

H. Public enlightenment regarding the financial needs of the schools.

VII. *Community Participation*

Education should prepare each generation to meet the social, economic, and political problems of an ever-changing world. The school should contribute to the betterment of private and public life, law observance, and intelligent participation in civic affairs. To foster participation in school affairs by the community, the Association advocates:

A. A continuous program to interpret completely and accurately the aims, practices, and achievements of the schools.

B. National, regional, and local cooperation among parents, teachers, and other interested citizens to bring the school, the home, and the community into closer working relationship.

C. Community and school visitations and conferences, and the utilization of community resources by the school.

VIII. Education and Democracy

The preservation, defense, and perpetuation of democratic ideals in our republic depend upon a citizenry educated to interpret and defend our American heritage. The Association opposes vigorously the tenets of communism or the tenets of any other philosophy of government which deny freedom of thought and which ignore the intrinsic worth of the individual human being. The Association reaffirms these convictions:

A. Education of all children is the primary responsibility of society.

B. All schools should teach the rights, privileges, and responsibilities of living in a democracy.

C. Teacher participation in democratic living and in the civic affairs of the community is essential to the further advancement of our democracy.

D. American schools should teach about communism and all forms of totalitarianism, including the principles and practices of the Soviet Union and the Communist Party in the United States. Teaching about communism does not mean advocacy of communism. Such advocacy should be prohibited in American schools.

E. The Association condemns the careless, incorrect, and unjust use of such words as "Red" and "Communist" to attack teachers and others who are not Communists but who merely have views different from those of their accusers.

F. Members of the Communist Party should not be employed in our schools nor hold membership in our Association. Teachers proved to be members of the Communist Party should be dismissed. Communist or-

ganizations, and communist front organizations should be required by law to register with the Attorney General of the United States.

G. Adequate preparedness is necessary for national security. The American people should be alert to the need for such security. The federal government should provide adequate national defense to assure peaceful working relations with other nations of the world.

H. The schools should develop moral stamina, physical vigor, mental health, scientific knowledge, basic technical skills, language facility, and civic competence.

I. The Association opposes legislation which in the name of national security would set up parallel educational agencies that absorb, supplant, or duplicate the programs of educational facilities now in existence.

IX. International Relations

Youth should be given an international understanding which will encourage friendly relations among nations and serve as basic preparation to face the problems of living in an interdependent world. The Association advocates:

A. Systematic instruction about the structure, purposes, accomplishments, and problems of the United Nations, and encouragement by school officials of visits by teachers and students to the United Nations Headquarters.

B. Support of the United Nations by schools and teachers as the organization recognized by our government to maintain security and peace.

C. Appointment of qualified representatives of public education by the Department of State to the United States delegations to Unesco.

D. Cooperation with those educational activities of Unesco which are suitable for the schools of the United States.

E. International interchange of teachers adequately financed by local, state, and federal governments with necessary information made available to the schools.

F. Financial assistance for missions by selected educational personnel from other countries to the United States and by American teachers to other countries.

G. Cooperation by teachers and their associations with the World Confederation of Organizations of the Teaching Profession.

H. Teacher education to include insights needed to teach international understanding.

I. Assistance from the more fortunate nations and their teachers for the educational reconstruction of countries devastated by war or other major catastrophes.

X. *Separation of Church and State*

The American tradition of separation of church and state shall be vigorously and zealously safeguarded. The Association respects and upholds the rights of groups, including religious denominations, to maintain their own schools financed by their supporters so long as such schools meet the educational, health, and safety standards defined by the states in which they are located.

Index

Abrams, Albertina, ix

Academies, 10-12, 14, 62ff

Accreditation and accrediting agencies, 75, 88, 90, 104, 314, 352

Adair, Cornelia S., ix, xi

Adams, Charles Francis, 99

Adams, Charles K., 73

Addams, Jane, 48

Adams, John Quincy, 209

Adler, Felix, 259

Adult education, 31, 51, 53

Adult Education Association, 278

Adult Education Service, 379

Agassiz, Louis, 6, 13, 14, 100, 154, 255, 271

Agricultural education, 93-94, 101

Alcott, A. Bronson, 14, 156, 158, 169-170, 173, 189

Alcott, Louisa, 170

Almy, Doris E., viii

American Association for Health, Physical Education, and Recreation, 121

American Association for the Advancement of Science, 20

American Association of Museums, 321

American Association of Colleges for Teacher Education, 88, 351

American Association of School Administrators, 121, 133, 145, 146, 274, 282-286, 309. *See also* Department of Superintendence

American Association of Teachers Colleges, 88, 351

American Association of University Women, 287n

American Bankers Association, 243

American Council on Education, 104, 321

American Education Fellowship, 203

American Education Week, 316, 317, 321, 377

American Educational Research Association, 272, 384

American Federation of Teachers, 321, 339

American Historical Association, 71

American Home Economics Association, 275

American Institute of Instruction, 12, 20, 24, 218, 255-256

American Legion, 316-317, 321

American Library Association, 319-320

American Lyceum Association, 20

American Medical Association, 121, 315-316

American Normal School Association, 41, 44, 88

American Philological Association, 218, 219, 228

American School Citizenship League, 118

American School Institute, 129

405

Set in Linotype Caledonia
Format by Marguerite Swanton
Manufactured by The Haddon Crafstmen, Inc.
Published by HARPER & BROTHERS, *New York*